The Anthropology of Catholicism

The Anthropology of Catholicism

A Reader

Edited by

Kristin Norget, Valentina Napolitano, and Maya Mayblin

UNIVERSITY OF CALIFORNIA PRESS

University of California Press, one of the most distinguished university presses in the United States, enriches lives around the world by advancing scholarship in the humanities, social sciences, and natural sciences. Its activities are supported by the UC Press Foundation and by philanthropic contributions from individuals and institutions. For more information, visit www.ucpress.edu.

University of California Press
Oakland, California

Library of Congress Cataloging-in-Publication Data

Names: Norget, Kristin, editor, author. | Napolitano, Valentina, editor, author. | Mayblin, Maya, editor, author.
Title: The anthropology of Catholicism : a reader / edited by Kristin Norget, Valentina Napolitano, and Maya Mayblin.
Description: Oakland, California : University of California Press, [2017] | Includes bibliographical references and index.
Identifiers: LCCN 2016026840 (print) | LCCN 2016028907 (ebook) | ISBN 9780520288423 (cloth : alk. paper) | ISBN 9780520288447 (pbk.) | ISBN 9780520963368 (ebook)
Subjects: LCSH: Catholic Church. | Anthropology of religion.
Classification: LCC BX885 .A59 2017 (print) | LCC BX885 (ebook) | DDC 306.6/82—dc23
LC record available at https://lccn.loc.gov/2016026840

Manufactured in the United States of America

26 25 24 23 22 21 20 19 18 17
10 9 8 7 6 5 4 3 2 1

To Adaeze, Kamau, Ezra, and Willa

CONTENTS

ACKNOWLEDGMENTS

This book has been a labor of love. It was born across two continents and three different cities, and from somewhere in the constant back-and-forth between everyday spaces of family and work. Long Skype conversations, even with intermittent dropped lines, and exchanges during sporadic crossed paths at conferences allowed us to brainstorm and plan its beginnings. The seeds of early thoughts on anthropology and Catholicism were sown in a 2009 Latin American Studies Association meeting panel in Rio de Janeiro, then inspired by the very generous comments of our panel discussants, Manuel A. Vásquez and José Casanova. A key moment spent together in a lovely five-day hiatus in March 2014 in Valentina's warm Toronto attic, fueled by wine, pasta, and long walks, allowed us to consolidate critical ideas and the basic structure. But it was the belief all three of us had in the need for this book that kept us going over the long months. Somehow once we got started the book seemed to take on a life and momentum of its own. Far more than an intellectual project, it has been about experiential cross-continental learning.

We cannot mention all the people who have been enabling, in different corners of the world, the thinking for and the making of this book. But we would like to thank, above all, our editor Reed Malcolm for having faith in this project right from the start and for shepherding us so expertly through every turn and glitch. We are also grateful to John Berkman, Elizabeth Castelli, Simon Coleman, Stacy Eisenstark, Connie Gagliardi, Chris Garces, Zuha Khan, Chris Krupa, Ashley Lebner, David Lehmann, Carlota McAllister, Kelly McKinney, Ken Mills, Jessica Moll, Andrea Muehlebach, Michael D. Murphy, Robert Orsi, Stephen Scharper, Jeremy Stolow, and Donna Young. In addition to the three anonymous reviewers whose feedback and criticisms have improved the manuscript immensely, we would like to thank Andreas Bandak, Jon Bialecki, Tom Boylston, Magnus Course, and Diego Malara for their prompt and invaluable comments on earlier drafts of the Introduction.

Jennifer Campbell and Daniel Ruiz-Serna provided research assistance at critical moments of production. Elisabeth Magnus was our superb and patient copy editor; many thanks also to PJ Heim, who did a wonderful job as our indexer. We are also grateful for funding from the Social Sciences and Humanities Research Council of Canada (SSHRC), which covered various aspects of readying the final manuscript for submission.

Introduction

The Anthropology of Catholicism

Maya Mayblin, Kristin Norget, and Valentina Napolitano

In one of his final books, the late American Catholic priest and sociologist Andrew Greeley attempted to elaborate what he called "the Catholic imagination." The working of this imagination, he wrote, is "most obvious in the Church's seven sacraments but the seven sacraments are both a result and a reinforcement of a much broader Catholic view of reality."[1] This reality, stressed Greeley, is essentially enchanted—one in which an immanent God "lurks in aroused human love and reveals Himself to us through it" and in which "God leaves all kinds of hints of Her presence, but slips away just at the moment we think we might have caught a glimpse of Her."[2] Greeley's brand of Christian sociological apologetics would likely have drawn skepticism from anthropologists, for whom such a universalizing view of Catholic subjectivity would be anathema. But it is a project of this kind of scope and ambition that this volume is in curious sympathy with. If there were such a thing as a "broader Catholic view of reality," what would it look like? What sorts of theoretical conversations would it provoke both within and outside itself? And more to the point, what exactly would a set of fine-grained ethnographies reveal about Catholicism as a global phenomenon, as an object of immense historical depth and significance, as a political form, and as a "lived religion" constituting everyday worlds? Would they move Greeley to modify some of his suppositions?

Global Catholicism has seen some tumultuous events in the last century alone, but the number of studies by anthropologists about Catholicism remains woefully small. Thus, in a self-conscious effort to get a critical conversation about Catholicism off the ground, this volume pulls together work by scholars past and present to explore the many dimensions of Catholicism as a "world religion" in the broadest sense. This book is the first time that anthropological approaches have been brought together explicitly under the umbrella term *anthropology of Catholicism*. Moreover, it is the first volume of its kind to occur in conversation with the anthropology of Christianity that emerged as a self-conscious intellectual movement about fifteen years ago, and at a historical, global conjuncture that impels us to rethink "religion" by emancipating the concept from its long-unacknowledged Christian underpinnings.[3] Within its pages, Catholicism comes to light both through and beyond the "sacramental imagination," as a political and institutional form, a contested set of practices, and an embodied and ethical orientation to the world. We believe that bringing these essays together makes it easier to see not only what makes Catholicism distinctive from other kinds of Christianity but also how Catholicism opens windows onto areas of debate within the discipline of anthropology more widely. Far from promoting the anthropology of Catholicism as a sub-sub-subdiscipline within the anthropology of Christianity, we echo Thomas Csordas's call in this volume to bring studies of Christianity "back into the larger fold of comparativist anthropology of religion." In other words, an anthropology of Catholicism needs to develop within the discipline of anthropology more broadly as well as playing a productive role in interdisciplinary dialogues beyond anthropology.

The work of fresh ethnographic exploration and new anthropological conversation around Catholicism has certainly begun, but there is still a way to go. We need more studies, more ethnographic data, and, above all, deeper reflections on the ethical and political complexities of Catholicism today. In the following pages, our aim is to sketch out some of the themes we feel have been, and still promise to be, particularly productive for anthropologists of Catholicism to explore. Broadly speaking, these themes include power and institutionalism, "syncretism," gender, materiality, and concepts of mediation. Although the subheadings that follow do not aspire to be comprehensive in scope, we hope they will highlight key concepts and ideas—some old, others new—that Catholicism can teach us a lot about but that ethnographers have yet to plumb and repurpose for a contemporary audience.

THE INVISIBLE FAITH

As anyone who researches and writes on Christianity knows, it can be a daunting task to find anything to say that has not already been said or intimated before. Over two thousand years of writing and scholarship precede any present-day scholar of Christianity, sometimes illuminating but often overshadowing the places she wishes to go. For ethnographers of the contemporary whose primary means of investigation is participant observation in ordinary life-worlds, it can be hard to escape a nagging sense of déjà vu. Such a sense is compounded within the discipline of anthropology by the knowledge that studies of people who define themselves as Christian are also nothing new. All the same, it is generally accepted that while anthropologists have been exploring Christian cultures since the discipline's inception, prior to the emergence of an explicitly formulated anthropology of Christianity these writings did not cohere together around Christianity as an object or produce much grounds for cross-cultural comparison. In this ethnographic "prehistory" phase, so the story goes, not enough attention was drawn to the Christian-ness of people, in part because, as Fenella Cannell posited, Christianity was not a legitimate topic for anthropology[4]—even if it shaped the personal lives of key anthropologists of the mid-twentieth century, including E. E. Evans Pritchard, Godfrey Lienhardt, Victor Turner, and Mary Douglas.[5] The interesting thing about this prehistory, however, is that much of it—particularly pertaining to Europe and Latin America—was in fact about Catholicism. Why then Catholicism's apparent invisibility as an object of study in its own right?

A key example of such invisibility can be found in a brilliant essay by Julian Pitt-Rivers on "grace" that we reproduce in abridged form in Part One.[6] Although the term *grace*, in this essay, is acknowledged to have Christian theological roots, Pitt-Rivers draws our attention to this point almost in passing. Grace interests Pitt-Rivers, not because it is in any sense constitutive of a Christian or even Catholic self, but because it is a monotheistic analogue for *mana* or *hau*—a force immanent in the social. Indeed, Pitt-Rivers's discussion was never an explicit attempt to generate conversation with other scholars of Christianity, and hence it has little to say about the subtle variations that exist between different Christian understandings of grace. Protestant/Catholic conflicts over theologies of "grace" are arguably reflected in different cultural practices and values concerning gifts and exchanges, but Pitt-Rivers does not focus on this possibility. However, it is worth noting that Pitt-Rivers's discussion of grace draws deeply from his experience as an ethnographer of the Catholic town of Grazalema in southern Spain. What he produces, therefore, is arguably a distinctively Catholic European prototype for grace, in which the Eucharist, Mass, confession, prayer and penance, and material substances like incense, wine, and oil are its primary channels into the world. Furthermore, Pitt-Rivers observes the way that "honor" and grace articulate and depart from one another, tied as they are to a gendered division of affect where grace is the province of women, the reverse of a masculine honor that inheres in will and ambition. Pitt-Rivers thus reproduces the notion of a gendered divine panoply (in which the Virgin stands as a central symbol) that is distinctively and undoubtedly *Catholic.*

In such earlier anthropological forays around Catholicism, of which Pitt-Rivers's text on grace is one example, Catholicism itself remains implicit and deferred. Yet these texts deserve to be revisited, we argue, not only for what they might reveal about the hidden grammar of Catholicism, but also for what they show us about how studies of Catholic contexts moved scholars to be theoretically very innovative. In his provocative essay in this volume, Simon Coleman offers us a valuable conceptual architecture for understanding the questions presented by Catholicism within a wider anthropology of religion. The idea of a Catholic grammar in particular provides a fruitful tool for appreciating how Catholicism and Protestantism can share a broader Christian language but also diverge in significant ways. In the wider ecology Catholicism is not necessarily performing drastically different salvific and other functions from other Christianities, yet the modalities by which it performs these functions are peculiar and raise particular sorts of questions.

With regard to the question of Catholicism's relative "invisibility" in earlier ethnographic studies, we need to consider the profound tendencies of both Catholic and Orthodox forms of Christianity to structure communities at all levels—to exhibit, as Chris Hann and Hermann Goltz put it, a "high degree of congruence with secular, national identities."[7] In earlier ethnographic accounts of southern Europe, Catholicism is present as a system that has become so deeply constitutive of life-worlds that it barely registers as distinct. If the Catholic Church remains powerful in this region of the world in its "invisibility," it is in no small part a reflection of its ostensible dominion over all secular powers and forms of government in most of Europe between the fall of the Roman Empire in the fifth century and the Protestant Reformation in the sixteenth.

We might speculate that Catholicism's presence-as-nonpresence in many Mediterranean ethnographies is indicative not only of its success as a cultural form but also of its politico-historical legacy and subsequent naturalization in the institutional sense.[8] As with other dominant sociocultural positions in Western societies—maleness, for example, or whiteness—that are similarly undeveloped as prominent categories because of the power already wielded by those who occupy them, Catholicism's relative invisibility could, in the southern and eastern European context at least, be linked to its historical connection with deeply entrenched systems of power. However, as David Mosse reminds us in his contribution to this volume, if we have an impression of Catholicism as a coherent and universal cultural system it is because it has been "hard won" through the conscious formation of religion as a distinct category. Hence the original problematic concerning Christianity's late theoretical foregrounding in anthropology, as formulated by Fenella Cannell and Joel Robbins, requires more qualification in the case of Catholicism.[9] In other words, we contend that there is something particular about Catholicism's proclivity to cultural invisibility that makes it, as a form of Christianity, peculiar and thus worthy of study.

CATHOLICISM ACROSS TIME

One of the curious things about Catholicism is its endurance in the face of crisis. It would be easy to assume that, given secularizing trajectories or the wildfire spread of Protestant evangelical and Pentecostal forms of Christianity across the globe, the modern Catholic Church is in decline. Shifting away from the effervescence of pilgrimage and "folk-syncretic practice" in the 1960s and 1970s, a raft of studies in the eighties were particularly gloomy. These studies were produced during the emergence of neoliberal economies worldwide, at a time when anthropology was entrenched in debates concerning rationality, modernities, and the failure of these originally perceived liberatory projects of "development." As Pentecostalism started to attract attention, studies emerged that predicted Catholicism's ossification and demise.[10] In the secular Western media, the critique of Catholicism as a medieval, archaic form of religion converged with a slew of sex and financial scandals within the church. In our own fieldwork settings in Brazil and Mexico through the 1990s and early 2000s, we ourselves witnessed the rising numbers of converts to evangelical Christianity, some of whom bitterly maligned the corruption and lack of relevance of the Catholic Church. Given this picture, what becomes remarkable is not Catholicism's decline but its endurance and continuity despite such pressures—whether institutional, social, or cultural—from Catholics and non-Catholics alike. To what should we attribute this remarkable resilience in the face of doubts and scandals that tear at it today? This is one of the questions that a contemporary anthropology of Catholicism needs to ask, particularly if it wishes to break new theoretical ground.

A strong theme in the more recent anthropological literature on Christianity is that of "rupture," "discontinuity," and "breaks with the past."[11] According to Robbins, many forms of Christianity do stress radical change, to the extent that rupture and discontinuity are real experiences in many converts' lives. Robbins's observations, drawn from his own fieldwork among converts to a Protestant millennial form of Christianity in Papua New Guinea, led to his famous critique of anthropology as a discipline overly attracted toward what he called "continuity thinking." When claims of rupture are made by Christian research participants, he argued, these are too often treated with suspicion by anthropologists who "suspect that those who make these claims are not Christians at all or at least that they fail to live up to their own self-professed Christian ideals concerning discontinuity and change."[12] Although Robbins's critique caused debate about the nature of "rupture" to flourish within the discipline, attention to rupture's conceptual counterpart, "continuity" or "endurance," has been slower to emerge.[13] For the anthropology of Catholicism this remains a problem, for continuity emerges time and again as an ethnographic concept in its own terms in the guise of "tradition"—a value that derives partly from the theological principle of apostolic succession. Catholicism's rhetorical reliance on original, transcendent truth, on the enduring character and depth of tradition, and on the very notion of apostolic succession—the thread of permanent repetition that constitutes church authority—points not toward a continuity of "simple" reproduction but toward one of considerable labor. Such labor is present, for example, in recent moves on the part of the Catholic Church to mend long-standing fractures to its "one, holy and apostolic" body.

Since the 1950s, for example, it has allowed married Anglican vicars to convert and join the Roman priesthood, and since 2009 ordinary married Church of England converts have been allowed to be ordained as priests. Under Pope Benedict XVI attempts were also made to bring Orthodox Church leaders back into the fold through high-profile ecumenical meetings and, in 2007, through the drafting of a "joint document" in Ravenna, Italy, that addressed (or perhaps zigzagged around) the question of papal primacy over all Catholic and Orthodox bishops.

This question of continuity is given careful ethnographic illustration in Eric Hoenes del Pinal's discussion in this volume of Charismatic lay leaders' negotiation of their relationship to the mainstream church. As Hoenes shows, renewal movements that seek to remain Catholic but to differentiate themselves from the mainstream remain constrained by the fact that ultimate spiritual authority (and a rich material resource base) derive from an umbilical link to "the one true church." Indeed, a close reading of the history of key Catholic renewal movements such as the Charismatic Catholic Renewal suggests that success and survival depend not so much on foregrounding a radical discontinuity with the past as on maintaining an optimal balance of difference and sameness in relation to a mainstream spiritual center. In such contexts what is paramount is not "rupture" but endurance, despite or even as product of an ever-expanding *Mater Ecclesia*.

This is not to deny that the schismatic possibility of forming alternative centers lurks *in potentia* in all forms of Christianity in the Christian tendency to endorse ideals that can never be fully realized.[14] Indeed, as the essays here reveal, Catholicism, like any other form of Christianity, is continually subjected to critique and renewal, as well as to accommodations and evolutions. Robert Orsi's chapter in this book looks at one of the most profoundly faith-rattling issues for contemporary Catholics, the scandal of sexual abuse of children by Catholic clergy. Orsi's compassionate account of the anguish of survivors of abuse at the hands of Catholic clerics in Chicago allows us to see that (as Truth and Reconciliation Commissions the world over have shown us) "healing" is a complex and vexed process fraught with ambivalence. There is an interesting linkage between Orsi's and Maya Mayblin's chapters in that both take up the question of Catholic responses to the sex abuse scandal. Whereas Orsi's focus is on abuse survivors, Mayblin explores how the ellipses and equivocations surrounding the potent matter of sexuality in the church intersect with Catholic understandings of sin in ways that complicate the politics surrounding the ordination of women.

Orsi's and Mayblin's chapters are among the first ever anthropological treatments of such topics and could be read as portents of institutional change. Indeed, if the decreasing number of "practicing Catholics" (particularly in the West) is to be considered alongside the steady—if highly contentious—increase of ordained Roman Catholic women priests worldwide, it might be assumed that the Roman Catholic Church is, at the present time, in the muted throes of schism.[15] Yet it is perhaps too early to tell if we are seeing the crest of one tradition breaking to reform as another.[16] Returning to the *longue durée*, it is worth noting that Catholicism has ridden out many such waves, and as the essays here and beyond reveal, Catholicism remains remarkable in its capacity to contain dissent, even taking its strength from a range of divergent, sometimes wildly disarticulated practices, whether monastic, clerical, or lay.[17]

CATHOLICISM ACROSS CULTURES

Catholicism's longitudinal axis—its sheer age and its conscious self-elaboration as a faith revealed only in and through a singularly enduring material institution is crossed by its latitudinal axis of diversity in terms of practice.[18] It might be noted that Catholicism is spatially and organizationally elastic in that it can stretch to contain a bewildering variety of devotional structures and theological positions without breaking. Indeed, Catholicism's strength seems to be based as much on its rhetorical toleration of locality and difference as on its universalizing, and highly centralized, "infallible" core. At least part of Catholicism's remarkable resilience of form derives from the many modalities (theological, praxeological, and infrastructural) by which it is able to collapse the "many" into the "one," only to allow the "many" to concertina out again, should the context demand.[19] Consider, for example, how a single (Roman) center of authority translates, over time, into a multitude of private lay organizations and missionary orders; how a single God (though at once Father, Son, and Holy Spirit) may be accessed through a plethora of saints; how a single Virgin Mary embraces an array of different names; and how a single priest embraces in his role as "spiritual father" a multitude of lay. This paradoxical capacity for singularity and multiplicity to coexist may not be unique to Catholicism, but it points to something peculiarly "gymnastic" about Catholicism's engagement with the world.[20]

In the vast territories of the European colonial empires in Africa, Asia, and the Americas, the violence of conquest bled irredeemably into the project of conversion, so that the two often constituted the same thing. Nevertheless, the clergy's periodic openness to a degree of deviation from church teachings, its readiness to mimic indigenous sacred forms or to adopt these to ease catechistic or other religious teaching, and the inherent indeterminacy of religious evangelization meant that conversion was never quite the before/after story that emerged in Protestant settings. And this has made "syncretism"—traditionally, the blending or meshing of separate religious systems into a new integral tradition—a key theme in ethnographies of Catholic settings everywhere, especially in Latin America, the region embracing more avowed Catholics than anywhere else in the world.[21]

Syncretic strategies produced by the church "from above" with the specific aim of enfolding "the many" within the "one" are arguably as old as Catholicism itself, although they became more elaborated during the sixteenth century, when human-ist philosophies emerging in Europe afforded missionaries scope to tolerate and even incorporate indigenous, plastic modes of engaging with the sacred.[22] Post–Vatican II missionary projects continued this tradition under the banner of "incul-turation," promoting concern for the retrieval and reinvigoration of indigenous or local sacred concepts and practices within an "official" Catholic framework.[23]

By way of attention to the nature and evolution of the missionary encounter, David Mosse's work unpacks the complex historiography of Catholic accommoda-tion to local sacred forms in the context of India.[24] In India, missionaries came to depend upon a series of subtle and continually crystalizing distinctions that had never been necessary before: first among these was a conception of Christian truth apart from the cultures and languages in which it would be expressed, and second was a conceptual separation of the indigenous social world into the "idolatrous" and the "purely civil." A key but contingent evolution was a concept of "culture" that allowed early Jesuits to clothe the faith in semiotic forms acceptable to India's powerful elite castes (in sum, to survive so far from its European center, Catholi-cism had to blend with and support the hierarchical forms it found on the Asian continent). Only in the nineteenth and twentieth centuries did the church in India set about describing itself much more as a separate domain of "religion" in the sense of the word that emerged subsequent to the Reformation. Catholicism, in this context, was never, argues Mosse, a "transcultural" essence but rather an emergent field of concept and practice, the product of particular regional histories having particular effects.[25]

Catholic missionaries have arguably long used forms of ritual and linguistic accommodation as an evangelical strategy. Yet only in the wake of Vatican II did an elaborated Catholic theology of "inculturation" come into being. The results and uptake of this theology did of course vary. European missionaries were not immune to the frequently racist assumptions of the cultures from which they came, and the diversity of their responses to what they found in the missionary encounter reflected this. Thus idioms of both "savagery" and "civilization" trailed alongside projects of inculturation—something evident in the very different levels of respect that European missionaries had for the "cultures" they encountered in Asia as opposed to Africa. In a cogent critique of the post–Vatican II "incultura-tion" doctrine in Africa, Ludovic Lado points to the various ways in which the supposed dialogue between the Catholic Church and "African religions" "is not a dialogue between equal religions." There have to be questions about the appropri-ateness of this sort of "dialogue," argues Lado, for "all that is really happening is that Christians are talking about African religions. There is no way for the African religions to talk back."[26] Writing of the contemporary Mexican context in a similar vein, Kristin Norget draws our attention to the carefully orchestrated syncretic public rituals of an inculturationist church where an "eclectic collation of Catholic liturgical staples" are juxtaposed with "authentic" native folkloric elements "whose ethnic signification [is] emblematic and non-specific."[27] In this manner, she argues, inculturation works in practice to hold the Other within the Catholic Church's "paternalistic fold."[28]

The current demographic reality is that most of the world's Catholics now live outside Europe, in the global South, and many of them in indigenous communities. In these terms indigeneity—the politicized valence of "Otherness" in church discourse—is Catholicism's nemesis or elastic end point. Yet as recent contestation around the theological endurance of a fifteenth-century papal bull on the dominion over American indigenous people would suggest, vestiges of the church's colonial-evangelical drive remain problematically present to this day.[29] In Valentina Napolitano's discussion of the "Atlantic Return," the unresolved tensions of past colonial endeavors come subtly to the fore in issues surrounding Latin America migrant itineraries. While growing numbers of Latin American migrants in Rome present something of a troubling inversion of the original colonial-evangelical project, they also mark an ongoing challenge to Eurocentric notions of Catholic identity. In this subtly layered ethnographic account we see how transnational migrants work to renew and re-hew the institution from within, even as they tell "stories of a struggle for inclusion and autonomy."[30] Public performances of the church's new evangelization replete with inculturated elements of indigeneity (dances, music, language, material culture, local saints) have, over the course of the twentieth and twenty-first centuries, become indicative of Catholicism's cosmopolitanism—its way of dealing with cultural differences through a self-conscious recognition and legitimation of "other" practices and symbols—*contra* the globalism of Pentecostalist charismatic and evangelical movements, which tend to incorporate such differences by reversing their moral charge.[31] The signifying force of indigeneity in such contexts may be skewed by a legacy of epistemic coloniality built into Catholic theological reasoning, but this does not necessarily foreclose the indexical potency of such signs. As Matthew Engelke and Matt Tomlinson put it in their discussion on the "limits of meaning" across Christian cultures, new signs, like compass needles, "can swing back magnetically to their previous associations, transforming both prior and future contexts and meanings."[32] Thus, in Liana Chua's discussion of Catholic Borneo in Southeast Asia, the "Bidayuh culture" that is featured on major calendrical feast days is aesthetic and object centered, much like the sanctioned versions on offer to tourists in gift shops: "Bidayuh baskets, brass gongs, and swirling, geometric paintings reminiscent of Kayan and Kenyah artwork."[33] Nevertheless, it leaves the door ajar for "deft conceptual criss-crossing" that allows the faithful to preserve an all-important element of continuity with the "old ways."[34] A complex understanding of "syncretism" in the context of Catholicism, as a conscious and controlled strategy of incorporation offset (or complemented) by unplanned processes of synthesis and erasure can be found in the work of Andrew Orta.[35] Orta analyzes the *ayuno* performance of Aymara Catholics (an intracommunal event correlated with the start of the planting season) on two analytical dimensions: first, as an adjunct performance of a practice newly officialized by the inculturationist Catholic Church, and second, as an example of a cultural practice that exceeds the legible meanings intended by the missionaries. Such rituals, argues Orta, "enact a form of meaning that is always irreducible to the commensurability, legibility, and fixity of Christian meaning."[36]

Questions of "commensurability, legibility, and fixity" have been (and continue to be) as relevant for the church in Europe as they are for the church of the global South. Debates about "syncretism" refract throughout Ernesto de Martino's classic work on southern Italian *tarantismo* for example,[37] and in an essay on Portuguese Catholicism Caroline Brettell broached the issue through the notion of "contract." Catholicism, she argued, is everywhere "an accommodation"—a "contractual relationship between the doctrinal definition of religion adhered to by the parish priest and other church officials and the ideas about religion and community behaviour that are the will of the people."[38] Take, for example, the priest in the northwestern Portuguese village studied by Joao Pina-Cabral, who attempts to assume greater control of the fiesta of St. Sebastian (his chosen saint), yet is defeated by his parishioners when they refuse to attend.[39] Although the racial and political undertones of this kind of power struggle are different from those to be found in colonial and postcolonial contexts, the on-the-ground dynamics of clerical capitulations to Other wills and Other customs may be very much the same.

Consequently, inasmuch as all social interactions involve a certain degree of slippage (or "charitable" accommodation), "official" versions of Catholicism, replete with established vocabularies, material practices, and social authority, *are* indeed compromised, as are "popular" practices in their turn.[40] A useful framework for thinking about this has been provided by Webb Keane, who distinguishes between, on the one hand, "available vocabularies, material practices, norms for argumentation and the authority to take them up" and, on the other, that which is as yet unformed: "the ineluctable specificity of circumstance" or "the surface of things."[41] Keane's purpose with this is to move our understanding of human ethics and actions, moment-by-moment decisions and occurrences—what, indeed, we might call "culture"—away from abstract principles and instrumental rationality and toward "collaborative acts of framing" and the "divergent possibilities" of experience. As Rosalind Shaw and Charles Stewart write, "Conundrums of agency and intentionality make syncretism very slippery, but it is precisely its capacity to contain paradox, contradiction and polyphony which makes syncretism such a powerful symbolic process."[42] But is simply recognizing Catholicism as a living system of "polyphony" enough? Is it possible to distinguish between syncretism as a transparent descriptive term for social life in general from syncretism in the religious context of Catholic practice? Scholarship on Catholicism surely demands some sort of creative refashioning of the term, one that can combine both the theological and sociological possibilities of the word—a reappropriation in which syncretism is neither an inevitable, teleological social process simply unfolding nor an entirely willed modus operandi on the part of church.[43] In many ways what is required for a contemporary anthropology of Catholicism to flourish is a *new, syncretic* definition of syncretism (for new analytical purposes). By this new syncretic definition, *syncretism* denotes what arises when explicitly formulated inculturation (a conscious, strategic *theology of* blending) combines with the implicit everyday praxes of *creative lenience* (a mixture of will, responsiveness, environment, and happenstance).

CATHOLICISM AS INSTITUTION

For some time now, "lived religion" has functioned within religious studies as a kind of catchall concept that emphasizes people's own experience of their faith as they carry out their religious practices in the realm of the everyday. Popularized especially by Robert Orsi's work on Italian Catholics in Chicago and New York City, the concept was introduced as a corrective to the preoccupation with text-focused analyses that dominated religious studies, helping to paint a vibrant picture of Catholicism as very much socially and culturally contoured.[44] Such an approach may seem obvious to anthropologists, but one of its less explored consequences has been to highlight some of the axiomatic tensions between individual experiences and institutional prescriptions. Rather than mapping this tension onto a problematic opposition between "great" versus "little" religious traditions, we suggest that to understand Catholicism as "lived religion" challenges us to include not just people's own views and ways of exercising their faith but an appreciation of Catholicism as a continually crystalizing system of patterns, replete with infrastructures, dogmas, and "official positions" that must be made and responded to in differing ways.[45]

Recent sociology of religion in western Europe shows evidence of a growing rejection of mainline organized forms of religion.[46] Western moderns are more likely to self-identify as "spiritual" than religious, and much of this appears to be down to a popular mistrust of institutions. Such mistrust has been echoed, perhaps unconsciously, in much contemporary ethnography on religion, where the overwhelming focus is on newer charismatic practices, cognitive experiences, and individual phenomenologies of the sacred.[47] Within the anthropology of Christianity in particular the attention paid to language, individual transcendence, and the materiality of Christian belief has deflected attention away from those "mundane power relations within and between churches which depend in turn on wider secular macromaterialities."[48] Hann's call to complement the insights we have gleaned from recent explorations of materiality and language with more attention to "larger frames" is part of one ongoing project to reorient the anthropology of

Christianity back toward political economy.[49] In a similar vein, John Barker notes the importance of attention to infrastructure for a comparative anthropology of Christianity because, despite its infinite variations, "One of the defining character- istics of the 2,000-year expansion of Christianity across the globe is the planting of enduring institutional structures operating at local, regional and international lev- els."[50] Hann and Barker are surely right in urging anthropologists to grapple with the economic, bureaucratic, and political bases of Christian organizations. But given the remarkable fact that Catholicism is both the largest and the oldest reli- gious organization that the Western world has ever known, we suggest that a full engagement with Catholicism necessitates more than this; it necessitates a return to the analytical concept of "institution," and thus to fundamental questions about the relation between individual and collective, between structure and agency, between the very nature of society itself and the forces that construct and reproduce it.

We need to ask both how and why Catholicism continues to be the single largest and most politically dominant Christian denomination in the world. This is no easy task, yet we might begin to move toward a better understanding by rethinking and refining our current uses of terms such as *institution* and *organization*. In her study of Marian apparitions in Transcarpathian Ukraine, Agnieszka Halemba critiques the interchangeability with which social scientists tend to use these two terms. Halemba argues for a clear analytical distinction between them, based on "the respective level of recognition of a given pattern of social behavior as separate from other aspects of life."[51] Religious organizations—various as they are—all have explicit rules and are objectified "not primarily by researchers but by the people involved in their opera- tion."[52] Organizations, she points out, have rules that are explicitly defined—often even codified in writing. But their most important feature is that "they are perceived by social actors as entities that can act as if they were persons."[53] In contrast, the meaning of *institution* is more slippery. Researchers may use the word to refer to patterns of repetition, reproduction, and stabilization in human interaction that people themselves do not necessarily objectify as "special" or "set apart" from the rest of their lives. Hence whereas marriage, kinship, witchcraft, and neoliberalism may be identified by social scientists as "social institutions," their rules may be largely implicit and hence may need to be extracted by a researcher from actions and accounts. Adopting this heuristic distinction allows us to ask more precise questions: What could micro-level ethnographic explorations of Catholic organizations (struc- turing mechanisms clearly objectified by the actors involved) tell us about the nature of Catholicism as an institution? Following this, how could recent sociological understandings of institutions as "ingenious combinations of personalities and materialities" help us understand how Catholicism (as individual experience, as reli- gious organization, *and* as social institution) endures over time?[54]

An understanding of the Catholic Church as an agent in its own right apart from the individuals who locally make it up is necessary, we argue, not merely because it is theoretically interesting but because it is ethnographically *and theologically* sali-ent. Anthropologists, however, have long resisted this point. Durkheim's superor-ganic "group mind," as Mary Douglas once pointed out, has for a while now been "the central, repugnant paradox" for social theorists who maintain that agency is to be located in persons, not groups or institutions.[55] Yet anthropologists of Catholi-cism need to engage this question of group agency head on if they wish to deal with the mysterious superorganic body that Catholics view as the church—"One, Holy, Catholic and Apostolic." In a theological passage of "Image and Pilgrimage," Victor and Edith Turner reflect on the concept of the church as a "communion of saints." This entity they describe as "not in principle a kin group, but a group of all those, whether kin or not, who possess the same object of belief." The church, while uni-fied under Christ, is divided in Catholic doctrine into three dynamic parts: the Church Militant (the visible society of faithful on the earth), the Church Suffering (composed of souls in purgatory), and the Church Triumphant (composed of saints and angels in heaven). In this system, note the Turners, "Isolated prayer does not exist; every act of prayer refers to other members."[56] These three divisions, continu-ally interconnected and forever praying and interceding on one another's behalf, combine to form a single, corporate body that bears resemblance to what anthro-pologists might call a "cosmic" or "social" order, a "society," or even an "ontology"—an unquestionable set of premises about the nature of being.

The importance of distinguishing between Catholicism as church, as organiza-tion, and as institution is made more complex—but also more interesting—by the fact that such terms and concepts are used extensively among clergy and theolo-gians themselves.[57] Do "methodologically atheist" sociologists and Catholic theo-logians mean the same thing when they talk about the Catholic *institution*? If not, how do their usages differ? How might the different senses of the word be com-bined for a renewed, truly anthropological understanding of Catholicism as a complex social structure? In what follows we suggest that what we could general-ize as, on the one hand, theological, and on the other, sociological, understandings of institution, while not identical, are fundamentally and inextricably linked.

In a central writing, the political philosopher Carl Schmitt elaborated on what he saw as the particularity of Roman Catholicism in contrast to Max Weber's ver-sion of Protestantism. Catholicism, Schmitt posited, is inextricable from institu-tional power in such a way that if we do not understand the Catholic Church as an institution, we do not understand the nature of Catholicism in the world.[58] Sch-mitt's assertion that "all significant concepts of the modern state are secularized theological concepts" has been worked through by philosopher Giorgio Agamben, whose particular brand of political theology reveals the richness of Catholicism, not only for our understanding of Western concepts of sovereignty and governance, but also for contemporary theorists interested in "recentering" power a generation after Michel Foucault's emphasis on the dispersal of power.[59] Agamben's claim that politics and theology are inherent within each other—that there is no theology without some practical, political application—was foreshadowed by political and theological writings on Catholic liberation theology.[60] More recently Agamben's work has been taken up in productive ways by Chris Garces in the context of Catholic Ecuador and by Napolitano in the context of the "Atlantic Return."[61] Such works suggest that reflections on the enduring interrelation of theology and politics will continue to be a promising area for the development of an anthropology of Catholicism.

Yet questions of power and politics address but one aspect of Catholicism's nature as social institution, for its institutional status stems as much from its organizational nature as it does from its theological core. Thus we are prompted to further explore the organizational and bureaucratic structures through which particular norms of action are subtly defined. The uniqueness of Catholicism's geopolitical center in Europe (the Vatican), its visible head (the pope), and its vertical, complex organizational structure must be stressed here, for in these features alone Catholicism contrasts somewhat with the horizontal thrust and comparatively decentralized organization of other religions. In the figure of the pope Catholicism differs not only from Protestant forms but also from theologically closer Orthodox Christianities. The pope condenses in his person—through the notion of his infallibility—some of the key features of the institution: its continuity, its authority (through the direct and exclusive link to the Apostle Peter), and perhaps most importantly its role as the pinnacle of human continuity with the divine.

In its concrete infrastructural manifestation, the church is a vast, articulated bureaucracy spread across the globe, internationally recognized as a state with its own legal system of canon law, independent financial holdings, and even passports.[62] The centralization of the production of official theology and canon law in pontifical universities is part of Catholicism's epistemological constitution and governmentality, making Catholicism unique among forms of Christianity.[63] Such organizational features are ethnographically very interesting, yet to date anthropologists have collected very little data on them.[64] What we do know—more from historical sources, public reportage, and autobiographical accounts—is that the Catholic Church is often lived and experienced by those on the inside as a *total institution*.[65] Arguably, it was this peculiar "totalness" that moved Talal Asad to make one of the most important theoretical interventions in the modern anthropology of religion. According to Asad, drawing from Foucault, the famous Christian "inner disposition" first emerged, not from free-floating sets of meanings and symbols, but via harsh monastic disciplines that had strong physical and psychological impacts on individual subjects.[66] Such monastic disciplines were made possible because Catholicism was more than just an interlocking set of spiritual ideas: it was also an expansionary *organization*—growing fast in terms of infrastructure, political influence, technocracy, and bureaucracy, an organization enabled then and for the subsequent two thousand years by its connection with empire.

Even today, with weakened powers of physical juridical governance, the Catholic Church continues to deliver legitimacy and protection and to control its subjects through the extraction and redistribution of material and labor resources. As a total institution it works like a "passionate machine," continuously recalibrating its sovereignty over material and immaterial territories.[67]

For priests, religious, and moral theologians working "inside" the church, the question of discipline remains, to a certain degree, unchanged. According to bodies of circulating statistics based on anonymous surveys, levels of clerical dissent on key rules such as mandatory clerical celibacy and the ordination of women are extremely high.[68] However, the existence of conscious dissent among church officeholders in particular remains somewhat theoretical, as open expression of such views in the modern church continues to carry consequences such as internal ostracism, public condemnation, bureaucratic blockage, divestment of liturgical office, and finally even excommunication.[69] The practical and economic impact on the lives of paid Catholic servants can be severe, particularly for those who lack alternative training, social capital, or professions to fall back on. Consequently, clerics frequently keep silent about their dissenting views. They may rationalize such silence in practice by invoking critical distinctions between sacred ideals and imperfect institutions; the liturgical and pastoral demands of public office and the private demands of conscience; and the name of the church as a singular, sovereign body and individual callings to particular religious orders or lay movements. The positing of such cognitive distinctions and separations, and the ability they possess to "contain" clerical dissent, could be understood as yet another element of Catholicism's institutional flexibility.

Conflict and suppression at the church's own center are reiterated in fractal fashion in the relation between center and periphery, or—to use Coleman's phrasing in his essay for this book—those "ineluctable relationships between clergy and laypeople." A key example of this operation of power can be seen in attempts to control sacred spaces and persons, both in infrastructural terms through the establishment of shrines and spiritually through processes of canonization. Histories of sainthood and shrines the world over reveal how the church as an organization reproduces itself through charismatic ruptures that cannot be wholly routinized but must nevertheless be contained. Studies of shrines and of canonizations offer interesting windows onto what sociologist Francesco Alberoni has described as "the nascent state": sites of experimentation destined for either absorption or ejection by a dominant institution.[70] As Halemba's study of Marian apparitions in Transcarpathia reveals, religious organizations are put in a difficult position vis-à-vis the experience of direct divine intervention. In such contexts the organization as superorganic agent cannot "simply surrender and quietly leave the scene"; rather, its officials "go to great lengths to reclaim religious institutions and experiences that flourish outside or at the edges of their organizational borders."[71] Yet such organizational efforts are continually complicated by attitudes toward charisma itself: while some see the church merely as a "manager of" and conduit for charisma, others see charisma as a feature of a power necessarily superior to and independent from church structures.[72]

Just as ethnographies on emergent sites of Marian apparition illuminate initial attempts between clergy and lay at negotiation—movement toward absorption—studies of canonization ceremonies can present us with the end stage of such negotiations—what we could call a kind of *beneficent cannibalization*. In Kristin Norget's account of the beatification of the Oaxacan Martyrs, Juan Bautista and Jacinto de los Angeles, we see the mechanics of organizational cannibalization up close.[73] In the case of the Oaxacan Martyrs, all elements of indigeneity became "scripted" until the final celebration was one in which "the Otherness of that culture had been thoroughly tamed." Norget draws our attention to the "profligate production" of saints across the Americas, particularly during the papacy of Pope John Paul II (who gave the Catholic Church more beatified martyrs and saints than all his twentieth-century predecessors combined) as a form of "emplacement": a process of "vital mapping" in which distanced and disembedded Otherness submits to the church as "author of a univocal enunciation of indigenousness."[74]

If recent years have witnessed an interesting rash of canonizations, they have also witnessed an intriguing return to official practices of exorcism. In Csordas's contribution to this volume we see this process of absorption in 2005, with the launch of a training course for exorcists at a pontifical university in Rome, and in June 2014, with the Congregation for the Clergy's official Vatican recognition of the International Association of Exorcists, founded in the 1990s. In this renewed field of practice, networks of doctors and scientists work to parse evil from mental illness, thus setting it squarely in Catholicism's domain. Csordas's work on exorcism reveals how the Catholic Church's discourse on evil works to mediate anxieties underlying broader social transformations, crises both within the church and in the world at large. However, it also points us back, in a curious way, to an organizational mechanics of absorption, revealing how contemporary issues are continually emplaced within Catholicism's rhetorical sphere of command.

DISCIPLINE AND TOLERANCE

In Talal Asad's famous exegesis on the concept of religion, the emergence of the Christian self turns on the institution's undeniable capacity to discipline and punish.[75] Yet this is only half the story. To fully comprehend the nature of the institution, we need to be equally attuned to its capacity for toleration. Catholicism's complex organizational history is as much a history of exceptions, shortcuts, and leniencies as it is a history of rigor and discipline.[76] Like any abstracting state machinery, Catholic institutions encompass blurred or "gray" zones whose opacity may support specific projects and actors. Indeed, we argue, this subtle combination of discipline and tolerance is the key to Catholicism's capacity to absorb difference and opposition and thus to endure as the world's largest religious organization.

Theologically it has been noted that the lived and imagined religious world of Catholics is often characterized by a sort of flexibility and spiritual economics very different from Protestant ideals of unmediated sincerity. This flexibility has led some scholars to characterize Catholicism as a "both/and" rather than "either/or" sort of religion.[77] Another way to describe it, as political philosopher Carl Schmitt famously did, is as a *complexio oppositorum*.[78] Some of the chapters in this volume address various aspects of Schmitt's concept, which, at its core, describes Catholicism's containment of different and multiple forms of life via the figure of the pope and the impersonal nature of his office as vicar of Christ, an office that rests on both divine (theological) and human (political) powers. In Schmitt's reading the church has a unique capacity to hold any possible plurality of interests and parties because there is no other realm of life and sociality that she—the gendered pronoun used by the church—cannot embrace. As Andrea Muehlebach has argued in the context of northern Italy, the *complexio* allows us to see how an apparently "secular" ethical system may operate as a mode of Catholic governmentality, mediating broader life-worlds especially in the context of neoliberal labor regimes.[79] Whereas Muehlebach draws our attention to the encompassing (or cannibalizing) nature of the *complexio*, Andreas Bandak in his contribution to this volume draws us to it through the metaphor of a "force field." In Bandak's chapter on Syrian Catholicism, where Catholicism has a small but historically important presence, we see the *complexio* manifest in moral personhood fashioned through various engagements with prayer, surrender, and debt. For Bandak, Schmitt's concept is to be understood, not as, in any way, a resolution, but rather as an animating force whose perpetual existence is generative of Catholicism, as manifest in passions and debates.

CATHOLIC PIETY AND THE QUESTION OF "BELIEF"

If the "ethical turn" within the anthropology of Christianity (and Islam) has shaped our understanding of modern religious subjectivities, it has done so primarily through uncovering the complex worlds of pious individuals, for whom the propositional content of religion *really matters*. From Saba Mahmood's pious Islamic women to Tanya Luhrmann's hardworking, Bible-studying evangelicals, the anthropology of religion seems of late to have taken a rather earnest turn, with an overwhelming number of studies focused on subjects whose religiosity requires exceptionally high levels of conscious, individual reflection and personal time commitment.[80] Although Catholics and indeed studies of Catholicism in this vein do exist, it is also fairly axiomatic that Catholicism as a marker of identity is not always and everywhere primarily about "belief." Across Brazil, for example, Protestants are commonly distinguished from Catholics by the term *crentes* (believers). Devout Catholics regularly use this term when referring to their denominational brethren in a matter-of-fact fashion, in part because no shame is perceived. To be a Catholic in Brazil today is invariably to be aware of Protestant critiques about the superiority of "sincerity" and interior belief over routinized forms of ritual and practice. Nevertheless, the fact that many Brazilian Catholics will comfortably self-identify as nonbelievers—albeit in a muted and implicit fashion, through their labeling of Protestants as the "believers"—is significant. This may be, at least in part, because in the context of contemporary Brazil, where Catholicism remains hegemonic in cultural and historical terms, even the socioeconomically poorest of Catholics continue to occupy a position of dominance. As Clara Mafra shows, working-class Pentecostals in a peripheral urban district of Rio de Janeiro continue to recognize Catholics as "distributors of modernity": "They are the ones, 'those up there,' who are concerned about the transcendent and who are consequently careful to distribute modern infrastructures and practices to 'those down here.' Charity, favours, clientelism, and sponsorship—important points of equity in the national culture—can be traced back to Catholic principles of saintliness."[81]

Mafra argues that Brazilian Pentecostals juggle two "semiotic ideologies"[82]—"sincerity and saintliness"—the former deriving from Protestant emphasis on interiority and "belief" and the latter more associated with Catholic-inflected notions of material codependence, intercession, and redemption. This intermingling or "oscillation" of semiotic ideologies in the formation of the Brazilian Pentecostal self is indicative not only of Catholicism's traditional alignment with Brazil's powerful, dominant classes but also of the powerful effects of Catholicism understood not as religion but as a set of ontological assumptions about the world.

Even in "postsecular" contexts where Protestantism was culturally dominant in the past, a range of self-categorizations used by "nominal Catholics" provides an interesting reference point. In the English language, people will refer to themselves as "Catholic, but nonpracticing." One also encounters "lapsed Catholics," "cultural Catholics," "ethnic Catholics," "cradle Catholics," and "nonobservant Catholics." Such denotations suggest that Catholicism is open to identifications that index aspects of personhood beyond religious belief—kinship, territoriality, ethnicity, belonging—identifications that remain variously distanced, critical, and uncertain with regard to Catholicism's key propositional content. In Coleman's study of middle-class English visitors to Walsingham, described by him as "relatively disengaged, agnostic 'Christians,'" accounts of pilgrimage "lack a self-consciously coherent stance to ritual or religion." His informants' accounts reveal Catholicism's metonymical connection with childhood, with parental boundaries of expectation, and with memory and the circularity of time.[83]

Following Danièle Hervieu-Léger's wider argument about the links between religion and "chains of memory," and more recent work on religion as "heritage," we might then view the new anthropology of Catholicism as offering vital insights on the connection between ritual, kinship, notions of permanence, and human engagements with mundane, worldly time.[84] Such a project, as Coleman argues, may require us to focus our ethnographic gaze "away from the most obvious centres of religious action, to look for the seemingly incoherent in religious behaviour and attitudes, to move away from core, 'hard' ritual practices and toward apparent ritual and aesthetic peripheries."[85] Indeed, we suggest that for an anthropology of Catholicism to develop, there has to be some way of better understanding the many Catholics who populate these lapsed peripheries, particularly in regions where "cultural" or "nonpracticing Catholics" make up the vast majority of Catholics. What are the ties that connect these sorts of Catholics to the center? And how do national belongings and fantasies intersect these ties?[86] How do labeling practices participate in or shift according to context, casting comparative light on religious identity as a field of debate? The challenge, as we see it, is not to assume such labels as the product of an ever-increasing tendency toward secularism but rather to scrutinize them from within Catholicism's own living forms. What allows Catholicism to encircle not only doubt and dissent but also *indifference* within its single embrace?

MEDIATION AND DEFERRAL

A clue to Catholicism's relative toleration of a degree of indifference among its flock can perhaps be found in its divine economy or *oikonomia,* its bureaucratic and legal bent, and its enshrined division of labor between clergy and lay. In its simplest terms Catholicism is ordered by a priestly caste, an ordained elite who, as David Lehmann puts it, "do the hard work" while "the followers follow."[87] In Catholicism the priesthood manifests as a form of traditional authority that dominates, as Weber described it, by "the authority of the eternal yesterday."[88] In their analytical foray on orthodox religious worlds and their particularities, Andreas Bandak and Tom Boylston offer some productive insights on this form of organization by describing it as a "community of deferral."[89] In Orthodox, Catholic, and other heavily institutional forms of Christianity the division of spiritual labor between priests, lay, and other religious virtuosi distributes the burden of piety and religious knowledge. Cultures or "communities" of deferral therefore allow some individuals to take a more passive role in relation to piety. In practice, therefore, rather than striving for absolute correctness, subjects may orient themselves toward a "lack of incorrectness" without sacrificing their claim to Christian identity.[90] The point here is not so much that in Catholicism an emphasis on ritual and a more elaborated "sensorium" fills in for an absence of *doxa* but rather that an absence of theological certainty among individuals is acceptable. Catholicism does not exact high levels of reflexive certainty from everyone, or at least from every individual *all of the time.*

Equally important for this system to work, we note, are the ways that spiritual labor is divided and shared out among the lay themselves along axes of gender and generation. For it is here that Lehmann's depiction of priests as the "hard workers" is often inverted. In the perspective of "the lay grandmother from Calabria," for example, it is she who does the hardwork. The priest only has to perform Mass, whereas she has to attend to the souls, mouths, and stomachs of her family. He receives a comfortable wage, whereas she must perform devotional tasks and work to make ends meet.[91]

In this volume, the spiritual labor of lay people is exemplified in dedicated Mexican and Peruvian procession goers carrying heavy effigies, paying promises on behalf of themselves and their families.[92] Spiritual labor is also enacted by Hillary Kaell's Canadian subjects, who, as she describes in her chapter, tend to the giant wayside crosses sprinkled throughout the Quebec countryside. In Kaell's postsecular setting, where the pull exerted by Catholicism's social hegemony or strength of presence has weakened and where the highly publicized scandals recently faced by the church have further compromised the center's moral leverage for Catholics at its margins, wayside crosses work increasingly as markers of sensible faith in the face of the loss of a stable, directive center.

Returning to Bandak and Boylston's "community of deferral," we might see lay spiritual labor as, very often, designed to form chains of mediation capable of connecting a sacred core to its runaway peripheries. Consider the role of Sara, a twenty-three-year-old pilgrim in Elaine Peña's study on transnational (Mexico-US) devotion to the Virgin of Guadalupe: Sara performs pilgrimage wearing a white T-shirt covered in handwritten requests for protection from friends and relatives unable to make the journey themselves.[93] Consider, also Kaell's North American pilgrims to the Holy Land, whose obsessive shopping for Holy Land gifts to distribute to grandchildren is ultimately an attempt to encompass grandchildren—with or without their conscious acceptance—within an overall economy of divine materiality and spiritual salvation.[94] Both examples suggest an important role for kinship and affect and at the same time return us to an analytical concern with "collectives," "social bodies," and the endurance of institutions. Long ago Henri Hubert and Marcel Mauss elaborated on the importance of mediation, in the context of sacrifice, as a technology for keeping the divine at a safe (but efficacious) distance.[95] But what else do chains of mediation achieve? If we extend our focus beyond the individual ritual of sacrifice to consider mediation across and between generations of Catholics both dead and alive, perhaps across whole communities—in the case of the patron saint, perhaps even across traditionally Catholic nation-states—we start to see Catholicism's impressive capacity to travel through time and space.[96] As Napolitano asks in her chapter, does this allow us to open up a focus not on "religious movements" (be these reformist, charismatic, or conservative) but on the movement of the religious (as superorganic, yet immanent Catholic body) through history?

We here suggest that Catholicism's proclivity to form chains of mediation is part of what enables it to exceed the intentionality of individuals. The fact that in Catholicism grace may be both partible and distributable through objects and persons returns us again to the Catholic notion of a communion of saints, and hence to the manner in which Catholicism (as church, as "organization" and as "institution") is able to stretch across time and space.[97] In this conception Catholicism is better approached, not as an "official" religion crisscrossed by "folk" practices, but as a living *ecology* in the most holistic sense: that is, as an alignment of "living signs" and the individual agents who populate them. Thinking of Catholicism in such ecological terms helps us to recognize, following Douglas and Eduardo Kohn, that Catholicism is a *lived* institution and hence a "thinking self" in the sense that "representation exists in the world beyond human minds and human systems of meaning."[98] To speak of a Catholic ecology is not, we should clarify, to misrecognize the capacity of any ecology to produce destructive and exploitative patterns. Catholic ecologies are historically layered and have politicized and financial forms even as they display elements of "flow" and "mutuality" with their physical environments.

GENDER

If "folk" divisions of spiritual labor in Catholic cultures were well documented in early accounts of Catholic communities, the gendered and political salience of such divisions was underanalyzed. In earlier ethnographies of the Mediterranean in particular, lay virtuosi were present through the stereotype of the "black clad, rosary telling women."[99] As Cannell notes, the women in such ethnographies were mainly disregarded by this earlier generation of ethnographers as "those to whom society has assigned the role of appeasing the church by a demonstration of orthodox religious observance." Men, by contrast, were more interesting subjects for study, given their supposed "cultural autonomy" manifest, partly, through "flamboyant anticlericalism."[100] A lesson can be learned from ethnographers of Greek Orthodoxy who offered something of a corrective to this view by juxtaposing the sociopolitical marginality of Greek women against the formidable affective force of their ritualized performances.[101] Nadia Seremetakis's impressive work on the women's work of lament revealed the scope for social commentary and critique embedded in Catholic and Orthodox forms of "elaborated suffering."[102] More recently Napolitano has drawn our attention to the complex tension that besets

Latin American women migrants' devotional labor for their European Catholic hosts.[103] On the whole, however, few key texts within the more recent anthropology of Christianity have focused on the question of gender, and those studies that have addressed gender directly have mostly been authored by women.[104] Thus it would seem that women scholars of Christianity have generally been left to tackle the "the gender question" in much the same way that Catholic women are left to clean church buildings once mass is over and the priest has left.

In the seminal work of William A. Christian, Catholic practices of dividing up spiritual labor are analyzed through the lenses of gender and life course. Christian observes that as a woman of the Spanish valley ages, the colors she wears become more muted until, finally, in widowhood she "abandons the last remnants of light" and wears black, "not unlike the cassock of a priest."[105] For Mayblin this movement of Catholic religiosity within and across not merely the social or collective body but the individual gendered body *over the life course* is significant, for it links to a central logic undergirding Catholic conceptions of the divine as sexually ambiguous.[106] In Mayblin's thesis, definitions of masculinity, femininity, and their attendant erotic associations "become blurred the holier a body becomes." This "blurring," manifest so often in hagiographic accounts and popular discourse on saints, is refracted again in the asexuality of the worldly celibate priest, and then again in the aging and/or sexually ambiguous bodies of lay virtuosi.[107] Hence we see how, particularly in rural, traditional "folk" Catholic communities, lay people's devotional activities increase as their bodies grow more distant from the phase of sexual reproduction. As Christian intimates, older virtuosi become, in a rather practical and mundane sense, freer for the channeling of grace in their lives. Relationally they become more like celibate priests: more available to God, the saints, and the souls surrounding them.[108]

The gendered division of spiritual labor in Catholicism remains, we argue, a key issue for the future anthropology of Catholicism. Interestingly it was made explicit especially in Pope Leon's 1891 encyclical *Rerum Novarum* and was developed further in the Second Vatican Council (1962–65). However, the stakes of this division, tied as they are to power, prestige, and political visibility/invisibility of office, are reaching an apotheosis in debates surrounding the ordination of women. In Part One's excerpt from Caroline Walker Bynum we see how for thirteenth-century female mystics ecstasy or possession served as an alternative to the authority of priestly office. The visions that women received at Mass, most notably Eucharistic visions, writes Bynum, "occasionally projected women, in metaphor and vision, into access to the altar, even into the role of celebrant—things strictly forbidden to them." These medieval women's aspirations were to a certain extent curtailed and circumscribed, not just by the church, but by the wider social environment of patriarchal gender norms in which they were situated. While the church's stance on gender has changed little over the subsequent millennium, the wider social environment most clearly has, a shift evident in Mayblin's chapter for this volume on the Roman Catholic Women Priest movement. Here we see how the paradoxes surrounding the interdiction on women's ordination refract through shifts in discursive register, silently shadowing the current crisis concerning sexual abuse in the priesthood. This complex crisis, argues Mayblin, is unique inasmuch as it exceeds any one particular locality, constituting a crisis of diffusely globalized and even secular proportions.

BODIES AND MATTERS FOR A NEW ANTHROPOLOGY OF CATHOLICISM

Mediation is one of anthropology's current leitmotifs, a window for examining cultural production and reproduction within globalization as these are shaped especially by new media technologies. Many of the ethnographies featured in this book return us to the critical theme of mediation, in some ways hardly surprising given Catholicism's sacramental vision, in which material things (water, oil, medallions, images, flower blossoms, relics, etc.) and human/divine beings (Christ, the Virgin, the saints) are channels and sources of God's grace. The analogical imagination of Catholicism thus inheres in metaphors and metonyms of fleshiness/carnality, blood, passion, and their sublimated undersides that ebb, flow, and circulate in fascinating ways. The doctrines of the Incarnation (from the Latin: *in* + *caro*, flesh: *incarnare*, to make flesh), in which Jesus Christ, assuming human flesh, body and soul, unites divine nature with human nature, and transubstantiation (which presupposes the "realness" of the transformation of blood and body into wine and wafer) index a view where invisible *mysterium* and material *tremendum* unite. In Jon Mitchell's chapter we return to the doctrine of the Incarnation via his discussion of the Catholic body. Mitchell's discussion argues for the persistence, in modern Catholicism, of "porous" selves for whom the boundaries between natural and supernatural, material and immaterial, body and soul are indistinct. Such an idea, he stresses, is hardly "archaic" but demonstrative of a "modernity" that, *contra* Weber, does not eschew enchantment.

While several of the contributions to this book draw upon Catholicism's proclivity for certain forms and aesthetic formations, the chapter by Norget provides insight on the potential vitality and political leverage to be wrought by Catholic institutions through "baroque" frameworkings. If there is a tendency to think about Christianity as a coherent system of meanings and ideas capable of transcending local variations of culture, Norget presents us with the interesting possibility that there might be something inherently transcendent—something inherently *Christian* even—in Catholic forms of the baroque. An anthropology of Catholicism here challenges us to consider certain aesthetic forms, not merely as a happenstance worldly vehicle for "Christianity" (here understood as a prescribed set of abstract ideals) to inhabit, but as intrinsically Christian in their own right. The chaos, contradiction, and inherent excess of the baroque are not merely indicative of a certain period's aesthetic sensibility; as Norget points out, the baroque also works as sort of transhistoric mobile *theological architecture.*

If material culture, in its mobility and portability, is an important way in which institutions reproduce themselves across time and space, no object is perhaps more emblematic of this for Catholicism than the humble rosary. Ellen Badone's contribution, based on research at a French shrine in Brittany, probes deeply into the phenomenology of Rosary recitation to reveal both its meditative *and* its mediative aspects. Notable here is what Badone describes as a more encompassing "Catholic spirit of death." This is not a horrific, sterile death but a fertile one, with the principal imaginational referent being the passion and death of Christ. Badone's contribution, like the essay for this volume by medieval historian Niklaus Largier, demonstrates the importance of the *longue durée* perspective for understanding Catholicism's sensory forms. Catholic anthropology rooted in the medieval age, Largier shows us, was not dependent on romantic or modernist notions of a nature that enables the subject's cultivation of an inner religious imaginary. Instead, medieval practices of prayer, contemplation, and a poetics of sensation participated in the creation of a "theater for the soul," thus inverting the usual commonsense understanding of our senses as mediating our encounter with the outside world. Largier's historical phenomenology inspires a much-needed reengagement with questions of mediation, experience, and modes and substances of embodied belonging that are central themes in the development of the anthropology of Catholicism.[109]

Nevertheless, if there is an important challenge for an emerging anthropology it will be, as Michelle Molina warns us, not to make Catholicism part of a "just-so story" in which Catholic materiality "triumphantly resists the Western colonial legacy while simultaneously dethroning Protestant theology's dominion over religious studies terms and concepts."[110] Just as Protestant Calvinists are not the only Christians in the world to stress "interior belief," the work of scholars like Birgit Meyer on African Pentecostalism amply shows that Roman Catholics are not the only materialist Christians in the world.[111] Indeed, as Meyer stresses in her essay for this book, the neatness of the imagined Protestant/Catholic dualism in terms of mentalist/materialist religiosity rarely translates in terms of everyday practice. Rather, "These dualisms could be seen as the poles of a continuum that includes Protestant *and* Catholic religiosities."

The popular stereotype of Catholicism as Protestantism's nonascetic cousin is interesting inasmuch as it points us back to the Cartesian dualisms of Western thought.[112] The point here is not to rail against Cartesianism, for as a "native philosophy" and as a hermeneutic it has a role, but to remind ourselves that Catholicism's relationship with candles and ritual sensoria is much debated among Catholics themselves and periodically subjected to reform. In *Natural Symbols* Douglas

tackled just this theme through an analysis of the clerical rejection of Friday absti-
nence. "Thus was the old ritual abolished," she writes. "Friday no longer rings the
great cosmic symbols of expiation and atonement: it is not symbolic at all, but a
practical day for the organization of charity."[113] Douglas's *Natural Symbols* could be
read, on some level, as a personal reaction to the iconoclastic wave that swept
through her church in the 1970s, following Vatican II.[114] Indeed, it was in this same
period that Stanley Brandes conducted research in the Spanish village of Becedas,
where similar abolishments were under way. In the excerpt included in Part One,
we encounter the religious sensorium of Becedas villagers in a phase of diminish-
ment, its traditional cycle of rituals in steep decline. For Brandes, such changes were
the result of the Vatican's continuing attempt to adapt the church to contemporary
needs and conditions "to make religion more comprehensible to the ordinary
believer, to divest Catholicism of much of its mystery and mysticism." Douglas
would doubtless have agreed with the Becedas villagers that the eradication of ritual
represented a destruction of what Brandes calls "the eternal verities of religious
action."

ABOUT THE STRUCTURE OF THIS VOLUME

The essays gathered in this volume consider the above themes in ways that we
consider critical to the construction of a new anthropology of Catholicism. The
classic works of Part One are designed to give the reader a sense of Catholicism's
important presence in the ethnographic canon that preceded the "anthropology of
Christianity" as it later became known. While the selection of these works is far
from exhaustive, we hope it will go some way toward tracing out an alternative
genealogy for the field and setting the stage for the theoretical and ethnographic
engagements in Part Two. The Part One excerpts are presented chronologically not
by date of publication but in order of the period in which the author began working as an anthropologist. Each excerpt is prefaced by a short introduction locating
it within the wider anthropology of Catholicism. In Part Two we have gathered
works that we consider exemplary of a new wave of ethnography on Catholicism—
a wave inspired in part by the discipline's efflorescent theoretical interest in Christianity's forms but also by increasing desire on the part of anthropologists of
Christianity to enter into dialogue with scholars of neighboring disciplines whose
thought-provoking works on Catholicism provide continual inspiration. While
most of the essays in this section are by anthropologists, we also include contributions by nonanthropologists, reflecting the necessity of an interdisciplinary
approach to Catholicism's *longue durée*. Finally, Part Three features five established
scholars, Simon Coleman, Birgit Meyer, Niklaus Largier, Thomas Csordas, and
Robert Orsi, whose "thought-pieces" set out to identify issues and challenges for
an anthropology of Catholicism today.

This book then takes up Greeley's project of elucidating a specifically "Catholic imagination" but in a way that goes well beyond the theological gates. To elaborate the "Catholic imagination," as we hope to have shown in this introduction, is not to reduce Catholicism to a simple structure that is the same everywhere, but rather to engage with the ways certain principles—of continuity and universality, of affect and authority, of tolerance and diversity—ripple and refract across space, across time, across bodies and relationships. Such a project, we suggest, offers insights not just into the institution of Catholicism and the diverse groups of people of which it is composed but also into the anthropology of religion more generally.

NOTES

1. Greeley (2001, 1–2).
2. Greeley (2001, 7).
3. See Robbins (2014) for reflections on the anthropology of Christianity as a conscious theoretical project.
4. Cannell (2006, introduction).
5. For more on the importance of Catholicism to the Oxford School of anthropologists, see Al-Shahi (1999); Larsen (2014); Fardon (1999).
6. Pitt-Rivers ([1992] 2011).
7. Hann and Goltz (2010, 5).
8. Douglas (1986).
9. Cannell (2006); Robbins (2010).
10. For example, Burdick (1998).
11. Robbins (2007); Meyer (1999); Engelke (2004); Bialecki, Haynes, and Robbins (2008).
12. Robbins (2007, 10).
13. For discussion on "rupture," see Engelke and Robbins (2010) and Badiou (2003).
14. Bialecki (2014), quoted in Robbins (2014, s163).
15. Since the first female ordinations in 2002, some three hundred women across the world have been ordained as deacons and priests, and approximately twelve have been made bishops. Although Roman Catholic women priests exist in Columbia, South Africa, and even Taiwan, numbers have been growing most in North America and western Europe. For more information, see the website of Roman Catholic Womenpriests at http://romancatholicwomenpriests.org.
16. See Bialecki (2014) for a discussion of denominational evolution.
17. See Certeau (1986) for inspiration on the *longue durée* as an analytical angle.
18. On Catholicism as a "transversal institution," see De la Torre (2002).
19. See Barker (2014), who argues that studying institutional configurations provides anthropologists a strategic point to consider local versions of Christianity as both "One *and* Many."
20. See Mayblin (2014a) for an elaboration of the inherent "gymnasticity" of Catholic semiotic form, particularly in relation to the gendered body.
21. For an excellent anthropological dissection of the term *syncretism*, its etymology, and the history of its application, see Shaw and Stewart (1994). Their discussion pivots on the difficulty many anthropologists have had embracing a term that has acquired—in some quarters—pejorative meanings. They point out that problems with syncretism from an anthropological point of view at least do not lie with any substantive objections to the semantics of the term, "since hardly anyone would deny that different religious traditions have amalgamated in the past and continue to interact and borrow from one another today" (3); rather, they lie with the word itself and its history of application, which

took a particularly negative turn in the nineteenth century when religious scholars used it to signal "disorder," "confusion," and reduction to a "lowest common denominator." Like Shaw and Stewart, we acknowledge that "syncretism" is a historically constituted concept that comes with certain political baggage that scholars should be aware of. Nevertheless, the concept remains semantically useful in the context of Catholicism as a religion whose own forms are themselves inherently plastic.

22. See, for example, Díaz Balsera (2005); von Vacano (2012); Mignolo (2002, 2011).

23. For example, Angrosino (1994); Cannell (1999); Chua (2012); Orta (2004, 2006).

24. See Mosse (2012) and his chapter in this volume.

25. On South Indian Catholicism and "syncretism," see also Henn (2014).

26. Lado (2006).

27. Norget (2009, 342).

28. Norget (2009, 342).

29. See Pope Alexander VI, 1943, *Inter Caetera*, which validated the possession of the kingdoms of Portugal and Castile in the Americas. Repeated requests have been made to the Holy See to refute such a bull, to no avail yet: Apache-Ndé-Nneé Working Group (2015).

30. Napolitano (2016, 125).

31. D. Lehmann (1999).

32. Tomlinson and Engelke (2006, 16).

33. Chua (2012, 143).

34. Chua (2012, 143).

35. Orta (2004, 2006).

36. Orta (2006, 180).

37. De Martino ([1961] 2005).

38. Brettell (1990).

39. Pina-Cabral (1986, 131).

40. On charitable accommodation, see Davidson ([1984] 2001).

41. Keane (2010).

42. Shaw and Stewart (1994, 21).

43. In this analytical understanding, syncretism opens up political questions around forms of living and "living in common." For an interesting take, see Roland Barthes (2012, 48), who argues for a "third way" of living together, one that is neither dyadically exclusive, not alienatingly distant. See also Giorgio Agamben's (2013, 58) discussion of the Catholic life of cenoby—lived medieval rhythms that unfolded without any shared telos or common goal. Agamben argues that certain cenobic forms of living emerged in the spatio-temporal tension between life and precepts. Neither of these latter two exist prior to each other, but they acquire a meaning through particular forms of living.

44. See, for example, Hall (1997); Orsi (1996, 1985).

45. A "two-tiered" model religion, made up of discrete spheres known as "great" and "little," was first elaborated by Redfield (1956). The model was later critiqued by writers such as Brown (1981) and Christian (1981), who argued that it perpetuated the misconception that the spheres were disconnected from one another or else characterized by a downward percolation of concepts from "great" to "little." For an excellent summary and in relation to synonymous terms such as *popular, folk*, and *informal religion*, see Badone (1990, 3–8). Going beyond received notions of "lived religion," as Napolitano (2016, 178–79) and Jacqueline Rose (1998, 3) remind us, also requires attention to "unlived" fantasies—those wishful or unconscious acts that remain unacted upon.

46. See Davie (1994); Day (2006); Lindsay and Gallup (1999); Vincett and Woodhead (2009).

47. An important example of this trend can be found in contemporary mainstream cognitive and psychological studies of religion. See, for example, Luhrmann (2012).

48. Hann (2014, 183).

49. See Hann (2012).

50. Barker (2014, s179).
51. Halemba (2015, 9).
52. Halemba (2015, 9).
53. Halemba (2015, 10).
54. Quote from Durão and Lopes (2011, 364).
55. Douglas (1986, 15–16).
56. Turner and Turner (1978, 159).
57. Theological treatises on the nature of religious institution are numerous. Many proceed by investigating the supposed dialectic of opposing principles such as institution/charisma, Christology/pneumatology, and hierarchy/prophecy. In an essay titled "Ecclesial Movements and Their Place in Theology," Ratzinger (2007) dissolves such binaries, arguing that the church is not constituted dialectically, as some sociologists would suggest, but organically. The priesthood, he argues, is not a bureaucratic adaptation or an "office" so much as a "divine gift." The apostolic succession is not a move away from charisma but, on the contrary, a total dependence on the spirit. For interesting sociological discussions of this theology, see, for example, Stark (1965) and Thorsen (2015).
58. Schmitt ([1923] 1996); Weber ([1905] 2001).
59. Agamben (1998); Hansen and Stepputat (2006).
60. The classic theological work of liberation theology is Gutierrez ([1971] 1973). Well-known political science perspectives, which have dominated social scientific literature on the movement, can be found in Berryman (1987) and Levine (1992). Anthropological analyses on liberation theology include Lancaster (1988) and Norget (2004).
61. Garces (2010); Napolitano (forthcoming).
62. In 1964 the Holy See acquired status as a permanent "observer state" at the United Nations. Through its choice to remain an "observer state" rather than a full-fledged member state, it has been able to exert a different type of influence in decisions made by the UN Assembly—such as spearheading important motions like a world ban on the death penalty.
63. For key work on the formation and reproduction of governmentality, see Foucault (1997), T. Mitchell (2002), and N. Rose (1998).
64. Some anthropological exceptions include Irvine (2010); Lester (2005); and Corwin (2012). For a social history of the cloister, see Rapley ([2001] 2009); for a vivid autobiographical account, see Armstrong (1997).
65. Erving Goffman (1961, 17) defined total institutions as "social establishments" of the most "encompassing" type: "A basic social arrangement in modern society is that the individual tends to sleep, play, and work in different places, with different co-participants, under different authorities, and without an over-all rational plan. The central feature of total institutions can be described as a breakdown of the barriers ordinarily separating these three spheres of life."
66. Foucault (1993); Asad (1993).
67. On the Church as "passionate machine," see Napolitano (2016).
68. Pew Research Center (2015).
69. For an autobiographical account of excommunication from clerical orders see, for example, Loisy (1924); for a more recent theologian's experience, see, for example, Curran (2006).
70. Alberoni (1984).
71. Cf. Christian (2012).
72. Halemba (2015, 274–75).
73. For an interesting Uganda case, see Behrend (2011).
74. Norget (2009, 348–49).
75. Asad (1993).
76. Mayblin (n.d.).
77. Tracy (1981).

78. Schmitt ([1923] 1996); see also Marder (2008) for a detailed discussion.

79. Muehlebach (2009).

80. See Luhrmann (2012); Mahmood (2005).

81. Mafra (2011, 456).

82. On the nature of "semiotic ideology," see Keane (2007).

83. Coleman (2014, 287).

84. On the concept of "chains of memory," see Hervieu-Léger (2000). Hervieu-Léger emphasizes how religion is partly constituted precisely through the process of the transmission of its tradition in time. An elaboration of the idea of "religion as heritage," which sees religion even in "secular" societies as visible and recognizable because of its character as a national heritage or tradition, may be found in Hervieu-Léger (2008).

85. Coleman (2014, 290).

86. For affective dispositions and national fantasies nested within Catholicism, see Bandak (2013) and Napolitano (2009).

87. D. Lehmann (2013, 658).

88. Weber ([1948] 1998); see also C. Taylor (2007), who discusses the historical legacy of this religious division of labor for the development of the secular.

89. Bandak and Boylston (2014).

90. Bandak and Boylston (2014).

91. Diego Malara, personal communication, January 2015.

92. For example in Napolitano's and Norget's chapters in this volume.

93. Peña (2011).

94. Kaell (2012).

95. Hubert and Mauss ([1964] 1981).

96. On Catholicism as transnational and encompassing, see Casanova (1997).

97. See Mayblin's chapter in this volume for a discussion of grace as partible yet "barrier sensitive."

98. Douglas (1986); Kohn (2013); quote from Kohn (2013, 31).

99. Cannell (2006, 9).

100. Cannell (2006, 9).

101. See Caravelli (1980); Cowan (1990); Dubisch (1995); Du Boulay (1974); Seremetakis (1991).

102. Seremetakis (1991). For discussion of "elaborated suffering" as moral work, see Mayblin (2010).

103. Napolitano (forthcoming).

104. For example, Brusco (2010); Drogus (1997); Eriksen (2008, 2012, 2014); Martin (2009); Mayblin (2010, 2014a).

105. Christian ([1972] 1989, 161).

106. Mayblin (2014a).

107. Mayblin (2014a, 278).

108. Christian ([1972] 1989).

109. For recent discussions by anthropologists of Catholicism and the body, see Blanes and Fedele (2011); Egan (2011); Bacchiddu (2011); Ballacchino (2011).

110. Hughes (2012, 16).

111. See Meyer (2004).

112. See also Engelke's (2007) discussion of matter in Christianity as "the problem of presence."

113. Douglas (1970, 47).

114. See Fardon (2013).

PART ONE

A Genealogy of the Anthropology of Catholicism

1

Excerpt from "St Besse: A Study of an Alpine Cult"

Robert Hertz

The works of French sociologist Robert Hertz (1881–1915) are now staple readings in general anthropology. This study of the cult of a saint in the Italian Alps is lesser known than Hertz's celebrated essay on the symbolism of death and sin, "Death and the Right Hand" (1907), yet it remains a model of classic ethnography. Hertz was raised in a devout Parisian Jewish family, studied at the École Normale Supérieure under Émile Durkheim and Marcel Mauss, and later became a critical member of the famous Année Sociologique group. The influence of the Année—its concern with theoretically driven, detailed, holistic, and integrative analyses of social phenomena—can be seen in his essay "Saint Besse: Étude d'un culte alpestre" (first published in 1913 in the French *Revue de l'Histoire des Religions* and translated into English in 1988).[1] The essay is a painstaking, eloquent ethnohistory, locating Saint Besse intimately in divergent paths of regional history and local tradition, where Saint Besse's shrine in a rocky Alpine overhang is, quite literally, embedded in the landscape. The essay portrays beautifully the independent spirit of popular Catholicism, especially in the flexibility of the hagiography of Saint Besse, which allows each community—whether mountain peasants or village dwellers, even church authorities—to lay claim to the saint through the qualities he is seen to manifest: the courage of a soldier, the moral stature of a bishop, and the devotion of a pious shepherd. The work is methodologically unorthodox for a Durkheimian, for Hertz not only draws on oral and archival sources, popular, local, and ecclesiastical traditions, but also has left his Parisian armchair for direct, "participant observation" in the field. In the Italian Alps, as elsewhere, a vibrant popular Catholicism evolves from pagan, telluric sources, sometimes articulating with official Catholicism, sometimes not. In typically Durkheimian fashion, Hertz describes the tremendous power of Saint Besse to knit together diverse communities of people morally and physically through

Robert Hertz, "St Besse: A Study of an Alpine Cult," in *Saints and Their Cults: Studies in Religious Sociology, Folklore and History*, edited by Stephen Wilson, pp. 55–100. © Cambridge University Press, 1983. Reprinted with the permission of Cambridge University Press.

collective religious devotion. In Hertz's focus on Saint Besse as a material source and mediator of social identity we can read this work as a precursor to many other great ethnographies on Catholic saints (popular and more official), whether in Europe, Latin America, or elsewhere. But we can also read in the essay the political and moral vision of a socialist, activist—and Jewish—scholar who saw in a popular rural Catholic saint cult the vitality of community life that he might have seen as missing in his own social milieu of pre–World War I France.

. . .

Every year on 10 August, at the head of a remote valley in the Italian Graian Alps, a devout and joyful crowd gathers right up in the mountains at a height of more than 2,000 meters: this is the festival of St Besse, the protector of Cogne and of the Soana valley. To the rare outsiders who witness it, it offers a picturesque and poetic spectacle. Inside and around the little chapel, built against a steep rock, throngs a motley band of pilgrims. The bright colors of the costumes of the Canavese region stand out against the gray of the rocks and the monotonous green of the pastures. As soon as the procession and the service are over, animated groups spread them- selves out, eating, drinking and singing as they relax after the morning's hard climb. Their noisy revels, however, barely manage for these few hours and within a small space to disturb the silence and peace of the immense mountains.

But neither the grandeur of the surroundings nor the especial charm of this ceremony can make the historian of religions forget the problems posed by the festival of St Besse. What meaning do the faithful give to their annual presence in this place, and to the rites that they carry out here? And, beyond the perhaps illu- sory reasons provided by the believers themselves, what is it that brings together every year in this solitary spot, at the cost of a painful climb and often a long journey, a whole host of men, women and children, who come from the neighbor- ing valleys and even from the plain of Piedmont?

Simple observation of the festival did not provide an adequate answer to these questions; and thus it proved to be the point of departure of a long and complicated inquiry. First of all it was necessary to interview a large number of those devoted to St Besse, or rather to let them talk freely. Then, several educated people, who know the region well from having been born there or from having resided there for some time, kindly agreed to reply to the questions which I put to them. Finally, if St Besse has up to now been the object of no monograph, one can glean some information, at least indirect, about him from the historical and hagiographical literature. It is from these three sources that the information analyzed in the present study has been drawn. . . .

II. THE DEVOTION TO ST BESSE

If you ask local people who St Besse was, when he lived and what he did, you will usually obtain from them only vague and incoherent replies. However, as far as the status of the saint at present is concerned, they will answer you with unanimity and precision: St Besse is a saint who has "great powers" and who performs "many miracles." His name arouses in them above all, not intellectual curiosity, but feelings of tender veneration, gratitude and hope. To honor their great patron, they will vie with each other in telling you stories in which his power is conspicuously manifested. Some of these are drawn from everyday life and concern their close relatives: the sister of one is sure to have been cured by St Besse "alone" of an old and chronic illness; the child of another, who had gone on the pilgrimage hobbling on his crutches, had left them at the shrine. Other stories touch on the marvelous, the fabulous: in the mountains, a man could not free himself from a snake which held him prisoner, he vowed to carry out a novena in honor of St Besse, and at once the snake slipped away. What the saint has done for so many others, he will surely accomplish for us, if we worship him as we should. Anyone who has a favor to ask must participate in the festival of 10 August. Anyone whom misfortune strikes or threatens "makes a vow" to St Besse: he promises to attend his festival the following year or even for nine years in a row. Anyone who fails to fulfill a vow should beware: some "accident" will certainly befall him! But if he perseveres in his devotion, he will not be disappointed.

The power of St Besse is not limited to any particular category of favor: he is a saint who "gives firm protection in all circumstances." He is invoked against sickness in people, and in livestock, as well as against the spells of witches; for there are still very evil witches in the valley. Nevertheless, according to some, there is a class of things which is the particular province of St Besse. As the images represent him in the guise of a warrior, he is, in a special way, the patron of soldiers. No man who has to leave for the wars, or simply for the barracks, would fail to attend the festival and to bring away from it a "stone of St Besse," which he will wear on his person constantly. This is why none of the men from Cogne, who have taken part in wars from those of the First Empire to the African campaign, has ever been killed in battle, so far as anyone can remember. Yet, since the institution of compulsory military service, the main task of the warrior saint has not been to protect his devotees against shot and shell but rather to exempt them from being soldiers altogether. Youths about to draw lots for the annual conscription contingent have only to attend the Saint-Besse festival: they will not then be chosen and will not have to join the regiment! But this tendency of St Besse to specialize in military affairs is, as we shall see, a secondary phenomenon, and one that is perhaps peculiar to Cogne.

The stream of favors, which the patron of the two valleys pours out over his worshippers, originates in a precise point in the landscape, which is the setting for the annual festival. The chapel of St Besse is attached to the side of a huge block of shale, an enormous natural standing-stone, which sticks up in isolation in the middle of the high pastures, its face forming a vertical or overhanging cliff thirty meters high. On top of this rock, called St Besse's Mount, is a cross and a tiny oratory. It is to this place that the faithful come each year to draw on the precious virtue which helps them to vanquish life's misfortunes.

Although the saint's protection of his own is effective throughout the year, it is only on the day of his festival that he communicates the benefit of his power to the faithful assembled around him. Doubtless one can anticipate the salutary effusion of his grace or favor by means of a vow; but the vow, far from dispensing one from visiting the shrine, by realizing its benefits in advance makes the visit absolutely obligatory. It is on 10 August that the debts contracted towards the saint during the past year are paid; and it is on 10 August that one goes to be provided with a fresh supply of grace for the year to come.

In every festival, each party must have his due. The saint has his, and the faithful have theirs. And first of all, St Besse receives from his visitors the homage of their presence. The greater the gathering of pilgrims, the "finer" the festival is judged to be and the more the saint is honored. Beyond this, the pilgrimage itself represents a real sacrifice. It is no light thing in the mountains where the summer season is so short to set aside one or two days, not to field work but to the cult of the saint. To reach Saint-Besse, moreover, from Cogne means a journey of eight to nine hours over a difficult route which crosses a col at an altitude of over 2,900 meters. From Campiglia, the nearest village, there are 700 meters to climb on a rough track, which takes two hours; the stages of this route are marked by small chapels and some people increase the merit of the ascent by making it in bare feet. The pilgrims who assemble for the festival, therefore, braving bad weather and fatigue, have brought the saint a precious offering of their time and their trouble by the mere fact of their coming.

The celebration of mass in the little chapel, sumptuously decorated and brilliantly lit, renews and augments the sanctity of the place. The sermon given by the priest exalts the greatness of St Besse, his glory and his power, as well as reminding his worshippers of their religious duties. But the central event of the festival is the procession. In good order, the whole community of the faithful leaves the chapel, grouped according to sex, age and religious dignity; they only return to it after having "done the round of the Mount," that is to say having made a complete circuit of the rock, proceeding, of course, from left to right and reciting the prayers of the rosary as they go. To add to the luster of the ceremony, the parish of Campiglia, on whose territory the shrine is situated, provides St Besse with an accompaniment of all kinds of banners and holy images; but these are only accessories. By contrast, two other elements are essential to the procession. These are, on the one hand, the two *fouïaces*, ornaments composed of ribbons and fabric in bright colors, mounted on wooden frames, and almost entirely covering the faces of the young girls who carry them on their heads; these *fouïaces*, regarded today as the "trophies" of St Besse, in the past contained consecrated bread which was distributed after the procession. On the other hand, and above all, there is the massive statue of St Besse, dressed as a Roman soldier and holding the palm of martyrdom in his hand. Four or eight young men carry it on their shoulders carefully and seriously, as befits those entrusted with a trying but honorific and praiseworthy task. Is it not right that the emphasis in this ritual promenade should be placed above all on the hero of the day, on the master of the "Mount," on glorious St Besse himself? Back in the chapel, alone, he receives the adoration of the faithful, who prostrate themselves before his statue and devoutly kiss his feet.

Beyond these personal or liturgical prestations, the faithful send or bring material offerings to the shrine. On the Sunday preceding 10 August, in all the parishes participating in the festival, a collection is taken after mass, known at Cogne as a "picking," and the proceeds of this are given to the treasury of the chapel. But many of the faithful prefer to bring the gift which they have promised the saint in their own hands and in kind. Each one of them offers at the shrine his or her most precious possession, for a man a calf or a lamb, for a woman her finest shawl or even her wedding dress. It is true that this sacrifice is not necessarily definitive. At the end of the service, the president of the festival auctions all the objects which have been offered to the saint. If the pilgrim is really attached to the "gift" which he has given, there is nothing to stop him from recovering possession of it, provided that he pays the price for it. An ingenious procedure this, which assigns to the saint the essence of the offering, that is its money value, while allowing the devotee to buy back the cherished object of which his devotion had temporarily deprived him. Giving up the spirit in order to keep the substance, is this not, in the last analysis, the very basis of religious sacrifice?

The gathering of people, the rituals and the procession, the pious offerings have all raised to its highest pitch and fully activated the sacred energy that emanates from the shrine. Before abandoning themselves entirely to the joy of being together and of happy feasting, the faithful have set their hearts on obtaining for themselves their share in the festival, by drawing on the abundant and lively source of grace that is offered to them. In the past, consumption of consecrated bread, which used to be carried in the *fouïace* and was distributed after the procession, incorporated the benefits of the ceremony in their flesh. Some people, men and women, still, it seems, rub their backs against the rock to cure themselves from pains or from sterility. But it is also necessary to take home visible tokens of the protection of the saint, which will extend over space and prolong through the whole year the efficacy of the festival. So, at the doors of the chapel, several stalls are set up, where a mixture of sweetmeats, musical toys and objects of devotion is displayed; one can buy there small images of the saint, crude little pictures or medals, which are like small change to the gold reserve of the great statue in the shrine. At one time, when the cross on top of the rock was of wood, people went to scrape it in order to collect a little dust, to be used as a remedy in case of illness. The faithful today do not have this resource; for the old cross was blown down in a storm and has been replaced by an iron one. But they still have a means of remaining in communion with the saint that is more direct and more certain.

We have seen that the chapel of St Besse is an integral part of the great rock which dominates it. A ladder set up behind the altar gives access to the heart of the Mount itself. The faithful go up the ladder and chip the rock with their knives, detaching small pieces which they piously carry home with them. These are the "stones of St Besse." They are regarded as if they were relics of the saint. At ordinary times, they are simply kept in the house like a talisman; but, at times of special danger, such as a war, for example, people wear them on their persons. If a member of the family is ill, the stone is put into the water that he is given to drink; he is even made to swallow a few particles of it. It is a sovereign remedy; but, in the words often on the lips of the faithful, "It mustn't be mocked, *you've got to have faith and trust.*" When the festival is over and the gathering breaks up, when the pilgrims in small groups get back to their scattered hamlets, bearing with them a few fragments from the mighty rock and imbued with its special power, one could say that St Besse himself goes down with them to their settlements and that, dispersing himself while retaining his being, he takes up his place for the year to come in each of the houses where he is adored.

The festival thus profits both the faithful and their patron. It exalts the prestige of the saint; it maintains and increases the honor of his name and the renown of his shrine. Without the festival, it would be as if St Besse did not exist and he would quickly lose his place in this world. As for the faithful, they bring away from their visit to the Mount a little of that fortifying and tutelary sanctity which is necessary to them in order to live their hard lives. Just as the deep valleys breathe out towards the sky a soft warm vapor which, after being condensed on the mountain side, falls back on the valleys in life-giving drops, so the humble parishes of men send up towards the venerated shrine the living breath of their devotion, which, transfigured in that holy place, returns to them in a rain of blessings. . . .

VI. THE GENESIS OF SAINT BESSE

. . . St Besse must have had an extraordinary power of attraction and cohesion to hold in check the centrifugal forces that were tending to break up the little community of his worshippers. What then is the real nature of this focus of so intense and so persistent a devotion?

We have seen that the legends, popular and semi-learned, of St Besse are mainly intended to account for the mysterious quality attributed to the Mount: they both seek, via different symbols, to introduce the sanctity of a holy man, more or less intimately, into the heart and substance of the rough stone. The real basis of the cult, even today, is the belief in the sacred character of the rock, around which the cult gravitates. Is it not likely that, in very ancient times, this fundamental belief was still free of the layers of representation that have come successively to cover it over and that it stood out clearly and directly in the consciousness of the faithful? It is certain that the ancient inhabitants of a great part of Europe practiced rock cults; it is probable that they practiced them, as so many primitive peoples still do, in complete good faith, without feeling the need to justify themselves in their own eyes, and without seeking at all costs to make the power of the rock which they venerated issue from the ideal perfection of a holy man. It would be easy to produce a crowd of examples taken from simpler societies in order to support such a conjecture. But there is no need to look in the Antipodes for what we can find close at hand without even leaving French territory. In 1877, Messieurs Piette and Sacaze were able to observe, almost intact, in the far Pyrenean valley of the Larboust, this cult of rocks against which several church councils fulminated from the fifth to the seventh centuries; these writers listened to "respectable old men" expressing with feeling their "great faith" in the sacred stones, which the people of the valley went to "touch" with all reverence in order to obtain fertility for their fields and for themselves. Here, the rocks are still the immediate and the avowed objects of devotion; or, if people feel the need to represent their power in concrete form, they do so in the guise of special spirits, "half angels, half serpents, inhabiting the sacred rocks." According to Messieurs Piette and Sacaze, the priests of the Larboust valley were rigorously combating this persistent paganism, as the Council of Nantes in 658 already prescribed; they had the sacred stones destroyed secretly and scattered the smallest fragments far away, thus running the risk of provoking disturbances among their parishioners who were scandalized by such sacrilege. In general, and particularly in the Alpine region, the Church has adopted a less rigorous attitude towards the "worshippers of stones": it has not razed to the ground the sacred rocks, but has simply placed crosses on top of them, flanked them with little chapels and associated them in one way or another with Christian belief and practice.

If we were able to compare at leisure the cult of St Besse with that of the many other saints of the region, male and female, who are adored and celebrated in the immediate neighborhood of a rock, we would find, on the one hand, an astonishing uniformity in the ritual practice and in the elementary representations which it implies, and, on the other hand, an almost infinite diversity in the legends which are supposed to explain the existence of the cult and to define the sacred being to whom it is addressed. So many shrines, so many different justifications for a devotion which is always and everywhere the same. Here are employed the themes, familiar to us, of a mortal fall or of a burial-place; but, elsewhere, a holy bishop, finding the gates of Ivrea closed one evening, went to sleep on a rock, leaving the imprint of his body on it for ever. This stone is sacred because the Theban Valerian made it his oratory and left the mark of his knees on it, while that one is sacred because the Theban Solutor was martyred there and sprinkled it with his blood. If rocks are the goals of the two most frequented pilgrimages of Piedmont, it is because St Eusebius once hid his miraculous Black Madonna at one, while at the other a pious local woman at the start of the eighteenth century hollowed out a niche in which she placed a statue of the Blessed Virgin. But how can one accept that "causes" so particular and so contingent could have produced an effect so general and so constant? How can one see in these "explanations" anything but superficial and variable translations of the ancient fundamental belief which saw in certain rocks the seat and focus of a divine power? . . .

Over the centuries, St Besse has taught his devotees to rise above the restricted horizon of their daily life, if only for a few moments, by loading on to their shoulders with joy the heavy burden of the ideal, and to retain even in times of distress "the faith and the trust" that overcome evil. In communicating to them little pieces of his substance—the small stones brought out each year from the immense rock—he made them understand, in the concrete language which they alone could grasp, that each one of them derived his strength and his courage from a superior being, who include[s] all individuals present and to come and who is infinitely greater and more durable than all of them. When the sacred rock becomes once more an ordinary rock, quite empty and purely physical, who will there be to remind the people of the valley of these truths, which are as substantial as the stone of which the Mount of Saint-Besse is made?

CONCLUSION

If it is true that the religious life of a people is a manifestation of its profoundest being, the cult of St Besse has the merit at least of taking us inside the consciousness, otherwise so distant and so closed, of the mountain people. Beyond this, St Besse, however limited his domain, is not confined to one or two Alpine valleys: one finds him transplanted into the capital of a vast diocese, into Ivrea, where for several centuries he has been honored with a very popular cult. Now, as all experienced critics confess, the personality of the saint of Ivrea is a mystery that scholars have tried in vain to elucidate by searching in the episcopal archives or by comparing late and contradictory texts. Have we perhaps been more fortunate by taking as our point of reference, not the sumptuous cathedral of the town but rather the humble chapel of Monte Fautenio? If this attempt has succeeded, in part at least, then one must conclude that every time circumstances are right, the hagiographer will do well not to neglect those precious instruments of research, a pair of stout shoes and a walking-stick.

What is more, the local cult of St Besse allows us to study the formation of a religious legend, in conditions that are particularly favorable. Nearly everyone agrees today that the Lives of the saints are the product of two distinct forces, the inventive spontaneity of the people and the work of learned compilers. Critics, working to recover the historical truth beneath the jumble of legends and concerned above all to purge the belief of the faithful of all adventitious elements, have in general been very severe on popular legends and on the writers who have echoed them. . . . These scornful judgments might be well-founded, if it were a question of the "people" emerging from a condition of mythological innocence into a sort of semi-civilized state and setting out to write history. But would it be fair to assess "the imagination of the child" by simply considering the more or less fantastic historical compositions of primary school children? Moreover, since the anonymous author of the legend is not the person who writes it down, one is nearly always obliged to imagine what the "popular" narrative was like from the literary version given by the compiler. And by what signs can one tell that the latter, in any particular part of his work, is just retailing what is authentic to the people, that he really is "the echo of the popular voice"? Any verification is usually impossible, because no element for comparison exists. Even the oral traditions of the countryside today, when they are closely connected with the cult of Christianity, are so saturated with representations of ecclesiastical origin that it is quite chimerical to regard them as "popular." However, it happens that by rare good fortune, some of the devotees of St Besse have retained in a pure state the original tradition on which the learned have set to work. In this privileged example, where we are able to collate the model and the copy, the popular legend appears indeed to be indifferent to historical truth and to Christian morality; but it lays no claim to either, since it exists on a totally different level of thought; yet, in its own sphere, it is perfectly coherent and perfectly adapted to its milieu. On the other hand, we see the compilers of the various literary versions recasting and reconstituting the oral tradition in an attempt to make it fit into a Christian framework. If the official legend of St Besse offends common sense, logic and the truth of the facts, the blame does not lie with the "people," but with those who have sought to "correct" them. Of course, it would be rash to draw general conclusions straight away from the results of this particular comparison; but the experiment which St Besse allows us to make should put us on our guard against the temptation of regarding hagiographical texts as the faithful reflection of the popular beliefs on which they are based.

Finally, there is a very good chance that observation of an Alpine cult reveals to us very ancient forms of religious life. As has often been said, the mountain is a marvelous preserver, on condition of course that the tides of the plain have not yet swept over it. The Italian Graian Alps are a paradise in this respect; they form a kind of reserve where the ibex, which has disappeared from the rest of the Alps, is found in large numbers and where the rarest Alpine plants abound. In the pastures around the shrine of St Besse, the edelweiss is about as common as the daisy in our lowland meadows. Nor is the sociologist less fortunate here than the zoologist or the botanist. In the same way that in the Alps the primitive rock emerges sometimes from the accumulation of more recent strata which cover it elsewhere, so one can see standing out here, in a few small islands, and for only a little longer, vestiges of Europe's most ancient civilization. At the extremities of the high valleys, beliefs and ritual gestures several thousand years old are perpetuated, not in the form of survivals or of "superstitions," but in the shape of a real religion with its own life and which is publicly celebrated beneath a transparent Christian covering. The main interest of the cult of St Besse is without doubt that it offers us an image, fragmentary and slightly veiled, but still distinct and very much alive, of the religion of prehistory.

NOTE

1. Isnart (2009).

2

Excerpt from "Tarantism and Catholicism"

Ernesto de Martino

Ernesto de Martino (1908–65) could be described as one of the founding figures of Italian ethnology. Until his work was translated into English, he was fairly unknown to English-speaking anthropologists. Since then, however, the importance of his contributions to the field has received wider recognition. In the book *Terra del Rimorso: Contributo a una storia religiosa del Sud* (*The Land of Remorse: A Study of Southern Italian Tarantism*), de Martino unravels how alterity may be found "at home," through a study in the southern peninsula of Salento of rural people seasonally affected by *tarantismo*, a form of possession attributed to the bite of the *tarantola* spider.[1] The affliction is cured by the performance of "choreutic" dances followed by pilgrimages and offerings made to Saint Paul. For de Martino, *tarantismo* is the living presence of an other-than-Catholic history—an echo of earlier pagan, erotic ritual forms. Tarantism can be understood only when placed within the context of Catholicism's regional history, its broader social and economic conflicts, and tensions around gender, kinship, and sexuality within the home. The cult is one that the Catholic Church has "purged" but also resignified and appropriated in an effort to contain its vitality. As de Martino shows, however, the church's engagement with the cult in the first half of the twentieth century colludes with scientific and medical—particularly psychiatric—discourses. The relevance of this work for a modern anthropology of Catholicism is plain in its historical breadth and the richness and detail of de Martino's ethnographic research. But it is also interesting for the way it highlights how questions of science, magic, and enchantment have posed challenges of different types for the modernizing, bureaucratic church.

· · ·

There is no doubt that the tarantism which our team was able to observe in the Salento during the summer of 1959 featured all the signs of a profound cultural disintegration, especially since one of its fundamental characteristics, the musical-choreutic-chromatic exorcism, showed clear signs of wear. It was rather exemplary that in the case of Caterina and Immacolata of Taviano, however much the ideology of the *taranta* had remained intact, the musical exorcism was never carried out because it had long since fallen into disuse in Taviano. Matilde of Cutrofiano had danced with the sounds in her youth, but now she merely sang something to herself without a band. Giorgio of Galàtone and Giovanna of Maglie had to interrupt their dancing because of the *carabinieri,* who acted in the first case to halt unauthorized money collection and in the second case on orders by the health official. For economic reasons, too, dancing with the sounds was no longer practiced as it once was: a *tarantata* from Termite, age fifty, "bitten" twelve years earlier, had danced every year except the last because, "although her blood needed it," she was unable to pay the musicians. Analogously, perhaps for the same reason, Concetta of Cànnole, age thirty-six, *tarantata* for twenty years, had danced for sixteen consecutive summers accompanied by musicians and assistants who yelled and clapped their hands in tempo or else joined her in the dance. But in the last four summers she had contented herself by dancing without musicians, doing the best she could all by herself. Moreover, there was an increasing shortage of musicians willing to play with expertise and diligence throughout the strenuous musical exorcism: only the band in Nardò led by the barber-violinist and the tambourinist offered the *tarantati* and their families what was needed for a proper exorcism during the critical season.

Finally, the variety of music used to probe the *tarantato* and ascertain what music was suitable for "his" *taranta* (one of the aspects of tarantism which the traditional literature had always mentioned) now appeared drastically narrowed. The band of Nardò itself employed an extremely limited repertory in the exploration. This impoverishment weakened the link between the crisis episodes and a certain number of traditional melodies offered to the *tarantato* to induce him to dance. During our fieldwork, we often gathered data on extemporaneous reactions not only to religious music but also a great variety of musical passages belonging to the current repertory of village bands, records, radio, television and cinema. So, for example, Carmela of San Pietro Vernotico had to rush out of the movie theater upon hearing *Lazzarella.*

Limiting ourselves momentarily to the sphere of religion, the decline of the traditional exorcism conducted through musical, choreutic and chromatic symbols appeared connected to the relationship between the *taranta* and St. Paul, which was promoted by the influence of Catholicism. Indeed, this was an extremely confused and contradictory relationship involving the coexistence of a St. Paul as protector of *tarantati,* implored for the grace, a St. Paul who sent the *tarante* to punish some misdeed, and a St. Paul-*taranta* or *taranta*-St. Paul who could be exorcised with music, dance and colors. Finally, during the dialogues with a hallucinatory voice either the *taranta* or St. Paul appeared, and at times something appeared which could be both. In short, what was taking place seemed to have two different symbolisms—that of St. Paul, protagonist of the episode of Malta, and that of the *taranta* which bites and re-bites—which unsuccessfully sought to merge in a new cultural equilibrium. The figure of the Saint, supported by the Church and its clergy, had attracted the people's attention to itself, thus diverting attention away from the *taranta* and its symbolism and imparting greater emphasis to the relationship of the Saint with the visionary aspect of tarantism, to the point of completely dropping the home musical exorcism. The attraction in favor of St. Paul was noticeable in many of the cases already examined (for example, that of Caterina and Immacolata of Taviano), but it was reflected in an exemplary manner in the case of Donato of Matino, a sixty-three-year-old man who had been a *tarantato* for fifty-three years. In the first years, Donato had regularly danced with "the sounds" of Matino, but then his relationship with St. Paul had come to dominate to the point that he spoke with the Saint "like a brother."[2] Finally Donato ceased dancing with "the sounds" entirely, limiting himself each year to making a spectacular entrance in the chapel of Galatina: he crawled on his back, yelling with his fists raised in the air (this was precisely one of the images in the photos taken by André Martin some years earlier). The old peasant asserted that in these annual "dances" in the chapel, to which the ceremonial aspect of his tarantism had been reduced for some time—"instead of the poison, he now got the Saint out of his system"—since the poison of the *taranta* had to be considered eliminated after so many years. In other words, Donato's tarantism had been transformed into a very eccentric devotion for St. Paul expressed with "the behavior of the poisoned victim" and by transferring to the Saint the "venting" that was previously stimulated by the "poison" of the *taranta*.

This slow process of Salentine tarantism's disintegration had been taking place in the chapel of Galatina for approximately two centuries. Aside from the mythical antecedent of Malta, the miraculous power of the well in Galatina was connected to a local legend, presented in the following version by Dr. Nicola Caputo of Lecce in the first half of the eighteenth century:

> It is said amongst the citizens (of Galatina)—whose belief has no support other than the testimony of an uninterrupted tradition—that one night the apostle St. Paul, who sailed our seas after Peter's preaching, was passing by the promontory of Santa Maria of Leuca and came to Galatina incognito for fear of persecutors, with the aim of visiting neophytes. He was welcomed there and received information at the home of a devotee, which still exists today and for this reason is called the House of St. Paul. The citizens of this town tell various things in relation to the legend, but the most important thing they say is that to reward the piety of this religious man, St. Paul

obtained the power to heal for him and his descendants, a power obtained from God through the merits of Jesus Christ; they could heal by making the sign of the cross on small wounds of those who had been bitten by poisonous animals, such as scorpions, vipers, phalangids and the like, making them drink water from a well of the House of St. Paul. It is said that when the descendants of this devotee had died out, some victims of the bite of the *taranta,* scorpion or viper came to the well—it, too, is still visible—while the poison was still in action, and asked to be healed by St. Paul, whence they were immediately cured after drinking the water; they returned home with glad hearts and gave thanks to their benefactor. This is the tradition of the citizens of Galatina, who relate various healings of this sort. Whether or not the story is to be believed in its entirety is not for us to judge, but it is in too great a contrast with the faith of these citizens to maintain that it is an entirely false story and that all of these events are to be attributed to the natural virtues of that water.

Thus, around the first half of the 1700s, there was a House of St. Paul in Galatina with a well of miraculous water, and the *tarantati* gathered there in the summer to ask the Saint for his grace and to drink the water. Caputo also notes that in the Salento many sorcerer-healers traveled from place to place boasting of their descent from St. Paul's family, showing marks which resembled snakes under their tongues, below their knees, or on their arms or legs. They swindled the public, selling false medicines to treat illness. A century earlier, Gerolamo Marciano spoke of tarantism, the cure for the bite of the *taranta* and poisonous animals through spells and poems; he recorded how "even today some silly women and vagrants lie, saying that they are of the house of St. Paul." The tradition of snake charmers and healers bragging to be descendants of the Apostle who mastered the poisonous snake in Malta was widespread in the Salento and throughout Southern Italy; even today, folklore provides us with information about so-called *Sanpaolari*. In the sixteenth century, Ferdinando Ponzetti, a doctor who became apostolic secretary in 1499 and bishop of Molfetta in 1527, wrote at length about these self-styled members of the "House of St. Paul" in his *Libellus de venenis.* One of them told the author that he knew how to cure victims of the bite from afar, operating on someone who was capable of providing him with the details of the bite; he enjoined the patient not to move, made the sign of the cross on him in the name of the Father, the Son and the Holy Ghost, had him drink water mixed with Lemnian earth, and pronounced a spell—in the end, this provoked vomiting and the immediate recovery of the distant patient.

In any case, around the first half of the eighteenth century there had already been a well for a long time and a House of St. Paul where the *tarantati* gathered. According to the precious information offered by an unpublished manuscript by the local scholar Luigi Cesàri, the well and the house were part of the territory which belonged to the Chapter of Galatina, and it is likely that ever since that time the Chapter profited from the offerings of the *tarantati* who flocked to drink water from the miraculous well. In 1752, a wealthy local gentleman, Don Nicola Vignola, purchased the territory for seven hundred ducats, reserving for the Chapter the privilege of all offerings in money, votive candles, and so forth, upon the condition that the seven hundred ducats be used for Masses in honor of St. Paul, which would be celebrated by priests descending from the new owner, and if there were no descendants, by the Chapter. In fact, quite soon there were no more priests descending from the owner, and the celebration of the Masses was turned over to the Chapter. Then the Vignola family decided to erect the present chapel, expecting that the celebration of the Masses—that is, the income from the seven hundred ducats—would pass to the independent administration of the chapel itself. The Chapter of Galatina objected vehemently, and a dispute followed between civil and ecclesiastical jurisdictions which lasted for decades. Don Vincenzo Vignola requested and easily obtained royal consent for the opening of the chapel, but papal consent was slow in coming, and although Don Vincenzo had connections and supporters and did not neglect to soften the opposition with gifts of fruit, poultry, sheep, fish and game, he did not succeed in obtaining anything. On the contrary, to add insult to injury, the Chapter of Galatina had assigned some Oblates the task of collecting the offerings of the *tarantati* at the well, and it conceded the begging of alms on contract, drawing stipulated sums from the mendicants, all of this taking place on someone else's property—that of Vignola. . . .

This was the very chapel which exists today, with its gallery, the painting of St. Paul, the sacristy, the well; the only thing missing was the niche with the statue of the Saint protected by an iron grating to shelter it from the aggressiveness of the *tarantati*. From what we were told by the local clergy, however, the niche and the statue in the chapel dated to a more recent period, when the disturbance caused by the *tarantati* during religious functions led to the transfer of the statue from its former location in the Mother Church to the chapel. In the report of the pastoral visit of 1837, the doctrinal justification for welcoming the *tarantati* into the sphere of St. Paul's cult was limited to taking note of the popular belief in the miraculous virtues of the well's water for the *real bite* of poisonous animals, clarifying how such a belief must in any case be viewed as a miraculous cure worked by God, thanks to the Apostle and the prayers of the faithful and the clergy. A different and more elaborate attempt at doctrinaire justification was found in a Latin hymn to St. Paul, of recent origin, in which the bite of the phalangid or viper became an opportunity to remember the fundamental symbolic order of Christianity: Christ as liberator of humanity from original sin and Paul as an apostle of this liberation among the Gentiles. The following refrain was repeated in the hymn: *Oremus ut fideliter / qui Galatinae sumpserit / tuam aquam sit innoxius / Morsu phalangi et viperae.* In the other strophes, however, the realistic meaning of this bite gave way to a symbolic meaning, to the "ancient serpent" which Christ had defeated, and which the Apostle to the Gentiles had once again dominated in the episode of

Malta: . . . *Caecus Damasci commorans / Es tu potitus lumine / Sic nos videre perfice / Serpentis antiqui dolos./ Oremus ut fideliter,* etc. . . . *Ut ad Melitam naufragus / Cives ferarum sospites / Fidem Fovens nos libera / A criminis contagio / Oremus ut fideliter,* etc. . . .

It was up to our investigation to evaluate whether or not this attempt to absorb the *tarantati* in a Christian symbolism had actually succeeded beyond the Latin hymn. With this aim we had to observe what occurred in the Saint's chapel on the afternoon of June 28 and on the morning of June 29 in 1959. The team witnessed the scene in the chapel hidden in the gallery *ad audiendum sacrum* mentioned in the report of the pastoral visit of 1837—a concealment that was necessary in order to prevent the observers to the greatest extent possible from disturbing the phenomenon under observation. Seated behind the balustrade, covered by a drape which gave some apertures onto the scene, we spied on what happened below for several hours, while every so often the photographer jumped up, emerging like a puppet from the balustrade for just the amount of time necessary to frame and photograph some salient scene. The social worker, on the other hand, had the task of wandering in the bedlam, mingling with the *tarantati* and their families to gather data which were impossible to obtain from our vantage point. The Salentine *tarantati*—the vast majority were women—gradually assembled, their crises having a simultaneous onset in the restricted space of the chapel. The musical exorcism seen a few days earlier at the home of Maria of Nardò was fresh in our minds: an exorcism so orderly and systematic, so clearly articulated in its consistent choreutic cycles, so regulated by the rhythm of the tambourine and the melody of the violin, so dramatically engaged in the evocation and release of obscure psychic urges through music, dance and color. But now, before our eyes, there was only an intertwining of individual, horizonless crises, disorder and chaos. The chapel lacked the music, the colored ribbons, the engrossed atmosphere of the home and the wide range of symbolism put into motion by the on-going musical exorcism: in the absence of this traditional apparatus of evocation and release, the *tarantati* foundered. From time to time they seemed to sketch a dance step, clapping the rhythm with their hands or even their barefoot soles, or they briefly attempted to break into songs which were sometimes gay and at other times melancholy, rhythms of tarantellas and funeral dirges. But it was as if they were clinging for a few moments to the debris of a shipwreck surfacing on the waves of a tempestuous ocean, and then they lost their grip, quickly sunk again by the imminent crisis. The scenes which we saw from above in our gallery *ad audiendum Sacrum* gave us the impression of colored chips of a shattered kaleidoscope, one that was no longer capable of composing geometric designs as before: states of abandon on the floor, uncontrolled psychomotor agitation, attitudes of anxious depression, bursts of aggressive frenzy along with hysterical arches, slow crawling in a prone position, sketches of dance steps, attempts at prayer, song and retching. Everything which we had already been able to see during the home exorcisms was repeated, but with no dynamic bond or teleological framework, as with a demolished building where one finds the exact same things which furnished the rooms when the building was still standing. This desperate agitation was dominated by the stylized cry of the *tarantati*, "the crisis cry," a variously-modulated *ah-eee* [a.i.:], which could be better described as a whine than as a human cry. The *tarantati* asked ardently for grace before the statue of the Saint in its niche or in the presence of a painting above the altar which depicted him with the serpent, recalling the episode of Malta; they rolled on the ground traveling the space between one image and the other; they mounted the Eucharistic table to draw nearer to the painting; they struck the iron grating which protected the statue's niche with their fists or their shoulders; they asked for water from the miraculous well, and they were carried to the sacristy, where they vomited or urinated. At a certain point, a sing-songy invocation rose up toward us, making us feel most brutally the inextricable knot of cultural contradictions which had been tied in this chapel in its two centuries of history. The invocation went like this: *Santu Paulu meu de le tarante, / che pizzichi le caruse "nmezz" all' anche / Santu Paulu meu de li scorzoni / che pizzichi li carusi int'i balloni.* We recalled the couplet which the Jesuits Nicolello and Galliberto referred to their brother Kircher in the seventeenth century: *Deu ti muzzicau la tarantella? / Sotto la pudìa de la vannella.* But while in the seventeenth-century couplet the symbolic "bite on the genitals" was attributed to a libertine little *taranta*, in the invocation which rose up to our gallery from the floor of the Chapel of St. Paul three centuries later, the Apostle to the Gentiles had taken the place of the libertine little *taranta* and was made responsible for the shameless bite which tormented youth of both sexes. Judging by this substitution of the libertine *taranta* with St. Paul of the *taranta* or *scorzoni*, the Catholic attempt to Christianize the behavior of the *tarantati* did not seem to have gone much further: the Latin hymn remained in Latin, and at least in this regard had not shaped tradition. *Omnia omnibus factus sum, ut omnes facerem salvos,* the Apostle had proclaimed to the Gentiles; but now, made into a *taranta* with the *tarantati*, he risked becoming a prisoner of his own transformation, letting the boundless apostolic fervor of *ut omnes facerem salvos* sink into nothingness. In any case, the attempt had gone much further in a negative direction by disintegrating tarantism into a series of horizonless crises and grotesque hybridisms with no future. Transported into the chapel, amputated from the musical exorcism and all of the symbolisms of evocation and release put into motion by that exorcism, tarantism was divested of any trace of cultural dignity or symbolic potency and receded to the level of individual morbid episodes, subject to the evaluation of a psychiatrist rather than a historian of religious life. For the ethnographer, what was taking place in the chapel took on at most the meaning of an instructive "cultural experiment"—as only fieldwork can provide for at times—an experiment which permitted the observation of the phenomenon *in statu moriendi* after having surprised it more or less intact in the home musical exorcisms. This made a comparison possible which yielded useful indications as to the functioning of the mythical-ritual symbol and the conditions of this functioning.

The death throes of tarantism in the Chapel of St. Paul were, as stated, carefully recorded by the team. . . .

PAOLA OF TUGLIE (4:45PM–4:55PM)

Paola of Tuglie, the Sicilian who emigrated to the Salento, lies on the ground with her eyes shut. She suddenly interrupts her motionlessness, jumping up and letting out "the crisis cry"—a shrill, prolonged *ah-eee;* she hurls herself against the niche and falls back down to the ground where she stays for a few minutes, emitting her stereotypic lament at intervals. Then she requests "water, water!," and someone brings her some in a carafe. She seems to calm down, but shortly thereafter she resumes her lament, striking the ground with a palm and then with a fist in light, rhythmic blows, as if to accompany the tempo of a tarantella ringing in her ears or perhaps simply to satisfy a hunger for rhythm. Her family says that she has a "tempestuous *taranta*" which drives its victim to "rampage." Indeed, she rises from the ground to hurl herself against the niche, banging against the protective door with her fists, and the chapel is filled with the usual roar which mixes with the shrill *ah-eee* of her strident voice. She quickly rolls to the opposite wall, gets on all fours and crawls behind the altar into the sacristy to urinate in a corner. . . .

As fate would have it, we witnessed still another episode in the death throes of tarantism in the Chapel of St. Paul: the closure of the well on the order of the mayor, who acted on a report by the sanitation officer. As we have stated, the well of St. Paul had played an important part in the Catholic attempt to absorb tarantism; for centuries, the *tarantati* flocked there, and the chapel had been built in such a way that the sacristy enclosed the mouth of the well, in whose water people saw "St. Paul's animals" swarm: serpents, scorpions, *scorzoni, tarante,* and other insidious animals that creep on the ground, bite and poison. Those who drank the water vomited the poison and recovered. But in June 1959, the sanitation authority of Galatina had argued that the water was not miraculous, but quite the contrary: dangerous, filthy, contaminated water. . . .

The *tarantati* reached the sacristy [in the Chapel of St. Paul] in their white garb, stopping astonished in front of the bricked-up well, the sepulcher which denied their lips the miraculous water and denied their eyes "St. Paul's animals" which were teeming in there. Then they went away to vanish into the turmoil of the chapel, restless shadows emerging from the kingdom of the dead. This "kingdom of the dead" was in reality the past to which they were miserably thrust back by a very prosaic "ordinance" by the mayor of Galatina; but the pity of the historian could not let them be swallowed up by the whirlpool of past centuries without having attempted to restore their palpable flesh and the dignity of their lives in the only way a historian can—through the recollection of the past. The ethnographic investigation had obtained some appreciable results: tarantism appeared to be a culturally conditioned mythical-ritual symbol, as a horizon of evocation and release for unresolved conflicts operating in the unconscious, as a cultural framework equipped with its own autonomy with regard to the occasions and existential conditions which sustained it. Specifically, the real bite of a poisonous arachnid during the harvest of the fruits of summer must have represented an important existential conditioning of the symbol in a more or less distant past in history. The analysis had evidenced a series of indices which testified to this autonomy—local immunity, the annual repetition of the crisis-exorcism connection, the predominant female participation, the familial distribution, the incidence of the crisis during puberty, the varied symbolism which was connected to the episode of the "first bite." The analysis had also highlighted how tarantism had been profoundly disarticulated and weakened as a cultural phenomenon, partly because of the Catholic influence and partly because of changed social and economic conditions. This was demonstrated by its current limited geographic diffusion, the relatively scarce number of *tarantati,* and the decadence of the musical exorcism and the scenes in the chapel. On the other hand, the ethnographic fieldwork did not have sufficient means for ascertaining in depth the elements of the myth-ritual nexus which had lapsed with time and were thus no longer ethnographically observable. Even utilizing the memories of the oldest informants, the historical probe employable in the field could not go beyond a half-century, a negligible interval for a phenomenon for which the oldest evidence dated back around six centuries. Thus, an exploration into the past became necessary in search of a less threadbare image of tarantism, one that was more intelligible and meaningful. The historian-ethnographer now had to make way for the historian-philologist, who could cover the passage of centuries gone by through the means of written documents or other equivalent traces. During the ethnographic investigation it had occasionally been necessary to appeal to verification and supplements from the philological investigation; now the roles were inverted, in that the written documentation was essentially relied upon, with possible verifications and supplements sought in the results obtained through the fieldwork. In this way, a second journey through time began, a journey in the direction of what "the land of remorse" had once been.

NOTES

1. *Rimorso* in Italian means "remorse and nostalgia," but it can also be read as *ri-morso,* or biting again. The book is about both of these meanings and the latter in a metaphorical as well as literal sense.

2. In the original, *come frate e sora,* a dialect expression literally meaning "like brother and sister."

3

Excerpt from "The Place of Grace in Anthropology"

Julian A. Pitt-Rivers

Julian Pitt-Rivers's masterful essay was originally published in 1992 as the culminating piece in *Honor and Grace in Anthropology*, a volume that this renowned ethnographer of the Spanish Mediterranean and student of E. E. Evans-Pritchard at Oxford edited with his colleague J. G. Peristiany, almost a decade before his death in 2001. The essay reveals the erudition and breadth of his ethnographic vision. Why, asks Pitt-Rivers, despite its implied presence in wide-ranging ethnographic contexts, have anthropologists ignored the concept of grace? "Grace is a whole," he argues, a socially constituted concept that we cannot understand outside of social interaction and principles of exchange and reciprocity. Unlike Mauss's classic explanation of the gift within an economy of return, however, grace is a kind of "nonreciprocity" or gratitude. Pitt-Rivers observes that grace is much older than Christianity, yet he roots all current forms of the idea of grace in the Christian concept and its etymological roots in Latin (*gratia,* or favor, or a gift freely given), tying it with individual salvation. Grace, therefore, is "a free gift of God" that implies no obligation on the part of the receiver. God bestows grace, "the friendship of God," on humankind out of his free benevolence, for their eternal salvation. Pitt-Rivers's insistence on understanding grace as exemplary of a "reciprocity of the heart" (versus the law of contract) and the "affective side of life" echoes recent scholarly awareness of modes of being and ethics—even religiosities— that cannot be explained through recourse to rational, economic models. It pertains to a consciousness of life as that which binds us together, modes of conviviality, commensality, and interrelatedness that underpin Catholicism as a living form.

   Inasmuch as grace as a concept constitutes an otherworldly force or originary substance that sets things in motion, it bears a family resemblance to ethnographic concepts like *mana*

J. A. Pitt-Rivers, "Postscript: The Place of Grace in Anthropology." In *Honor and Grace in Anthropology*, edited by J. G. Peristiany and Julian Pitt-Rivers, pp. 215–46. © Cambridge University Press, 1992. Reprinted with the permission of Cambridge University Press.

or *hau*.[1] Although Pitt-Rivers's discussion of grace was never an explicit attempt to generate conversation with other scholars of Christianity, his framing of grace as a proto-Christian version of *mana* began a process that would eventually make Christianity a "legitimate topic" for mainstream anthropological theorizing.

. . .

It remains an enigma that the notion of grace should have escaped the anthropologists for so long. This is only the more remarkable in view of the attention they have given, in recent decades, to the problem of reciprocity. Can one explain systems of reciprocity adequately without considering the possibility of non-reciprocity, i.e. gratuity? Reciprocity is the basis of all sociation, in the form of systems of exchange, of women and of food, of labor and services, of hospitality and of violence. Anthropologists attach importance, rightly, to the detail of personal conduct in their understanding of human relations. And are not thanks the common coinage of encounters between persons? Yet what do they imply? What is their logic? Not even Goffman nor the ethnomethodologists have told us. . . .

The meanings which a single word has in different contexts, or had in the forgotten past, are guides to the premises which underlie its daily conscious usage, but daily usage is indifferent to contradictions arising between its various senses, and leaves them to be sorted out at the level of action. (This is the case of honor also.) Thus it is not necessary to analyze a word in order to know how to use it correctly.

Moreover, the implications of the concept differ from place to place; expressions of gratitude are wont to follow different rules of etiquette in different social milieux, as in different cultures, and it is only by reflecting on all potential differences that one comes to understand the concept as a whole, and I maintain that grace *is* a whole. Thanks can in some situations be interpreted as a reluctance to pay what the recipient expects as his due; in others, on the contrary, to thank is to recognize indebtedness and represents a promise to return the gift or service in the future. (Such cultures might be described as "Maussian," for they have already understood "the necessity to return presents," as Mauss put it in the subtitle of his great essay on the gift.) But the etiquette concerning the return of gifts contains more subtleties than Mauss explained. . . .

There are, then, two parallel modes of conduct, ideally, even if they are not always easily distinguished, which correspond to the old opposition between the heart and the head; that which is felt and that which is known, the subjective and the objective vision of the world, the mysterious and the rational, the sacred and the profane. They are governed, respectively, by the principle of grace and by the principle of law, that is to say, predictable regularity, as well as justice and the law which impose order in human affairs—from which pardon (grace) authorizes a departure. Under the heading of "grace" it is possible to group all the phenomena that evade the conscious reasoned control of conduct.

ETYMOLOGY: THEOLOGICAL ORIGINS AND
EXTENSIONS

Let us look then first of all at the notion of grace in general before dealing with its different aspects. From the Greek root "Charis" (χάρισ), we get charity, charisma, eucharist and so forth; from the Latin, derived from it, gracious, gratitude, congratulations, etc. The origin of the word is religious; it is a theological idea which has found various spheres of extension outside the realm of theology. Benveniste (1969, 199) traces it to an Indo-Iranian root: the Sanskrit, *gir,* a song or hymn of praise or of grace, or to give thanks. He notes also that, like all other economic notions, its economic sense derives from the totality of human relations or relations with gods rather than the contrary. Gratuity is the core of the notion, that which is undertaken not in order to obtain a return but to give pleasure.

We must certainly start with the theological concept of grace, for it appears that the structure of the religious notion is able to account for the elaboration of the popular senses, though whether popular theology is derived from the reasoning of the learned or whether the latter have based their doctrines on the popular premises which they absorbed in infancy—an argument that has raged for a century with regard to other aspects of culture—is an issue that we need not raise now, but it is worth observing that, unlike honor, grace seems never to have quite forgotten its etymological roots. Without entering into the subtleties of the numerous varieties of grace and the excessively optimistic or pessimistic doctrines which have been condemned as heresy from time to time, we can give, as its starting point, the pure gratuitous gift of God.

Louis Ott (1955) defines it as "a free gift of God unmerited by men" ("un don gratuit de la part de Dieu et immérité de la part de l'homme"). According to St. Thomas Aquinas it is especially the gift of the Holy Spirit, but it is also, in the Pauline view, associated particularly with Christ whose death redeemed us from original sin. As pardon obtained through Him, it is the key to salvation.

It develops within us as a *habitus*,[2] an acquired disposition to cooperate with the will of God, and this involves human will also, upon which the will of God operates, in St. Augustine's opinion. It is a supernatural accident created in our nature in such a manner as to adapt it to divine life, in the Thomist doctrine. Ott (1955, 314), again, says: "The unfathomable mystery of the doctrine of grace is to be found in the intimate collaboration and reciprocal intervention of divine power and human freedom. All the controversies and heresies regarding grace have their point of departure in this." ("Dans la collaboration intime et l'intervention réciproque de la puissance divine et de la liberté humaine se trouve le mystère insondable de la doctrine de la Grâce. Toutes les controverses et hérésies relatives à la grâce ont là leur point de départ.") And he discusses the relations between grace and freedom (348ff.).

It is clear that the discussions center upon the role of human will which is insufficient by itself to attain salvation, but which cannot be dispensed with—without falling into determinism. If individual will is the essence of honor, the essence of grace is the will of God, which necessarily restricts the individual's will in some degree, but the attainment of grace can only be achieved with the cooperation of human will since God requires his beneficence to be returned; the rites of the Catholic Church require the appropriate intentions on the part of the beneficiary in order to be valid. The Catholic solution to the paradox of theodicy resides in this mysterious conjunction of the will of God and the will of man.

Grace is connected with the will in another way also, for it is associated with purity. To be "in a state of grace" is to be sinless, to be redeemed, through confession, from the state of sin into which our all too human will has led us. To be in a condition to receive grace one must be cleansed of sinfulness, not only of original sin, of which one was discharged by the grace of the Holy Spirit at baptism, but of the sins which result from a will inadequately accorded to the will of God. Yet such provisions are necessarily insufficient to assure the attainment of grace, since the will of God on which this depends is by definition arbitrary. On account of this unpredictability, grace comes in popular usage to mean good fortune, that which cannot be foreseen. . . .

Though grace is a free gift of God, unpredictable, arbitrary and mysterious, there are nonetheless means of obtaining it: first of all through the sacraments. This is the main function of the rites of the Church, indeed of any church. Sacrifice is always a tentative to embark upon an exchange of grace with the Deity. The offering invites a return-gift of grace, the friendship of God, as it has been called. The Eucharist, the commensality of the mass, confession, prayer, and penance, the usage of "gratiferous" substances: incense, corn, wine, oil, and salt and water too, are all employed in the enterprise of obtaining grace, whether for the salvation of the souls of the faithful or their material prosperity. But the passage of grace is never guaranteed, even by the state of grace, the purity of intentions or the correct administration of the rite, because grace is a mystery which remains in the free gift of God.

If God is the source of grace, this does not mean that humans cannot generate it, and dispense it to others. The dictionaries' lists of meanings provide an abundance of examples, which we can leave the reader to examine at his leisure. The central core remains always the notion of gratuity, on the social as on the theological plane, and the essential opposition is to that which is rational, predictable, calculated, legally or even morally obligatory, contractually binding, creating a right to reciprocity. Grace is a "free" gift, a favor, an expression of esteem, of the desire to please, a product of the arbitrary will, human or divine, an unaccountable love. Hence it is gratuitous in yet another sense: that of being not answerable to coherent reasoning, unjustifiable, as when an insult is said to be gratuitous, or when a payment is made, over and above that which is due. . . .

GRACE, POSITIVE AND NEGATIVE, IN GRAZALEMA

The connotations of grace are as varied as those of honor, the more so in Spanish than in English, it appears; for this reason, and also because I have previously examined the concept of honor in Andalusia (Pitt-Rivers 1977), I shall deal with grace as it operates in that part of Spain where its logic, thanks to its richness, can be seen more clearly. The variations in the daily use of grace, as of honor, distinguish different national cultures, and to some extent regions and classes as well, while the theological variants are matters of doctrine rather than usage and depend upon individual thinkers, cults and heresies—and historical periods.

Let us see then how the word *gracia* is used in the everyday life of a small Andalusian town, Grazalema (Pitt-Rivers [1954] 1971), starting with its role in popular theology. It figures in the subjectivity of the townsmen and above all, townswomen as a state of grace, forgiveness subsequent to confession, the achievement of atonement which makes a person eligible to receive divine grace through the sacraments, or in answer to prayers. It is the essence of redemption through baptism; the rite of baptism assures the entry of a new-born child into the religious, that is to say, the human community. It expunges the sin of Adam through the application of the water, the salt, and the chrism, the unguent vehicle of grace which figures also in the last rites. It establishes the tie of spiritual affinity between the god-child and the god-parents who give the child its name. A person's first name is sometimes called his *gracia*. The god-parents, *padrinos*, are also called *padres de gracia*, spiritual parents or parents of the Christian name, in opposition to natural parents whose duties towards their children stand in marked contrast to those of the god-parents. The tie of spiritual affinity still exists in the popular view, with all the obligations of respect and the usage of the third person in speech between the *compadres* (parents and god-parents in relation to each other), despite the recent abolition of this tie in the dogma of the Roman Catholic (but not the Orthodox) Church (Pitt-Rivers 1976).

The grace of God is obtained through other sacraments, and prayers are offered to God and to the saints, above all to the various manifestations of the Holy Virgin, for their intercession to obtain divine favor in the form of personal advantages, cures, or miracles. Promises *(promesas)* were made to reciprocate the favor, if the prayers were answered, by wearing a robe recalling that of the image of the saint who had obtained the miracle or by performing a penance such as bearing a wooden cross, going barefoot or on knees during the processions in the celebration of Holy Week. . . .

Grace, like honor, is not at all the same thing for both sexes. While masculine honor is a matter of precedence in the first place and the man of honor strives to establish his name in the forefront of his group, the honor of women is rather a matter of virtue and sexual purity. The distinction is clearly marked in Sicily under the titles of "Name" and "Blood." The first is active and positive, a matter of attaining or inhering status and prestige or, in the plebeian community, the respect due to an honorable member. The second is negative and passive, a matter of avoiding any action that might stain the reputation of the family. Male honor is something to be won, increased, and defended against a rival; female honor is something to be conserved and protected from the evil tongues of the envious.

Grace is rather the reverse of masculine honor which depends upon individual will and ambition and this aligns it with female honor. In the first place women have, as it were, a prior claim to grace, not merely on religious grounds (they are more active in religious practice than men), but in the attribution of it in most of its forms. Aesthetic grace is purely feminine: men are not expected to have grace of movement, though they may dance with grace, and professional dancers are commonly assumed to be effeminate.

The *curanderas* (curers), also called *sabias* (wise women), possess an individual grace which comes to them from the saint of their devotion and enables them to cure through the grace in their hand and the performance of ritual gestures (signs of the cross on various parts of the patient's body), anointment with blessed oil, and prayers, muttered rather than declaimed because addressed to the divine powers rather than to the patient or the audience. The whole rite bears a general resemblance to baptism or to coronation, but the divinities to whom the prayers are addressed show the rite to be anything but orthodox Christianity. They include, apart from Jesus Christ and the Virgin Mary (in the manifestation which is the particular devotion of the *sabia*), the holy salt, addressed as a divine personage ("Salt, Salt, they call you salt, but I call you Holy Salt . . . "), the Seven Lions, Venus and Astarte, and others of an equally heterodox character. Aided by the holy oil, the evil leaves the patient's body and enters the arm of the curer who endures the pain for the next twenty-four hours or so.

Were a *sabia* to accept a gift of money in recompense for the cure she had performed, she would immediately lose her grace, for it belongs to God and would be withdrawn if she were to use it to obtain material gain. In return for her grace she can accept only symbols of grace, blessed candles to burn in front of the Virgin or holy oil, for she is operating upon that second circuit in which only grace can be returned for grace.

Given the ambivalence of magical powers, a general phenomenon in anthropology, it is not surprising that the first people to be suspected of witchcraft were the *sabias*. Could they not use their grace for evil ends also? Nothing appeared more plausible, for just as cursing is the reverse of blessing, so magical damage is the reverse of magical healing. It suffices to invert the intention to produce the opposite result. Witches are commonly credited with the power to inflict damage on man or beast, to do love-magic, to foretell the future, to drive men mad, etc., in brief to operate upon the health or sentiments of their victims.

Witchcraft everywhere depends upon envy, the will to do harm. But to do harm to an enemy is quite legitimate conduct; it is part of the game to take vengeance against the man who has damaged you or your reputation in order to recuperate your honor, "restore it to a state of grace." Witchcraft, however, is the attempt to take vengeance, not openly, but by covert dishonorable means, negative grace, invoking the aid of the Devil. For this reason the curer who enjoyed the greatest popularity in Grazalema never tired of repeating that she did "nothing but the things of God" and gave every outward sign of her piety. In brief, witchcraft can here, as anywhere else moreover, be defined as an *habitus* of negative grace. Just as positive grace is opposed to reasoned empirical means of doing good, so negative grace is opposed to overt vengeance and employs the supernatural. The grace of the *sabias,* the source of their magical power, was something inherent in their bodies, like their sex. And it must be added that the female sex produces maleficent manifestations at the time of the period. Other forms of involuntary evil attributed to certain women were the Evil Eye and that quality, called *calio* in Grazalema, which makes them permanently dangerous as though they were menstruating. (A similar belief is found elsewhere in the region, though under different names, which all however recall the notion of heat: see Pitt-Rivers [1954] 1971, where a more complete account is given.)

Witches can in fact be of either sex, though in Grazalema their techniques are totally distinct. Women cure by their grace which comes from God and if they bewitch it is, implicitly, by a misuse of that grace which has power even when perverted to nefarious ends, rather as the black mass, by inverting the symbols, uses the powers of religion to accomplish the work of the Devil.

Men have no grace in this sense; they cure and they bewitch not by the mysterious power of grace but by techniques which are supposedly rational and depend upon knowledge (though this is not general throughout Spain; men who cure by grace are to be found in the northern half of the country and as far south as the provinces of Alicante and Caceres). Thus apart from the practitioners of "scientific medicine," doctors and chemists, all of them men, those of folk medicine were limited to bone-setters and herbalists (the latter could also be women). The techniques of witchcraft practiced by men consisted of spells, and above all of spells to invoke the aid of the Devil through reading a book of magic. Since poltergeists were the work of the Devil, they were necessarily caused by "reading" and consequently by men only, though their victims were all women. Thus the distinction established by Evans-Pritchard between witchcraft and sorcery with regard to the ethnography of the Azande was exemplified in Grazalema, with the additional rider that witches were all, and by definition, female, while sorcerers were all male. None of the *sabias* knew how to read. Newspapers and notices on the municipal noticeboard were the main reading matter, that is to say, reading concerned the male sphere of relations with the administration and news of the outside world.

Hence reading was an essentially male activity. News regarding the inner sphere of the community was passed by word of mouth at the fountain whither every household had to send a member every day to wash clothing if they wished to keep up with events. . . .

The signs of grace are not confined to women, but they tend to reinforce its connection with the female sex: to begin with, in popular theology the source of grace was the Virgin Mary, who is announced as such in the Ave Maria. Hence all women named Maria have grace and this accounts for half the female population, for they are named after a specific manifestation of the Virgin, and are generally called, for abbreviation, only by the name of that manifestation. Hence Dolores, Carmen, Luz, Pilar, Mercedes, Milagros, Imaculada, and the place-names of her appearance. Lourdes, Fatima, etc., are all in fact Maria. But in any case it is said that all women are Mary simply by virtue of their sex. Good luck is also grace, prosperity on earth as well as salvation in the hereafter, for they are all given by God. In this sense it corresponds to *baraka,* as in a number of others which the reader may have noted. . . .

To summarize, in the sense of benefaction, gift, demonstration of benevolence, concession, graciousness, pardon, or indulgence, grace is inspired by the notion of something over and above what is due, economically, legally, or morally; it is neither foreseeable, predictable by reasoning, nor subject to guarantee. It stands outside the system of reciprocal services. It cannot be owed or won, specified in advance or merited. Hence it can mean remission of a sin or a debt, mercy, pardon, or forgiveness and thus it is opposed to justice and the law. As gratitude it is the only return-gift that conserves the nature of the initial prestation. You cannot pay for a favor in any way or it ceases to be one, you can only thank, though on a later occasion you can demonstrate gratitude by making an equally "free" gift in return. Like hospitality, which is a manifestation of it, or like violence, its contrary, a demonstration of malevolence, it can only be exchanged against its own kind (Jamous 1981). To attempt to reply to violence by invoking the sanctions of the law is behavior not approved by the code of honor (Pitt-Rivers 1977).

Grace, then, allows of no payment, no explanation, and requires no justification. It is not just illogical, but opposed to logic, a counter-principle, unpredictable as the hand of God, "an unfathomable mystery" which stretches far beyond the confines of theology. The opposition is clear and applies in every case: grace is opposed to calculation, as chance is to the control of destiny, as the free gift is to the contract, as the heart is to the head, as the total commitment is to the limited responsibility, as thanks are to the stipulated counterpart, as the notion of community is to that of alterity, as *Gemeinschaft* is to *Gesellschaft,* as kinship amity is to political alliance, as the open check is to the audited account. . . .

The concept of grace which lay at the basis of my explanation cannot be assumed to exist elsewhere, even if Mauss's essay suffices to establish that the gift corresponds to a general sociological category. The basic opposition between human attempts to foresee and control the future through calculation and a law of contract, on the one hand, and the inscrutability of the will of God, whose grace is a mystery, on the other, is missing in primitive cultures. The Christian concept of grace is above all concerned with individual salvation, from the religious point of view, and this I put forward as the root of the extended senses of the word. It might be thought to follow therefore that there is nothing like grace to be found where there is no salvation, that is to say, outside Christianity. However we have suggested that, lacking such a fertile theological soil to grow in, a concept very similar to grace is found in Judaism (*hesed*) and in Islam (*baraka*). Reciprocity of favor, like friendship, which is nothing more than this, is universal whether between man and God or between men. It is the other term of the opposition that is missing; legal contract is specific to societies that keep written records. . . .

HONOR AND GRACE: THEIR MEDIATIVE FUNCTION

We have tried to encompass the totality of grace and explain the coherence of the whole concept and the relation between its different meanings. In defining a notion of such variety, it is not enough to study only the concept by itself, one must place it within sets of wider range and look for its connections with others. The one of particular interest for this book is that which forms, with grace, its title, honor, for it seems to deal with problems in the same field: the destiny of a man and his relations with other people and with God. It shares with honor the same tendency to be evanescent and self-contradictory. Sometimes the two words are almost interchangeable: you pay honor in offering grace, for it is an expression of sentiment freely willed. You expose your honor in doing so, precisely because there is no obligation to return grace unless it comes from the heart—and you are dishonored if you get a "brush-off," in which case you are justified in being offended. Hence it can be seen that exchanges of honor are very similar to exchanges of grace. To be favored or privileged is to be honored, exalted above those who are not favored. Rituals of honor are continually marking distinctions of this sort. . . .

The unverifiability of intentions and the state of the heart, which are necessary to both honor and grace, the paradoxes which assail both and the uncertainty of divine judgment which refuses to submit to mundane reasoning, have encouraged societies with writing to replace the reciprocity of the heart by the law of contract and provide sanctions for its enforcement. Taking reciprocity out of the field of grace detaches it from the sentiments and objectifies it, making it abstract and depersonalized. As soon as the monarchy was strong enough, it suppressed the judicial combat and took justice out of the unpredictable hands of fate, curtailing the problem of theodicy. Yet the affective side of life cannot be obliterated. Despite their contrary aspects grace and honor remain and contribute each to the composition of the other. . . .

But grace is closer to God than the ambition to succeed, and for that reason he who has renounced all pretension to honor by demanding (and exploiting) pity enjoys a privileged relationship with the Almighty. Grace, not honor, is the ideal enjoined by the Beatitudes. Indeed the contradiction is spectacular, the lesson clear: one must renounce one's claim to honor as precedence if one is to attain the fellowship of the Holy Ghost, or more precisely one must invert it, adopt the counter-principle represented by the honor of women, whose sex excludes them in theory from the agonistic sphere. (The resemblance between feminine honor and grace has already been noted.) In somewhat similar vein the sacred status of priests imposes upon them the renunciation of violence and worldly ambition as well as the right to play the male role in relation to women.

One might be tempted to jump to the conclusion that this opposition between masculine honor and grace is a product of the moral revolution imposed by Christianity—this was what Nietzsche thought—yet grace is much older than Christianity and Mauss (1966, 15) had already noted the generic connection between the gods and the poor through whom they can be approached; we also know from classical Greece that Zeus was accustomed to adopt the disguise of the beggar who enjoyed his special protection. The opposition is therefore more general than its connection with Christianity. The sacred status of beggars can be found in India also. . . .

However, once the hierarchy is established, the competition is over, and from that moment the man who has achieved power, preeminence, the dominant position, wishes only to legitimize it in the public consensus. His honor changes its nature and from striving to achieve precedence it becomes honor validated in the view of others, honor as virtue, recognized by his subordinates and dependants, whom he protects. This simplistic paradigm of power would have no interest if it did not correspond to a transition from agonistic honor to grace which we can detect in other circumstances. It would appear that there are in Western civilization two opposed—and ultimately complementary—registers: the first associated with honor, competition, triumph, the male sex, possession, and the profane world, and the other with peace, amity, grace, purity, renunciation, the female sex, dispossession in favor of others, and the sacred. . . .

Hence that which appears at first as an anomaly if not a contradiction becomes, once viewed in the perspective of the life cycle, a relation of complementarity and in the end concordance, for, since grace is the will of God, it is by His grace that the triumphant hero received his endowment in the first place, was predestined to win. If one ends up dishonored, it was for lack of grace in the first place. Honor stands before the event; his honorable qualities produce the victor. Grace stands behind it; the will of God is revealed in the outcome. Each is therefore a precondition of the other. If you lack grace you will not attain honor, in which case you will lack the means to be gracious. . . .

Both honor and grace are mediative concepts; they interpret events in accordance with the prevailing values of society, putting the seal of legitimacy on to the established order. Together they constitute the frame of reference by which people and situations are to be judged. They are indistinguishably blended in the Basque concept of *indarra,* in which natural, cultural, and social forces come together; the life force of men, plants and the wine, the grace of the Holy Virgin, and the legitimacy of property rights in houses. Elements of both honor and grace are found in Polynesian *mana,* and other "legitimizing concepts" can be found in the ethnographies of other parts of the world. They supply the point of junction between the ideal and the real world, the sacred and the profane, culture and society.

References

Benveniste, Emile. 1969. *Le vocabulaire des institutions indo-européennes.* Vol. 1. *Economie, parenté, société.* Paris: Editions de Minuit.

Bourdieu, Pierre. 1987. *Choses dites.* Paris: Editions de Minuit.

Jamous, Raymound. 1981. *Honneur et baraka: Les structures traditionelles dans le Rif.* Paris: Editions de la Maison des Sciences de l'Homme.

Mauss, Marcel. 1966. *The Gift.* London: Cohen and West.

Ott, Louis. 1955. *Précis de théologie dogmatique.* Paris: Editions Savator.

Pitt-Rivers, Julian. [1954] 1971. *The People of the Sierra.* London: Weidenfeld and Nicolson.

———. 1976. "Ritual Kinship in the Mediterranean: Spain and the Balkans." In *Mediterranean Family Structures,* edited by J. G. Peristiany, 317–34. Cambridge: Cambridge University Press.

———. 1977. *The Fate of Schechem or the Politics of Sex.* Cambridge: Cambridge University Press.

NOTES

1. *Mana* is a major concept in Polynesian cultures, denoting an energy or life force of supernatural origin. *Hau,* a Maori term denoting a form of energy or spirit that binds givers and receivers, was made popular by Marcell Mauss ([1954] 1990) in his famous book *The Gift.*

2. A note here in Pitt-Rivers's original reads: "The term has been borrowed by the philosophers and, finally, by the social sciences. For its utilization in the latter, see Bourdieu (1987, 23): 'a system of acquired schemas functioning practically as categories of perception and assessment or as classificatory principles as well as organizing principles of action.'"

4

Excerpt from "The Dinka and Catholicism"

Godfrey Lienhardt

Like Julian Pitt-Rivers, Godfrey Lienhardt (1921–93) was a student of E. E. Evans-Pritchard at Oxford. His great ethnography *Divinity and Experience: The Religion of the Dinka,* published in 1961, is regarded as one of the great social anthropological studies of religion. In his research (1947–50) on this southern Sudanese nomad population (neighbors of the Nuer, the people researched by Evans-Pritchard), Lienhardt approaches religious symbolism, imagery, and leadership as informed intimately by the Dinka's own everyday experience of the world. He altered dominant social anthropological perspectives on religion of the time by drawing attention to the discrepancy and contradictions that existed between people's everyday experience of "religion" and their conscious, reflexive articulations about those practices.

The attention to skepticism and ambiguity is evident in this essay (first published in 1982, and reproduced here almost in its entirety) that reflects on the interaction between the Dinka and Italian Catholic missionaries, who had been in the Sudan since the mid-nineteenth century. Lienhardt begins by asking, "What kind of translation, as it were, of experience is required for a Dinka to become a nominal or believing Christian?" He responds to this question with circumspection, stressing the challenges in any missionary encounter, which he aptly characterizes as not one of simple straightforward instruction and conversion (or rupture), but one fraught with gaps in understanding and divergent intentions on both sides. Many of these gaps inhere in language, both idiomatic and semantic terms, with many ideas being "caught in translation," leading Catholicism to "stick" unevenly and in unpredictable ways across the Dinka world. Thus the Dinka accepted the Church mostly, Lienhardt suggests, through ideas of progress and mostly material development that were quite foreign to Dinka experience and, somewhat ironically, also to the ideas and principles taught by the

This essay was published in *Religious Organization and Religious Experience*, J. Davis (ed.), pp. 81–95, Copyright Elsevier (1982).

missionaries. Catholic doctrine and eschatology were thus absorbed into the Dinka life-world through a kind of "linguistic parallax" (a displacement or change in the perception of objects in space from different points of observation). Lienhardt erroneously characterizes the church as "the bearer of a theoretically unified body of theological and social doctrine"—a portrayal similar to widespread views even today. But the acuity of his attention to the intricacies and uncertainties of the exchange of meanings that is part of missionization—and to the political economic realities shaping the encounter—distinguishes this work as a pioneering study in the anthropology of missions, especially in colonial Africa. In this respect Lienhardt's essay might be seen as a precursor to a great tradition of poststructural-ist works on African religious missionaries, postcolonialism, and social transformation.[1] His focus on Catholicism, however, provides us a glimpse of the dynamics of "syncretism" in situ as a process that cannot be understood outside its social, historical, and political context.

· · ·

To describe the Southern Sudan as Christian (as journalists, political commenta-tors and religious sympathizers have often done) misrepresents the situation. Most educated Southern Sudanese were indeed the products of a Christian form of edu-cation, as are today the many more western-educated southerners who provide the political leadership and administration of the South; but in the 1940s proselytizing Southern Sudanese Christians, except for those few in the service of the Church itself, were not conspicuous. It was not primarily as Christians that southerners fought against the northern Government until almost ten years ago, but as non-Arabs and non-Muslims against Arab and Muslim domination. In that world, what kind of translation, as it were, of experience was required for a Dinka to become a nominal or believing Christian?

The Church is the bearer of a theoretically unified body of theological and social doctrine. The two are already represented in the reported reaction of the early missionaries mentioned in the quotation with which I began—the wearing of the crucifix and the intention to demonstrate their charity. They bear the symbols of their faith, and hope to recommend them by their works. The doctrinal symbol of the crucifix caused immediate difficulties, for Fr. Dempsey (1955, 103) says that the Shilluk "ran away from men so cruel as to wear on their breasts a cross with a man fixed to it" and expresses his view, as a missionary priest, that for the Shilluk (and for the Dinka this is equally true) educational and medical and other practi-cal services of the Church necessarily must precede any hope of evangelization (124ff.). He recognizes also that the freedom of movement taken for granted by the Shilluk population (and the pastoral Nilotes are much more mobile) creates a dif-ficulty for missions, for the Church's forms of organization elsewhere presuppose a settled population, a Catholic community with priestly guidance and leadership. Thirty years ago certainly the practice of Catholicism was associated with towns and mission stations, providing a very different form of social life from that of the villages and the cattle-camps. For traditional Dinka, towns have always been places of ill-repute, attracting social riff-raff, and Dinka of good family did not wish their children to be corrupted by such company as they might find near established mission-stations. Hence there were scarcely any Christian chiefs. Catholicism had not grafted itself on to the local leadership.

The Dinka indigenous leaders combined religious with political status; but although some of the priest-chiefs, "masters," of the fishing spear, had a higher reputation for their religious power than others, there was no hierarchy of authority. Each priestly family provided spiritual and political guidance for the people of the area in which it was dominant. Its position was validated by elaborate myths, basically common to all Dinka, which set the priestly clan in a religious tradition closely bound up with the ecological conditions and basic experiences of life and death of the Dinka in their own places in Dinkaland. The myth itself represents the first priests as descended from the union of a spirit with a woman who could not have a child by human agency, and the first priest gives a teaching, performs various miracles and shares his power among his followers. The Dinka thus already had a story of the founding of their religious belief and practice which corresponded at some points to the Christian story of the birth and earlier career of Christ, and to the authority inherited through the Apostles at his death. Although such correspondences might appear advantageous for those wishing to persuade the Dinka to accept the Christian version, they could also appear simply as alternative and foreign versions of religious truths already familiar on their own terms to the Dinka, and unlike the Christian version, intimately connected with their own way of life. Ideas of a high God, of sin, of sacrifice, of redemption by blood and God's forgiveness (to mention only a few of the components of Christian doctrine) were also central to Dinka religion. Dramatic religious conversion, ideas of turning away from idolatry, being freed from spiritual bondage and excited by new cultural expressions of religious fervor (characteristic of the effects of fundamentalist missions in particular among peoples defeated by foreigners), could scarcely be expected on any large scale among the Dinka. The pastoral Nilotes have a very non-material—indeed anti-material—conception of the nature of religious forces, and at one level or thought could easily accept the commandment that "thou shalt have no other God before me," or the Moslem "There is no god but God," and they make no "graven images," the effectiveness of which could be questioned by an appeal to a more spiritual or scientific interpretation of religious forces.

The Dinka knew also that in different parts of the country there were many differing versions of the validating myth of their own priesthood, each giving its own account of the original characters and action in relation to local clans and communities. As there was no hierarchy of religious control, so there was no idea of a hierarchy of doctrinal authority. I took down many different versions of this myth among people who knew that I had been told stories different from their own.

I never heard of any concern to establish one true version, for myth is "what people heard from the people of long ago," and different peoples heard different things.
Only within each community was it accepted that some versions were more correct
and fuller than others, and here the more authoritative version, the "true doctrine,"
as it were, was that of on the whole older men, recognized to have taken a special
interest in tradition, and to have had it handed on in more complete form from
fathers and grandfathers who had themselves been similarly specially instructed.
But the very idea of missionary activity, of teaching and propagating a more comprehensive religious truth, was absent, except in the case of the few "charismatic
leaders," called "prophets" in the anthropological literature, whose teaching did
not deny the basic tenets of traditional Dinka religion, but revived them with their
own personal revelations and divine guidance. They claimed revelation from God,
so another theme in Catholic doctrine represented, for example, by the statement
of Cardinal Fumasoni-Biondi, "The Catholic Church comes from above and not
from outside," was also familiar to the Dinka themselves.

Thus there were enough parallels between Catholic theological and social doctrine for the Christian message not to appear entirely new, but (and this must be a
particular problem for evangelists in such circumstances) Christian arguments
against Dinka religious and spiritual conceptions could involve calling into question
also the Christian ones to which they were analogous. Why (to take just two examples) if Dinka accepted the Christian miracles, should they reject similar miracles
attributed to great religious leaders in their own indigenous tradition? Why leave
their own established religious leaders who called upon their people to become reconciled with God and each other, who made blood sacrifices to cleanse them from
sin, who often called for peace, in order to follow others with a similar message?

The higher philosophy of missions, as it was represented in the 1950s, was
intended to take account of such questioning, but, it seems to me, assumed native
populations more readily convinced than the Dinka that the Christian message
incorporated all that was good and true in their own religious experience, and
hence somewhat misunderstood the way in which Christianity was in practice
propagated, as though it were a matter of confronting "lower" with "higher" spiritual ideals. I quote a few passages from the papal encyclical on the missions, *Evan-
gelii Praecones,* promulgated by Pope Pius XII in 1951, as representing the official
Catholic approach at the time of which I am writing:

> The Church, from the beginning down to our own time, has always followed this
> practice: let not the Gospel, on being introduced into a new land, destroy or extin-
> guish whatever its people possess that is naturally good, just or beautiful. For the
> Church, when she calls her people to a higher culture and better way of life, under
> the inspiration of the Christian religion, does not act like one who recklessly cuts
> down and uproots a thriving forest. No, she grafts a good scion upon a wild stock,
> that it may bear a crop of more delicious fruit.

The "wild stock" of Dinka religion involved a fundamental identification of each clan with its own tutelary divinities, addressed as "you of my father" in all Dinka prayers. That conception of religious communion by descent, and symbolized by animals and other creatures and objects which the Dinka therefore held in reverence, was difficult to use as a stock upon which to graft Christianity, for it went so deep into Dinka personal and social life that to reject it would be to reject the very idea of an abiding spiritual truth, transmitted from generation to generation *per omnia saecula saeculorum,* upon which the Church based its own claim to religious authority. . . .

This program is in a liberal tradition of Catholic thought which must recommend itself to those who find no authority in Christian teaching for the condemnation of indigenous dancing and drinking, for example, which seems to figure so largely in the message of some Protestant sects. But it presupposes a comprehension of "pagan philosophies" as formulated by systematic thinkers like the Greeks, Chinese or Romans, and thus doctrinally comparable with Christian teaching. The earlier missionaries among the Dinka could not possibly have any such comprehension of a Dinka philosophy. The Dinka themselves did not think doctrinally, and the missionaries, partly by the very nature of their convictions and vocation, could not suspend their own belief to reach the comparative level of thought required to reinterpret the encyclical in local terms. Thus despite the Catholic view that the Church comes from above and not from outside, and the Church's claim to be teaching *quod ubique, quod semper, quod ab omnibus,* in the eyes of the Dinka the Catholic Church could not but appear to come from outside, in the form of "red foreigners" (their term for Europeans) often bearded, and dressed in special garments unlike those of European officials. They provided in the schools and missions a way of life and teaching foreign to the Dinka, and turned those they could influence into a different kind of person from the herdsman, warrior, and husband of many wives and father of many children, who represented the Dinka ideal. The introduction of Christianity involved in some ways a more, and in some ways a less, radical reformation of Dinka ways of thought than the encyclical, and other Christian aspirations on the same lines, assumed. The familiar Malinowskian, functionalist view of all social institutions as intricately interconnected would have suggested that eradicating "bad" beliefs and customs, and retaining and adding to "good" ones, was a more complex task than this liberal tradition of Christian thought allowed for.

The Nilotes regarded the missionaries like all foreigners as inferior to themselves in all but technological and medical skills, and were as secure in their own standards as the missionaries in theirs. So the missionary presence was valued above all for one contribution to Dinka well-being which reflective and influential Dinka slowly came to see as necessary for their cultural and political survival—education. The Dinka were made increasingly aware that much though they might have preferred to live without external interference in their traditional mode of life, that interference had already begun to endanger their independence. They saw that they needed enough of their own people capable of thinking in foreign ways, of meeting foreigners on their own ground while remaining Dinka in their loyalties, to understand and circumvent encroachments on their own autonomy.

Education, and therefore evangelization where it took effect, started in the Dinka language, moving on to elementary English and now Arabic. . . .

. . . In the 1950s, outside mission stations and among people speaking wholly in Dinka, one rarely heard any word which could be understood as a version of the word "Christian" as if referring to religious commitment only. Schoolboys and people around missions whether Christians or not, were *mith abun*, "the children of the mission," *abun* presumably being a loan word from the Ethiopian *abuna*, a father and Bishop. Baptism was *doc plu nhialic*, "blessed with God's water," an idea quite familiar to Dinka in their own religious practice, though here become a specialized term for the Christian rite. Thus missionized Dinka were seen as belonging to another kind of family, different from their natal family, and when away from it, forming a community with customs, and linguistic usages, of their own. Then "the children of the missionaries" were fed and brought up by the missionaries instead of their own parents. A redefinition of vernacular terms makes possible the construction of a framework of reference coming from Dinka family life, now applied to the Church, seen as a kind of family, but not a Dinka family. . . .

To traditional Dinka, that idea of progress was quite foreign. There was little evidence that life had ever been different from what it was today, nor, until the coming of the Europeans, that it was ever going to change in the future. But by the 1940s, it had become apparent to many thoughtful Dinka that in lacking education their people were lacking some of the essential skills for political survival in the modern Sudan, and they came to accept the idea that they were in some ways which put them at a disadvantage in the modern world, backward. This idea was suggested to them, with no disrespect for their own culture, by missionaries and government officials alike, since both were anxious that the Dinka should be able to speak for themselves in councils of state outside their own homeland when the Sudan became independent.

I do not doubt that some Dinka were converted by a love of God and drawn into the Church by the attraction of some Christian principle, by prayer, by individual, introspective activity of the conscience, or by the example of such priests and other Christians as they had among them. But in general, the road to Christianity, or at least to a Christianized way of thought, and the incorporation of some Dinka into the wider civil and ecclesiastical organizations of the modern world, came with the acceptance of the idea of progress through education. And "getting ahead," as is shown in this and other songs, was interpreted in terms of familiar Dinka intertribal rivalries and encouraged by them. So the acceptance of the

Church came through foreign secular ideas of progress and development, for the most part material, which had little to do with the main evangelical purposes or teaching of the missions.

The usage of the expression for "to go ahead, to go first"—in Dinka *lo tweng*—for "to progress" or "to get on in the world" is a small but telling example of the way in which at many such small points a foreign system of thought was introduced, not simply as a replacement of the traditional system but as an alternative to it, through a kind of linguistic parallax. The SOED definition of "parallax" (*Astron.*) is "apparent displacement of an object, caused by the change (or difference) of the point of observation." Far from thinking themselves "backward" among their non-Dinka neighbors in the Sudan, the Dinka thought themselves superior to them, as indeed did their Nuer neighbors to the Dinka. *Tweng,* "ahead," meant either further on in a journey, or senior. Age-sets were divided internally according to seniority into three generation groups, according roughly to the relative ages of the young men who had been initiated at about the same time, and the period at which it seemed appropriate to give an up-and-coming generation its own name as a separate set. The senior in each generation were *nhom tweng,* literally "head forward" and this both "ahead" "higher" and "in front" (as with quadrupeds, especially cattle); the middle were *ciel,* "in the middle"; and the junior *cok cien,* "foot behind" and thus "in the rear." These groups were in periodic competition, self-assertive juniors trying to wrest the leadership from their seniors when the time came for establishing their own superior prowess and vitality, in order to be recognized as the seniors of one generation of sets instead of the juniors of another. This followed roughly the biological cycle of adolescence, aggressive unmarried manhood, settling into middle-age and then retiring from much dancing, courting and fighting into the wisdom of elderhood.

When the idea of acquiring more foreign knowledge and competence—a continuous process over the generations—has been placed in the context of trials of strength between Dinka age-sets, a sporadic activity repeated in each generation, the "point of observation" has modified the understanding. The Dinka view of age-sets, based upon a cyclical notion of local history, begins to be displaced by a dynamic view of history, accompanied by a philosophy of progress, and with teleological overtones. Through the association of generational competition for local status with ideas of cumulative development and advance, "getting ahead" begins to be directed towards some distant, more universal end, defined in foreign terms. A social process is metaphorically translated into social progress. Here social philosophy is affected by the linguistic parallax I have mentioned, and the possibility of thinking that mankind should strive towards some *civitas dei,* some superior form of society conceived of by the Catholic Church as, differently, by rationalist evolutionists, but never before by the Dinka, begins to be introduced.

A similar process of translation from indigenous to foreign concepts involving a reformulation of experience and thought may be seen in relation to theological doctrine. The Dinka concept of *wei*, meaning breath, life, what animates, is discussed in another paper (Lienhardt 1980) and I shall mention it only briefly. This word for breath and life may be the nearest approximation to anything that could be meant by "soul" in the Dinka language. But the Christian "soul" goes with a whole set of eschatological doctrines, conceptions, and ideas of human personality, which have no relation to the meanings of the Dinka word *wei* as breath/life. Added to this is the use of *wei*, as in *wei santo* (using the Italian adjective) for the Holy Spirit. There can be no doubt that Dinka with a Christian education use their own words in this parallactic way. I wrote in the earlier paper: "Missionaries, using *wei*, breath and life, as the best approximation to translate 'soul,' have presumably successfully reshaped the Dinka word for their converts into a unitary term for a moralized and spiritualized self-consciousness of each separate individual in relation to a personalized God" (Lienhardt 1980, 75).

But though Christian doctrine would require a Dinka Christian to assert that an ox had no "soul," I doubt if even the most scrupulous Christian Dinka would ever be able to assert that an ox had no *wei*, since this is what the strong animal has in superabundance, far more than human beings, and what is released to give them the power and vitality they ask for when the beast is sacrificed. . . .

. . . The Dinka "God" is often addressed as a father; but in the indigenous usage it is the relationship of respect (*thek*) for the father that the Dinka "God" *nhialic* brings to mind, rather than the affection of a father for his children.

So a transmission of Christian doctrine, and all the organization, both of society and of experience which go with it, first through the Dinka language, and then through English, involve a complex reorganization of meanings and their relationships. The associations of particular religious terms, either in Dinka or in Catholic teaching, are mutually defining, and in order to convey a new set of meanings in the same language as the old, an alternative pattern of associations is introduced. . . .

References

Dempsey, James. 1955. *Mission on the Nile*. London: Burns and Oates, 1955.

Lienhardt, Godfrey. 1980. "Self, Public, Private, Some African Interpretations." *Journal of the Anthropological Society of Oxford* 11 (2): 69–82.

NOTE

1. For example, Comaroff and Comaroff (1991, 1997); Ranger (1986).

5

Excerpt from "Iconophily and Iconoclasm in Marian Pilgrimage"

Victor Turner and Edith Turner

Before he died, the well-known anthropologist of African religion Victor Turner (1920–83) turned his attention to Catholic forms of pilgrimage and, with Edith Turner, traveled across the world visiting Marian shrines. Victor and Edith Turner were themselves Catholic. The book that resulted is a classic of early anthropological writing about Catholicism and has done much to lay down an analytical "grammar" for thinking about it. In this chapter the Turners draw attention to the long-standing tension in Christianity between iconoclasm and iconophily—a topic that resonates deeply with contemporary debates about semiotics.[1] In this chapter the Turners explore the potent affordances of material form through an analysis of shrines, images, and statues. Of interest here are the multiple and sometimes contradictory layers of personification and signification that accrue to devotional objects and places over time, through repeated human interaction. The shrine's semantic field has a diachronic axis as a well as a synchronic one—both axes further layered with political and historic events that inscribe themselves upon the place. Both in and out of structure and time, shrines condense symbols, practices, histories, and culturally specific influences and affordances. An analytical question running through this chapter is thus whether the power of the divine is compressed within and hence generated by the image or whether the image simply represents the power of the divine. This, of course, is something of an age-old theological problem in Christianity, which the Turners as Catholics themselves are eminently aware of. In their treatment of this issue, however, they remain steadfastly anthropological, taking seriously the sensorial plasticity of devotional objects and their inherent capacity to exceed the roles intended of them by official theology. Rather than "materiality" or "aesthetic formations," the Turners describe devotional objects as "outward vehicles" for

From Victor Turner and Edith Turner, "Iconophily and Iconoclasm in Marian Pilgrimage." In *Image and Pilgrimage in Christian Culture*, ed. Victor Turner and Edith Turner, pp. 140–71.© Columbia University Press, 1978. Reprinted with the permission of Columbia University Press.

symbols. "Outward vehicles," they argue, have a tendency to become more bound up with the *orectic* pole of signification than the *normative* pole. Here the "orectic" encompasses the emotional, sensorial, and affective field of semantics, whereas the "normative" encompasses the abstract, ideational field. The Turners see this as a basic religious structure common to all religious traditions, although the respective stability of each pole is reversed in different cultures. Thus in non-Christian "tribal" societies the orectic pole is more stable than the normative one, whereas in hierarchically organized, scripturally complex religions such as Christianity the normative is more stable than the orectic.

Although the language the Turners employ is reflective of the structuralist and symbolic-humanist fields they were very much embedded within, their work is relevant to a renewed anthropology of Catholicism for the way it helps to make sense of the relationship of parts to wholes, and for the creative attention it draws to the circulation of ideas and affects within Catholic institutional territories.

. . .

In the course of this study, we have seen that pilgrimage shrines, in principal centers of peace and communitas, are often involved in social and political conflicts of great vehemence and intensity. This paradox has particularly marked the famous Marian shrines; the flux of Marian devotions has indeed been related to some of the major political and theological changes in Western History.

Let us begin *in medias res,* with an event which vividly illustrates the issue of iconophobia versus iconophily, which in a more general sense is a pervasive theme of this chapter. The event was the burning of certain statues of the Virgin in London in 1538, by order of Henry VIII's vicar general Thomas Cromwell, at the instigation of Bishop Hugh Latimer of Worcester. Earlier Latimer had asked in a sermon: "What thinke ye of these images that are had more than their felowes in reputation? that are gone into with such labour and werines of the body, frequented with such our cost, sought out and visited with such confidence? what say ye by such images, that are so famous, so noble, so noted, beying of them so many and so diuers in England. Do you think that this preferryng of picture to picture, image to image, is the right vse, and not rather the abuse of images?" (quoted in Jusserand 1891, 355).

In the political climate of the 1530s these comments stood every chance of being translated into violent action. . . .

Latimer's communications could involve us in the study of centuries of Christian infighting, but we wish to call attention only to his central argument against the images at pilgrimage shrines; namely, that the excess of public devotion to them was an abuse of the Church's directives. The Second Council of Nicaea (the seventh ecumenical council, A.D. 787) had decreed that both "the figure of the sacred and life-giving cross" and "the venerated and holy images" were to be "placed suitably in the holy churches of God," but that the honor paid to them was to be "only relative for the sake of their prototypes"; they were to receive "veneration, not adoration."

The council's definition was itself a response to the first great wave of iconoclasm in Christian history. About A.D. 726 the Byzantine emperor Leo the Isaurian had published an edict which led to the destruction of images and the persecution of their defenders. After the Second Council of Nicaea, iconoclasm erupted afresh in the Byzantine Empire, and the destruction of monasteries and images went on until 843, when the policy was reversed by the empress Theodora. . . .

Bishop Latimer was not a complete iconoclast like Leo the Isaurian before him, or Oliver Cromwell after. His argument was directed against the *abuse* of images, and could claim the Nicene declaration itself as its precedent. . . . The general intent of the Church's recommendation was that sacred images were not to be particularized, "realistic" representations, but should have a semiheraldic, stereotyped character befitting their function as collective representations. They were not to be taken as "natural symbols," but as "conventional signs." Yet since they represented human beings (in however conventional a way), and were objects of private devotion in side-chapels and niches, as well as serving as architectural and liturgical elements (for instance, the crucifix on the altar), it was inevitable that certain individual images would become personified. This tendency was reinforced by the use of images as sacramentals in the home—material objects (such as crucifixes and pictures of saints) signifying spiritual truths and processes.

As all know, every symbol has a signifier and a signified. The signifier is the sensorily perceptible vehicle of a conception. The personifying process here involves a changing relation between signifier and signified. For example, a specific image of the Virgin Mary is a signifier meant to represent not only the historical woman who once lived in Galilee but the sacred person who resides in heaven, appears at times to living persons, and intercedes with God for the salvation of mankind. The popular tendency is to see the Virgin's supernatural power as intimately bound up with the particular image, rather than to see the image as just another symbol of that power. The signifier's connection with the theological signified thus becomes greatly attenuated. As we have seen in earlier chapters, the outward form of a symbol is connected more closely with its orectic (or emotional/volitional) pole of significance than with its normative (or ideological) pole. Association and analogy connect the sensorily perceived symbol-vehicle, or image, to referents of a dominantly emotional or wishful character. Images, if not idiosyncratic in form to begin with (for example, as the individualized products of a particular artist), often acquire, in the course of time, idiosyncratic physical features, due to discoloration of the original materials (numerous "black" Madonnas, such as the one at Montserrat in Spain, are the result of exposure to the sooty smoke of candles, for instance; others, of the oxidization of silver, as at Rocamadour), or accidental defacement, or due to their being traditionally vested in clothes of a particular period or region. The more particular the form of the symbol-vehicle (and the more attention is paid to its form), the likelier the signifier is to take on a life of its own, apart from its intended or original meaning, or "signified." New significance may then be generated as devotees associate the particularized, personalized image with their own hopes and sorrows as members of a particular community with a specific history. The original intended signified, related to universally accepted theological principles, may be partially replaced by a new signified, derived from some critical historical event in the community. The original signified is not completely replaced, but rather fused with and partially altered by the new signified; or it may coexist with the new as part of a mosaic of meaning. The "new" signified may not in fact be historically new, but may represent a resurgence of archaic ideas and beliefs. It is not idolatrous worship of the signifier, at the expense of the signified, that is here in question—as theological polemic has too often asserted. Rather is it the creation of a semantic arena in which a multiplicity of signifieds—original, new, archaic—are for a time in conflict. By "original" we here mean theologically primary, which we distinguish from the "archaic," relating to an earlier, suppressed religion. The conflict is between what is often called the instinct of the masses—that is, the deep patterns of the people's cultural tradition—and the conscious efforts of agents of religious orthodoxy to purify the signified of "folk" ideas that are heterodox or theologically irrelevant. Iconoclasm is the simplest, if most draconic, solution; to purify the meaning, it destroys the vehicle. It does not recognize any *necessary* linkage between signifier and signified. It denies that there are "natural symbols." But it has the major, long-term disadvantage of destroying a public center of social and cultural integration. In the short term, this may be precisely what the iconoclasts desire: to destroy the integration provided by a rival world view. But they have then the problem of devising a religious system without visible, tactile signifiers, or of developing signifiers of an impersonal, neutral, or abstract type. Mass literacy is propitious for such a development, for the signs of written language have a less immediate emotional impact than do symbolic objects, gestures, sounds, and actions, which are like the books of the illiterate.

Johan Huizinga, Émile Mâle, and many other scholars have described the propensity of the late Middle Ages to crystallize its religious thought into images. For anthropologists, of course, this propensity is not confined to the European Middle Ages, but is found in innumerable tribal religions, as well as in the folk practices of the other great historical religions, even where "idolatry" is forbidden or discouraged by the orthodox establishment. But Huizinga ([1924] 1956, 165) took too simple a view of the relation between signifier and signified when he wrote the following:

> The naïve religious conscience of the multitude had no need of intellectual proofs in matters of faith. The mere presence of a visible image of things holy sufficed to establish their truth. No doubts intervened between the sight of all those pictures and statues—the persons of the Trinity, the flames of hell, the innumerable saints—and

belief in their reality. All these conceptions became matters of faith in the most direct manner; they passed straight from the state of images to that of convictions, taking root in the mind as pictures clearly outlined and vividly coloured, possessing all the reality claimed for them by the Church, and even a little more.

What Huizinga did not see was that behind the visible image stood not a single significatum with which it was immediately identified, but an entire semantic field, an area of multivocality, the "referents" of which were drawn from the most disparate sources. First, there was the system of theological doctrines on which the Church insisted. Though Huizinga conceded, "The Church did not fail to teach that all honours rendered to the saints, to relics, to holy places, should have God for their object" (165), he did not realize how much this doctrine and others, such as the communion of saints, have influenced the development of the cultuses of Mary and the saints, and how completely they are comprehended by peasants and proletarians. We have been astonished, in places as far removed as the cities of Stockport, in Cheshire, England, and Izamal, in Yucatán, to find how well the poor and unlettered know their basic theology, where pilgrimage is concerned. Sermons, homilies, tracts, advice in the confessional, discussions among the laity on religious and ethnic questions, keep fundamental doctrines alive, doctrines which are indeed embedded in the very rituals of the liturgy. But, of course, the doctrinal ideas share the semantic field with derivatives from archaic, even pre-Christian ritual traditions, as we have seen with the pilgrimages to the Guadalupe and Los Remedios shrines in Mexico, and to St. Patrick's Purgatory in Ireland. But the archaic notions do not belong to the normative pole of the symbol's meaning. Rather do they supply vivid pictures, or "images" if you like, which give emotional coloring to the symbol, and root it deeply in the past of the group's social experience. As a devotional image continues to be venerated over the years, its semantic field incorporates further significata, some resulting from the "development of doctrine," others from historical experience. For example, the belief that on several occasions the Remedios and Guadalupe Virgins saved Mexico City from plague, floods, and drought now forms part of the "meaning" of these images, particularly at their orectic pole. Guadalupe's meaning also encompasses the times when her banner was associated with the struggles for national independence and peasant rights. For the cultural anthropologist, a symbol's meaning is much more than its legitimated interpretation (see Turner 1967, chaps. 1 and 2). Beyond the *exegetic meaning,* there are other levels. The *operational meaning* concerns not what people say about a symbol but how they act with reference to it, who so acts, and the social structural context of such action— we also include here the symbol's "social history"; that is, the stereotyped memories of great events with which the symbol has been connected. Symbols also have *positional meaning,* for they are rarely isolated units; they enter into relations with other symbols in clusters and systems of signifiers and signifieds. Some symbols are dominant, others ancillary, in these constellations. Symbols may appear in the dyadic relations, or in triadic relations. In the case of an important image of the Virgin, for example, the theological referents of the signified may belong to a sub-system of the total theological system. Similarly, the signifier itself (in this case the image of the Virgin) may form part of a symbolic complex (such as a painting of Virgin and Child), or a set of images, each located in some significant relation to the main altar of the Church. In these instances, the relation between the component symbols would be of key importance. The natural dependence of a child on its mother might be countered by the Child's standing on the Madonna's knee and giving a priestly blessing, for example, indicating that the infant is God and, hence, that the mother is the Theotokos, the Mother of God. In the twelfth century, the infant was often portrayed with an adult's face—representing the Divine Word; the doctrines of the hypostatic union and the Incarnation were also implied. To cite another example—Gary Gossen (1972) has shown that the arrangement of saints' images in a church with a Tzotzil congregation in Chiapas, Mexico, is influenced both by pre-Columbian cosmological notions and by Christian doctrine. Eva Hunt has observed (in a personal communication) that pilgrimage shrines among the Cuicatec Indians in Oaxaca tend to be grouped in fives (a quincunx, with a shrine at each cardinal point, east, south, west and north, and one in the center) and have successive feast (and market) days, following a pre-Columbia pattern. All three levels—exegetic, operational, and positional—must be taken into account if we are to form an adequate interpretation of a symbol's meaning.

Huizinga ([1924] 1956, 166) was correct, however, in arguing that in the waning Middle Ages "an ultra-realistic conception of all that related to the saints" developed in the popular faith. The relation between signifier and signified had worn thin, and a too literal view of images resulted—a constant danger among all kinds of symbolic forms and actions. But Huizinga exempted from his stricture the devotion centered on Christ and His mother, which he considered was still profound (166). This profundity had marked the pilgrimage devotions of the High Middle Ages, whose zenith was the thirteenth century. A balance seems to have been then attained between the normative and orectic poles of symbolic meaning; the outward form was still translucent to the inner meaning, while archaic customs and Christian theological ideas and imagery inter-resonated harmoniously. . . .

Though the phenomenon of pilgrimage has a common processual form, each pilgrimage has a particular history, which is affected by world and regional history. The duration of a ritual process—whether a puberty rite, a harvest festival, or a communal pilgrimage process—is defined as being outside the historical timestream; often the ritual is performed in a marginal site: a circumcision lodge, a chapel outside of a town, etc. It has, like music or drama, ahistorical diachrony. But the ritual processes are enacted by groups whose nonritual activities place them firmly within the historical process. Their rituals become subject to political manipulation and pressure, respond to the ecological cycle and to economic fac-tors, and thrive or succumb in relation to currents of secular thought. The symbol-ism and conceptual structure of ritual processes are by no means immune to these historical and nonritual vicissitudes. . . .

It is the doctrine of the Assumption of the Virgin which is probably of the great-est importance in connecting Marian devotion with pilgrimage. This holds that both the body and the soul of Mary were taken into heaven when she died, in anticipation of the universal judgment. . . . In accordance with the tendency to seek homologues between events in the lives of Jesus and Mary, missals and prayer books often note that the Assumption was for Mary what the Resurrection was for Jesus. Mary was with her Son in Her sufferings and she is with Him in his triumph: she already has that fullness of glory that we hope to have at the end of time. By "fullness of glory" is meant that reunion of body and soul in heaven which, for all other humankind, must await the Last Judgment. At the folk level, the doctrine of the Assumption underlies the belief that Mary can and does manifest herself to the sensory perceptions of selected mortals in apparitions, defined theologically as certain kinds of supernatural vision; namely, those that are bodily or visible. Her body having disappeared from the world at the Assumption, it is argued that she can reappear in the body, in a more concrete way than a saint whose body remains buried or whose relics are believed scattered in different places. Mary continues to connect earth and heaven in a "bodily" or "visible" way. This and many other beliefs are clearly inferred from doctrine as much as from persistent folk beliefs. . . .

Pilgrimages in general, and Marian pilgrimages in particular, owe much of their theological rationale in Catholic and Orthodox Christendom to the doctrine of the communion of saints. . . . In its fully developed form, the doctrine of the communion of saints is a sophisticated cultural expression—a "conscious model," perhaps, of ideological communitas. Like tribal religion, it emphasizes the unity of the living and the dead of a given social group. But there is one salient difference. A tribal group or one of its segments (a clan or lineage, say) stresses ties of ascribed *kinship*, which provide *obligatory* links between the living and the dead, with ritu-als of ancestor veneration used as a means of communication between them. The Church, however, is not, in principle, a kin group, but a group of all those, whether kin or not, who possess the same object of belief. The communion of saints, while stressing the unity under and in Christ of the Church throughout the ages, divides that Church dynamically into three parts: the Church Militant, the Church Suffer-ing, and the Church Triumphant. The Church Militant represents the visible soci-ety of the faithful on earth, including sinners as well as the just. The Church Suf-fering is composed of the souls in purgatory. The Church Triumphant is composed of the saints in heaven, the angels, worthy souls from before the time of Christ, and worthy non-Catholics. These three components communicate directly or indi-rectly with one another and with God. The living of the Church Militant pray to

God and to members of the Church Triumphant on behalf of the members of the Church Suffering, and to God in honor of the saints. The saints intercede with God for the suffering and the living. The suffering, the souls in purgatory, pray to God and the saints for others. It is held, though, that the holy souls of purgatory cannot effectively intercede for the living until their "temporal punishment" is over; this inability is, in fact, regarded as part of their suffering. Christ, the head of the total Church, intercedes continually for the living and the dead. In this system, isolated prayer does not exist; every act of prayer refers to other members. There is, in theological language, a universality of purpose. Every deed of each member is held to affect for good or ill the whole body.

In this system, Mary plays a special role, which gives her a pivotal position in Catholic pilgrimage. She is the first of the blessed, and hence the most efficacious intercessor in relation to God the Father. She is a link binding men to God, since she is the Mother of God. As the "second Eve," she is also, as we have seen, the spiritual mother of all living humankind. Like the other saints, she is no mere model for a virtuous life but is a living and functioning member of the Church. She is liable to put in an appearance, unexpectedly and of her own free will, at any moment and in any place. As regards pilgrimage, the doctrine of the Assumption, while it deprived the Church of her bodily relics, gave her complete mobility through the universal Church, as a potential patron of nations, dioceses, religious societies, and so on. She embodies the communitas of the Church, and is innocent of any blame for sometimes being enlisted by particularistic groups with bloody axes to grind.

This brief sketch must suffice to indicate the central semantic structure of the normative pole of Marian pilgrimage symbols. That pole of meaning has remained remarkably constant throughout history, while there has been much variation at the orectic pole; that is, in the culturally defined feelings and motivations associated with the symbol-vehicles. In this respect, the dominant symbols of Christianity, and indeed those of the other historical relations, which are also maintained by literate specialists, are sharply distinguished from the symbols of tribal societies. In tribal religion there is a high consistency of orectic significance (for instance, in Central Africa the red gum exuded by certain trees stands, in a wide range of societies, for blood and the emotions connected with its shedding), but at the normative pole meanings vary considerably (the red gum stands for matriliny and motherhood in some groups, for patriliny in others, and for hunting cults in yet others). The normative consistency of symbols in the historical religions, in contrast, may be due to the development, in the Western European tradition, of a specialist class of theologians, and to social, political, and cultural centralization; both these developments contribute to uniformity of normative reference and to the generation of universal patterns of doctrine, overriding local differences. Local differences then tend to be expressed at the opposite semantic pole, and to color the ways people feel about the symbols. Such differences also manifest themselves at the level of the signifier; that is, in the form of sensorily perceived symbol-vehicle. Even here, however, theological pressures contribute to the stereotyping of images, attributes of saints, and so on, so that they will not be at cross-purposes with dogmas, doctrines, and scriptural models. Local feeling may manifest itself in the materials used—such as the *tilma* on which Our Lady of Guadalupe is painted, the ocote wood from which the image of Our Lady of Octlán is carved, or the *pasta de Michoacán* of which the little figure of the Virgin of Zapopan is made, to cite examples discussed in our chapter on Mexico—or it may be manifested in tales about the origin or history of a given image. . . .

In summary, pilgrimage in the normative frame of the total medieval ecclesia stands at the communitas pole and not initially at the social structural pole of the sacred system. Marian devotions cluster at each pole but it is not without significance that Mary has become easily the foremost saint venerated at the great international, national, and supraregional shrines. For she is the great vessel, the *vas,* of salvation, through whose motherhood the doomed children of the fallen Eve are reborn, transformed—ideally as the result of free will responding to heavenly grace. Mary is not only—in the words of Gabriel's greeting, endlessly repeated in the Rosary down through the ages—"full of grace," but is also to be regarded as a personification of the Church in its nonlegalistic aspect, a collective mother in the order of freedom. It used to be said among Catholics: As Mary goes, so goes the Church. We would qualify this to mean: As communitas goes, so goes the Church. The huge crowds that still frequent the Marian shrines of Lourdes, Guadalupe, Fátima, Knock, Einsiedeln, and Czestochowa—to name but a few—testify to the endurance of this belief. The danger is, of course, that Mary, in principle representing global communitas, has in practice become, in each of her numerous images, exclusive patroness of a given community, region, city, or nation. Wherever she has become such a symbol of xenophobic localism, political structure has subverted communitas.

References

Gossen, Gary. 1972. "Temporal and Spatial Equivalents in Chamula Ritual Symbolism." In *Reader in Comparative Religion*, 3rd ed., edited by W. A. Lessa and E. Z. Vogt, 135–48. New York: Harper and Row.

Huizinga, Johan. [1924] 1956]. *The Waning of the Middle Ages.* New York: Doubleday, Anchor Books.

Jusserand, J. J. 1891. *English Wayfaring Life in the Middle Ages (XVI Century).* Translated by Lucy Toulmin Smith. London: T. Fisher Unwin.

Turner, Victor. 1967. *The Forest of Symbols.* Ithaca, NY: Cornell University Press.

NOTE

1. Keane (2007).

6
‾‾‾‾‾

Excerpt from *Person and God in a Spanish Valley*

William A. Christian

The book *Person and God in a Spanish Valley,* by anthropologist and historian William A. Christian, is a classic twentieth-century study in the anthropology of Catholicism. It embraces key spatial and temporal dynamics of Catholicism through the analysis of devotional behavior across a range of intersecting axes and contexts. Among these, gender, class, and moment within the life course are shown to be of particular importance in shaping the quality and concerns of individual faith. In chapter 3, of which this is an abridged version, Christian shows how different styles of payer point to different economies of affection, obligation, forgiveness, and indebtedness. "Putting God in one's debt" clearly illustrates that Catholicism is not only a practice of devotion but also an economy of circulation of affects and indebtedness. Devotional prayers can work either to keep humans and the divine separate or to bring humans increasingly close to the divine. However, *Person and God* also does much to emplace Catholicism within a broader history of agrarian politics and reform in northern Spain and is a remarkable work for its mastery of historical perspective as well as its fine ethnography. In particular, it offers some important anthropological insights on the local repercussions of the Second Vatican Council (1963–65), revealing shifts toward new forms of priesthood, less concerned with a hierarchical reproduction of the church (and its connection to land patronage) and more inclined to a lay participation. The effect of such changes in Catholic doctrine and orientation on long-existing systems of "triadic patronage" in the area is one of the key questions that this work addresses.

Among the numerous monographs on Mediterranean villages that came out in the 1970s, Christian's is perhaps unusual in the degree to which it *fore*grounds Catholic forms of reasoning and practice, rather than *back*grounding them to discussions of patronage and kinship and political economy. The importance of *Person and God* for a modern anthropology of Catholicism cannot be overestimated, for it has been key in establishing a core "analytical grammar" for understanding popular Catholic practices that subsequent generations of scholars continue to revisit. Indeed, the work has figured as an important reference point in various twenty-first-century writings on the anthropology of Christianity,[1] having achieved something of a status as "the go-to" citation for discussions about the presence of an "earlier" anthropology of Christianity.

. . .

An understanding of how individuals and communities use the divine repertoire will be furthered by a summary of the kinds of communication with the divine that are common to the valley. These communications vary from quite generalized, affective messages to very specific, instrumental requests:

1. Generalized affective prayers
2. Prayers for the fulfillment of the annual round
3. Prayers for forgiveness
4. Prayers for salvation
5. Instrumental prayers

Implicit in these routines are images of the divine and a theory of divine action. . . .

Until the turn of the last century, and in some villages until the 1930's, the parish priests were local boys without a great deal of education. They often kept cows themselves and sometimes wore regular work clothes. The Episcopal Visits recorded in the parish account books bristle with written admonitions for priests to wear their cassocks and collars at all times. Such priests, because of their membership in the kin network and their insertion in the culture, were usually not terribly innovative. Their emphasis was on a proper fulfillment of the obligations of the community and the individual to God and the maintenance of the devotions and brotherhoods launched by the missionaries.

By the turn of the century, more adequately trained priests from elsewhere in the diocese were assigned to the valley; they brought with them, as we have seen, successive waves of new devotions. Their main struggle was to ethicalize the religion, to change it from an instrumental set of outward observances into a deepened, more inward spiritual life. The relationship they emphasized was that of the individual and God, and they encouraged the personalization of the relationship. This was a movement all over Europe, and the sentimental style of lithographs, the statues of saints with the baby Jesus, sweetness, and light characterized the whole period.

As the century progressed and the Church became visibly threatened by the force of reason and revolution, a toughness developed, a note of belligerence. But all through these different tones and colors, the philosophical groundwork of the

Council of Trent remained. This groundwork, which on the level of the individual had as its chief effect the provocation and maintenance of cycles of purification and redemption, should be seen as overlaid on a far older set of principles and activities. These are the activities that deal with the very land itself, that see the landscape as brimming with meaning and coherence. While the generalized devotions, designed as aids to salvation, belong to the post-Tridentine period, the old chapels belong to the pre-Tridentine (one is tempted to say the prehistoric) period of valley life.

The two modes of devotion exist side by side; indeed they interpenetrate and make mutual adjustments. With few exceptions the priests tolerated the elaborate if informal system of instrumental promises and concomitant mortifications aimed at the chapel images. And some of the people acceded to the clerical pressure for purification and redemption. The chapel images became agencies for redemption as well as practical protection. Conversely some of the generalized devotions presented by the priests and the orders as auxiliaries to salvation, such as Our Lady of Mt. Carmel, the souls in purgatory, and the Sacred Heart of Jesus, were adapted by the people for use as patrons and shrine images, utilized for practical aims.

This interpenetration has slightly blurred what is an essential difference, both historical and philosophical, between shrine images and generalized devotions, instrumental and purificative religion. The older set of divinities are not as much intercessors with God as they are intercessors with nature, for they are located in specific places in the village landscape, from which they can be moved only under certain rigorous ritual conditions. They mark off boundaries between village and village and boundaries between cultivated and uncultivated land. Throughout Spain they mark critical points in the ecosystem—contact points with other worlds. Mountain peaks, springs, and caves seem to be contact points with the worlds below and above; boundary shrines with other earthly worlds. With their periodic devotions at these sites it would seem that the villagers were at once confirming the boundaries of their world, assuring the continuity of the annual cycle of seasons, and attempting, through propitiation or the use of promises, to gain some control or some influence upon the entry of foreign material or foreign power into their world. Since they themselves are not capable of fully regulating their environment, there must be other powers beyond who are capable, and the chapels are located at the most logical transaction points with these powers beyond. Individual promises and individual regular devotions served the same ends for the individual as the village ceremonies did for the village—to influence the course of crises and ensure the normal unfolding of the life process. The religion brought in by the priests, penetrating to most of the people in this region only after the Counterreformation, emphasized the Christian message of salvation and a series of purificative actions and ethical principles useful to that end. Communication with other worlds was to be mediated by the Church and its ministers.

With the breakdown of community boundaries through mobility and the media, with the industrialization of Europe, the rise in standard of living, the circulation of alternatives to the Catholic life, and by way of one brand of Catholic response to these events, the Catholic Action movement and the Second Vatican Council, a new model for communication with other worlds has developed in the valley. It has been brought in by radio, television, students, returning emigrants, but above all by the young emissaries of the Council, the younger priests. Often hostile to the older priests, certainly opposed to many of their sociopolitical assumptions and devotional practices, and critical of their nonaggression pact with the local pantheism, the younger priests are having a decided impact on the valley. The impact can be measured by the incredible reaction of the village and its gods—through a series of apparitions of the Virgin Mary in San Sebastian in the early 1960's. The impact can also be seen in the partial conversion of the youth to the ideas of the young priests and in the revalorization of democratic, mutualistic relations on all levels.

The new doctrine of these young priests virtually renders divine images irrelevant, or at least radically challenges their usefulness. As they are often products of village Catholicism themselves, many younger priests maintain a reverence and affection for Mary. But they do not regard either Mary or the saints as essential intermediaries with God. Much less do they regard the geographically located shrine images as special points of access to the powers beyond. Instead they have found a new intermediary between God and man: man himself.

The priorities of God-person, person-person relations for the older priests could be diagrammed as follows:

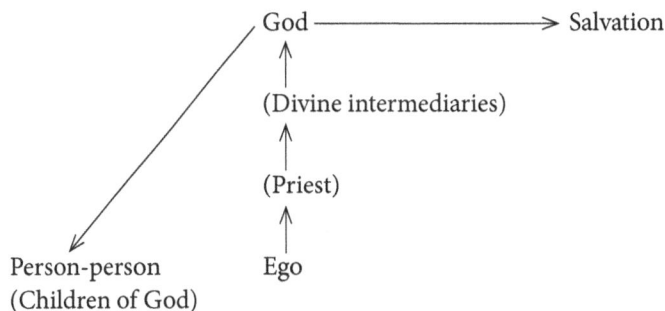

The use of intermediaries helps the person to form a bond with God. As a consequence of that bond he or she is then a member of the family of mankind and is also on the road to salvation. The prime emphasis is upon the relation of God and person and the eventual salvation of the individual.

The priorities of the villagers, *grosso modo,* are as follows:

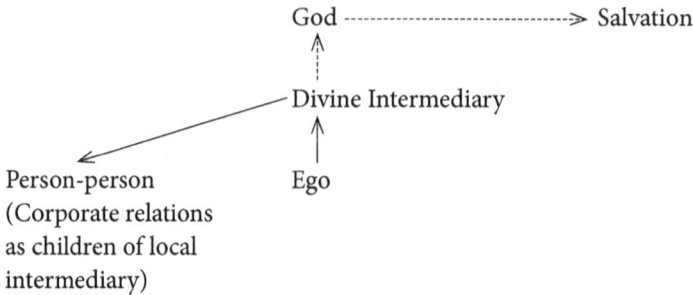

God ---------------------------------> Salvation

Divine Intermediary

Person-person   Ego
(Corporate relations
as children of local
intermediary)

The intermediaries are useful in, of and for themselves. Salvation comes through a combination of their direct action and their intervention. Again, there is a kind of byproduct of community, based on the effect of a specific local intermediary as corporate parent or protector.

It will be seen how these two systems, sharing the same basic configuration, could live with each other. However, neither can live with the priorities of the younger priests:

EGO ⟶ PERSON-PERSON (Brotherhood in Christ) ⟶ GOD ---> SALVATION

In this third system other people are the intermediaries on the path to God. There are no divine intermediaries. The bottom is knocked out of the system of promises. Salvation becomes the byproduct of the good life, not its goal. The priorities are completely reversed. Now in San Sebastian the money in the alms box that used to go for masses to the souls in purgatory (from promises, for the salvation both of the souls themselves and the villagers' temporal and eternal needs) goes to the diocesan charity fund. Living dependents replace dead ones; living intermediaries replace dead ones, whether souls in purgatory or saints.

This new system invalidates to a degree all the old distinctions between the sacred and the profane. The unvalued, uncontrolled relationships of peers, not even mentioned as religious obligations in the Claret handbook, are revalorized. The young priests associate with and encourage the teen groups, for instance. These were the most unsacred associations in the old system. In fact, under the old system, as we saw in Tudanca, the teen groups were a temporary counter culture which said mock versions of the Lord's prayer and mocked all authority by their actions. Because the mocedad was a mutualistic, democratic organization it had no place in the authoritarian symbol system, a system that was reinforced by, if not derived from, the two systems of priorities diagrammed above for older priests and villagers, in which the vertical God-person (or divine intermediary-person) relation sets the pattern for all religiously valued relationships.

The young priests revalue also the relationship of men among men. We have seen how, because the peer group was not valued in the old religion, this greatly contributed to the men's dismissal of the old religion as irrelevant. Now, especially in the cities, men are finding the religion more relevant. This has not yet happened in many of the villages because of the traditional hostility of men to priests and because the young priests have no idea how to approach the older men. Similarly, because person-person relations are most highly valued, certain kinds of mutual, community activities are preferred by the younger priests to the old habits of meditation and contemplation.

Because salvation is no longer a direct goal (a young schoolteacher told me she thought worrying about salvation was like loving a father for the money he was going to leave you), emphasis is no longer placed on purification, decontamination, and the domestication of instinct. Instead of an emphasis upon the suppression of the bad aspects of human nature, the young priests try to bring about an active transformation of self that permits one to do new things, instead of not doing wrong things.

Again, because priest-parishioner relations, like other relations in the society, are seen as mutualistic and nonauthoritarian, the priests shed their cassocks and work with people in the fields, or as bartenders at fiestas. In contrast, the older priests maintained a ritual purity, a distance from the population that enabled them to be effective negotiators with the divine. The younger priests say "we" instead of "I and you" in their sermons. Generally misunderstood by the villagers, they attempt to share as much of their lives with the people as they can, to break down the old isolation. (In fact, so far all that has resulted from their efforts is their conversion to the role of village-wide patron—their use as intermediaries between the village and outside bureaucracy that leaves them with fully as much power and authority in the village as their predecessors, if not more. In a sense, they have taken over the old role of benevolent noblemen.)

Naturally, the images of God have changed also. The younger priests encourage the concept of Christ as friend or model, although they do not find objectionable the notion of Mary as mother (that model still stands). Two sermons preached by two types of priests in two separate villages on the same day show the shift in emphasis. The text assigned by the diocese for the sermon was the miracle of the fishes and Christ's words to Simon Peter, "You shall be a fisher of men." The moral of the text to be drawn was that each of us has an apostolic mission on earth. The older priest emphasized Christ's power in performing the miracle and drew a parallel in Christ's role with men, that Christ alone gives us the power to go out into the world. In contrast, the younger priest spoke of the ideas and example of Christ, not his power, in stimulating a Christian life. One emphasized divine help, the other divine inspiration.

Ultimately the position of the younger priests leads them to a denial of the doctrine of original sin and a revalorization of human nature, which they see partakes of Christ. Thus, the kind of human brotherhood they bear witness to is less a brotherhood of the children of God, as in former theology, and more a brotherhood in Christ himself, based on the sacrament of communion.

As a result of this new doctrine, certain things are lost. The impact on the villages is beginning to be felt, but not yet with full force. First of all, there is a philosophic loss. Under the old system, both the philosophy of the village and of the Church made it possible for people to perceive a world behind their world. Immanence was a reality. Virtually every shrine in the indigenous traditions and virtually every devotion brought in by the priests was started by revelation, by the appearance of a divine figure on the earth who demonstrated the usefulness of the devotions, who pointed out the ceremonies and rituals that were to be fulfilled, who in essence sealed sacred contracts upon which were made conditional the natural unfolding of life. This is the true message of most origin legends of shrines. Behind all events was meaning for those who had eyes to see and whose hearts were open. In the daily lives of the active villagers, these meanings were only fleetingly perceived. They were accorded a special status in the universe of truths—they were left in an anteroom of suspended disbelief. To this category of neither truth nor falsehood applied the sacred condition of certain animals, like the mule, the ox, the swallow, and the bee. Certain plants—roses, heather, juniper, oak, it varied from village to village—were granted a special status. Some places in the landscape were seen as closer to the divine than others. Only with old age, on the part of some of the women virtuosi, were people able to move into and entirely inhabit this other world, brimming with excitement and meaning, in which every leaf that unfolded in the spring was a testimony to the power and love of God. Involved here is a sense of belonging, of communion with the landscape and habitat. That lexicon we discussed in the first chapter—the lexicon of persons' names and place names—had added to it the names, nicknames, and places of the divine. It was a part, perhaps the most essential part, of the village culture. To this world was added the wonderful mysteries of the Church, the divinely instituted infinity of devotions, and techniques to be investigated by the traditional means of observation, contemplation, and meditation. Thomas Merton writes, "The earliest fathers knew that all things, as such, are symbolic by their very being in nature, and all talk of something beyond themselves. Their meaning is not something we impose upon them, but a mystery we can discover in them, if we have but eyes to look." As an old man in Tudanca told me, "Everything in the world has its place, its assignment, although we do not know what they are." And my closest friend, old Antonia in San Sebastian, says, "Everything, even the tiniest thing, has its mystery."

There are degrees of belief in immanence. They form a continuum that runs from a world in which there is no coincidence to a world in which the laws of probability and randomness are fully operative. Most of the villagers fall, in respect to their beliefs, somewhere in the middle of the continuum. A few of the more traditional priests and many of the older villagers can decipher signs and portents everywhere. I am not at all sure that community centers and television sets adequately substitute for this degree of delight and wisdom. By their hardnosed rationalism the young priests live in a world where there is little or no participation of God in day-to-day affairs.

Another loss, for those in the society who cannot participate in peer groups, are the divine intermediaries. As we have seen time and again, lonely people find companionship in their personal patron, who provides them with comfort, reassurance, and love. Again this will hit older people, especially women, the hardest, but it will also affect the housewife isolated from her husband and the infirm isolated from the work cycle. The effect for those married may be somewhat mitigated by the fact that the young priests are also at work in changing the structure of marriage to make it egalitarian and affectionate.

Perhaps because it can be an instrument of unity, perhaps because they recognize that it is too sensitive an issue, the young priests have not, as of yet, moved on the village shrines and village patrons. The only case I know of is a young priest who had to fill in at the last moment as the preacher in his home village at the annual ceremony of Our Lady of Mt. Carmen. "I had no notes, but had some ideas I had been thinking about, and told the people that the saints and the advocations of the Virgin are found nowhere in the Bible, that salvation must come through Jesus Christ and that we must imitate him. I haven't been back to hear their reactions. I would not dare say that anywhere else, but I would in my own village." He went on, "In the Bible it says, 'We asked for bread and you did not give it to us.' We as priests are responsible for the parish; we cannot go on fooling the people, keeping the truth from them. Many times I have thought that if in Spain we said one rosary less and read the Bible more, we would be better off."

The seminaries are now almost wholly in the hands of the reform movement. If the pace of change is maintained as fast as at present, there may be a progressive removal from the liturgy of ceremonies to divine intermediaries. This would probably serve to alienate the priests even more from the villages they are attempting to change. They do regard the patronal images as a hindrance because of the way they limit the scope of the Christian society and the Christian family to the village or valley culture. They see the need for spreading the concept of familyhood to include all people, which might mean abandoning the idea of patronage on all but a universal scale. Since many of their parishioners will be moving to the city, since the village as a sacred landscape is already being abandoned and rejected for an urban or cosmopolitan culture by the villagers, who still inhabit it, the priests are attempting to teach a more versatile, more universal religion that will not be limited in its applicability to a certain place.

What is to be feared is that the supports of the old society will be knocked away before the new society can be built. The priests by their sermons and by their spiritual direction in the confessional could destroy the Church's ideological support for the village philosophy long before they could have much concrete effects on social relations. In fact, in the case of the young priests I knew best, the impregnability of the village social structure and devotional system so discouraged them that they all went off to the cities, like Santander and Torrelavega, where a more fluid, dislocated social situation made their ideas much easier to put into effect, perhaps with a greater usefulness. But more young priests keep coming in, and one can only hope, for the sake of some of the villagers, that they act with patience and humaneness in making the great transformation.

NOTE

1. Cannell (2006).

7
———

Excerpt from "The Priest as Agent of Secularization in Rural Spain"

Stanley H. Brandes

Stanley Brandes is an American sociocultural anthropologist whose work spans both European and Latin American peasantries. In this article Brandes describes a kind of Catholicism characteristic of peasant villages of the Iberian peninsula: locally inflected by rites and practices particular to specific regions, and organizationally overlapping with kinship and territorial corporate groups. At the broadest level, the essay offers a set of reflections about processes of modernization and secularization, viewed through a classic set of anthropological oppositions: collective/individual, rural/urban, great/little. More specifically, however, it tells us something interesting about the impact of Vatican II reforms on the ground. Brandes argues that what might be read as "secularization" is, in the village of Becedas, a function of processes *internal to religion itself.* Today, in light of works such as Charles Taylor's *A Secular Age,* this line of argument has become quite familiar. Yet as Brandes's ethnography suggests, ruminations around the polemic between belief and unbelief have not merely been the preserve of scholars and philosophers; they have inflected the lives of ordinary Catholic peasants as well. Through Brandes we see how Becedas villagers narrate, in their own idiom, the development of the idea of "the secular" as something that is contingent upon the history of Christianity in the West.

By exploring the disjuncture between Catholic "great and little" traditions Brandes touches on one of the most interesting pressure points within the anthropology of Catholicism: the division of labor between the clergy and the lay. Such a division may map with varying intensities onto other distinctions, such as those between elite and folk, or educated

From Stanley Brandes, "The Priest as Agent of Secularization in Rural Spain." In Joseph B. Aceves, Edward C. Hansen, and Gloria Levitas, eds., *Economic Transformation and Steady-State Values: Essays in the Ethnography of Spain.* Queens College Publications in Anthropology. Flushing, N.Y. 11367: Queen's College Press, 1976, Number 2, pp. 22–29. © Stanley Brandes. Reprinted with the permission of Stanley Brandes.

and uneducated, and even onto distinctly differing ethnicities and cultural backgrounds. Whether or not clergy are perceived as "cultural outsiders" in the communities they serve, where a person stands within the institutional hierarchy matters. That is, Catholic subjectivities are incontrovertibly shaped by an individual's relationship to or position in relation to the church. Belonging to the priesthood thus diminishes the possibilities for certain abstractions and sensorial trajectories, just as it makes others imminently actualizable. In the particular context being described here, the priest, Don Sixto, sees "folk Catholicism" a bit the way a radical Protestant sees Roman Catholicism: as a Christianity contaminated. His work is one of purification: separating true belief from "blind adherence to custom." For parishioners, however, there is no a priori concept of a religion "contaminated." There is only a corpus of devotions whose gradual elimination leaves a sense of spiritual vacuum. By foregrounding a "perspectival" approach split between the view of the priest, the people, and the anthropologist, Brandes allows us to grasp the structural tensions that propel different versions of what is correct and what is proper in Christian forms of practice. Brandes's article might be read in some ways as a tentative exploration of the interesting and often fraught role Catholic priests perform in their day-to-day ministry as mediators between the center and the periphery, and old and new, in the great march of Christian modernity.

. . .

In an article that recently appeared in the *European Journal of Sociology*, David Martin (1969, 192) optimistically claims that "a general theory of secularization is (close) to realization . . ., in spite of the field being poorly developed." I would put the matter differently: if the study of secularization is poorly developed, it is because we believe, with Martin, that the process is already well understood, and are therefore either unwilling or unable to scrutinize it with a fresh eye. The price of such overconfidence has been a replication in the literature of minor variations on the same basic secularization themes—themes which, on the basis of my knowledge of religious change in rural Spain, I wish to question or at least to cast in a new light. . . .

What all these theories have in common, of course, is that they perceive religious change as emanating from socioeconomic change. Specifically, they reflect the notion that rural peoples are losing colorful and quaint religious traditions as a result of the invisible, yet powerful and inexorable, modernization and development process. This is the idea which I, at least, had assimilated from the literature on peasantry, and which I carried with me when I first settled in the small Castilian community of Becedas in April 1969. In this paper I hope to show that religious decline is, rather, a function of activities of the clergy and of the state.

Becedas is a tightly nucleated settlement of some 800 people, located about 200 kilometers west of Madrid in the foothills of the Gredos Mountains, one of the most elevated regions in the Iberian peninsula. A socially and economically egalitarian community, Becedas' most important structural bonds, outside the nuclear family, are provided by friendship, neighborship, and corporate age sets. Occupationally, the vast majority are small landholders, each working tiny dispersed parcels and cooperating with fellow villagers in the regulation, care, and use of communal resources. Like most Castilian communities, Becedas has suffered heavy out-migration in recent years, which explains why its present population is only two-thirds of what it was in 1950. . . .

During my initial field trip to Becedas, I concentrated on the study of social change, particularly on the impact of migration on village economy and society. If, at that time, I would have been asked to rank my subsidiary interests, religion certainly would have fallen low on the list. Nonetheless, I knew that I was in a region rich in religious traditions, and of great religious and political conservatism, which presented little or no resistance to the Franco regime and exhibited much less than the usual Spanish share of overt anticlericalism. I also became aware of the gradual abandonment of this religious tradition, and routinely recorded the course of its demise. Not only did I find a decline in the ritualistic manifestations of devotion, particularly in the number and elaborateness of religious processions, but I also encountered a not-so-subtle religious cynicism which was all the more striking for being confessed to me, a known non-Catholic, against whom a community of believers might be expected to take a more or less united stance. Whenever I asked friends and acquaintances why they were missing Mass, or why a certain procession was not being held, the answer came surely as an incantation: "*Se nos quitan la religión ellos mismos*" (They themselves are taking religion away from us). The age, sex, or political background of the informant made no difference: the explanation was always the same. And when I asked, in response, "They who?" the answer, usually given in hushed voice and with furtive air, could also be predicted with certainty: "*Claro, los curas.*" "Why the priests, of course."

Looking back on my early field notes, I realize that I dismissed this explanation of declining religious traditions as a rationalization. After all, here were peasants in a modern world, caught up in a rapidly developing economy, influenced daily by hundreds of cultural messages and products from the nation's capital. No wonder they were becoming secularized. . . .

Fortunately, near the end of that first field trip, I had a long conversation with Don Sixto, priest of Becedas, which dispelled my initial impressions. This conversation, along with an examination of information gathered in a revisit to the community in 1972, has convinced me that, in essence, the villagers are right. Seen from their eyes, it is the priests and their associates who are responsible for religious decline. To understand why, let us begin by distinguishing between two conflicting views of the religious sphere: that of the anthropologist and priest on the one hand and that of the peasant villagers on the other.

To both the anthropologist and the priest, the religion of peasant communities like Becedas consists of a combination and fusion of two types of elements. First, there are always portions of religion which belong to what Robert Redfield (1960) dubbed the "Great Tradition," that is, the codified, written beliefs and practices, which are followed closely by the elite, and which form the underlying substratum of beliefs and practices adhered to by all individuals who share the same given culture. In Roman Catholic communities, including Becedas, such "Great Tradition" elements consist of belief in the Trinity, the Virgin Mary, all the saints, heaven and hell, purgatory, and so forth. "Great Tradition" practices include weekly attendance at Mass, at least one confession and communion annually, plus participation in the relevant sacraments—baptism, first communion, confirmation, marriage, and extreme unction. In this category, too, fall observance of all the universally recognized and required Catholic holidays and feast days, such as the Sunday sabbath, Holy Week, Corpus Christi, and the Day of the Immaculate Conception (December 8).

In contrast, anthropologists, along with priests, usually juxtapose the "Little Tradition"—practices and rituals recognized at the local level which are neither a codified, required feature of the larger religious tradition nor much accepted beyond that local level. In Spain, such "Little Tradition" elements include an elaborate annual round of feast observances not considered mandatory by the universal Church, as well as numerous and diverse pre-Christian practices originally accepted by the Church and subsequently integrated into local religious lore through the process of syncretism. Some of these elements, such as decorating house façades with embroidered sheets on Corpus Christi, are—or until recently were—widespread throughout rural Spain. Others, such as fire-walking in Soria (Foster 1955) or devil-dancing in Cuenca (Foster 1960, 209–12), are restricted to a handful of villages at most. Until recently, every Spanish community exhibited a multitude of such local traditions, more numerous or elaborate in some areas than in others, but always present in some degree to supplement or modify the ubiquitous Great Tradition.

Now, while the anthropologist and priest may distinguish between the Great and the Little Traditions in the religious sphere, peasant villagers themselves make no such distinction. To the people of Becedas, at any rate, there is just "religion," a wide complex of sacred beliefs and practices which include both types of elements, all of which have universal validity, unrestricted by time or space. Villagers themselves recognize no incorporation of pre-Christian forms into their religion, nor can they perceive the numerous small modifications which have taken place over the centuries as a result of diffusion, structural adaptation, and legislation. Politics may be ephemeral, but religion is eternal, to be strictly observed in its correct and proper variant—the variant found in their own small locale. It is with the recognition of this native point of view that we must approach the vast religious changes which have taken place in Becedas over the past decade.

About ten years ago, two types of religious change began to affect the community and seriously disrupt the seemingly timeless continuity of Becedas religion. First, there was the introduction of changes in the Great Tradition sphere. In rapid sequence, and largely as a result of the Second Vatican Council (1965), numerous elements in canon law became modified. The Mass and sacramental prayers could now be recited in the vernacular, not only in Latin. The altar table could be pushed from its centuries-old position against the wall, requiring the priest to pray with his back to the congregation, out toward the front of the choir, permitting him to perform Mass face frontward. Saturday night Masses were introduced and could be substituted for Sunday morning Mass. Dietary regulations were altered so that meat might be eaten on Fridays. Not even the holiest of acts, communion, was above modification. No longer was it necessary to fast from midnight the evening before receiving the host, then kneel and passively accept it from the hands of the priest. Now one could even eat breakfast—or dinner, depending on which Mass you were going to—an hour before standing at the altar, picking up the wafer one-self from a consecrated plate, and placing it in one's own mouth.

All of these changes, as well as many others, have of course emanated from Rome, and are part of the Vatican's continuing attempt to adapt the church to con-temporary needs and conditions. In this connection, one of the main goals has been to make religion more comprehensible to the ordinary believer, to divest Catholi-cism of much of its mystery and mysticism. Though the goal may be universal, the way in which it is interpreted and implemented at the local level varies from parish to parish. Some priests undoubtedly explain each change to their congregations as it is adopted, thereby further fulfilling the aims of religious understanding and assuring that the alteration will not come as a shock or be interpreted as whim.

Such is not the case in Becedas, where, for the most part, Don Sixto has simply imposed the changes (in which he believes wholeheartedly) without explanation. Though himself of peasant stock, Don Sixto has a somewhat condescending, impatient air in his relations with his flock, and I am sure places little faith in their ability to understand the meaning of papal decrees. As a result, his parishioners, who have acquired a very short-sighted view of recent religious changes, believe them to be peculiar to their own region, and initiated by Don Sixto and other priests of the area in an attempt to dilute age-old, sanctified practices. At least some peasants clearly believe that Catholics in other parts of Spain, let alone the world, are not victims of the same sacrileges as they are. Their error derives from lack of information and from the condescension. Given such conditions, it is no wonder that they believe that the clergy, and Don Sixto in particular, are shame-lessly and overtly doing away with their religion.

Parish priests have little or no control over modifications in canon law. In this regard they are simply instruments for the implementation of Vatican policy. They do have a great deal to say, however, concerning the retention or elimination of Little Tradition elements in their own parishes. Here, in this second religious sphere, the degree and kind of change is highly dependent on the character and personal predilections of the individual immediately in charge. For many years,

Becedas was assigned an extremely affable, sympathetic priest, a local historian in his own way, who collected examples of regional traditions and who, with the wholehearted backing of his parishioners, adhered with meticulous care to what we would call village folk religion.

In 1966, however, Don Sixto became the new village priest. With complete candor Don Sixto admits to his goal of religious purification. He wants to cleanse Becedas religion of what he regards as superstition, and trim it down to the bare legal necessity as defined by Rome. In our terms, he wants to divest it of all Little Tradition elements. Above all, he wants villagers to act on the basis of faith, not blind adherence to custom.

"I am an enemy of processions," he once told me bluntly. "Why?" I asked. "Because they do not enhance devotion," he continued, "and I am against all which does not enhance devotion." Of the fourteen annual processions in the traditional Becedas fiesta cycle, perhaps five continue to take place. Don Sixto informed me of how, in the most calculated manner, he began to do away with the processions year after year, one by one. His final goal is elimination of all but two processions: Corpus Christi and the village patron saint, Santa Teresa. He eliminates the processions gradually, he says, so as not to alienate or shock the community too much. . . .

In addition to processions, other Little Tradition practices have also been altered by Don Sixto. For instance, until several years ago it was village custom to hold funeral Masses on three consecutive mornings following a person's death. Similarly, memorial Masses were held on the anniversary of a death for three consecutive years. Since 1971 Don Sixto has steadfastly refused to hold more than one funeral Mass and one memorial Mass, despite the entreaties of his parishioners, who feel the loss. In fact, Don Sixto's behavior is totally incomprehensible for its economic irrationality. "Did you ever see a priest who rejects money?" villagers ask, "Don Sixto imposes poverty on himself by refusing to let us hold our Masses." . . .

Don Sixto knows the Little Tradition well and can identify it much more exactly than can the anthropologist, even though he does not refer to it with our terminology. Villagers are aware that he is working to get rid of it, though *they* do not distinguish between these changes and those which come from Rome. To them, there has just been a consistent shrinking of religious responsibilities and activities. Even if Don Sixto's tenure did not coincide with the canonical changes promoted by Vatican II, his elimination of folk religious occasions would have been enough to brand him as sacrilegious. Because his actions in the folk sphere have been combined with alterations of the Great Tradition, he must be considered a near-enemy of religion. Thus, when villagers say that the priests *quitan la religion* (take religion away) they are indeed giving an accurate rendition of the situation. For their priest has destroyed the eternal verities of religious belief and action, and in so doing has given rise to a well founded religious cynicism. Even when villagers go through the motions of religion, they no longer consider the Church a legitimate outlet for their sacred feelings, for the Church is today represented and manned by its own worst enemies.

I want to conclude with a few points of clarification. First, I recognize that the course of religious change in Becedas may be different from that in many, if not most, Catholic communities. The Roman Church has survived in large part because of its adaptability to a continually changing social milieu. Recent Church reforms, and the attitude of clergymen like Don Sixto will undoubtedly operate to retain within the fold many people who might otherwise have left. In relatively isolated, conservative places like Becedas, however, where religion and the clergy have never been perceived as an enemy, these actions may boomerang.

Second, I realize that I may be describing only a tiny portion of the total causal chain in the process of secularization. We might, for example, argue that ultimately it is the world economy which brought about the ecumenical movement, which in turn created the Papal reforms, which finally gave rise to the spirit of religious purification motivating Don Sixto's actions in Becedas. This is all true, perhaps, but not nearly as interesting, to my way of thinking, as perceiving the secularization process from the ground up. If we agree that the main goal of ethnography is to see the world through the eyes of our informants, then it is the clergy, not the economy, which is bringing about religious decline in Becedas.

Third, I am aware, as no doubt many readers are, that the Becedas case may simply represent an instance of secularization resulting from a system of imposed religious heterogeneity. . . . Yet can we really say that where a Great Tradition and a Little Tradition meet, as in this case, we have true religious heterogeneity? And even if we construe the situation as heterogeneous, does such diversity automatically bring about religious decline? . . .

After all, in villages like Becedas, religious festivals and processions are the only occasions on which *all* community members meet and on which they can assert their mutual loyalties and affection. Yet let us not automatically interpret the disappearance or alteration of ritual as a consequence of social atomization and economic individualization. For the process may be just the reverse.

References

Foster, George M. 1955. "The Fire Walkers of San Pedro Manrique, Soria, Spain." *Journal of American Folklore* 68 (269): 325–32.

———. 1960. *Culture and Conquest: America's Spanish Heritage.* Viking Fund Publications in Anthropology no. 27. New York: Wenner-Gren Foundation.

Martin, David. 1969. "Notes for a General Theory of Secularization." *European Journal of Sociology* 10 (2): 192–201.

Redfield, Robert. 1960. *Peasant Society and Culture.* Chicago: University of Chicago Press.

8

Excerpt from "Women Mystics and Eucharistic Devotion in the Thirteenth Century"

Caroline Walker Bynum[1]

In this chapter the renowned medievalist scholar Caroline Walker Bynum brings our attention to a striking historical occurrence: in twelfth- and thirteenth-century Europe the concern with and attachment to Eucharistic devotion was overwhelmingly female. Why this gender bias, and at that time? Christian women were predominantly "inspired, compelled, comforted and troubled by the Eucharist" and in many different forms—from miraculous apparitions, to experiences of ecstasy connected to the attendance and ingestion of the Eucharist, to the showing of sensorial excesses in its presence. Bynum shows how material and physical receptions of the body of Christ were expressed not only as forms of ecstasy but also as gendered modes of living the *Imitatio Christi*. This thirteenth-century corporeal, female experience of the Eucharist is connected to a particular moment in the life of Christ—the transition between life and death. Positioned as "brides" and hence as the erotic counterparts of Christ, women and female mystics exploited the full potential of Christ's own corporeality rather than his otherworldly nature.

Bynum's work constitutes a formative reference point for scholars of Catholicism across a range of disciplines for the obvious reason that it deals so elegantly with themes of substance, gender, bodies, and devotional forms of Catholic practice. Her work continues to be an original source of inspiration for anthropologists because of its remarkable sensitivity to religion as an embodied, practice-generative engagement with the world. Bynum should also be considered as important for the "new" anthropology of Catholicism for her pioneering work on the gymnasticity of gender and for the attention it draws to the sublimated erotic tension that exists between institutional doxa and mystical aesthetics.[2] In Bynum's work, gender is not presented as merely one among a number of potential analytical foci for

From Caroline Walker Bynum. "Women Mystics and Eucharistic Devotion in the 13th Century," from *Fragmentation and Redemption*. New York: Zone Books, 1992 (pp. 121–50). © Zone Books, 1992. Reprinted with the permission of Zone Books.

elaboration of Catholicism; rather, it *is* the very ontological architecture of the religious, and hence an essential topic for scholars seeking to understand Catholicism as a translocal force.

· · ·

... The attention which thirteenth-century women paid to the eucharist has been noticed before. But scholars have tended to correlate eucharistic concern either with order (particularly the Cistercians or the Dominicans), or with region (particularly the Low Countries or southern Germany), or with type of religious life (particularly nuns or recluses). If one reads widely in thirteenth-century saints' lives and spiritual treatises, however, it is glaringly obvious that laywomen, recluses, tertiaries, beguines, nuns of all orders and those women (especially common in the early thirteenth century) who wandered from one type of life to another were inspired, compelled, comforted and troubled by the eucharist to an extent found in only a few male writers of the period. In this essay I want not only to illustrate the importance of women in the development of this aspect of thirteenth-century piety, but also to explain why women's religiosity expressed itself in eucharistic devotion. ...

[In fact] even in accounts by male authors written for male audiences, we find the eucharist and the attendant theme of the humanity of Christ associated especially with women. . . . To thirteenth-century women, the mass and the reception or adoration of the eucharist were closely connected with mystical union or ecstasy, which was frequently accompanied by paramystical phenomena. To some extent, reception of Christ's body and blood was a substitute for ecstasy—a union that anyone, properly prepared by confession or contrition, could achieve. To receive was to become Christ—by eating, by devouring and being devoured. No "special effects" were necessary. In the eucharist Christ was available to the beginner as well as to the spiritually trained. This is what the German beguine Mechtild of Magdeburg means when she says:

> Yet I, least of all souls,
> Take Him in my hand,
> Eat Him and drink Him,
> And do with Him what I will!
> Why then should I trouble myself
> As to what the angels experience?

Simply to eat Christ is enough; it *is* to achieve union. . . .

The eucharist was, however, more than an occasion for ecstasy. It was also a moment of encounter with that *humanitas Christi* which was such a prominent theme of women's spirituality. For thirteenth-century women this humanity was, above all, Christ's physicality, his corporality, his being-in-the-body-ness; Christ's humanity was Christ's body and blood.

Both in a eucharistic context and outside it, the humanity of Christ was often described as "being eaten." To popular twelfth-century metaphors for union (often ultimately of Neoplatonic origin)—metaphors of light, of darkness, of wine diffused in water—women added the insistent image and experience of flesh taken into flesh. Lutgard of Aywières rejected an earthly suitor, calling him "thou food of death"; she later nursed from the breast of Christ so that afterward her own saliva was sweet to the taste, and she received Christ as a lamb who stood on her shoulders and sucked from her mouth. Angela of Foligno nursed from Christ and saw him place the heads of her "sons" (the friars) into the wound in his side. Anna Vorchtlin of Engelthal exclaimed, upon receiving a vision of the baby Jesus: "If I had you, I would eat you up, I love you so much!" Mechtild of Magdeburg spoke of mystical union as "eating God." And Ida of Louvain was able to eat Christ almost at will by reciting John 1.14. For, whenever she spoke the words *Verbum caro factum est*— which she inserted into the Hours whenever possible—she tasted the Word on her tongue and felt flesh in her mouth; when she chewed it, it was like honey, "not [her biographer tells us] a phantasm but like any other kind of food." This example makes clear to the modern reader how insistently Christ's humanity was thought of as flesh, as food (*corpus, caro, carnis*), eaten in the eucharist, a substitute for the meat many women denied themselves in long fasts. Moreover, the incorporation of self into Christ or of Christ into self was so much a matter of flesh swallowing flesh that women who were not able to eat still received and digested Christ's physicality. For example, when the host was placed on the breast of the dying Juliana Falconieri it simply sank into her body and disappeared. The humanity of Christ with which women joined in the eucharist was the physical Jesus of the manger and of Calvary. . . .

[Moreover,] illness and asceticism were rather *imitatio Christi,* an effort to plumb the depths of Christ's humanity at the moment of his most insistent and terrifying humanness—the moment of his dying.

Mary of Oignies, in a frenzied vision of the crucifix, cut off pieces of her own flesh and buried them in the ground to keep the secret of what she had done. Lukardis of Oberweimar drove the middle finger of each hand, hard as a nail, through the palm handled and loved; sexual feelings were, as certain contemporary commentators (like David of Augsburg) clearly realized, not so much translated into another medium as simply set free.

Asceticism and eroticism sometimes fused so completely that it is hard to know under which category to place a mystic like Ida of Louvain, who went mad from desire for the eucharist and had to be put in chains, or Beatrice of Nazareth, who consulted a spiritual adviser to find out whether God would sanction her effort to drive herself literally "crazy" as a way of "following" him. We misunderstand the power of the erotic, nuptial mysticism of Low Country figures like Hadewijch and Beatrice of Nazareth if we project onto their image of lover seeking Lover stereotyped notions of brides as passive and submissive. Their search for Christ took them through a frenzy they called insanity (*orewoet* in Flemish, *aestus* or *insania amoris* in Latin).

Erotic imagery is unimportant in some women's writing. And nuptial language is often most elaborate in *male* biographers, who may have had their own reasons for describing women they admired and loved in erotic metaphors. But the image of bride or lover was clearly a central metaphor for the woman mystic's union with Christ's humanity. In the twelfth century, Hildegard of Bingen actually dressed her nuns as brides when they went forward to receive communion. And Hadewijch and Mechtild of Magdeburg, women given voice by the emergence of the vernaculars, found in secular love poetry the vocabulary and the pulsating rhythms to speak of the highest of all loves. . . .

Part of the answer [to a fusion of asceticism and eroticism] seems to be that women's ecstasy or possession served as an alternative to the authority of priestly office. . . . In the visions that women received at mass, they sometimes acquired metaphorical priesthood. I have discussed elsewhere the fact that women's visions sometimes gave them general authorization to prophesy and teach and hear confessions. What should be noted here is that eucharistic visions occasionally projected women, in metaphor and vision, into access to the altar, even into the role of celebrant—things strictly forbidden to them. For example, a woman who had loved Juliana of Cornillon very much in her life saw her after death at mass, assisting the priest. Angela of Foligno, feeling that the celebrant was unworthy, had a vision of Christ bleeding on the cross and angels said to her: "Oh you who are pleasing to God, behold, he has been administered to you . . . in order that you may administer and present him to others." Benevenuta of Bojano saw the Virgin administering the chalice in a vision. And, in addition to the infrequent visions in which women actually see themselves or other women as priests or acolytes, there are hundreds of visions in which Christ himself gives the chalice or the host to a nun or beguine or laywoman who is unable to receive, either because of illness or because the clergy prevent it. Moreover, criticism of corrupt clergy was—in the eyes of both women and men—the special role of religious women; and female eucharistic miracles were a favorite vehicle for this. . . .

There is no question that this aspect of thirteenth-century religious women was particularly stressed by men, that it was men in particular who saw women as an alternative to and a criticism of wealth, power and office. Woman, both as symbol and as fact, was "liminal" to man in the technical sense given the term by Victor Turner. In her visions and her devotions, woman—particularly the mystical bride of Christ—was the point where the powerful male found a reversal and a critique of exactly those things about which he felt greatest ambivalence. In saints' lives from the twelfth to the fifteenth century, women receive striking political visions for the assistance of men. Hildegard of Bingen, Elizabeth of Schönau, Mary of

Oignies, Lutgard of Aywières, Elizabeth of Hungary, Catherine of Siena, Birgitta of Sweden and Joan of Arc are the most obvious examples. . . .

[Furthermore,] if food was sometimes a symbol of self and of the world, invoked at moments of decision or conflict, the fasting and nausea of medieval women were not simply world rejection, nor were they simply control of self substituted for control of circumstance. Angela of Foligno, desiring to punish herself for hypocritical piety, wanted to parade through the streets with rotting fish and meat tied around her neck; she described herself as tempted by the devil to give up eating entirely. Later, she came to see these reactions as pathological and found the eucharist to taste like especially delicious meat. Thus, not-eating was complemented by holy eating. Food was filth; it was also God. The woman's revulsion at her own body, even when it took what appeared to her and her contemporaries to be bizarre forms, was given a theological significance more complex than dualism. The peasant saint Alpaïs of Cudot did not, after all, die of "anorexia." She survived for forty years on the eucharist and became a living proof of the efficacy of the sacrament. The point of even the oddest of these stories was ultimately not rejection of the physical and bodily, but a finding of the truly physical, the truly nourishing, the truly fleshly, in the humanity of Christ, chewed and swallowed in the eucharist.

. . . If we look at the thirteenth-century theological context, it is clear that women's concern with matter, with physicality, with imitation of the human Christ, must be located against the background of the war against heresy. Controversy over the eucharist reemerged after centuries of silence in the late eleventh century; and twelfth-century theologians themselves (for example, Hildegard of Bingen) saw denial of the eucharist as one of heresy's major threats. Modern scholars have frequently argued that the central theological purpose behind the proliferating eucharistic miracles was support for the doctrine of transubstantiation. Recent historians have also suggested that thirteenth-century eucharistic devotion was part of the general effort of theology and spirituality to propose an alternative to Cathar dualism. We can see such motives reflected, for example, in the writings of James of Vitry and Thomas of Cantimpré, who held up women saints, with their concentration on Christ's body and blood, as a counter to the Cathar view that the physical world is the creation of an evil God. The cardinal legate who helped Juliana of Cornillon propagate the feast of Corpus Christi supported it explicitly as a weapon against dualism. Furthermore, it seems clear that confessors urged women toward eucharistic piety in an effort to keep their devotional life not only orthodox but also firmly under ecclesiastical control. We must, however, look beyond any conscious effort to propagandize against the Cathars if we are to understand the extent to which thirteenth-century spirituality is a response to the threat of dualism. Indeed, it is possible to argue that the theme of the positive religious significance of physicality runs throughout thirteenth-century theology. . . .

In fact, eucharistic practice as reflected in art and architecture underlines the extent to which reverence for the host was reverence for the divine *in the material*. Not only did the thirteenth century see the growth of the practice of reserving the host in pyxes or tabernacles; the eucharist was also sometimes reserved in a reliquary, mobile tabernacles were modeled on reliquaries, and pyxes were sometimes displayed alongside reliquaries. The practice of burning candles or lamps before the host was borrowed from the manner in which relics were revered. Thus, the host was clearly treated as a relic of Christ; tabernacles were thrones or tombs for Christ's body. And it is interesting to note that our earliest evidence for visits to the reserved host seen as a relic of Christ, a fragment of his physicality, comes from an English rule for female recluses and from the life of Mary of Oignies.

Changes in the twelfth-century notion of *imitatio* also lie behind women's eucharistic devotion. Scholars have stressed that the twelfth-century search for the *vita apostolica* was a search for perfect poverty; somewhere in the course of the century (in a by-no-means unidirectional development), the apostolic life came to mean preaching. What scholars have failed to underline, however, is the extent to which imitation—of the martyrs, of the apostles and of Christ—became more and more literal. Thus, by the late twelfth century, *imitatio* had moved far beyond the Cistercian notion of affective meditation. Whereas Bernard of Clairvaux taught that we identify with Christ by extending our compassion to his humanity through pitying the suffering humanity of our neighbors, Francis and Mary of Oignies *became* Christ on the cross while a seraph looked on. Indeed some male descriptions of holy women explicitly stress that *imitatio* is fact, not memory or imagination. We are told, for example, that Margaret of Cortona and Lukardis of Oberweimar became one with the Crucifixion *rather than* simply remembering or pitying Christ's suffering. Margaret of Ypres's extreme self-flagellation as a means of joining with Christ was called a *recordatio* (remembrance); but in such a passage the very meaning of the word "remember" has changed. Beatrice of Nazareth, more theologically sophisticated than many of her fellow women mystics, spoke of the three grades of moving toward Christ: turning toward grace; growing in the memory of Christ's passion; and, finally, inhering in Jesus.

This sense of *imitatio* as *becoming* or *being* lies in the background of women's eucharistic devotion. The eucharist is an especially appropriate vehicle for the effort to become Christ because the eucharist *is* Christ. The fact of transubstantiation is crucial. One *becomes* Christ's crucified body in *eating* Christ's crucified body. Thus, reception of the eucharist leads so naturally to stigmata, visibly or inwardly, that contemporaries hardly worried about how to account for their appearance. *Imitatio* is incorporation of flesh into flesh. Both priest and recipient are literally pregnant with Christ. The metaphor of the good soul as Christ's mother, which had a long lineage, became in the thirteenth century more than metaphor. Caesarius of Heisterbach described a priest who swelled up at the consecration, pregnant with Christ. Ida of Louvain swelled with the eucharist. By the fourteenth century, Dorothy of Montau repeatedly experienced mystical pregnancy and was almost required by her confessor to exhibit it as part of her preparation for communion. . . .

If anything, women drew from the traditional notion of the female as physical a special emphasis on their own redemption by a Christ who was supremely physical because supremely human. They sometimes even extrapolated from this to the notion that, in Christ, divinity is to humanity as male is to female. . . . [Hence] Mary was, of course, important in women's spirituality. Particularly in southern European saints' lives, the theme of *imitatio Mariae Virginis* is strong. The biographer of Douceline of Marseilles, for example, actually sees Douceline as imitating the poverty of Mary, whereas her beloved Francis imitated the poverty of Christ directly. But the reverence for Mary that we find in thirteenth-century women mystics is less a reverence for a "representative woman" than a reverence for the bearer and conduit of the Incarnation. The ultimate identification was with Christ as human. Some women saints swoon with Mary before the cross; *all* women saints swoon on the cross with Christ himself. . . .

Contrary to what some recent interpretations have asserted, thirteenth-century women seem to have concluded from their physicality an intense conviction of their *ability* to imitate Christ without role or gender inversion. To soar toward Christ as lover and bride, to sink into the stench and torment of the Crucifixion, to eat God, was for the woman only to give religious significance to what she already was. So, female devotion to the eucharist—and to the dying or the infant or the bridegroom Christ—expresses a special confidence in the Incarnation. If the Incarnation meant that the whole human person was capable of redemption, then what woman was seen as being—even in the most misogynist form of the Christian tradition—was caught up into God in Christ. And if the agony of the Crucifixion was less sacrifice or victory than the redemption of that which is human (matter joined to form), then the Crucifixion could be imaged as death or as eating or as orgasm (all especially human—bodily—experiences). Women mystics seem to have felt that they *qua* women were not only *also* but even *especially* saved in the Incarnation.

NOTES

1. For reasons of editorial consistency this excerpt does not contain footnotes and bibliographic references appearing in the essay's original version.

2. For an elaboration on "gender gymnastics," see Mayblin (2014a).

PART TWO

Contemporary Works in the Anthropology of Catholicism

9

"Complexio Oppositorum"?

Religion, Society, and Power in the Making of Catholicism in Rural South India

David Mosse

The notion of *complexio oppositorum* ("complex of opposites") has been used to describe the capacity of the Catholic Church to embrace all forms of state, government, and culture. Carl Schmitt used this idea in developing a theory of hegemony in imperialism, which necessarily involves tying together incompatible cultural materials into one formation. As the "paradigmatic imperial force," Catholicism is able to contain within itself antimonies such as royalism/capitalism, autocracy/democracy, conservatism/liberalism, tradition/progress, nature/spirit, militarism/pacifism, arrogance/humility, natural good / natural evil, and "limitless ambiguity" / "precise dogmatism," among others. Schmitt's point was that Catholicism has the capacity to hold such tensions and to unite within itself thesis and antithesis without the Hegelian drive toward a "higher third."[1]

Schmitt argued specifically that Catholicism resists the resolution of opposites through some theological abstraction above or Protestant interiorization within; instead, it permits oppositions to clash, and from this confrontation Catholicism derives its political energy and preserves an "externality."[2] The *complexio oppositorum* implies, therefore, a position against abandoning the world. It resists the abstraction of God from the world and its struggles and antagonisms, and it implies a political idea of Catholicism that keeps the church in the public sphere.[3] This chapter examines a tradition of Catholicism (in South India) no less involved in a complex of opposites but without imperial capacity, and so with very different implications and a specific route to political engagement.

Too often Catholicism (or Christianity) is attributed an independent coherence, power, and ideological encompassment, and missionization is conceived in terms of the transmission of a set of distinctive beliefs—teachings on salvation or new monopolies of mediation that demand of its receivers a radical reorganization of existing religiosity. But the unity and coherence of Catholicism—its capacity to embrace rather than to be embraced by various cultural elements—are not to be presumed. That is to say, Catholicism cannot be taken as the known entity and container of politically fruitful oppositions. In the instance of South India, we have to examine how Catholicism was to find its place within a given sociopolitical and religious order and adapt to an existing structure of categories.

It is equally mistaken, however, to focus on processes of localization without an account of the distinctive Christian institutional, social, and semiotic (or religious) processes. It then becomes a historical and empirical question, how Catholicism is made locally through (or often against) hybridization, ambiguity, or contradictions, and how Catholic agents (including missionaries and priests) had to work to forge a domain of action for themselves. In this sense, Catholicism can be considered an accomplishment of missionization as a cultural encounter, not its premise. And this accomplishment itself has profound societal impacts. In short, Catholicism is not a "transhistorical essence" or translocal cultural regime with agency of its own. It is an emergent field of debate and practice, the product of particular regional histories having particular effects.[4] The apparent coherence, universality, and authority of the church were (and still are) produced through struggle and contingent action, which succeeded in forging a separate realm of Catholic religion only by concealing these messy processes and constitutive exclusions.[5]

Looking at ways in which, on the one hand, Catholicism is profoundly localized into and produced through other cultures and, on the other, how Catholicism opens up space for variant types of thought, altered ideas of person or modes of signification or radical social action, allows departure from false dichotomies of cultural continuity or discontinuity in the anthropology of Christianity.[6] It is then possible to return in a more historicized way to Schmitt's question of how Catholicism and its "complex of opposites" produce a political engagement.

To explore the way in which Catholicism is constituted through a complex of opposites, at one moment incorporated into existing conceptual and societal structures, and at another a source of countercultural critique, I will turn to the story of Roman Catholicism in an interior Tamil region of South India begun by Jesuit missionaries in the early seventeenth century. Periodically from the early 1980s I have stayed in a village I call Alapuram in modern-day southern Tamil Nadu whose Catholic members are inheritors of this tradition, although this is also a region in which religious affiliation as Christian (or Hindu) is far less important to villagers than their shared social life, structured and ritualized around endogamous (separated and ranked) identities of caste or *jati*. From the early eighteenth century until the 1930s, here Hindu villagers participated along with Christians in large-scale festivals of the Catholic saints organized at churches that are themselves understood in terms of the Tamil temple, or *kōvil*, and its ritual forms. Such village festivals with their order of ceremonial offices and entitlements—shares in the village produce and in the worship of the protector saint—articulated a local political economy and structure of political power through connections outwards to warrior overlords, sovereigns, and state.

Catholic ritual practices around life transitions such as birth, puberty, and death likewise used an existing scheme to map the necessary processes of dealing with life's dangerous residues onto social differences and specialist caste identities and services. In such ways, the social belonging of caste was central, and the church's ritual forms only secondarily distinguished Christian from Hindu. As I will explain, Catholic practice also involved Tamil conceptions of divinity and reproduced an order of castes within the sacred space and rites of Catholic churches that both honored rank and position and subordinated and excluded certain castes in relation to others.

From an ethnographic point of view, the starting point here is not Catholicism, or Catholics as a social group. The question is not, for example, "Do Catholics have caste?" or "How did Catholicism 'accommodate' an indigenous culture of caste?" It is instead, "How has caste society accommodated Catholicism as part of its mechanism?" Rather than disrupting existing authority and social investments, Catholicism provides another means for their reproduction. But this is only part of the picture because Catholicism is nonetheless produced as a culturally and ritually distinct domain. The question is, then, "How have caste persons (relationally defined) engaged with this Catholic religious domain?" and specifically "How did the distinct personal, social, and semiotic possibilities of Christianity eventually lead to a new politics of equal rights?"

I will return to these questions, but let me begin with the missiological preconditions for (or rationalization of) what became a dynamic caste-mediated synthesis of Catholicism and indigenous social and religious practice in Tamil South India. This takes us back to a seventeenth-century Jesuit innovation.

BRAHMANIZING CATHOLICISM

In 1606 the arrival of Italian Jesuit Roberto Nobili (1577–1656) in the temple city of Madurai signaled an important shift in Catholic mission in the region. Until then Christianization—under Padroado and mostly confined to the coastal areas controlled by the Portuguese trading power—involved an assault on indigenous religion and demanded from converts a radical separation from the culture of "paganism." From other points of view, Christian conversion brought an association with *parangis,* or Westerners, and their unclean and impure habits, seriously limiting the appeal of Christianity and horrifying the Brahman religious elite.

As a means to overcome barriers to Christian dialogue with those he perceived as the influential cultural elite, Nobili developed a radically new approach to mission that sought, not the extraction of Christian souls from paganism's grip, but the conversion of a civilization through the restoration of a lost truth—the fourth *veda* of salvation. The learned Brahmans' theological texts were to be regarded not as heathen religion but as a kind of "defective Catholicism."[7] They offered insight into natural law upon which revelation could be planted.[8] Nobili thus initiated a project allowing Christianity to take Indian civil form, although his famous method of *accommodation*, often celebrated as an early instance of "inculturation," was in fact primarily a means to enhance the status of Christianity in the eyes of Brahmans and other elite groups that Jesuits sought to influence.

Breaking the association of Christianity with polluted and polluting "outcastes" specifically necessitated allowing continuity of caste identities, separations, and discriminations. The legitimacy of such an approach in Rome depended upon acceptance of Nobili's (at the time unprecedented) separation of indigenous (Tamil) life into elements that were "religious," that is, pertaining to idolatry or superstition, and those that were merely "civil" and could be joined to Christian faith. As Županov argues, Nobili offered an *ethnographic* perception that substituted the condemnation of superstition and paganism with the discovery of "Brahmanism" as a universe of social practice onto which Christianity would graft true religion.[9] One could say that Brahmanic practices concerned with purification and caste separation were "secularized" so that Christianity could be Brahmanized. However, it is equally important to emphasize that ultimately Nobili's Jesuits were not so much interested in "accommodating caste" to Catholicism as in preparing the basis for Tamils to engage with Christian truth and salvation (religion) *beyond the social.*

Nobili was singularly unsuccessful in converting Brahmans in the Tamil cultural heartland. Nonetheless, it was as a kind of Brahmanic "high religion," whose rites existed alongside the public orderings of caste (taken by Jesuits as morally indifferent matters or *adiaphora*), that Catholicism took root in the seventeenth- and eighteenth-century Tamil countryside.[10] Churches headed by Jesuit renouncer-teachers became patronized by minor warrior-kings and Hindu rulers in the remoter plains areas. Here Brahmanic gloss and Jesuit ritualism may have been consonant with the status ambitions of warrior chiefs aspiring to become royal personages; but Catholic centers attracted patronage even more because they incorporated immensely popular sacred places, miraculous tombs or saint shrines, conceived in indigenous terms, some of which preceded the Jesuit mission, having filtered inland from the older fishing Catholic communities on the Coromandal coast.

These were seats of powerful divinities with large followings at which aspiring big men or warrior kings could hardly afford not to be recognized as primary patrons. Around these constituency-building saint shrines were elaborated systems of entitlement and honors, which also served to incorporate in-migrating groups into an expanding surplus-generating economy. In short, the early expansion of Catholicism in this region was tied up with processes of statecraft, honor politics, agrarian settlement, and caste competition that were not of the Jesuits' own making.

THE MISSIONARY MAKING OF CATHOLIC RELIGION

The village of Alapuram offers historical insights into the local cultural politics of Catholicism through Jesuit diaries and letters, the earliest around 1730. This records a popular pilgrimage center focusing on the miraculous tree shrine of Saint James or Sandiyakkappar under the patronage of regional kings. By the late eighteenth century this and other such centers had been drawn into the orbit of the Jesuit mission. Saints such as Sandiyakkappar were established power divinities in a local sacred and political geography—divine personages in royal form, worshipped by their Christian and Hindu devotees as protectors in their royal seats or kōvils. As noted already, the Tamil temple form in which public worship of the saint took place articulated formalized caste orders, economic rights, and connections to political overlords through systems of service, gifts, and honors.

Acting within this system, eighteenth-century Jesuit missionaries were key players: "Brahmanic" renouncer-teachers; power-holding domain-building big men; allocators of politically important ritual honors; and arbiters of status conflicts between competing caste groups.[11] The Catholic mission was equally subject to shifts within a volatile political system of which it was now a part. The consolidation of British rule from 1800 coupled with the ecclesiastical ruptures of the suppression (1773) and later restoration (1814) of the Society of Jesus (in no small measure to do with controversy over Nobili's "accommodations") set in motion important changes.

At first, Catholicism was further embedded in the local political order by factors such as competition between missionary rivals (French Jesuits of the new Madurai Mission and Padroado "Goans" who claimed jurisdiction of shrines and churches after Jesuit expulsion) coupled with conflicts between caste groups arising from shifts in local economic and political power. New property regimes, cash cropping, markets, and migrations led prospering cultivator castes with status ambitions to make claims against an old caste political order through the system of festival and other honors at Catholic shrines. By comparison with Hindu temples, the political dynamic of Catholic centers was especially productive of social power, not least because competition between missionaries (Jesuit, "Goan," and Protestant) for local support resulted in the further elaboration of ranked caste orders around Catholic worship. But this politics also entrenched the subordination and exclusion of the "untouchable" castes known then as Pariahs and now as Dalits.

In the second half of the nineteenth century, British rule allowed the French missionaries of the reinstated Jesuit order gradually to institutionalize Catholicism as a domain of religion, which was in missionary and bureaucratic conception separate from politics—a domain within which they would themselves be "over-lords." As such, Jesuit parish priests sought to erode the existing rights and honors in church systems held by Hindu rulers, village headmen, and caste big men, as well as other entitlements born of caste and village membership. They used the colonial courts in disputes with elements of the old political order that held a fundamentally different conception of churches as the seat of social power.

Over the course of a century, from the 1850s, and through an array of contingent actions—administrative, legal, ecclesiastical, ceremonial—Jesuit priests successfully merged within themselves the sacred and political order to forge the church as a newly separate realm of religious governance. Jesuits, for example, appropriated the royal functions of endowing shrines, patronizing the main processions, receiving first respect (*mutal mariyātai*), and becoming the arbiters of caste rank. Paradoxically, they used the ritual and symbolic forms of the Tamil *kōvil* to assert the church over the *kōvil*. In effect, Jesuits dismantled the earlier "outworldly" renouncer model of missionary priesthood and spirituality, which had resolved a complex of opposites by separating out the "civil" as the realm of ritual-political practices, and began to put in place an enclave domain of church authority within Tamil society. This meant confrontation and exclusion of the Hindu, of village politics and caste status.

It is more helpful, not to think in terms of a contested frontier between missionaries and other claimants on Catholic churches (as Jesuit missionaries conceived the matter), but to imagine that the very *same* physical spaces and ritual practices (the church and its ceremony, liturgy, and even the Eucharist itself) were subject to two different and largely incompatible frames of meaning: one defined by the Holy Church (*tiruccapai*) under clerical authority, the other defined by the saint's *kōvil*—as a source of social power in terms of which all spaces and practices, even those apparently central to Catholic rites (how, where, when or by whom scripture was read, lamps were lit, anthems were sung, the host was received, etc.), were inseparable from the order, services, and honors of caste society. There existed a dual system of Catholic public worship, although the power accorded to each varied.

If asserting institutional control over their churches was a challenge for Jesuits, how much more so was the disciplining of their parishioners' religiosity. Jesuit missionaries oversaw a complex and ambiguous realm of Catholic practice: a multitude of gods, saints, spirits, and sorcerers; hybridized conceptions of divinity; varied materializations of divine power; and a dual "representational economy": that is, the coexistence of more than one semiotic ideology (beliefs about signifying practices and the relationship between signs and their referents).[12] There was, as Ines Županov argues, an "endless conversion of meanings and relations of things" as preconversion beliefs and practices "returned to weave together and reinterpret Christianity in unpredictable ways."[13]

Following Nobili's method, seventeenth- and eighteenth-century Jesuits had sought to Christianize rather than replace Tamil religiosity, introducing or allowing a variety of sacred statues, relics, tombs, trees, and acts (pilgrimages, vow fulfilling, and animal offerings) to be worked on by an indigenous religious imagination. The Jesuit demand for radical distinction between "Christian" and "pagan" at the level of the signifier (Christian figures, substances, and signs), rather than the signified or the mode of signification encouraged a pantheon of Christian divinities in interdefinition with local (Hindu) divinity and its various powers and materializations, and in shared processes of ritual engagement and worship.

As French missionaries of the new Madurai mission endeavored to produce a more bounded institutional realm of Catholic religion, we find in their diaries parallel efforts to get their parishioners to separate the Christian from the pagan, as well as the interior from the exterior, the eternal from the everyday, faith from fantasy, and spirit from body. They worked to distinguish different beings and agency in a dangerously hybridized world and deployed their own spirit-object hybrids (crosses, holy water, recitations) to effect these categorical purifications and diagnostic separations.

The order and coherence of Catholicism as articulated by French Jesuits were not pregiven but indeed the outcome of such struggles with hybridity and heterodoxy. Among the most prominent were their battles against heterodox cults of spirit exorcism at popular shrines of Catholic saints. I have argued that such cults allowed the dramatic "externalization" of emotional struggle and spiritual battle at a time when, through new moral discipline of confession and communion, missionaries were effecting an "internalization" of guilt and affliction that bore down unbearably on the individual sinner.[14] The saint cults of exorcism not only were a rebellion against the harsh interiorizing and responsibilizing disciplines of the Jesuits but also mimicked the very missionary stance against pagan gods and human passions. The exorcist-saints did directly and dramatically what priests achieved only imperfectly, namely the purging of inner sin, desire, and passion from body and soul, objectified as demonic and visibly defeated. Missionary Catholicism was defined though these contests and the boundary marking they involved that served to establish the church as a distinct realm apart.

LOCAL RESPONSES—A DUAL MORAL WORLD

Of course, the Jesuit priest's was not the only point of view from which a complex and confusing spiritual realm involving Christian saints, Hindu deities, household or lineage gods, and spirits had to be made sense of. Tamil villagers had to find a way to negotiate relationships with an array of divine beings and across religious boundaries with Hindu neighbors while at the same time accommodating the teachings of their parish priests. They had somehow to isolate important social relations from the implications of the socially disruptive antipagan absolutism of the church in their midst—to accomplish a distinctive articulation with, but also radical opposition to, indigenous divinity.

In my book *The Saint in the Banyan Tree* (2012) I have identified some ways in which Catholic divinity is drawn into and organized through existing schemes and symbolic logics. In a localized Catholic imaginary, saints take on the character of royal personages, virgin goddesses, or tortured sages turning bloody histories of martyrdom into divine power. Moreover, this is a two-way street: Hindu gods and goddesses also acquire some of the character of Catholic saints, and the embattled forces of good and evil of Christian imagination appear in certain Hindu practices for dealing with demonic intrusions.

The Catholic religiosity recorded from my fieldwork in the 1980s was a dynamic field, not a stable religious synthesis; it involved assemblages animated by encounters across the boundaries between inconsistent frameworks of Hindu and Catholic, missionary and missionized. But what seemed clear was that the complex and heterogeneous array of Hindu and Christian divinity was ordered in terms of the relationships of an existing symbolic scheme, that, for example, separated out hierarchies of divine power, the dangerous from the benign, the violent from the nonviolent, the local from the cosmic, the ascetic from the royal, or the female from the male. In ways that cannot be elaborated here, Catholic divinity was imagined as part of a complex of relational divinity, continuous with but distinct from Hindu beings, incorporated through hierarchical spatial and ritual orderings. In this rural Catholicism, the "complex of opposites" takes the particular form of hierarchical incorporation, or, in Louis Dumont's apt phrase, "encompassing the contrary."[15] For Christians, Hindu divinity exists in subordination to, or as the relegated—dangerous, violent, impure—aspect of, a superior Catholic divine power. But beyond such relationships of control, manifestations of Hindu divinity are demonic and destructive.[16] The point is that Catholics ordered pluralistic divinity (and their continuing relationships with non-Christian beings) according to principles that are significantly Hindu.

It is worth noting that Catholic communities in the wider South Indian region map the relationships of divinity in different but socially significant ways. Thus Catholics in plains villages such as Alapuram, living in integration with Hindu kin, co-caste members, and neighbors, have produced hierarchical royal metaphors for the Catholic inclusion of Hindu divinity, rather than the rivalrous sibling ones common in more religiously separate Kerala, or the exclusionary demonization of Hindu divinity present in socially segregated coastal Catholic communities.[17]

Apart from having to make sense of a plurality of divinity and spirit agents, rural Catholics had to contend with the absolutist demands and teaching of the church, which refused any such hierarchical incorporation of "the other." Villagers worked to separate the domain of missionary absolutism from existing religious and social obligations and did so, I suggest, by allocating these to different notional and ritual spaces.[18] These spaces were also defined by an indigenous schema that set a particularistic, relational, incorporative hierarchical social and ritual realm (for example, the interior moral space of the *ūr,* or village) in opposition to a realm of the universal, the absolute, of renunciation and transcendence (that is, the exterior moral space of the *kāṭu,* or forest wilderness). These correspond to two contrasting ways of thinking about divinity. For example, the battle between Christian saints and Hindu deities at exorcism shrines takes place in the "forest," the realm of absolutes, in contrast to the incorporative hierarchy of Christian and Hindu in the "village" and its order of castes and ritual obligations manifest, for example, in the annual festivals. The domain of the church and its teaching is an equivalent nonrelational, essentialist "forest" space. The Tamil Catholic "complex of opposites" is then not so much held in tension, as Schmitt's conception suggests, as resolved in the imagination of two different kinds of spaces of religious pluralism, one characterized by thinking in terms of relationships (and relational identities) and the other in terms of essences (and absolutist identities).

Nobili's separation of noncontradictory parts—revelation and reason, religion and culture, Christianity and caste—was the foundation for a Tamil Catholic "dual moral world." On the one hand were the various social and ritual obligations involved in the Tamil "being in the world";[19] on the other were the entailments of participating in the realm of Catholic religion. This dual morality (described ethnographically by Mosse) finds its parallel in the Brahmanic model of the devotional sect or order whose equalizing rules of worship coexist with the obligations of caste separation and rank (at least in the Brahman Jesuit–influenced anthropology of Louis Dumont).[20] Catholicism was thus introduced into Tamil society by Jesuit teachers as a kind of devotional sect, separate from, but tolerant of, hybrid and hierarchical relations. This faith beyond the social was later manifest as the separating off of church compound and presbytery, protected from syncretic merging, social challenge, and caste politics.

As a structure of representation, the division of faith and caste has had a durable influence on the Catholic Church in South India. The secularization of caste (as morally indifferent *adiaphora*) was deeply conservative. Caste was desacralized so it could be tolerated among converts: there was no sin in caste. Caste and church were separate and ritually marked moral discourses. This is seen in all sorts of everyday village practices. To give just one example, the Catholic funeral rite first involves careful discrimination of purity and impurity, ritual roles and caste rank, and then abolishes all such distinctions in the priest's funeral mass over the body in the church. Evidently, the procedures that make a person Roman Catholic and those that are necessary to the Tamil "semiotic being in the world" articulate imperfectly,[21] so that improvisation is constantly needed, and ambiguity surrounds certain actions (e.g., animal "sacrifices" at saint shrines are simultaneously about propitiation, communion, and commensality).

I am pointing, then, to the historical making of a domain of Catholic religion by the actions of Jesuit missionary priests in relation to a particular social and political order and also to a structure of representation that separates out realms of the absolute and of the relational in thinking about divinity and society. This suggests an approach to understanding Catholicism in this part of South India. To return to an earlier point, the approach does not begin with Catholicism as the known entity, or Christian religious affiliation as a primary social identity. To do this would mistakenly lead to the residualizing of non-Christian practices as syncretistic, or Hindu "hangovers," or would proffer questions that are sociologically presumptuous, such as about caste among Christians (supposing Christian difference, or "Indian Christian" as a social identity, rather than the legal-political construction that it is). What is more productive is to examine ethnographically the relationship between participation in the realm of Catholic religion (including its particular meanings, semiotics, and practices) and Tamil modes of "being in the world." The latter involve the identifications of kinship, caste, and place that are socially prior to religion, enacted through a variety of relationships, rites, and reconciliations with humans, deities, and forces of fortune and misfortune, and the search for cures or caste distinction. The rituals that produce this mode of being in the world may be Christianized in signs but are not defined by faith or affiliation.

CHRISTIAN SOCIAL EFFECTS AND THE RISE OF DALIT POLITICS

The Tamil Catholic "complex of opposites" appears to produce quite the opposite of Schmitt's engagement in the public sphere: religion as a realm of absolutes is disconnected from the struggles of the world "below." This was a Catholic tradition that took root through the hierarchical social and religious orders of South India, and its potential to engage critically with that order was neutralized through efforts to locate religion *beyond* the social, and by the emergence of a stabilizing dual moral world. The question then arises, how is it that such a Catholic tradition could nonetheless (at a particular historical moment) become a source of social awareness, cultural challenge, and political mobilization?

The answer it seems to me has two parts: one concerns the social effects of participating in a realm of Catholic religion itself; the other concerns the manner in which Catholicism became implicated in the struggle for social recognition, political voice, and cultural identity among India's Dalits—those subordinated as caste "untouchables."

I noted that while never critical of caste belonging, Catholic teaching conveyed the notion that identity and occupation, the actor and the act, were quite separate. Since Tamil congregations were addressed by priests as a Christian collective, caste-free interactions such as cross-caste godparent relationships were among innovations finding no parallel in Hindu temples. One of the effects of the Jesuit mission was thus to place limits on the naturalization of inequality implicit in caste systems. Caste in Catholic form was desacralized as an "outer" thing, a public and political institution, a public form of knowledge, and more about power than person.

Missionaries, moreover, introduced a sharp distinction between individual sin and other life effects (pollution, bad time, inauspiciousness); and for them the exchange of substances (perhaps impurities) through food or diet, or through contact with "impure" others, was unimportant to the making of moral persons. Christians did retain the caste-dividing ritual structure of life-crisis ceremonies such as funerals but hollowed these out of specific meanings. The Jesuit semiotic considered signs to be readily detachable from referents in the civil realm of culture, and meanings were therefore contingent and changeable. Tamil village Catholics would thus be less likely to demonstrate the moral-bodily "indexical contiguities" emphasized in recent Indian ethnographic studies and would more likely evidence manipulable symbolic associations and negotiable meanings.[22] Thus Dalits who entered the church and received sacraments as Christians were able to treat their social exclusion as polluted persons as arbitrary and *symbolic* of their inferiorization as laborers and servants, rather than as substantially connected to, or an index of, their persons.

In fact, by the time of my fieldwork in the early 1980s, as Dalits achieved some economic independence, Christian villagers' capacities for symbolic manipulation or symbolic reversal became prominent in forging new interpretations of inferiorizing practices such as funeral service, festival drumming, or cattle scavenging— practices that continued out of economic necessity but were partly reframed within relationships of contract and choice rather than servitude and obligation. The village Dalit *dhobi* put it like this: "Work paid for in [neutral] cash [rather than obligation-loaded grain] has no pollution." This capacity for resignification become especially evident later (in the 1990s) through a Dalit cultural politics that tried to recontextualize defiling servile labor as publicly staged celebrations of Dalit performance arts (drumming and dance). This was part of a wider project of honoring an "outcaste" culture in which Christian seminaries took a lead.

There is a more general argument here, namely that two centuries of participation in Catholic religion introduced a negotiability, a changeability, a relativizing self-awareness or a sociological self-distancing from conventions into social forms in Tamil villages. We do not have to say that Christianity (and its institutional practices) *caused* these changes (which would be difficult to demonstrate). Rather, Christianity provided a coordination point for elements preexisting within Tamil moral traditions, brought together and articulated in ways that proved significant to contemporary Dalit activism.[23]

The second way in which Catholicism became implicated in opening a political space for Dalits arose from the earlier-mentioned consolidation of ecclesiastical authority and the de-exclusion of Dalits from the newly bounded Catholic religious domain. The link here is not self-evident. Forging a domain of Catholic (priestly) religious authority in the twentieth century involved progressively disembedding the church from local caste-political systems and moving the boundary between matters considered "sacred" and "civil." Or more precisely one might say that circumstances allowed that of the two systems of meaning and action, "church" was asserted over *kōvil*. As the domain of the Catholic sacred expanded, caste division was successively excluded (delegitimized) from the Eucharist, seating arrangements in the church, schools, and eventually cemeteries. This created a context allowing Dalits to make otherwise impossible claims to participate in public worship *equally as Christians*. Within their framework of the *kōvil* (in which the Jesuit separation of the religious and the civil had little salience), this meant participation in Catholic festival systems with public caste honor as religious donors rather than as humiliated village servants. This was otherwise impossible, first because Hindu temples excluded untouchables from worship and donorship, and second because the British colonial courts refused to intervene in "custom" or "religion" and so frustrated any claims against caste injustice.

The saint festivals were politically dynamic, in particular, because they bridged the divide between Catholic religion and caste society (or rather they brought together "church" and *kōvil* in a single set of contested practices). Jesuit missionaries intervened in these caste-ritual systems, making them matters more of the Catholic Church and less of the village *kōvil*. They weakened dominant caste influence erased the rights of non-Christians, and backed Dalit claims to inclusion as Christians. From the 1910s these festivals provided some of the first arenas for a Dalit politics of dignity, long before mobilization on the basis of civic rights and public access was possible. In villages such as Alapuram, Dalits in fact acquired wide networks and organizational skills in mobilizing around festival honors from the 1920s and '30s that were later turned to the ends of public protest in the 1960s, by which time the basis of Dalit claims had become the Indian Constitution rather than Catholic religion.

The way in which Christianity was implicated in the politics and emancipatory projects of Dalits was, however, significantly shaped by the different circumstances of various caste groups. I have referred to one case in which, by preserving the continuity of cultural-political forms (the Catholic church as *kōvil* with its caste-based festival honors), Jesuits enabled a particular subordinated group (the Pallar caste) to change its place within the agrarian order of Alapuram village. But this form of mobility was not available to other poorer and lower-ranking Dalit castes (such as the Paraiyar caste in the same village), who had effectively been excluded from the Jesuit mission for fear that their admission would prompt exit of the more valued upper-caste converts. Unable to bring about change in their relations with other groups (as Pallars had), Alapuram Paraiyars turned to Protestant

Christianity to find a means to signal change *in themselves* and to imagine a break with a shameful past, as part of a narrative of changeability and moral transformation.[24] This was marked by some outward signs of self-respect: in clothing, in work, or in storytelling that took the edge off dishonor. Paraiyars drew on the modernizing idioms of twentieth-century Anglican Protestant missions (rather than the traditionalizing ones of rustic French Jesuits) to reach beyond the present order in a language of urbanity (*nākarīkam*) that involved a civilizing of the self. So we can see that even within the same village Christianity was linked to projects of either cultural continuity (Catholic Pallars) or disjuncture (Protestant Paraiyars).

It was often the case that Dalit claims to caste honor as Catholics occurred within rather than against the social order. Catholicism was not inherently disjunctive. Nonetheless, in recent decades Catholicism has become significant for secular activists as part of a politics of Dalit difference. Several influences shaped this political production of cultural disjuncture, including the writing and vision of Dalit leader Dr. B. R. Ambedkar (d. 1956). Also significant was the new emphasis given to a Protestant framing of caste in religious rather than civil terms—that is, as a Brahmanic Hindu institution resting on scriptural tradition rather than as a form of agrarian domination and royal overlordship experienced in places such as Alapuram.[25] Religious conversion, which was earlier a means to new affiliations and dignity in response to oppressive dominant castes, was now an idiom of protest against a civilization and a state increasingly defined by its democratic majority as Hindu.

But even with the rise of Hindu nationalist forces in Indian politics in the 1990s, Catholic Dalit activism primarily sprang, not from the Christian critique of caste society, but rather from the much older and deeper internal contradiction within Tamil Catholicism—between universal ethics and caste particularism. The missionary disembedding of church from caste that was needed to forge a separate Catholic religious domain concealed the ways in which this religious domain was itself colonized by caste, as it were, from within (especially with the departure of European missionary priests). Catholic institutions were increasingly, in the model of *kōvils*, treated as the source of caste-based social power. Indeed, various fields of Catholicism—the priesthood, seminaries, educational institutions—expanded as sites for caste particularism and Dalit exclusion. By the time of the rise of Dalit movements in the 1990s, the early Jesuit dual moral complementarity of Christian faith and caste society had little relevance. It was the exposure of a structure of caste *within* the church—that is, evidence of pervasive discrimination in churches, schools and colleges, seminaries, convents, and the priesthood—that prompted a radical movement for Dalit Christian Liberation led, notably, by angry and humiliated Dalit Jesuits, the inheritors of the mission tradition that created the conditions for the compromised "dual ethics."

This Dalit Catholic activism arose from a complex of opposites: not from Christian ethics per se but from their negation in the church—that is, continuing systematic caste separation and discrimination. It came from the experience of Dalitness rather than of Christianity. The point shouted out was that caste was not among the morally indifferent things (*adiaphora*), relegated to the secular, the village, the past, the uneducated, the non-Christian. Caste was now viewed as an "idolatry" of Tamil Catholicism itself. Dalit priests refused the notion of a Catholic religion *beyond* the social. Either Christianity was anticaste politically, or it was rendered inauthentic by the oppressive tolerance of caste. Some bishops resisted, trying in various ways to reintroduce old complementarities and to return caste to the realm of secular politics apart from the spiritual life of the Catholic priesthood and accusing Dalit priests of playing into the hands of corrupting Dalit politicians fighting against the church. But the politics of caste was now irreversibly taking place *within* Catholicism; and at this point we can say that Tamil Catholicism was denied the resolution of opposites through theological abstraction or domain separation and that it derived a political energy from its internal contradictions.[26]

As the older structures of reconciliation of opposites collapsed (the dual moralities, and separate ritual spaces of caste and Christianity), the issue of caste invaded the church. By and large in seminaries, if not in parishes, facing the "sin" of caste is now a spiritual obligation. Dalitness has become definitive of Indian Christianity in the sense that the route to universal Christian truth now has to pass through the suffering of the Dalits, and any Christian theology of transcendence that has ignored this reality—including earlier Nobilian Sanskritic Hindu-Christian dialogue—is deeply suspect. From this perspective a recent head of the Jesuit province of Madurai (exceptionally, himself a Dalit) told me:

> Being a Dalit is more than original sin because baptismal water is able to wash original sin but cannot remove the stigma of being a Dalit. You say all human beings are made in the image and likeness of God, [but] is there a Dalit God? You bury the dead separately; is there going to be a Dalit heaven and a non-Dalit heaven? Or do we need a messiah who should be born as a Dalit? . . . My question is, when a Dalit priest celebrates Mass, is a Dalit Christ coming or a regular Christ, because some people don't want to receive Communion from a Dalit priest.[27]

Struggles that began within or against the church have generated ideas, writings, and activist organizations that have influenced the wider Dalit movement and Dalit politics in the state (even though today's Dalit leaders do not readily admit their tutorship by Jesuit priests). Some Dalit movement leaders are themselves Jesuit priests, and the campaigns against injustice, anti-Dalit violence, or the recovery of alienated land that they steer make expressive use of the performing arts, symbolic reversals, and "Dalit culture" shaped in Christian seminaries and elsewhere.

Drawing Christianity into the Dalit making of an outcaste culture, perhaps as a spiritual act of solidarity or a "preferential option for Dalits," is not so straightforward.[28] In this caste-divided social world, the church may be asked, "Whose culture is this?," especially by certain caste groups who feel that the culture of selected groups among the much-divided Dalit social category has been considered prototypically "Dalit" space to the exclusion of others. But then, when Catholic priests in compensation try to adopt the position of advocate for minority subordinated caste groups, they are easily accused of dividing and undermining the united Dalit movement.

Some Catholic priests (non-Dalit and Dalit) who have seen Dalit liberation movements being provincialized into a complex and fissiparous caste politics have made themselves prominent in translating caste concerns into other universalist languages, through scale-jumping participation in national or international forums that, for example, place caste within UN discourses on racism, slavery, and human rights. The task of these Jesuits, exactly contrary to Nobili their forebear, is to promote international moral outrage at caste inequality and discrimination. Global discourses such as human rights then return to be re-embedded as a language of local caste struggle (rather as Christianity itself did in earlier centuries).[29] Meanwhile, political opponents aim to delegitimize campaigns on human rights abuse or against Indian caste racism by translating human rights back into the discourse of religion with accusations about an agenda of Christian aggression, Western proselytism, and cultural appropriation.

How have the broad changes in Indian Catholicism impinged on Tamil village communities such as Alapuram? It is fair to say that while Catholicism is "Dalitized" in the seminary, it appears "globalized" in the village. Continuing a trend begun in the early twentieth century, Christian practice continues to be disembedded from structures of caste and diversified into religious styles reflecting various streams of global Christianity, whether Catholic or Pentecostal. While at present more universal, separate, and in principle "othering" of Hinduism, Christianity (even Christian radicalism) is not to any greater extent the basis of identity or division (even if socially divisive fundamentalist connections and discourses are manipulated in local disputes).

As caste itself is manifest less in public displays of ranked order and more as a form of private social and cultural capital, essential for negotiating access to new livelihood resources, especially higher education and employment, the church is reinvented as a mediator and allocator of chits for today's honors and aspirations (college places, posts, certificates, and scholarships) over which there is intense caste competition, comparable in a way to those over honors at saints' festivals in earlier decades and centuries.

One more encouraging observation is that a growing mass-mediated political discourse of "communal" conflict and violence embedded in divisions of caste and religion rarely translates into local-level intercaste or inter-religious conflicts in Tamil villages. Villagers no more allow the absolutism of religious and caste politics to shape everyday social relations than they allowed Jesuit missionary absolutism to demonize the gods of their neighbors. Artful translation between (in terms from Baumann) the dominant communalizing discourses and the demotic ones through which identities and interests are negotiated (by youth activists, movement leaders and others) ensure that these are kept apart.[30]

What we find here is a capacity to manage the threat of antagonistic social difference by negotiating between absolutist religious or caste discourses and the demands of everyday life in community—between realms of "forest" and "village"—so as to avoid disturbing rupture or conflict. This dual discursive capacity, which moves between incompatible meanings, morals, and modes of signification—has itself perhaps been acquired historically by Christians living in caste society and working out the reconciliation of everyday social life and the potentially (socially) perilous demands of Christian faith.

NOTES

1. Schmitt ([1923] 1996, 8–9).
2. Marder (2008, 30).
3. Central to this idea is the principle of *representation*. The church and its priests are representatives, and, as Schmitt put it, "In each of these great forms of representation, the complexion of life in all its contradictions is moulded into a unity of personal representation" ([1923] 1996).
4. Asad (2002, 118).
5. T. Mitchell (2002).
6. Robbins (2007).
7. Županov (1999, 115).
8. Mosse (2012).
9. Županov (1999).
10. On the Jesuits' attitude toward caste, see Županov (1999, 97–101).
11. See Županov (1999).
12. Keane (2007, 18–21).
13. Županov (2005, 25, 27).
14. See Mosse (2006; 2012, chap. 2).
15. Dumont ([1966] 1980).
16. Mosse (2012, 82ff.).
17. Dempsey (2001); Ram (1991).
18. Mosse (2012, chap. 2).
19. Daniel (2000).
20. Mosse (2012); Dumont ([1966] 1980).
21. Daniel (1984).
22. See, e.g., Daniel (1984); Mines (2005).
23. Pandian (2008).
24. See Mosse (2012).
25. See Viswanath (2014).
26. Cf. Schmitt ([1923] 1996).
27. Francis Xavier, interview, March 1, 2009, Chennai; Mosse (2012, 1–2).

28. Following Rome's approval of the Province Congregation's Postulate in 1987, the Jesuit "preferential option for the poor" was recast as an "option for Dalits." The Madurai Jesuit counter-Nobilian policy was to "reach out in a special way to the most marginalized and discriminated in Tamilnad society, namely Dalits" (Jesuit Madurai Province 2002, 64, 66).

29. Mosse (2015).

30. Baumann (1997).

10

Marking Memory

Heritage Work and Devotional Labor at *Quebec's* Croix de Chemin

Hillary Kaell

Our consciousness is shaped by a sense that everything is over and done with. . . . Memory is constantly on our lips because it no longer exists.

—PIERRE NORA, *REALMS OF MEMORY*

The cross is a symbol of history, it's our past. It's also a sign of vitality. When the wayside crosses are redone, are beautiful, are renovated, that says there are still Catholics here.

—RAYMONDE PROULX, AGE SIXTY-TWO, CROSS CARETAKER,
SAINTE-GERTRUDE-DE-MANNEVILLE

Memory and tradition are hardly central theoretical issues in the anthropology of Christianity. It is, after all, a field that has coalesced around ascendant and newly emerging forms of evangelical or charismatic Protestantism. This is certainly true in studies of US Christianity, where major foci include language ideology and Bible reading, the experience of being born again and evangelism, and political and social activism.[1] From the vantage point of Quebec, however, the scholarship looks very different. Sociologists and anthropologists working in this historic center of North American Catholicism regularly examine collective memory and the decline of institutional religious authority. Their work draws on a robust transatlantic discussion following the revival of Maurice Halbwachs's work by French thinkers, such as historian Pierre Nora and sociologist Danièle Hervieu-Léger.

Since its English translation in 2000, Hervieu-Léger's *Religion as a Chain of Memory* has stoked interest in Christian memory, especially in Europe.[2] It has also been criticized for its inherent Catholic bias.[3] Here *Chain of Memory* is a useful starting point precisely for that reason: its exploration of religious transmission and authoritative tradition highlights Catholic concerns too often sidelined in anthropologies of

North American Christianity. At the same time, drawing inspiration from the recent turn to more human-centered approaches in studies of secularism, I bring an ethnographic sensibility to bear on Hervieu-Léger's largely theoretical paradigm.[4] How is collective religious memory lived, felt, and talked about in rural Quebec?

This question is essential with regard to the *croix de chemin*—large devotional crosses planted across rural Quebec. These wayside crosses are handmade by local people, stand about fifteen to twenty feet high, and are situated on roadsides. They are often made of wood, painted white, and decorated with Catholic iconography based on the Passion. Traditionally, the crosses were built to commemorate an event, fulfill a vow (*promesse*), ask for protection, or provide a gathering place if the parish church was far away. Although scholars have repeatedly predicted their imminent demise, about 80 percent of the three thousand crosses surveyed forty years ago still remain, cared for by the rural people who live nearby.[5]

This chapter knits together the perspective of cross caretakers with that of ethnologists by comparing two interlocking *lieux de mémoire:* twenty-four months of intermittent fieldwork (2012–14) with contemporary caretakers and a survey of the archive amassed by ethnologist Jean Simard, principal investigator of a major government-funded inventory of the crosses in the 1970s and 1980s.[6] Both sites are emic, in that they are produced by and for French Canadians, and each one assumes that a cohesive national identity rests in part on promoting the rural past. Yet these perspectives also operate in a context that is "braided,"[7] where ethnologists and caretakers concur and diverge. Heritage professionals, including scholars, repeatedly imply that Catholicism is "over and done with," to quote Pierre Nora above, and that places of popular devotion have thus become secularized sites of national heritage.[8] Caretakers, by contrast, view the crosses as both patrimonial *and* still-active objects of devotional labor. As practicing Catholics, they maintain them in order to express and promote a relationship with God.

I explore these ideas through three key factors particularly salient to a Catholic conception of memory, drawn loosely from Hervieu-Léger's theoretical paradigm and Simard's body of work: perspectives on temporality, the role of institutions, and the rise of individual consciousness. Ultimately, I trace how Quebecois ethnologists and caretakers both lay claim to certain kinds of modernity—secular and Catholic—in the name of collective continuity.[9]

CATHOLIC QUEBEC IN A SEASON OF CHANGE

Halbwachs's great insight was that collective memories, even religious ones, never merely preserve the past—they establish identity in the present.[10] In *Chain of Memory,* Hervieu-Léger extends this idea as a rejoinder to the secularization thesis, a reigning sociological theory at the time. She argues that religion is a creative force that confers transcendent authority on the past in order to assure present meaning and future continuity. Drawing on Halbwachs's complementary forms of Catholic memory—the theological and the mystical—she posits that all religions rely on a central dialectic between the symbolic evocation of a chain of memory in an institutionalized liturgy and its actualization in a community's shared beliefs and practices. Her overarching definition of religion thus contains three symbiotic components: beliefs (individual and collective), tradition (the chain linking beliefs to collective memory), and institutional structures. Her conclusion is that modernity—or more precisely, the rise of a neoliberal state in France—promoted individualism and eviscerated institutional authority, including the rural "parish civilization" essential to Catholic memory.[11] The result, she opines, was that the chain was broken, precipitating religious crisis.

This view of history is echoed—arguably amplified—in Quebec, where a similar process of modernization was condensed into an intense period of change. In the 1960s, a "Quiet Revolution" swept the province, leading to vast political restructuring, economic modernization, social transformation, and rapid unchurching. The Catholic Church was largely divested of its previously central role in education and social services. Monthly mass attendance fell from 88 percent in the mid-1960s to under 20 percent today.[12] This revolution, though popularly perceived to be at odds with Catholicism, paralleled church-led modernizations spurred by the Second Vatican Council.[13] Among other things, the Quebec bishops exhorted the faithful to a deeper understanding of "true" Christianity, encouraged greater lay participation during Mass, and strongly discouraged many devotional "superstitions" of the past.[14]

In the midst of these societal upheavals, Jean Simard, a young ethnologist from Quebec City, was hired at Laval University. Simard had completed his doctoral training in mid-1960s France while the secularization thesis reigned supreme. He viewed modernity and religion as fundamentally incompatible, yet also developed a deep respect for Catholic devotional artifacts, which he viewed as popular art. Before securing a professorate in 1972, he worked at Quebec's Ministère de la culture et des communications on inventories of national heritage objects. At Laval, Simard honed a body of work based on the presupposition that culturally homogeneous people (French Canadians) inhabit definable territories (Quebec). In other words, Simard's ethnology reified an idea that other anthropologists, on the cusp of a turn to transnationalism, were in the very process of deconstructing.[15]

Simard was thus part of a trend that anthropologists of Christianity have only begun to explore: elites' conscious assimilation of religious heritage to shape emerging national identities in sites as diverse as South Africa, Poland, Korea, Brazil, and Japan.[16] Birgit Meyer's work on Ghana is especially helpful, since it delineates a historical trajectory similar to Quebec's: beginning in the late 1950s, state-led initiatives defined the modern nation by specifically reappropriating as heritage those religious traditions deemed irrational or embarrassing.[17] While "witchcraft" and "juju" are more fraught in Ghana than pre–Vatican II Catholi-

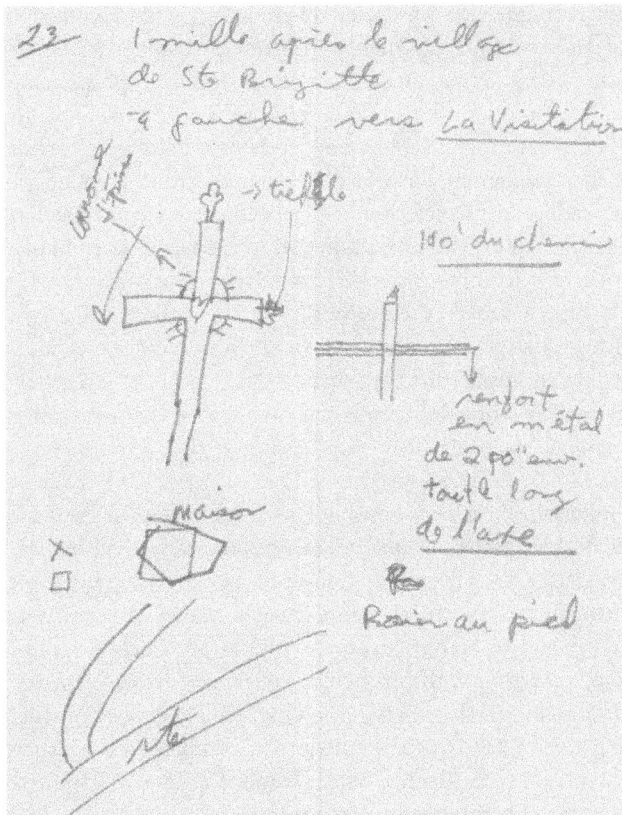

FIGURE 10.1. Page from one of the notebooks compiled by Jean Simard's students during the wayside cross survey, ca. 1975. Folder E/05533, Fonds Jean Simard (F1081), Archives de folklore et éthnologie, Université Laval. Author's collection.

cism is in Quebec, popular devotions were nevertheless viewed by Quebecois elites as problematic vestiges of the past. It was within this charged political, religious, and scholarly atmosphere that Simard's wayside cross inventory emerged.

LES ÎLES BIZARD AND JÉSUS

In June 1972, three university students, Nicole, Louise, and Luce, alighted on the islands of Bizard and Jésus. Their young professor, Jean Simard, had tasked them with conducting the inaugural survey of Quebec's wayside crosses in preparation for a seminar titled "Traditional Ethnography." Armed with fifty-cent notebooks and cameras, they fanned out across the islands.

The seminar in question was based on ethnology and folklore studies, distinct branches of anthropology in Quebec that emerged under Marius Barbeau, the most prominent early Canadian anthropologist. In 1911, Barbeau joined the Canadian Geological Survey under Franz Boas's protégé Edward Sapir to catalog the presumed last remaining specimens of "authentic" aboriginal culture.[18] In 1914, with Boas's encouragement, Barbeau also began to gather French Canadian songs and stories, leading to the creation of Quebecois *ethnologie*. His construction of the field relied on a few key assumptions, which he transmitted to his student Luc Lacourcière, who mentored Simard. First, Barbeau was convinced that French Canadian "peasants" lacked the inspiration to create; their value lay in how they faithfully transmitted an oral culture from medieval France. Second, he incorporated the strong antimodernist bent that colored his work with aboriginals: modern, commercial life ("hot-dog stands and coca-cola") was destroying an authentic French Canadian "essence."[19] It was up to ethnologists to preserve its traces as it disappeared.

Simard inherited these concerns but was also aware of nascent European programs to protect religious *patrimoine*. In 1972, the same year his students began their survey, UNESCO delivered its Convention Concerning the Protection of the World Cultural and Natural Heritage. Closer to home, Quebec's nationalist government had begun to actively promote folklore in order to reinforce a shared identity.[20] Collaborating with his former colleagues at the Ministry of Culture, Simard adopted a model then *en vogue* in Quebecois sociology of religion: sending out mobile teams of scholars and students to conduct massive surveys of rural areas.[21] Their task was to identify which wayside crosses constituted a "national treasure" that qualified for government protection.

Simard chose the islands of Bizard and Jésus as the trial site for two reasons: Barbeau had surveyed the crosses there exactly fifty years earlier, and now the area was undergoing rapid suburbanization. Places that had been rural farms just five years before were filled with tract housing and flanked by highways. When Nicole, Louise, and Luce set out, carrying Barbeau's maps and photographs, they sought to document the presumed destruction of the crosses he had catalogued in 1922. Their twenty-three-page questionnaire, designed by Simard and used for the next decade, focused almost exclusively on each cross's placement and material composition, down even to the screws. Did they have square, round, or deformed heads? The young women carefully ticked boxes beside each one.[22]

Countering their expectations, they recorded twenty-eight crosses—five *more* than Barbeau had found. However, nearly all were reconstructed or entirely new; only five crosses remained unchanged, which were the ones the researchers valued most. In those (few) sections of the survey that elicited more qualitative responses from local people, the researchers continually reiterated the loss of an original: Was this cross displaced? Did this cross replace another? Do you know of disap-

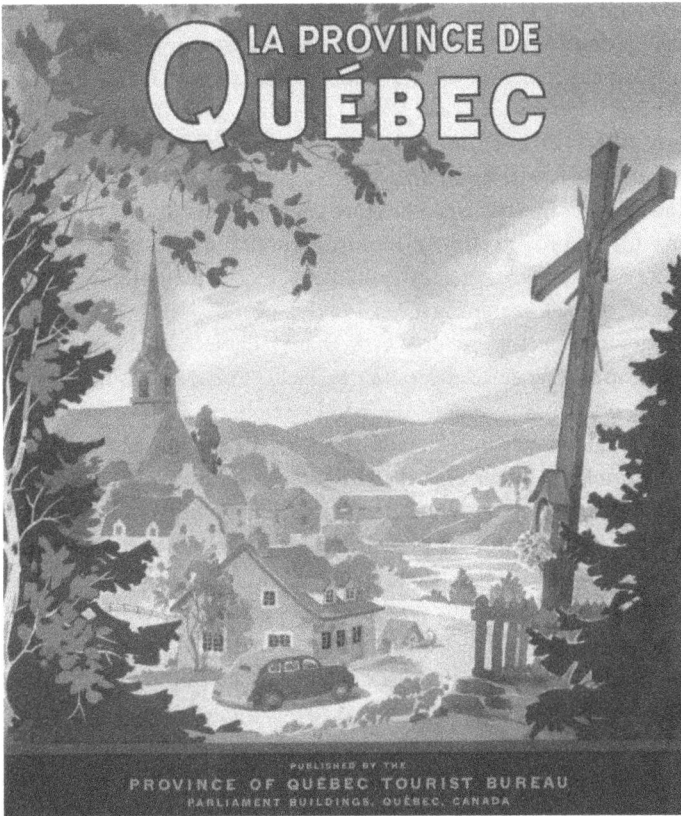

FIGURE 10.2. Brochure published by the Province of Quebec Tourist Bureau, 1935. It features a wayside cross as typical of rural Quebec.

peared crosses . . .? Despite clear evidence of active cross construction and religious adherence, the young women, echoing Simard, concluded their report by urging their urban, university-educated readers to take responsibility for the things rural people had built: the crosses are "part of the national heritage as a witness to an era, as well as a historic monument. . . . Those that still exist must be preserved, kept-up, and conserved."[23]

DIVERGENT VIEWS OF LOSS AND CHANGE

Fast-forward to today. Since the mid-1990s, thanks in part to Simard's efforts and to trends in heritage preservation worldwide religious *patrimoine* has become something of a priority for the provincial government.[24] Heritage studies also fit seamlessly with most Quebecois scholarship on contemporary Catholicism, which continually redounds to *ce qui s'est passé,* viewing the present through the lens of the past: What has changed? What remains the same? As a result, it often reiterates Hervieu-Léger's *"paradigme de la perte"* (paradigm of loss), a mode of scholarship that clearly reflects a (post)Catholic milieu. It is colored by the memory of a church that was omnipresent in many areas of civil society, including education.[25] Work on heritage further meshes with the close collaborations most Quebecois scholars maintain with the provincial government. Although studies now problematize the role of elite "heritage makers," others still regularly champion the government's "reinvention" of the Catholic past.[26]

This latter perspective reflects how many scholars, including Simard, view modernization and secularization as a ripple effect where ideas born in intellectual centers drift outwards to engulf the rural periphery. Thus forces destructive of traditional religious culture emanate from urban centers, but so do the saving powers of ethnology: the île Bizard and île Jésus survey, according to Simard, pro-duced almost instantaneous revitalization. Once the university students showed an interest, locals became aware of their crosses' value. When the students returned a month later, the crosses had been repainted and restored.[27]

If we reverse the lens, however, caretakers rarely, if ever, credit such experts with encouraging reconstructions. Nor do they see themselves as the passive recipients of ideas, swept up in a sea of change. Rather, they clarify that they and their predecessors have actively labored for Catholicism and as Catholics, with God's help. Wayside crosses, in fact, become the *ultimate* example of this process. I turn now to a clearer discussion of how their perspective overlaps with and diverges from that of Quebecois ethnologists, structured around three key themes in Hervieu-Léger's work.

Temporality

Time—how it passes, how it is remembered—is of the utmost importance to herit-age scholars like Simard. It is also central in Hervieu-Léger's model, which under-lines the essential role of rituals ("practices of anamnesis") that recall the past and thereby incorporate believers into a historical chain. Such collective remembering belongs to the "pure world of tradition," a concept she often invokes, which seems to imply a Lockean temporal mode: a linear trajectory that moves from a premod-ern period when traditional religion (Catholicism) was "naturally" transmitted between generations to a modern one where it is inevitably under threat.[28]

For many Quebecois scholars, the 1960s Quiet Revolution has provided a ready axis dividing these two imagined periods. Simard's inventory relied on it, since it was fundamentally an attempt to scientifically distinguish between the "tradi-tional" and the "modern" by categorizing crosses on the basis of age, material coherence, and type of carvings. This empiricism of the traditional subsumed the mythos of a French Canadian "essence," as per Barbeau, that was premodern, rural, and tied to the physical territory of Quebec. The crosses served as ideal metonyms for this complex of ideas, since they were handmade by local people and rooted in the ground. In Simard's "typology of significance," new crosses and the use of foreign materials (say, vinyl siding or British Columbian fir trees) were thus clearly undesirable. All twenty-five crosses that he identified as "national treasures" had elaborate wood carvings and predated 1921.[29]

Both ethnologists and caretakers connect wayside crosses to idealized memories of a rural past. Nostalgia, scholars note, is the attempt to situate oneself in a particular time and place and is thus constituted differently depending on one's social location.[30] Caretakers differ from ethnologists because for them rural Quebec is a memorialized past *and* an everyday reality. The past tense coexists with multiple cycles of destruction and care that define their agricultural environment. Each spring, crosses must be repainted and the gardens replanted. Every forty-five or so years, they become sufficiently *magané* (used up) that they must be replaced. Comparing this to generational change, Marielle Lemay, age seventy, says: "It's like an old person who dies. It's sad, but you say, well, there's an end to everything. That's just how it is . . . [and] it continues because you rebuild." Although many caretakers cherish and recreate selected decorative features from earlier crosses, they do not see their role merely as preserving and transmitting the things of the past in a way conforming to how Barbeau once viewed French Canadian oral culture. Caretakers view each renewal of a cross as a creative act.

Thus while heritage objects or heirlooms are generally valued for their singularity—the Vikings used *this* ship, my grandmother wore *that* locket—caretakers "pass down" crosses in ways that are more suggestive, defined by traces of the past. Clément Lavallière, age seventy, maintains a cross in the village of St-Janvier-de-Weedon that is typical of such creative (re)constructions. The original wood cross was erected in 1943 on a ridge above the village. By 1995, it had rotted sufficiently that five men, including Clément, decided to replace it. They maintained the size (seventeen feet), placement, and essential design but remade it in aluminum. They saved one design feature—a crest from the Marian year 1954—and reattached it. Three years later, the zinc bolts started to rust, so they ascended the ridge again. "We put in three hundred stainless steel bolts. I remember exactly because I was the one who changed them all," recalls Clément. "Now it's perfect. It will last a very long time." Then in 2002, they were given a three-hundred-pound steel corpus (Jesus's body) after a cemetery renovation. This was a major coup. "The corpus makes it very special. We're very proud of that," says Clément. Once again, they climbed the ridge, removed the cross, and added to it. They decided to paint the Christ white and found that car paint kept the rust at bay. The most recent addition, in 2004, was the initiative of a young electrician who donated neon lights "so that it would show up even more at night, be even more beautiful."[31]

FIGURE 10.3. St-Janvier-de-Weedon cross, renovated by Clément and other villagers in the Chevaliers de Colomb. Photographed in 2010. Courtesy of Monique Bellemare.

Most contemporary crosses are re-creations built on, or close to, the site of an earlier one. Yet, paradoxically for heritage experts like Simard, caretakers often express a connection to this history by employing new materials—electric lights, zinc bolts, or car paint—that augment visibility and durability. At stake are contrasting notions of continuity. For heritage experts, continuity means material coherence (the *same* materials, the *same* decorations). For caretakers, it is closer to Hervieu-Léger's living "chain"—recalling the past by projecting into the future: the aluminum cross will last "a very long time." Yet Hervieu-Léger ultimately views traditional Catholicism as transformed only in ways that produce its own destruction.[32] Caretakers, on the other hand, view Catholicism as evolving, especially with regard to expanded roles for laity, including women. At a personal level, their faith has also deepened since they were children. For caretakers, this twin progression is evidence of positive change—echoed in the improved technologies of wayside cross care.

So what does this mean for future continuity? Caretakers labor to augment a cross's durability yet usually evince little concern about whether it will be maintained when they are gone. There seem to be a few reasons why. Some caretakers emphasize the importance of belief in God rather than in the object itself. A larger number do care about the object *qua* object but are convinced that young people who seem indifferent today will naturally take over the role as they begin to head families and own property. Last, a significant number of caretakers refuse a linear view of time altogether by leaving room for something akin to Dipesh Chakrabarty's History 2, which continually interrupts the "totalizing thrusts" of capitalist/secularist history.[33] God punctuates the progressive march of time. Florence Bergeron, a seventy-three-year-old caretaker, puts it thus: "I have great confidence that the church still exists. . . . In what way will the religious reawakening happen? I don't know *how* it will happen, but [I] have faith. So we await it."

Institutionalization

Religious institutions are key nodes in Hervieu-Léger's chain. They anchor the very definition of religion, in contrast to idiosyncratic beliefs, because they transmit traditions and proffer authority. It is their failure in the modern era that has produced religious crisis. Pierre Nora's work, upon which Hervieu-Léger draws, implies a similar trajectory, mapping out how the state replaced the Catholic Church as the main site of identity formation after the French Revolution. Nora decries earlier historians who claimed to be empiricists yet actually privileged narratives that served nationalist ends. By contrast, Simard's body of work promotes collaboration between activist scholars and nationalist governments, offering significant insight into this relationship as a result.[34] What all these studies leave unexplored, however, is the way that people like the caretakers actually interact with institutional authorities.

Most caretakers self-identify as "practicing" Catholics; 83 percent attend Mass at least once a month. Nevertheless, they are ambivalent about the institutional church. Like many North Americans, they no longer conceive of it as infallible or impregnable, and they refer to the amalgamation of parishes, the defection of priests and nuns, and the sex abuse scandals as proof. Yet such feelings are never as final or all-encompassing as many theories of modernity imply. In large part this speaks to how, *contra* Hervieu-Léger, modernity in rural Quebec is not defined by "specialized circles of memory" where people clearly distinguish between family memory, religious memory, national memory, and so on.[35] Rather, caretakers describe a series of nested institutions, including church, nation, village, *rang*, and

FIGURE 10.4. Wayside cross in Saint-Télesphore, the home of Jean Robert. Typical of traditional wayside crosses, it is made of wood, painted white, and planted directly in the ground. Decorative instruments of the Passion include the ladder, lance, rooster, pincers, hammer, and stylized sacred heart. Photographed in 2014. Courtesy of Monique Bellemare.

family—all of which order the world and thus connect to God.[36] One result is that they often use "religious heritage" and "religion" nearly interchangeably. Jean Robert, a fifty-eight-year-old caretaker in the village of Saint-Télesphore, is a good example. The crosses, he told me, "are part of the *patrimoine religieux* [religious heritage]. That's undeniable." He continued: "They were planted in this region a hundred years ago and [before that] by [French explorer] Jacques Cartier . . . so I consider it an important element to conserve from our religious heritage. It represents, as I said, Jesus Christ crucified who came to save the world. It shows that religion, Christianity, is still present among us and that there are people who want it to continue."

The overlap between different institutions, as well as notions of religious herit-age and religion, comes to the fore vividly during the celebrations held on parish anniversaries, which often incorporate wayside crosses. In 2014, Saint-François-Xavier-de-Brompton held one such *jour d'antan* (day of yore) on its 125th anniver-sary. The villagers renewed three wayside crosses, and the parish priest, Father Guy Giroux, was invited to offer a short homily and sprinkle holy water on each one in blessing. The "pioneer families" that had originally built the crosses were honored and had their photos taken with the priest. The photos were later reprinted in the local weekly, which described a "day full of pride, emotions and remem-brances still anchored to memory."[37]

In villages like Saint-François-Xavier, the same individuals head important regional families, serve on the parish *fabrique* (lay council for parish finances), and are elected to local government. For caretakers, the most salient distinction is not therefore between religious and secular institutions but between those that are far away (the Catholic Church or the Quebecois state) and those that are close by (parish priests, small businesses, municipal governments, or *fabriques*). While caretakers are split about whether church and state help or hinder their efforts, they are uniformly positive about local institutions because "everyone here is Catholic," they often say. Though most of their neighbors are no longer "practic-ing" (going to Mass), caretakers contend that what makes a Catholic is belief in God, participation in life cycle rituals (e.g. baptism, marriage), and celebration of Christmas and Easter. Indeed, 92 percent of French Canadians still identify as Catholics, and 91 percent baptize their children (a number that rises to 97.3 percent outside of urban Montreal). Among sixteen- to thirty-five-year-olds, the least reli-gious group, 73 percent still believe in God.[38]

This nesting of local authority produces a kind of flexibility. Over the last twenty years caretaking patterns have shifted, but not from Catholic caretakers to secular ones, as Simard and other heritage experts assume. This shift is within intercon-nected local institutions—all run by believing (and usually practicing) Catholics. If the original builder is gone, *rang* neighbors may assume a cross's care. Where the parish school no longer maintains the cross, the Knights of Columbus may step in. This Catholic fraternal organization represents a particular innovation in wayside cross care. Since the mid-1990s, local chapters have started caring for hundreds of crosses across the province, including the St-Janvier cross described above.[39]

Consciousness

For Hervieu-Léger, modernity rests on a paradox. It was twentieth-century Chris-tianity's own "subjectivization of religious experience" that degraded the chain of memory upon which religion relied.[40] The promotion of individual consciousness is thus essential to modern religiosity even as it ultimately destroys it, at least in Catholicism. To this, Nora's work adds an element of nostalgia; moderns long for "the silence of custom" now that it is gone. Heritage scholars, like Simard, acknowledge this loss but also propose a partial solution: Quebecois historical consciousness can be developed anew by state-run programs that "reinvent" its Catholic past to serve the present.[41]

Caretakers concur with Hervieu-Léger and Nora, especially in how these scholars tie the loss of collective memory to societal and economic changes that have gutted formerly thriving rural areas. They also echo Hervieu-Léger's contention, following Halbwachs, that religious feeling is adversely affected by individualism and modern capitalism.[42] They differ, however, about the subjectivization of religious experience. Rather than breaking "the chain" of religion, caretakers view a certain kind of subjectivization as an improvement over earlier forms of Quebec Catholicism. Nicholas Girard, a sixty-two-year-old caretaker and deacon, expresses it well:

> Today when people say, "I believe" they don't say it because their neighbor is doing it. It's not a mass movement but a movement that is individual, each one chooses. And once that person chooses to say, "Yes, I believe," there is a faith within him. A faith that says, "Yes, I believe with my head. Yes, I believe with my heart. . . ." By contrast, if we think about the faith of my grandparents or great-grandparents—I'm not saying it wasn't good, my grandparents were strong believers—[but] there was a collective mentality there.

This characterization of French Canadian religious life before the 1960s is so widely believed, and has generated so much public criticism, that even caretakers who decry falling attendance at Mass do not advocate a return to the "collective mentality." As caretakers see it, wayside crosses serve an important symbolic function as a beacon of individual consciousness, now and even in their grandparents' era, since laypeople generally chose to erect them beyond the confines of the church. From a Weberian perspective, we might say that individual builders construct a moral Christian self through their labor. However, while Weber was concerned with the advent of wage labor, wayside cross devotional labor is morally significant precisely because it is voluntary; it is unrelated to wages, parish work, or even penance for sin.[43] Its sole purpose, say caretakers, lies in how each human builder seeks a direct relationship with God.

Given this fact, surprisingly few caretakers find it relevant to know why their cross was erected or even by whom. In Simard's surveys, 62 percent of respondents had no idea why the cross had been put up—though it was usually within a generation.[44] If asked today, people who care for crosses on public land often make recourse to generalities ("It was the style back then"), while those who maintain family crosses typically respond like Christian Blanchette, fifty-four, who cares for the cross on his farm, erected by his grandfather: "My grandfather was a good Catholic and very proud of his property, on the corner of the *rang* where almost everyone passed to get into the parish. When I knew him, he went to Mass every day and took care of the church and the cemetery. . . . That's why he built it. The *real, real* reason why, the *personal* one [the vow], I don't know. I never asked."

Scholars are aware that, at a philosophical and psychological level, memory and forgetting are coconstitutive: each one forges the mechanisms that bring the other into being.[45] Yet the study of domestic objects tells us that things passed down— photos, souvenirs, mementos—are meaningful because they materialize particular stories associated with particular people. Their sentimental value is lost if no one recalls why they were kept.[46] Most crosses can be classed as domestic objects because of their association with "the ancestors." So why, for caretakers like Blanchette, does the object retain meaning even when the stories that originally impelled its construction are lost? To some degree there is overlap with Simard's approach, which sees the reason for a cross's construction as largely irrelevant to its didactic value in recalling the archetypical peasant of an idealized past. At another level, however, caretakers depart from Simard: the *fact* of the original prayer is crucial, even if the details are not.

The best way to describe caretakers' perspective may be to acknowledge, along with scholars of material culture, that people do not translate every sensation into discourse, nor do they want to.[47] Put in these terms, caretakers' refusal to trace the narrative behind a cross's construction may actually signal how for them the "real story" concerns the object's power to mediate intangible presences—then and now. As Tom Beidelmann notes of rituals in Africa, secrets are powerful in part precisely because they intimate the existence of an unknown world, where a person speaks to the gods.[48] When the contents of a prayer conversation remain private, it may reiterate the existence of these beings locked in discussion. It thus becomes less important (even irrelevant) to caretakers whether the cross was erected to fulfill a vow, to sacralize the land, or to ward off calamities. That the original prayer remains secret only intensifies the *fact of relationship* between the pious ancestor and God, which works to repudiate the notion that Catholicism is inevitably bound up in the "collective mentality" that Quebecois, including caretakers, now view with ambivalence.

MARKING MEMORY IN QUEBEC

One of the most comprehensive scholarly volumes on Quebec's religious heritage, *Le patrimoine religieux*, begins with a preface by Jocelyn Groulx, director of the Religious Heritage Council: "Unfortunately, it is clear that as the major historic and founding [religious] traditions are less practiced and less passed down, the few remaining people will not be able to adequately assure the survival of this vast [material] heritage."[49] Funded by the Ministry of Culture, the Religious Heritage Council is in many ways heir to the work of Simard and other ethnologists of

Catholic "folklore." The tone of Groulx's contribution is thus hardly surprising: it calls for government intervention, couched in a persistent refusal to see Catholicism as a still-living religion, at least for French Canadians.

I foreground the work of heritage scholars and bureaucrats in order to demonstrate how a robust anthropology of Quebecois Catholicism must encompass two *lieux de mémoire* at once: contemporary religious practice and the heritage work that seeks to reposition Catholic devotionalism vis-à-vis national identity.[50] Hervieu-Léger's *Chain of Memory* offers a helpful framework, I argue, for highlighting key issues related to this milieu, especially in how it acknowledges the multiple nodes of relationship related to collective memory and also the pull that an institutional religious past (and present) may exert.

Indeed, it requires a careful hand to trace the interaction of heritage, culture, and religion in a place where Catholicism has been so closely associated with ethnicity, yet weekly Mass attendance has dropped precipitously and "memory" is on many people's lips. My point here is that the result is not necessarily (or inevitably) "belonging without believing" in a religious tradition that does only cultural identity work.[51] Rather, Quebecois ethnologists and caretakers each lay claim to particular kinds of modernity—secular and Catholic—in the name of collective continuity. As such, their perspectives are more than sites of contestation; they are parallel and overlapping, enmeshed in shared societal, economic, and political networks.[52] Through them we see how Quebec Catholicism encompasses multiple modes of simultaneous interaction—including heritage work and devotional labor operating side by side at the very same cross.

NOTES

All translations from French are mine. I use *Quebecois* and *French Canadian* for people with French ancestry. Though outmoded in public discourse, *French Canadian* is still sometimes used in scholarship for clarification, as I use it here. I also refer to cross "caretakers," although there is no precise equivalent in French, where they are called "owners" (*propriétaires*) or the person who looks after the cross (*qui s'occupe de la croix*).

1. Surveying this literature is beyond my scope, but it includes the work of Susan Harding, Victor Crapanzano, Tanya Luhrmann, James Bielo, Jon Bialecki, and Omri Elisha. Formative debates in anthropology of Christianity about conversion as continuous or discontinuous with the past are, of course, directly concerned with religio-cultural inheritance, but the "traditional" religion in question is rarely Christianity.

2. Knobauch (2001, 527–28); Sakaranaho (2011, 135–58); Brosius and Polit (2011).

3. Geaves (2009, 19–33).

4. For more human-centered approaches to studying secularism, see, e.g., Bender and Taves (2012).

5. This estimate includes new crosses and reconstructions. It is based on my survey of locally produced books about crosses and a 2012–13 telephone study where my research assistants contacted 398 parishes, of which 199 had crosses.

6. On "lieux de mémoire," see Nora (1996, 14). I conducted intermittent fieldwork from 2012 to 2014, during which time I attended group prayers, cross benedictions, and springtime cleanups. I

directed a telephone survey (see note 5) and conducted fifty one- to two-hour interviews with caretakers, over the phone and in person, and twelve interviews with leaders in historical societies and the Chevaliers de Colomb (Knights of Columbus). I surveyed *Colombien* magazine from 1922 to 2007 and available village weeklies from 2006 to present. The archive is the Fonds Jean Simard (FJS), F1081, Archives de folklore et ethnologie, Université Laval (Quebec).

7. This idea is adapted from Orsi (2005, 9).

8. Routhier (2006a, n.p.). Admittedly, religious heritage preservation is complicated, since Quebecois clergy and female religious often worked alongside academics.

9. I use the term *secular*, but ethnologists more accurately operate in a post-Catholic context, since Catholicism's structuring traces still influence their work.

10. Halbwachs ([1941] 1992).

11. Hervieu-Léger (2000, 73, 86–87, 127, 132–35); Nora (1996, 1).

12. Bibby (2008, 161, 175).

13. Routhier (2006b). On a similar point, see Hervieu-Léger (2000, 170).

14. Gauvreau (2013, 193).

15. Appadurai (1988, 16–20); Gupta and Ferguson (1992, 6–23). The ministry was created in 1963 as part of the modernization measures noted above. Simard's scholarship predated the "transnational turn" but then continued with little variation into the 1980s and 1990s.

16. Chidester (2005); Zubrzycki (2013); Endres (2011); van de Port (2005); Albera and Eade, forthcoming). Simard pointedly does not identify as "elite," viewing his work on popular art as "the people's vengeance" against the church. Simard (1979, 2).

17. Meyer (2010c, 10).

18. Dominguez (1986); Nurse (1997, 99).

19. Barbeau (1935, 290; 1962, 9); Nurse (1997, 30, 314).

20. Handler (2011, 49).

21. Routhier (2006b, 301); Jean Simard, interview by author, May 23, 2014.

22. Nicole Genet, Luce Vermette, and Louise Decarie-Audet, "Les croix de chemin: Ile Jesus-Ile Bizard," report submitted to Jean Simard, November 5, 1972, in FJS, E/05547.

23. Ibid., 16–17; Simard (1972, 20–22).

24. Kritzman (1996, xii).

25. Hervieu-Léger (1996). Cf. Perrault (2011). On the role of the church in civil society, see Mager and Cantin (2010); Snyder and Pelletier (2011). In terms of early sociology/anthropology in particular, see Hervieu-Léger (2000, 9–22).

26. On elites, see Drouin and Richard-Bazire (2011, 1). On reinvention, see Noppen and Morrisset (2005).

27. Jean Simard, Interview by author, May 23, 2014; Joly (2008, 43); Carpentier (1981, 391); Simard (1998, 50).

28. Hervieu-Léger (2000, 124–25, 127). Locke compared time to "the length of one straight line, extended *in infinitum.*"

29. Simard (1995, 7, 47).

30. K. Stewart (1992, 253–54).

31. Of fifty caretakers interviewed, only two saw their cross as *patrimoine* and explicitly not religious. Tellingly, both opted to build precise re-creations based on old photos.

32. Hervieu-Léger (2000, 111, 176).

33. Chakrabarty ([2000] 2008, 66).

34. Nora (1996, 3); Hervieu-Léger (2000, 129). Simard inherited his view from Barbeau, for whom *ethnologie* necessarily included public education to counter the moral threat posed by modernity and materialism—and, ironically, to encourage tourism.

35. Hervieu-Léger (2000, 127).

36. A *rang* is a rural grouping of houses. The term is a holdover from the seigneurial system, where rural houses are strung out along on what today is effectively a small country road. In Quebec, each *rang* had its own school, its own post office, and often its own wayside cross.

37. Côté (2014).

38. Meunier, Laniel, and Demers (2010, 92, 122).

39. There is no official estimate of the Chevaliers' involvement. Amateur historian Monique Bellemare has amassed a photographic repository of 688 contemporary crosses. Of these, 7.9 percent display the Knights' insignia. At that rate, they maintain 200 to 250 crosses province-wide. However, the number is likely much higher, since the insignia is not always displayed and since Bellemare's record may highlight crosses that are more ornate. Knights' crosses are usually undecorated.

40. Hervieu-Léger (2000, 170).

41. E.g., Noppen and Morrisset (2005); Nora (1996, 1).

42. Hervieu-Léger (2000, 128, 130–40).

43. Cf. Mayblin (2010, 110).

44. Carpentier (1981, 42).

45. Méchoulan (2008, 121).

46. S. Stewart ([1984] 2001, 150).

47. Morgan (2010, 68).

48. Beidelmann (1993). This idea connects to what scholars also note about Catholic objects (e.g., Orsi [2005, 55]).

49. Groulx (2009, n.p.).

50. Meyer (2010c).

51. Hervieu-Léger (2000, 162); Handler (2011, 48).

52. Kilde (2013, 192).

11

Containment and Contagion

The Gender of Sin in Contemporary Catholicism

Maya Mayblin

On June 29, 2002, seven women from Germany, Austria, and the United States were ordained to the Catholic priesthood on a boat cruising the Danube River in a ceremony presided over by Romulo Antonio Braschi, a legally ordained Catholic bishop who was no longer in formal communion with Rome. The women who experienced the laying on of hands on that Bavarian summer's day have since become known as "the Danube Seven." By 2008 three of the original seven had been consecrated as bishops, and as women bishops they have continued the pastoral work of ordaining women to the priesthood all over the world. Since then, more bishops have been consecrated, mostly in the United States and Canada. The Roman Catholic Womenpriests (RCWP) movement that blossomed from this ceremony is today a worldwide renewal movement within the church whose aim is to create an "inclusive, Christ-centered Church for the 21st century." According to the RCWP website, there are currently over 180 official Roman Catholic Womenpriest supporters worldwide, the majority of whom are in North America. However, the movement has the public support of hundreds of priests and theologians and, at a fair guess, the somewhat less public support of thousands more.

To become a priest in Roman Catholicism, one has to receive the sacrament of ordination in a valid form, that is, through the laying on of hands of a consecrated bishop who stands in direct apostolic succession to Saint Peter. The canon law that governs the administration of the sacraments (Canon 1024) limits the matter of ordination to men alone.[1] Licit ordination and valid ordination are here differentiated. To be valid, ordination requires only a laying on of hands in direct apostolic succession; to be *licit*, however, it requires that the ordinand be a baptized man. As such, the RCWP maintain that although their ordination is not licit it is certainly valid. The Vatican, on the other hand, claims that because their ordination was *il*licit, no ordination in fact took place.

According to the Vatican Information Service, in July 2010 the Vatican announced that priests who sexually abuse minors, view child pornography, or sexually abuse mentally disabled adults, along with those who ordain women, or women who attempt to be ordained, will now be included among the list of *delicta gravoria*, or the most serious crimes against church law.[2] In sum, ordaining women, or being an ordained woman, has been made as bad a crime in canon law as being a pedophile priest.

In 2013 I became acquainted with Morag Liebert, a Scottish member of the RCWP and, to date, the only Roman Catholic woman priest practicing in Britain. Morag was born and raised in Edinburgh and worked in the nursing profession before retiring to study theology. In 2008 she was ordained as a deacon at a secret ceremony in Munich. One year later, on October 24, 2009, she was ordained as a priest in an open ceremony in Edinburgh. Morag had trained with the RCWP as a "catacomb" student. Only after her ordination into the priesthood did she go public with her dissent. Her excommunication was upheld by Cardinal Keith O'Brian via an "interview" that Morag described to me as "gracious, very nice, and very civilized." Since her ordination Morag has carried on her own ministry, and she celebrates Mass to a group of followers once a month around her kitchen table. She is sanguine about her small congregation, which serves, on average, between two to five congregants, and is stoical about the slowness of reform emanating from the Vatican. "If I live to a hundred I still might not see the Vatican resolve the woman priest issue," she tells me. "But on the other hand I might. I don't know."

Morag was sitting opposite me on the sofa; her gray hair was gathered neatly into a bun and her unadorned hands rested on her lap. On that day she was wearing a pink hand-knitted cardigan, which glowed incongruously in the blue January light filtering through my office window. The cup of tea I had made her sat untouched on the table. Perhaps it had not been to her taste? Possibly—I mused to myself—we had been so caught up in conversation that she had forgotten all about it. We had met up so I could learn more about Morag's "inclusive" language of liturgy but instead had found ourselves discussing various scandals besetting the church. Was there a link between mandatory celibacy in the priesthood and the sexual abuse of minors? I asked. Morag did not know of any link. We debated the statistical research that suggests there is no significant correlation. According to some reports, the incidence of child sexual abuse among the Catholic clergy is proportionally no higher than among the adult male population in general. We noted, at any rate, that of the two sexes it was the male sex that tended in greater numbers toward sex offenses. There was a pause in the conversation, and it seemed to me that for a fraction of a moment the implicit logic that *ours* was the fairer, more Christian sex after all hovered in the air. If women are less likely to rape minors in quite such large

FIGURE 11.1. Catholic woman priest Morag Liebert.

numbers, I thought to myself, is it not obvious that they would make better priests? I stopped short of voicing the thought out loud, for it would clearly have contravened the *inclusive* mandate of the RCWP. Nevertheless, it struck me as strange. Deductions such as these are understandable given the current state of the church's public image, but since they count as sex-based *discriminations,* they are also taboo. As global institution and system of moral governance, contemporary Catholic doctrine preaches the absolute equality of all humanity at the same time that it remains structured upon an indissoluble difference between women and men.

My conversation with Morag prompted me to later reflect on why, in the public imagination, clerical celibacy and sexual abuse are instinctively linked. For regardless of the statistical evidence proving or disproving any link, sexual abuse in the Catholic

Church *is* connected in the public imagination to the issue of celibacy and to a need for reform of the priesthood. Going by the popular media alone, one would be forgiven for thinking that Catholics have a much bigger problem with child molestation than the population at large. Articles and opinion pieces point to the various features of the Catholic Church such as its celibacy rules for priests, its insular hierarchy, and its exclusion of women from ministry to imply that there's something peculiar about Catholic clerics that predisposes them to such acts. In 2002—a time when Catholic sex abuse scandals were making newspaper headlines—a Wall Street Journal NBC News poll found that 64 percent of those queried thought Catholic priests "frequently" abused children.[3] Whatever the finer dynamics at play may be, the sex/abuse/authority complex in its varying permutations and forms accounts for the common suggestion that celibacy is partly to blame for the abuse. The same complex, once again, in a slightly different configuration, accounts for another common assumption: that if women could become priests, or if priests could marry, there would be greater understanding of the stresses of biological reproduction and contraception would be allowed.

The knot in contemporary Catholicism's fabric—time and again—concerns Catholic teachings on sexuality and gender. Feminist theologians have noted that at the crux of this global sexual maelstrom are two rather contrasting models of Catholic humanity: an older dualistic model in which humanity is divided ontologically into two distinct sexes and a later, post-Tridentine model, influenced by certain theological transformations brought about by the Reformation, in which humanity is ontologically singular.[4] My goal in this essay is to explore some of the performative shifts that occur when Catholics speak about "humanity." I am particularly interested in how slippage between these two models maps onto discursive understandings of sin and grace as particular kinds of objects—objects that are *differently* contagious or containable to subgroups of persons. The imperatives to contain grace and share out sin are, as I shall explore, immanently strategic in relation to church hierarchy. Catholic models of humanity, although they maintain a certain theological coherence in the abstract, rarely work as a priori defining features of Catholic discourse. My discussion, I hope, can go some way toward understanding the conditions of possibility that sustain global Catholicism's current, paradoxical, state of affairs. Proceeding, I will draw on ethnographic and textual data from a broad range of sources, including research conducted among Catholics in Northeast Brazil between 2000 and 2012 and in Scotland between 2012 and 2015, as well some analysis of English-language Catholic websites and newsfeeds accessed between 2012 and 2015. The online essays and theological commentaries I have drawn from were all selected for the fact that they appeared to have been authored by Catholics who write in a professional capacity (whether as journalists or theologians) for "the public domain." By drawing my data from cyberspace as well as from people in real-life contexts, I present Catholicism as a dynamic set of discourses and debates, unfolding in multiple domains that criss-cross time and space. Although the wide-ranging approach to data gathering I have chosen to take here is not without certain drawbacks, it has allowed me to identify certain globally reaching manifestations of the sex-abuse-authority complex manifesting at this critical historical juncture.[5]

A DUALIST ANTHROPOLOGY OF HUMANITY

Early Christian thinkers developed an anthropology (in the sense of a doctrine of humanity in relation to God and salvation) that attributed an ontological division between men and women. The differing anthropology of men and women did not rest purely on the practical differences of biology but encompassed matters of spirit and metaphysical aspects of character. Were women to be included in the definition of humanity? The crucial question, one debated by church elders in 548 at the Council of Macan in Lyons, France, was whether or not they had souls. Upon one side it was argued that woman should not be called *homo*; upon the other that she should because, first, the scriptures declared that God created man, male and female, and second, Jesus Christ, son of a woman, is called the son of man. The conclusion, that Christian women did indeed have souls, was decided at the Council of Macan by a margin of just one vote,[6] but the obvious anatomical and social *differences* between the sexes remained semantically and symbolically troublesome. Centuries afterward, the suffragist writer Matilda Joslyn Gage noted: "As late as the Woman's Rights Convention in Philadelphia, 1854, an objector in the audience cried out: 'Let women first prove they have souls, both the Church and State deny it.'"[7]

What emerged from medievalist thinking was arguably a working Christian model of humanity that was ambiguously dualistic. Women and men pertained to the same genus but were nevertheless ontologically separated by a boundary of slightly indeterminate origin. That is, although they were commensurate with one another, able to unite in sexual union and so forth, they were not, strictly speaking, of *one* kind. Complete metaphysical and conceptual identity remained impossible. God, it seemed, had ordained that men and women remain separated by a force field of sorts, across which various substances and qualities would not traverse. Among the various substances that would not traverse this barrier were certain graces and sacraments that could be conferred on men but not women. After the conversion of Constantine, the development of a new monarchic episcopacy provided the ultimate testing grounds for this dualistic model. As presbyters and bishops consolidated themselves as an organized clerical caste of professional ministers, it was gradually accepted that only men could become priests. According to historian Gary Macy, women thus lost central leadership positions in the church around the sixth century, positions that they have not, to date, recovered.[8]

Certainly women have always had important roles in the church as martyrs, saints, and overseers of religious orders and lay organizations, but their leadership has never been sacramentalized. According to tradition, the sacrament of ordination confers a permanent and *indelible spiritual mark on the soul* of the ordinand that cannot be lost, repeated, or conferred temporarily. The grace transmitted during the laying on of hands during a ritual of ordination might be likened to a dye that stains as soon as it comes into contact with the deeply receptive bio-spiritual substrate of the ordinand. In a dualist anthropology the materiality of a woman's body is mysteriously unsuitable for ordination, so much so that even if an ordained bishop were to perform the rite of the Sacrament of Holy Orders exactly on a woman, the dye would not take. In the words of one thirteenth-century canonist: "In the female sex a pre-eminence of degree cannot be signified since she occupies a state of subjection: (1 Timothy 2) 'I do not allow a woman to teach, nor to have dominion over a man.' For because she had made a bad use of her equality, she was put into subjection: (Gen 3) 'you shall be under the power of your husband.' Therefore she does not receive the character of the sacrament which possesses pre-eminence."[9] A woman's body is constructed in such a way that there is no risk of contagion, as it were: her bio-spiritual substrate presumably repels rather than soaks up the sacramental grace. In more recent pronouncements: "It must not be forgotten that the sacramental signs are not conventional ones. . . . Adaptations to civilizations and times therefore cannot abolish on essential points the sacramental reference to constitutive events of Christianity and to Christ himself. . . . The incarnation of the Word took place according to the male sex: this is indeed a question of fact, and this fact, while not implying an alleged natural superiority of man over woman, cannot be disassociated from the economy of salvation."[10] In her tracing of the theoretical genesis and practical implementation of this dual anthropology, Wendy Fletcher-Marsh notes that a dualist anthropology also mapped rather readily onto a Gnostic division between matter and spirit—if not in any official way, certainly in terms of practice and teaching.[11] Because women were subject to menstruation, and more visibly mired in bodily productions such as childbirth and lactation, their souls were held to be inferior: "For the menstrual blood, which accompanies birth, is considered to such an extent unclean that, as Solinus states, fruits dry up and grass withers at its touch."[12] In this sense a woman's physical shape, her biological potential, was simultaneously product of and punishment for her proclivity to sin.

For conservative Catholics defending a male-only clergy, a dualist anthropology has long been the "go-to" model of humanity because it allows for the claim that ministerial authority can inhere only in certain kinds (viz. sex) of bodies. It figures the development of sexual organs in the womb as a mystical event that brings entirely separate species of being into existence—species that are not "alike" or "the same" no matter how much modern society wishes they could be.[13] The dualist model is often glossed as "medieval" by more progressive members of the church, but this is not to say that it hasn't altered its form slightly with the times. In 1988 Pope John Paul II attempted to sand the medieval edges off the model in his famous encyclical letter to women *Mulieris Dignitatem*. In it, a dualistic anthropology is clearly present: human nature exists in two basically different forms, a male and a female form, each of which displays specific physical and spiritual characteristics. Nevertheless, the letter itself begins by praising the many achievements of women in the social and political sphere and championing the notion of gender equality. Only after this important lip service does it move on to address the ontological nature of women as *secondary* creations. Referring to Adam's loneliness in Genesis, Pope John Paul II writes: "God intervenes in order to help him escape from this situation of solitude: *'It is not good that the man should be alone; I will make him a helper fit for him'* (Gen 2:18). The creation of woman is thus marked from the outset by *the principle of help:* a help which is not one-sided but *mutual.* Woman complements man, just as man complements woman: men and women are *complementary.* Womanhood expresses the 'human' as much as manhood does, but in a different and complementary way."[14] Ever since this encyclical, conservative Catholic commentators have played heavily on the ambiguity of "difference" as a semantic category, and much has been made of the notion of "dignity in difference." Dignity in difference continues to inflect church practice and comes to the fore in matters of lay ministry. With the decline in vocations and the increasing dependence of the church on forms of lay ministry, discussion sometimes arises as to the different forms male and female lay ministry might take. In mainline and more conservative parishes there is a preference that lay men take up roles as acolytes, servers, crucifers, thurifers, banner bearers, and masters of ceremony while women remain as flower arrangers and conservers and cleaners of the sacred vessels and vestments. In practice, the fact that women tend to outnumber men as congregants means that the roles are more evenly distributed. Nonetheless, it is fair to say that a dualist anthropology continues to inflect, substantiate, and challenge much contemporary Catholic theology and practice.

ANTHROPOLOGY OF HUMANITY AS HAVING ONE NATURE

By the early modern era, the dualist anthropology was giving ground to other configurations. In particular it was increasingly being acknowledged that although men and women were physically different they were, at the same time, one in Christ. While fundamentally Pauline in character, this singular model of humanity was arguably brought back to prominence by the Protestant thinker Martin Luther, whose insistence on the priesthood of all believers imputed a radical uniformity to humanity as a whole.[15] Of course Luther was no feminist—his aim was ultimately to invert or level the hierarchy existent between the laity and the clergy. Nonetheless, his reasoning had the effect of erasing other divisions and subgroups within humanity, including that between the sexes. Just as all humans were equally unworthy, so they were equally redeemed. The introduction of this radical Christian equality paved the way for various twentieth-century theologies that conceptualized humanity in nongendered terms—using core notions of spirit, love, and Kingdom.[16]

By the mid-twentieth century the general atmosphere for Catholic women, particular in Europe and North America, had become much more progressive. As the rise of the women's movement collided with the advent of liberation theology, Vatican II, and other progressive reforms, some Catholics started publicly campaigning for women to have more prominent leadership roles. In 1976 a Pontifical Biblical Commission reported that it could find no support in the biblical evidence for the exclusion of women from the ordained priesthood. Indeed, Vatican II theology emphasizes women as equal in human dignity with men, as in the following statement: "Every form of discrimination against persons, either because of religion, nationality, race or gender, must be overcome and eradicated as contrary to God's intent."[17]

In 1995 Pope John Paul II argued an urgent need to achieve equality in every area, including equal pay for equal work, protection for working mothers, fairness in career advancement, and access to the rights of citizenship. In addition to this, feminist theology has, for a while, been part of the curriculum in Catholic academia, and women are teachers in many Catholic seminaries. The climate of thinking, as theologian Elizabeth Johnson suggests, has moved toward envisioning maleness and femaleness "in a more holistic context . . . one human nature celebrated in an interdependence of multiple differences . . . a multipolar set of combinations of essential human elements of which sexuality is but one."[18]

The Catholic Church position that women cannot be ordained has been an escalating point of tension in Europe and the Americas, where, over the course of the twentieth and twenty-first centuries, Catholic women have seen other Christian churches accept the ordination of women. Formally, it is the singular model that guides the progressive politics of the RCWP, who argue that there is no reason why a woman cannot embody Jesus's humanity in the role of a priest. In the words of Eric Doyle, a Catholic theologian and early supporter of women's ordination, Jesus is the GodHuman "without confusion or separation": "His maleness is not formally relevant to his mediatorship. The Church is a unity of human beings, 'a people brought into unity from the unity of the Father, the Son and the Holy Spirit.' It is not formally relevant to this unity that human beings are infants, boys and girls, men and women. Nowhere, I would submit, in the formal structure of the Church's sacramental system, with the exception of matrimony, does the circumstance of maleness or femaleness have an essential role to play."[19] According to this more recent model, humanity is a singular unit. Within its unified contours can be found a "multipolar set of combinations" of gender, race, sexuality, build, height, skin color, and so forth. The differences produced, however, constitute *informal* variations—differences of degree rather than of kind in the ontological sense. An important distinction therefore needs to be made between "difference" as a feature of the dualist model and as it applies to the singular one. In the former model difference is formally relevant, in the latter it is not. In the singular model, difference progresses along and across various continua whose ends keep receding into the distance. There is no obvious middle point at which a cut of separation could be made. All cutting points are necessarily arbitrary.

Having delineated what appear to be two, apparently incommensurable models of humanity, I should go back to the nexus of problems and paradoxes that instigated their discussion in the first place. At root, of course, remains the problem of how Catholic women can be Godlike but not priestlike. The contradictions that flow from this official religious dictum are various and have come to encompass one of the most serious infractions against the Catholic faith occurring on the contemporary stage: the sex abuse scandal. My interest here is in how these differing models of humanity handle conceptions of sin and grace. A latent but noteworthy point about the two models of humanity outlined so far is that they create specific affordances where containment and contagion are concerned.

The situation is complicated by the fact that in Catholicism both sin and grace can be conceptualized as material properties that literally enter and embed themselves in human bodies. As properties these can be spontaneously present in individuals through God's bestowal (in the case of grace) or inheritance (in the case of sin), but as qualities percolating within the world they can also be "caught" or passed on from one human to another—for example, grace through a ritual of ordination, via the laying on hands, and sin through the spatial proximities created by living in society (which explains why ascetics seek to remove themselves from it). Original sin is tangentially problematic here—because it is inherited it is always already present in human DNA. Nevertheless, technologies of penance and atonement allow Catholics to differentiate between an original state of sin—which can be better imagined as a latent capacity or talent for wrongdoing inhering in all people—and actual sins, of which there are varying shades. If original sin is the tinder, actual sin (as in individual instances of wrongdoing and moral transgression) is the fire that results when the tinder is set alight. In this way individual humans can accumulate differing levels of sin and virtue. The result is an overarching economy of salvation and damnation.

Let us look then at how sin and grace can be contagious but also containable. My aim is to show how idioms of contagion and containment index contrasting models of humanity. What we shall see is that whereas grace has a tendency to cleave to particular persons, or groups of persons, creating the impression of profound divisions—even ontological gender distinctions—within humanity as a whole, sin tends to travel outwards smoothly and evenly, blurring the distinctions between types and subcategories.

SIN

In previous publications I have described the tendency of Santa Lucian villagers to distribute the sin and violence of married life equally between the sexes.[20] The example I used to make this point concerned a village man I called Seu Luca who murdered his wife with a scythe in a fit of jealousy. For the sake of argument I return to this example once more. The problematic, as I encountered it at the time of writing, was how to approach the case of a man murdering his wife without subsuming it to a feminist analysis concerned with proving the universal problem of female oppression. It was not that, on a personal level, I was indifferent to the politics of feminism—far from it. The issue was ethnographic. My own informants refused, despite my probing, to frame the problem in terms of "men versus women." Rather, what they saw in the morally abhorrent actions of one man, or insisted on emphasizing, was the sinfulness of all humanity. Wives, too, in their view, could kill: women killed men, men killed women. The kinds of deaths meted out differed only on a temporal plane. Ultimately, it was reasoned, sin has no gender. During a subsequent fieldtrip to Santa Lucia in 2011, I recorded some details about the first mass celebrated in the village chapel in the wake of this murder. The priest celebrating that mass had been faced with the difficult task of making sense of the mortal sin that had occurred, and I wanted to discover what form his sermon had taken. A number of individuals who remembered the mass told me that the sermon had been about the dangers of gossip. It was gossip about infidelity (*fofoca*), the priest insinuated, that had ultimately led to Dona Mariquinha's death, and, as such her death was something that the entire community shared equal responsibility for. The congregants were admonished to reflect on their collective guilt and hence, consciously or not, on their *collaboration in Seu Luca's crime*.

At the time it did not occur to me that this sermon displayed the same momentum as those speech acts that had surrounded the original remembering and retelling of Seu Luca's sinful act. But I think, on reflection, that it constitutes another typical example of the contagiousness of sin. In the eventful moment of that one sermon, the sin of one man was dispersed among all.

I want to draw a link here with the diplomatic "division" of sin among a populace that happened in another context. In 2011 I returned to Brazil, this time to carry out research among the Catholic clergy themselves. I interviewed—both formally and informally—twenty Brazilian Catholic priests about their perception of politics and the Catholic Church. During these interviews I collected a number of responses and reactions to the clerical sexual abuse crisis, which was, at the time, very prominent in the news. Below I quote a typical exchange on the matter:[1]

> *Maya:* How damaging for the church do you think the recent media attention is on pedophile priests?
>
> *Padre Bento:* Damaging, certainly. Those convicted priests carried the weight of the church on their shoulders, and still do. But the priest is no less fallible than the next man. People forget that. No human is without sin after all—the crisis reflects on us all.

In all but two of the interviews I performed, the priests responded to this question with some appeal to the notion of a single-nature humanity. The point they wished to get across was that priests—as men—were human after all. This lament, human after all, would also encompass women of course. Priests as human, then, not as the male sex, were susceptible to worldly temptation, and worst of all to evil in the form of sexual depravity. Laments of this sort elided the *maleness* of the sin in such contexts. I am not in any way arguing that women are incapable of sexual abuse— in point of fact they are; I wish merely to draw attention to the fact that the over-whelming preponderance of the male sex among the population of sex abusers never enters such debates. Human weakness, sin, moral failure: such negative characteristics rarely invoke a dualist anthropology. Their movement in the world is inherently contagious, and thus what sin ultimately evokes is always, in some sense, a single model of humanity.

The reactions of some of Catholicism's more conservative gatekeepers to the sex abuse scandal throw the "contagiousness" of sin into heavy relief. In an article summarizing the findings of an independent church child abuse report, the Catholic bio-ethicist Nicholas Tonti-Fillipini engages an encompassing register to such ends. That there are priests who abused prepubescent or adolescent children "is to be expected," he writes, as "they are prone to the same human frailties as the members of any other professional group." Abuse here is the by-product of an Augustinian *human* frailty that encompasses "any other professional group." The dispersal of this "frailty" among all professional humans lightens the load on the clerical division somewhat. But the author immediately goes on to evidence this by turning to statistics that reference the problem through the quadrant of gender: "In the United States, the evidence indicates that paedophilia (sexual attraction to prepubescent children) affects 0.3% of the entire population of clergy, which is *lower than the average for males,* and homosexual attraction to adolescent boys affects around 2% of clergy, about the same proportion that affects married males."[21]

It is not, therefore, that the evidence for abuse lacks a gendered angle. "The gender question" implicated in the clerical abuse crisis is simply not part of the *moral* angle—elided as always by the question of "human frailty." The same momentum is produced by polemics that blame the clerical abuse crisis on the problems of society writ large. As Catholic theologian Scott Stephens writes:

> According to the study, far more significant for explaining the magnitude and concentration of the sexual abuse crisis are those discernable cultural patterns which indicate the deepening of a certain social anomie during the same period. . . . Only someone who is willfully naive or intractably bigoted would refuse to acknowledge that the social antinomianism and fetishization of sexual liberation in the 1960s and 70s, along with the valorization of the pursuit of individual pleasure and free experimentation with transgressive sexual practices, created the conditions for a dramatic escalation in deviant behaviour—including paedophilia—both within and without the Church.[22]

Here the impetus to sexual assault is diffusely present in the "sexual liberation of the 1960s and 70s." If sexual sins index anything, they index a particular epoch rather than a particular sex. The fact that everyone, whether man or woman, lay or cleric, can be affected by the "conditions" for sin it creates implies an endless porosity between types and subcategories.

Take, for example, the following online discussion, where scholar and Catholic commentator Anthony Esolen weighs in on a debate about the meaning of the phrase *In Persona Christi*. It is on the meaning of *In Persona Christi* that the women's ordination debate hangs, and Esolen, being opposed to women's ordination, sets out to refute the idea that the ordained ministry "is some kind of plum reserved for the favored few, rather than a dread burden and responsibility." He supports his point by invoking various female sinners in the ancient world. Jesus, he argues, in his magnanimity, does not fixate on the sex of these sinners (as we might assume he was free to do) but talks always instead of the sins of "Man" in the inclusive sense of *anthropos*.

> It isn't as if you couldn't find cultural villainesses aplenty, in the ancient world. You have Clytemnestra, the daughter of King Servius (who is said to have ridden her chariot over her father's mangled body), Jezebel, Athaliah, Vashti, the goddess Ishtar, the implacable Juno. . . . Jesus avails himself of none of that. On the contrary, he seems to assume that "man" in his parables will quite naturally stand for males and for men-in-general. . . . Man is to woman as the general is to the specific. . . . There isn't anything SPECIAL about being a man, in that sense.[23]

In fact what Esolen tells us here is that there is nothing specifically male about *sinfulness*—because there are "villainesses aplenty" in the ancient world. Once again, it is the genderless human individual, in this rhetorical moment, who reigns supreme. Sin here works through a process of unbridled contagion—suggestive, of course, of a singular category. However, we are then confronted with a paradox, for if humanity is—as such commentators claim—of a single ontology, on what grounds can women be definitively excluded from priestly ministry?

AUTHORITY BESTOWED THROUGH GRACE

When it comes to the propitious business of representing Christ, a singular ontology recedes from view and humanity becomes strangely dualist and singular at the same time. As Timothy Teeter writes, anyone, male or female, can represent Christ, "but only men can represent Christ as he represents all of humanity to the Father."[24] Father Wojciech Giertych, a Dominican priest and papal theologian opposed to women's ordination, reflects on the difference between the sexes to argue his point. He states that men are more likely to think of God in terms of "philosophical definitions and logical syllogisms"—a quality "valuable for fulfilling a priest's duty to transmit church teaching." The argument continues that priests love the church in a characteristically "male way" when they show concern "about structures, about the building of the church, about the roof of the church which is leaking, about the bishop's conference, about the concordat between the church and the state." Women, Father Giertych adds, have their own unique characteristics, which presumably are *un*available or perhaps *less* available to men. For example, "Women are more apt to draw from the mystery of Christ, by the quality of their prayer life, by the quality of their faith. . . . Women have a special access to the heart of Jesus, in a very vivid way of approaching him, of touching him, of praying with him, of pouring ointment on his head, of kissing his feet." In other words, says Father Giertych, "Women don't need the priesthood because their mission is so beautiful anyway."[25]

By casting actions such as flower arranging and ointment pouring as a kind of "mission" parallel to the priesthood, Giertych reinforces the ontological nature of the male/female split. The overall effect is one of containment. Male and female virtues are equally dignified but equally contained. They do not travel, they cannot be shared.

But it is not just supporters of a male-only clergy who seek to contain the authority bestowed through grace. In general, I would argue, grace cleaves to the particular, to individuals, and even to spots and crevices in the landscape. It is harder to share. In Catholicism it is individuals who embody holiness—the paradigmatic example of course being the saint, who stands not only as the exemplar par excellence but also as the container par excellence of the sacred. Although the thermic properties of holy places and people *can* be transferred and shared out among people, holy authority and grace are not semantically contagious in the same way as sin. Grace can leak, be contained, be transferred in objects, and even be passed among humans through sheer proximity. But there is always some conscious or ethical labor involved. Without the ethical labor of humans, grace does not travel; it sticks to the person on whom it was bestowed. Grace, we might say, is barrier sensitive. Thus Catholics must travel to benefit from its spillover in the world. Hence the practice of pilgrimage, or the custom of traveling to obtain the blessing of an ordained priest or the healing of a renowned faith healer. Touch is often essential for transmission to work. Hence, in Catholicism the touching of a relic, or the laying on of hands—not only are these kinesthetic practices symbolic, they provide a quite literal technology of transmission.

THE GENDER OF SIN

At this point it could be helpful to turn back to the title of this essay and to ask, well, does sin have a gender in Catholicism? This question, I suggest, lurks implicit in the current political and theological maelstrom that surrounds the question of sex abuse, gender, and women's ordination in the contemporary church. From an anthropological perspective there is no absolute answer, of course—or at least answers when proffered are always embedded in a particular social context. Being provocative, I might say that on the whole sin is genderless, except when it is advantageous to proclaim that it is not. The puzzle of the two models disappears if we acknowledge that the models themselves are in fact subservient to the problems posed by sin and authority bestowed through grace. We might say that where authority wants to be contained, sin wants, instinctively, to be shared. The simultaneous upholding of *both* these models in contemporary Catholicism could be cast as something of a puzzle or a "mystery"—yet another example of Schmitt's *complexio oppositorum*. However, from a political perspective, at least, the copresence of these different ways of conceptualizing humanity is problematic. From a conservative perspective it might be said that the singular model is simply a twentieth-century accommodation to post-patriarchal culture in western Europe and North America and has no divine origin. It should therefore be ruled out. But this, one senses, is a practical impossibility—for one thing, the stricter the dualism, the fewer conditions there are for contagion to occur. Not a problem where grace and authority are concerned, of course, but where the diplomatic division of sin is concerned, it is. From a more progressive perspective, on the other hand, there can and should be only *one* working model of humanity: a singular one. But this makes difference of any kind a problematic of sorts. Which differences should be accommodated for and which shouldn't? If all categorizations are in some sense arbitrary, and all human qualities and predilections are endlessly contagious, does containment make any sense?

The dynamic I have described might be likened to one described by Jon Bialecki,[26] who analyzes two sharply contrasting forms of speech—one he glosses as "centripetal," which is "expansively" allegorical in nature, and the other as "centrifugal," which is literal in nature and works always to occlude "imaginative frontiers." Curiously, notes Bialecki, each form has been claimed as definitive in some way of Protestant language ideology. In Bialecki's view there is no inherent contradiction in this; simply, each author's rendering of speech as a total social phenomenon is ultimately partial. While each speech form *should* cancel out the possibility of the other's emergence, in practice opposing forms overlap and work as variants of one another. In short, what appear as "impure elements" in any semiotic system "may have their own uses in a religious and representational economy—and receive their own sanction as ethically proper communicative acts because of it."[27] More specifically, argues Bialecki, each form of speech is "in some ways the answer to a crisis."[28] The notion of crisis is highly relevant here, and I would like to dwell for a moment on it. Like Bialecki's Vineyard informants, whose shifts in language use map onto a particular sort of crisis (in the case he describes, a demonic crisis), for the Catholics I have described, shifts in register map onto a crisis of another sort: that concerning sex, abuse, and the nature of spiritual authority. The crisis I have sought to describe today is in some senses unique within the current anthropology of Christianity, for it exceeds any one particular locality, or group, or set of rituals. It is, we might say, a crisis of diffusely globalized, political and even secular proportions. Across a range of divergent but public stages, whether newspaper articles, pulpits, treatises, or blog commentaries, what is striking is how capacities for containment and contagion are never a priori defining features but always "an answer" to this crisis.

And so to conclude, like apparently competing language forms, apparently incommensurable models of humanity attempt to occlude one another but turn out, in the final analysis, to be codetermining. I am not suggesting that people shuttle consciously between incommensurable metaphors and models. My point is, rather, that containment and contagion are agonistically related to one another— both metaphorically and literally. For supporters of a male-only clergy, authority can be contained only if linked to particular categories delineated as sexes; this containment draws upon a dualistic model of humanity in which barriers are present and not all human qualities can be shared. However, as we have seen, when sin becomes an issue the same protagonists will appeal to a singular model of humanity in which contagion is enabled, in which human qualities such as sin and the concomitant failure of spiritual authority implied can be shared out.

This said, it is possible to see the work of the RCWP as one that seeks to put an end to this juggling by fixing the viewpoint once and for all. Humanity, the RCWP argue, should look the same whether from the perspective of sin or authority. Of course, this is the job of all theology, which by virtue of its own fixedness of written form is able to materially emulate the very trait it seeks to instill in human thought and action: consistency and perfection of a particular view. But as theology's ultimate target is a moving one, I suspect there will always be a degree of displacement involved.

NOTES

1. Congregation for the Doctrine of the Faith (2007).
2. Vatican Information Service (2010).

3. The poll was conducted April 5–7, 2002; results available from Roper Center at University of Connecticut, *Public Opinion Online,* accession number 0402247.

4. Børresen (1992); Fletcher-Marsh (1998).

5. On the drawbacks, see Wilson and Peters (2002).

6. Fletcher-Marsh (1998).

7. Gage (1893, 28).

8. Macy (2008).

9. Joannes Andreae, Novella V, fol. 125v, trans. John Wijngaards, quoted in Raming (1976, 49–50).

10. Sacred Congregation for the Doctrine of Faith (1976).

11. Fletcher-Marsh (1998).

12. Sicardus, Mitrale V, chap. 11.

13. Sacred Congregation for the Doctrine of the Faith (1976): "The priestly office cannot become the goal of social advancement: no merely human progress of society or of the individual can of itself give access to it: it is of another order."

14. John Paul II (1988).

15. Fletcher-Marsh (1998).

16. Fletcher-Marsh (1998).

17. Paul VI (1965).

18. Johnson (1996, 155).

19. Doyle (1983, 19–20).

20. Mayblin (2010, 2011).

21. Tonti-Fillipini (2013).

22. Stephens (2011).

23. Esolen is quoted in Hart (2008).

24. Timothy Teeter, quoted in Hart (2008).

25. Rocca (2013).

26. Bialecki (2011).

27. Bialecki (2011, 698)

28. Bialecki (2011, 698).

12

Opulence and Simplicity

The Question of Tension in Syrian Catholicism

Andreas Bandak

German bishop Franz-Peter Tebartz-van Elst was suspended recently from his office and diocese in Limburg. Over the years he had managed to spend 31 million euros of church funds on his home, which allegedly had every conceivable luxury and extravaganza, earning him the title "Bishop of Bling." According to news reports, there was huge relief among German Catholics when Pope Francis used this specific case to present a different image of Catholicism. By suspending the profligate bishop, Pope Francis signaled that the way of the church is not—or rather should not be—one of opulence and extravaganza. That Pope Francis chose this sanction is in line with his own initial steps in the Vatican, where the choice of his papal name at the onset of his office made it clear that his mission is one imitating Saint Francis of Assisi and thereby an ideal of simplicity and solidarity with the poor and needy. The new pope has also changed the papal abode to a more humble one in a church guest house as compared to his predecessors' apartments in the Apostolic Palace. Likewise, he has changed the papal automobile—the famous Mercedes "Popemobile"—to a used 1984 Renault 4. Such moves are in direct opposition to those of a bishop of bling.

While it may too early to judge how Pope Francis will fare in the coming years, the tension between opulence and the ideals of poverty and humility is a much more prevalent theme found in Catholicism—a motor, I will argue, for Catholicism itself. The central question this chapter asks is how both this particular tension and also tension more generally play out in lived Catholicism. In lived Catholicism various forms of sacrifices are made that, in the phrasing of David Morgan, amount to a material economy of the sacred.[1] In such a sacrificial economy, the individual, as well as the church as a body, is seen to partake in a process of restoration of self and society. Such processes are, however, fraught with inequity and paradox, or tension as I call it, as the church is situated in the midst of politics not merely of a world to come but more perspicuously of the world at hand. Here money and worldly riches are striven for, and are therefore a potential source of worry because of their capacity to lead away from what is regarded as the right path. The tension between simplicity and opulence is accompanied by another formative tension, namely between gift and economy. On the one hand, Catholicism underscores grace and gratuity from the ultimate gift and sacrifice that Jesus, Mary, and the saints have already delivered and that cannot be reciprocated. On the other hand, this gift places the Catholic community in an economy of a wider set of binding obligations and relationships of reciprocity. It is exactly the tension between a free gift and reciprocation that places another form of motion in the Catholic force field, a movement between impossible reciprocation and the instrumentalization of obligation. Following French Catholic thinker and radical phenomenologist Jean-Luc Marion, I aim to explore this givenness in the tension between gift and economy.

To explore these questions of tension, I will engage discussions among Catholic Syrian Christians in the years before the current uprisings and subsequent civil war.[2] My material consists of twenty months of ethnographic fieldwork between 2004 and 2010 in Syria and subsequent periods of shorter fieldwork among Syrians in Lebanon from 2012 to the present. In Syria, Christians are numerically a minority of no more than 8 percent of the population; furthermore, Christians belong to a variety of denominations, with Greek Orthodox and Greek Catholics being the two largest.[3] Several other Orthodox and Catholic churches exist besides these denominations, where the latter, beyond Maronites, Syrian Catholics, and Armenian Catholics, also number Latin churches. The case of Catholicism in Syria serves well as a reflection of how a situation outside the *locus classicus* of Catholicism inflects core concerns in different ways than what are most often thought of.[4] In this chapter, the Syrian case is used to dwell on the particularities of economy in a wider Catholic understanding as it crosses spiritual and material domains.

CATHOLICISM AND POLITICAL FORM

The tension of wealth and power versus poverty and simplicity has been a recurrent theme in the history of the Catholic Church. In classic times, the various Catholic monastic orders owning a lot of property and the mendicant orders of the Middle Ages living only off charity could be seen as instantiations of this specific tension.[5] The Catholic Church here could be seen both as world-making, in the sense of owning massive amounts of property and building an enormous material apparatus, and as a more spiritual machine disavowing worldly riches. In contrast to recent anthropological studies of Charismatic Christianity, Catholicism is a significant form of Christianity to explore in its own right even if—or more precisely because—it sits uneasily in the sample.[6] Whereas Max Weber famously presented a Protestant ethic as the basis for modern capitalism, Carl Schmitt, in his significant text "Roman Catholicism and Political Form," pays tribute to Weber by scrutinizing a different Christian logic.[7] Schmitt here argues that the formidable provocation of Catholicism is its intricate relation with, even foundation on, power. It is impossible, Schmitt posits, to understand Catholicism without understanding this very foundation. The church is power. To bring home his case, Schmitt recasts the epic scene, or novel in the novel, on the Great Inquisitor from Fyodor Dostoyevsky's *The Brothers Karamazov*. In this scene Jesus returns to earth but is shocked to see what the church has become. The church, rather than follow a spiritual path, has turned into a massive apparatus. However, Jesus's sorrow over what the church has become matters little to the Great Inquisitor, who ends up locking Jesus up in prison. To Dostoyevsky, this situation is abhorrent as it shows a church whose master is displaced and finds no room there. To Schmitt, however, the Great Inquisitor gets it right, as the church is conceivable only as a political form. Where Schmitt transposes Dostoyevsky's position vis-à-vis the Russian Orthodox Church to the Roman Catholic Church, he also reverses it. The church, to Schmitt, is to be understood in its power.

Schmitt's criticism that scholars tend to overlook or shy away from the inherent political form of Roman Catholicism is critical. An overarching characteristic of Catholicism has been its power structure, and to disregard it would be untenable. While Schmitt presents a significant insight, it may inadvertently stop further analysis if used merely to assert the importance of the power of the Catholic Church as an institutional feature in and of itself. Rather, I argue, the significance rests in the tension between this very form of power and the ideals of simplicity, poverty, and humility going against that same form. We are not helped much by being forced analytically to follow *either* the Great Inquisitor *or* Jesus rather than seeing these two figures in tandem creating a productive Catholic force field. It is exactly the uneasy relationship between power and spirit that allows for a Catholic framing and specificity. To be sure, Charismatic Christianity and other world religions present similar tensions;[8] but in Catholicism they point up a particularly Catholic feature—the church's ability to encompass enormous differences within itself without leading to schism and breakdown. This feature helps us understand the specificity of Catholicism in that the political form of the institution, office, bureaucracy, and material aesthetic produces countertendencies from within. Accordingly, the relevance of Schmitt's analytical assessment is not only manifested in a scholarly discussion of Catholicism but is an integral part of local discussions of the proper role of the church and its representatives. The tension is therefore not to be situated as an analytic outside Catholicism, a perspective from afar; rather, it is to be found inside the Catholic Church itself. The tears of Jesus over what the church has become in Dostoyevsky's rendition resonate rather well with Syrian Catholic perceptions of what troubles the hearts of Jesus and his mother.

THE TEARS OF MARY AND JESUS

In Syria one encounters scathing criticism of the use and misuse of money and church funds. Priests and, in particular, bishops have often been targeted as being preoccupied with personal gain and not with their flock. One afternoon in the home of a Damascene family, I encountered particularly trenchant criticism of the Catholic Church along these lines. I had had conversations with Kamal many times, but this time he took on his parish church, Kanisat Kyrilios. Our conversation had started with his current work at a restaurant. Kamal, in his late thirties and still living in his family home, told of his experience working abroad in Cyprus. Kamal recounted how many Christians want to find better jobs and therefore look for opportunities outside Syria. At this point in the conversation, I asked how many Christians were leaving Syria, implying that this might present a problem as a large proportion of young Christians hoped to leave or were actually leaving the country. "It's true," Kamal said. "The church should do something about it! The problem is that most Christians don't think about the collectivity, but only about themselves. . . . For instance, in our church, in Kanisat Kyrilios, frescoes are being made outside the church in the courtyard. Do you know how much they cost?" I attempted a feeble guess, but it was completely off target. "Seven thousand US dollars apiece or even eight thousand US dollars!" Kamal exclaimed with indignation, his eyes telling how outrageous such a figure was. "Mary and Jesus will not cry for expensive frescoes! No, give the money to the poor so they can build families and have children, this is what they ought to do!" Kamal repeated this point as if to emphasize it: "Give the money to the poor! Make families! And children." I commented on the total cost of the frescoes, as it was a whole series with at least fourteen pieces. Kamal looked at me. "Here you have some pastors driving the Mercedes 500 series! This is completely inappropriate!"

The topic of the use of church funds for expensive frescoes, or expensive Mercedes Benz cars, was by no means a rare one. Quite a number of cases in Damascus revealed a tension between an ideal of, if not outright poverty, then modesty and simplicity, and the actual use of money for personal gain by named priests and bishops or excessive building projects that were deemed inappropriate. In Damascus, the concern of many lay people was of the church becoming too preoccupied with buildings and the display of wealth, rather than "the living church," understood as the well-being of persons and families. As Kamal aptly remarked, Mary and Jesus will not cry for expensive frescoes.

The prevalence of this topic in Damascus during this period is significant taps into several critical domains. (Suggested alternative to above: The prevalence of

FIGURE 12.1. Relief in the courtyard of Kanisat Kyrilios, here
decorated as a nativity tableau for Christmas. Photo by author.

this topic in Syria during this period is significant as it points to several critical
domains.) First, the use of wealth for the renovation of churches and church-
related projects had been ongoing in many parts of Syria during the 1990s and
2000s. Such projects were generally welcomed, since many Syrian Catholics saw
the increasing influx of Saudi and Gulf money, as well as money from Iran, and the
resultant massive renewal of older mosques and construction of altogether new
ones in Muslim areas and mixed areas, but also in close proximity to more traditional Christian areas, as troubling in that it facilitated a general refashioning of

the Syrian landscape.[9] In many of the building projects entailing renovation of churches and church compounds, criticism was not voiced per se, as Catholics as well as other Syrian Christians saw that a Christian response was needed. However, several discussions were ongoing in Catholic circles in Syria as to which kinds of projects were stepping over the proper limits.

One such discussion revolved around church premises and the use thereof. In the 2000s, the Melchite Catholic Patriarchate, under Archbishop Gregorious III Laham, invested funds not only in the renovation of church buildings but also in the construction of a hotel on its premises in Harat al-Zaitoun in the old city of Damascus.[10] Likewise, the Melchite Catholic Church opened a minor restaurant on the premises of another of its famous churches, namely the Church of Our Lady of Damascus, Kanisat Sayyidat Dimashq, close to the central Abbasid Square. Such projects, unlike the renovation of church buildings, generated vehement criticism not merely from people outside the church but also within it. As with Kamal's stance on the frescoes in Kanisat Kyrilios, opening restaurants or hotels as part of church complexes was seen as a problematic way to ensure monetary gain. Money in and of itself is a source of moral speculation, since on one level or another it is instrumental to any kind of institution or life of an individual. Money, however, is no simple object, for it mediates both options that bestow blessings and good work on others and options that advance egoistic and self-serving purposes.[11] Perhaps this is precisely why money is often the source of tension in a Catholic register. Let us take a closer look at how this tension plays itself out in the Syrian context.

MONEY, OR THE PROBLEMS OF BARGAINING

Criticism of clerical leaders, even anticlericalism, is no new theme in anthropological literature on Catholicism. Here scholars such as Joyce Riegelhaupt and Ellen Badone have amply demonstrated that clergy may often find their profession reviled.[12] However, it is significant that criticism of church policies may come not only from those with little or no significant church attendance but also, and even particularly, among those who see the need for a church that will act as it preaches.[13] In a Syrian setting, this was often the case. We have already encountered Kamal and his call for a church that would work to alleviate the sufferings of the poor and needy. Related to this was a widespread concern with money and the seeking of illicit or immoral gain. This concern surfaced in discussions of the managing of church finances, and on a more popular level of the access to miracles and grace.

In an interview with Pierre and Abu Rafi, two devout followers of Our Lady of Soufanieh, I was asked to switch off the recorder, as Abu Rafi wanted to explain a recent occurrence in Kanisat Sayyidat Fatima, one of the Syrian Catholic churches in central Damascus, at some length. In the Church of Our Lady of Fatima, an icon had allegedly recently started to exude oil. The miracle of an icon exuding oil was

FIGURE 12.2. The Shrine of Our Lady of Soufanieh with a devotee praying in front of her icon. Notice the small white plaque on the wall with the inscription "No donation accepted." Photo by author.

not as significant for Abu Rafi as the reaction of clerical leaders: as the icon continued to exude oil, boxes for donations were placed in front of it. Abu Rafi looked at Pierre and me to underscore the indecency of the act. "And the oil stopped oozing from the icon!" he said emphatically. Pierre nodded, seemingly in agreement with the imminent conclusion; you can't buy a miracle. You may plead with the divine through prayers and petitions, but turning the situation into a direct monetary transaction is a disgrace, even more when the church establishment itself does it. The saints, Jesus, Mary, and even God himself are understood to disapprove of this kind of monetary transaction.

The conclusion drawn by Abu Rafi—and supported by Pierre—was by no means incidental. In their perception, miracles belonged to a different register from that of what money could buy. The story recounted was a direct expression of a theme central to the devotion to Our Lady of Soufanieh: that the grace of God is given for free and therefore needs to be passed on for free. In the shrine of Our

Lady of Soufanieh, which is also the home of the stigmatic and visionary Myrna Nazzour, one finds a prohibition on the direct donation of money. On the wall in Soufanieh a small white plaque reads: "Please, we do not accept donations!" The plate signals a particular relation to money, and an important one, as behavior surrounding money is delicate. On the one hand, ardent followers of Our Lady of Soufanieh, like Abu Rafi and Pierre, will emphasize how God, aided by Jesus and Mary, is the source of all good and cannot be bought. On the other hand, various forms of support are needed for the devotion to Our Lady of Soufanieh to flourish. The ideal of simplicity, then, is inflected by the devotion to Our Lady of Soufanieh and her followers in their emphasis on giving and not taking worldly riches. Followers have underscored this with stories on money donated to Our Lady of Soufanieh being sent on to official churches, and by constant criticism of clerical authorities for using coercion to collect money instead of making giving itself the logic of its ministry. Bassam, an engineer in his late forties, depicted such a situation when describing how even as a child he abhorred the sound of coins tumbling down collecting boxes during service, as this made God and divine blessing into a commodity. "Ching, ching, ching . . ." Bassam imitated the sound of money being collected, then covered his ears with his hands, displaying not merely discomfort but also visceral disgust.

What comes to the fore in this zealous—perhaps even puritan—version of Catholicism is a logic of giving that places emphasis on grace and indebtedness for what already has been bestowed upon the individual. You shouldn't bargain with God in terms of money. Rather, you ought to receive his divine gifts and then pass them on to others. The sacrifices made by God, Jesus, Mary, and the saints place the individual in bonds of debt that cannot be repaid by any single operation. Rather, they are seen to foster attention and care toward one's fellows, and primarily the poor and needy.

The devout followers of Soufanieh help us understand Kamal's notion of the tears of Mary and Jesus. Mary and Jesus are moved by humans, but not predominantly by their investment in buildings and displays of wealth. Rather, they are moved by a sacrificial economy where the giving of oneself to others is the direct consequence of the debt to Mary and Jesus for their suffering with or on the behalf of the individual. In the felicitous phrasing of Anna-Karina Hermkens, Willy Jansen, and Catrien Notermans, people, and not only Catholics, are moved by Mary.[14] People are moved by Mary but likewise want to move Mary to see to them and their situation. Movement and investment are in this sense intricately related, though investment typically is emotional before it is monetary. No wonder, then, that the central saints in this puritan Catholic Syrian landscape are figures such as Saint Thérèse of Lisieux, also known as the Little Flower or the Jesus Child, Mother Theresa, and Saint Francis of Assisi, all saintly figures known for their simplicity and sacrificial giving up of worldly desires in order to alleviate the suffering of the poor and needy. These figures stand as pure forms of what simplicity in a Catholic version could look like.

However, these figures do not reveal the difficulties ordinary Catholics have in complying with such extraordinary behavior—after all, money is part of life, and so are desires less zealous in intent. Before we return to the tension between simplicity and opulence, we shall focus on a particular inflection of simplicity in a Syrian context. Catholicism here, as in any given instantiation, reflects local concerns, and these, as we have already seen, are affected in a specific way when Catholicism is a minority position.

SIMPLICITY, THE SYRIAN WAY

To understand simplicity in a Syrian context, we must understand its particular national pretext. A particular national ethos of simplicity has prevailed during the Ba'athist era. When the Ba'ath party seized power in Syria in 1963, it highlighted both Arab nationalism and socialism as dominant features.[15] Pride of homeland was henceforth connected with a reluctance to display wealth in public. The Syrian citizen was considered a hardworking, honest, and simple, with no predilection for conspicuous flashing of riches in public. Simplicity, *basāṭa*, was considered a core value. Often-circulated stories of President Hafiz al-Assad, and later, much in the same vein, his son and successor Bashar al-Assad, depicted the president as a humble and simple man with no desire to lead a luxurious life.[16]

The Syrian notion of simplicity was aided by constant contrasts with neighboring Lebanon that presented almost everything Lebanese in terms of a superficial obsession with appearances, consumerism, and inauthentic values. Many poorer Syrians knew of this conspicuous wealth firsthand, since after the Lebanese Civil War Beirut and Lebanon were rebuilt by an underpaid unskilled Syrian workforce.[17] Just to give one example of this work of contrasting, it was telling to observe the reactions to the Israeli attack on Hezbollah in the summer of 2006. As a direct consequence of the Israeli shelling of southern Lebanon and the outskirts of Beirut, massive numbers of Lebanese sought refuge in and around Damascus. Public schools, churches, mosques, and even private homes were used as housing in the weeks of the air strikes. While Syrians generally understood the Lebanese to be in need of immediate help and hospitality, they soon depicted them as too demanding. Several Christian interlocutors, active in the Legion of Mary in the Church of Our Lady of Damascus, described the Lebanese they aided as ungrateful—demanding better blankets, specific and variegated food dishes, and even preservatives. In the opinion of the Syrian Catholics, the Lebanese thereby amply showed that they were leading an indecent life with no appreciation of the efforts made by those trying to aid them. Generally, Syrians oppose Syrian sobriety to Lebanese extravagance. Unlike the capitalistic Lebanese, Syrians under state socialism have kept a low profile with regard to bling and showing off. In some measure, they see Lebanon and its extravagance as despicable, even though this attitude has an undercurrent of tacit admiration of Lebanese cunning in business. Damascus is used to depict a kind of authentic rootedness as opposed to Beirut's inauthentic consumerism. Such national stereotyping allows Syrians to account for many malfunctions in Syrian society and to portray less money and even poverty as ambivalent signs of virtue.

Though this more general reading of Syrian society inflects a national stance emphasizing simplicity, the succession of Bashar al-Assad to the presidency in the summer of 2000 led to several significant changes. During the 2000s, an opening up of Syrian society to foreign investment, albeit still in a controlled form, led to an influx of consumer goods that, while not flooding the streets, still resulted in a hitherto unseen display of wealth in the larger Syrian cities.[18] Whereas previously the Syrian elite would go to Lebanon or Paris to shop or to live a more overtly decadent life, now they were increasingly able to obtain luxury commodities in Syria, with the erection of shopping malls in areas such as Kafer Souse, the grand Four Seasons Hotel complex with all sorts of luxury shops in downtown Damascus, and enormous car shops on the Northern Damascus highway. Many ordinary Syrians lamented what they perceived as a decline of morals and contamination of society with Western ideas of superficiality and consumerism, but they still participated in this economy of appearances. What was challenged here was exactly the national stereotype of simplicity. And this in Catholic circles was read as a specifically Christian problematic. In a Syrian context, then, simplicity could be argued to be "natural" for Christians or "a natural way to be Christian" because the ideal of simplicity was already a marked feature of Syrian self-perception and was fed by the competition with Lebanon.

THEOLOGY, ECONOMY, AND GIFT

For persons such as Kamal, Bassam, Abu Rafi, and Pierre, the ideal of simplicity was of central importance. And while this ideal played out in relation to a larger national ideal of simplicity, it also encompassed understandings of Catholic theology. Another feature of the tension between opulence and simplicity is revealed here: namely, that especially devoted lay people would frame the discussion in terms of Jesus's relation to commerce and wealth. The sayings attributed to Jesus make clear that possession of riches is difficult to align with walking the straight and narrow path. Jesus for instance famously posits that it may be easier for a camel to go through the eye of a needle than for a rich man to enter the kingdom of heaven.[19] The Syrian priest to apply this saying most forcefully has been the well-known Father Elias Zahlawi, who used it in several of his sermons in his parish church (the Church of Our Lady of Damascus) and at the shrine of Our Lady of Soufanieh.

During the fall of 2009, Father Zahlawi used several sermons to admonish his flock against what he called love of riches, *ḥubb al-māl*.[20] In one of his sermons delivered at the shrine of Our Lady of Soufanieh, Father Zahlawi started his exposition with Jesus's parable of the poor man named Lazarus.[21] Lazarus is a beggar living next to a rich man, hoping to get whatever is left over from the rich man's table. The poor man dies and is carried by angels to Abraham's side. The rich man also dies. No angels carry him to Abraham, though; he finds himself in torments in hell. Seeing Lazarus at Abraham's side, the rich man asks Abraham to pity him and send Lazarus to alleviate his suffering. "Son, remember that in your lifetime you received your good things while Lazarus received bad things, but now he is comforted here and you are in agony." The rich man then asks Abraham to send Lazarus to his family so that they can avoid his fate. Abraham responds in the negative; the rich man's family has the scriptures, and if they do not believe in them, not even a person returned from the dead could convince them.

Opening with the story of Lazarus and the rich man allows Father Zahlawi to take up the topic of riches today and to criticize at great length the passive adoption of Western values. The West, as the rich man, does not see the needy world. Having established this point, Father Zahlawi ventures a moral hierarchization. At the top is the East, the place where values still persist. At the bottom are Europe and the United States, which in this scheme have sold out their values entirely. Zahlawi does not just hint at this—he spells it out and ranks the United States as the worst case, followed by Europe. What Father Zahlawi presents here is an idea that Christianity is nearer its roots in Syria, and even more so in Damascus, where Paul first met Christ and became the first missionary to the Gentiles. Father Zahlawi then places Syria and the listeners under scrutiny, expanding on the implications for the listeners and for Syrian society if they choose the attitude of the rich man: egoism and a heartless, divided society.

To counter such tendencies, Father Zahlawi underlines giving. One can and must give to become rich. And here another central challenge, according to Father Zahlawi, is that many do not give but want to keep for themselves. Investment not only of money but of time, effort, and energy becomes central to spiritual improvement and maturation, but many are seen as unwilling to make this investment, and thus as cold and indifferent to God's gift.[22]

PRIESTS, POVERTY, AND POSITION

Among those listening to Father Zahlawi and his criticism of riches were Samir and his sister Rula, both in their forties and rather affluent. I caught up with Samir after the service and he invited me to join him on his visit to his sister. As we drove off in Samir's huge green pickup truck, Samir went back to a subject he had brought up before, that he was considering buying a new car. "Have you seen the Porsche

Panamera?" he asked me. I said I had seen it in magazines but not on the street. "It is really a nice car! Luxurious, fast, it has everything," Samir said. I commented on such a car being very expensive. "It's expensive . . . but it is really nice. I am considering buying one. Or if not that one, then an Audi S8 or a Mercedes S500." Given that we had just come from a service where the central message concerned earthly riches, talking about such luxury cars seemed out of place.

After some time, we ended up in Tijara, a mixed middle-class neighborhood. The area was decorated for Christmas with festooned lights and crèches. Samir pointed out that there were fewer Christmas decorations here than in more established Christian areas such as Bab Touma or Bab Sharqi. He then turned to a previous conversation topic on the clergy and its management of the churches. He declared the building and opening of restaurants in some of the churches to be a misjudgment on the part of the clerical leaders. He reflected for a moment and then put it sardonically: "Jesus drove the sellers out of the temple, and now they are bid to enter again by the church!"

Samir was referring to a significant biblical story. In Matthew 21:13, Jesus drives out the sellers and buyers from the temple area in Jerusalem, overturning their tables and benches and saying: "My house will be called a house of prayer, but you are making it a den of robbers." Samir sardonically made the clerical leaders the "robbers" in contemporary Syria. The biblical story makes clear that Jesus is holding the religious establishment accountable. Likewise Samir's juxtaposition of the two cases left no doubt as to who was inviting commerce to the inside of the church; the clergy and religious establishment. Samir's own predilection for fast and luxurious cars apparently was not part of this discussion.

As we digested Samir's cake, his sister, Rula, addressed the sermon delivered by Father Zahlawi: "It was not that spiritual, wasn't he just talking on a lot of different things . . .?" Rula opened the conversation to more and perhaps alternative perspectives. Where many had lauded the sermon, Father Zahlawi's criticism of the rich and those who strove for worldly wealth did not rest easy with her. Rula's concern here suggested that she was reluctant to go all the way with Father Zahlawi, and perhaps even that she had felt intimidated and had somehow found his message disturbing. "Is all wealth bad? Is money used for others not a good thing?" Rula implored as we sat at the table.

TENSION, OR A CATHOLIC FORCE FIELD

A more general look at Catholicism in Syria and beyond easily reveals that a puritan perspective with regard to money is not easily entertained in practice. And this is why we must attend to the constant work of tension, whether between economy and gift or between opulence and simplicity. These tensions are not external to Catholicism but rather endemic parts of a specific Catholic force field. Again, it is no novel insight that revenues and market competition have been an ongoing issue among Catholic monasteries.[23] In some periods of the history of Western Christendom, shrines' dependence on various forms of income has shown Catholicism to be a religious domain that is as financially motivated as any other in society. Christianity for a large part of its history has focused not only on transcendental aspects and spiritual matter but on a significant material aspect in that it has attested to God's perceived nature in architectural form, building God's majesty and splendor into landscapes.[24] Furthermore, such material testimonies to God have been made possible only by wider transactions involving payments of effort, labor, and money.[25] However, such materializations of God's splendor and majesty are countered by an impulse toward purification and simplicity that would reveal God's nature not in instrumentalization but in giving and serving others.

What we find here is again a tension, parallel to the one between opulence and simplicity: the tension between economy and gift. From an economic perspective, the relations between humans and the divine, and among humans, are a system of exchange and reciprocity with obligations, as in the classic Maussian idea of the gift, to give, to receive, and to return.[26] But the gift establishes relationships between giver and recipient, whether in the form of debt, gratitude, or coercion. When we look at the system as one of exchange, we home in on economy, even if what is exchanged or paid is not money but various forms of offerings and gifts. But as David Morgan says of Catholic devotion, "Praise is the coin one pays to entreat attention and favor."[27] In other words, it is the establishment of various forms of relationships that matters, relationships that reflect the whole range of human emotions and affectivity from sorrow, despair, agony, and fear, to happiness and joy, but also indifference and lack of interest.[28]

However, the radical phenomenological thinker and Catholic philosopher Jean-Luc Marion, inspired by Jacques Derrida, has raised a problem with anthropological readings of the gift: they tend to obscure and reduce the phenomenon of givenness as a more general human feature by conceiving of reciprocity as an already established general system and key analytic.[29] Marion thus takes a criticism formulated by Derrida into a Catholic domain. In Marion's radical reading, a gift must be understood outside and even before a system of exchange. It must be conceived outside reciprocity.

In a Syrian Catholic context, as in practical life more widely, the gift and the system economy never exist entirely outside each other. Gift and economy rather present a tension between different perspectives, where the gift establishes relations that are never merely economic, and where economy may never be devoid of moments where gifts suspend any given system of exchange. Or, as William A. Christian once presented in his seminal studies of religious life in rural Spain, different relationships with the divine coexist, some tending toward practical aid and others toward purification.[30] Where this may very well be valid as a characterization of Catholic traits, I will add that Catholicism is animated in a tense force field of gift and economy, and of simplicity and opulence. In this force field, people move, invest, and pass judgment. The features of such a force field do not work toward resolution but rather continue to ignite emotions and debate, devotion and critique. The tensions allow the Catholic Church to encompass vast differences, differences almost impossible to reconcile. It is exactly for this reason that Schmitt characterized Catholicism as a *complexio oppositorum*.[31]

In this chapter I have argued that tension is a central category to take up analytically and ethnographically with regard to Catholicism. Lived Catholicism is not uniform; rather, it should be seen as a *complexio oppositorum* in which tension keeps this complex of differences together. The central role of tension—between simplicity and opulence, and between gift and economy—is that it introduces a particular form of movement in what I have termed the Catholic force field. The Catholic force field is actualized in the tensions over how to situate relations to money and economy vis-à-vis gift and giving. Here tensions are always played out locally, and we see how Catholicism is stretched between an idea of the universal church and its local inflections. In a Syrian context, Catholics draw on the repository of saintly figures, emphasizing the ideals of simplicity and giving; however, this does not prevent the clergy from using giving and the bonds of obligation instrumentally. Debates over the use and misuse of money in a Syrian setting illustrate a Catholic tension in a general sense and provide a local inflection where the stakes are played out in a particular manner. The Syrians I described in this chapter may have difficulty determining what the proper role of the church is in their lives, but the tension in not actually getting things right is never merely a by-product of human failure; rather, it is often the very motor. Whereas Pierre ended up entering a monastery in Lebanon after being troubled by the developments in Syrian society, Samir continued to remain skeptical of the church and its economy while still driving his fancy cars. In this sense, a Catholic economy of the sacred is never able to do away with this tension; instead it is animated by it. Consequently the apparent contradiction between opulence and simplicity will not be resolved. Rather, it remains a productive matrix where Catholics and Catholicism itself is being constantly reconfigured. The Bishop of Bling may not be an ideal figure, but he is a necessary adversary for Pope Francis so that the tension between opulence and the ideal of poverty can be played out.

NOTES

The author wants to thank Tom Boylston, Martin Demant Frederiksen, Regnar Albæk Kristensen, and Maya Mayblin for productive readings and engagements with earlier versions of this chapter. Funding for fieldwork was generously covered by the Danish Research Council for Independent Research in the Humanities.

1. Morgan (2009, 49; 2012a); see also Mayblin (2010, 2014b).

2. On the current situation for Syrian Christians, see Bandak (2014).

3. For numbers, see Abdu (2003). The general demographic development for Christians in the region before the uprisings is discussed by Courbage and Fargues ([1997] 1998) and Pacini (1998).

4. Kamal Salibi ([1988] 2003) in his work on Lebanon and the role of Christians in its history describes how the various Christian Catholic denominations in the wider Levant made their terms with Rome. The Melchites were, in the eyes of Rome, heirs to the true patriarchs of Antioch, even though the schism of 1054 saw the Melchites outside the established communion (74). The Melchites in Syria and predominantly around the city of Aleppo were among the first to identify an Arab conscious-ness as well as to make a more formal recognition of Rome (Masters 2001). In 1683 the archbishop of Tyre's recognition of the pope's supremacy resulted in a split into what are today known as Greek Catholics and the Greek Orthodox. By 1724 the Greek Catholics had established an Arabized version of their church with a native Arab clergy replacing the otherwise Greek clergy (Salibi [1988] 2003, 39ff.). The Maronites, more numerous in Lebanon, formally recognized Rome as early as 1180, but Rome's interest in the Levant only grew as the Reformation threatened the true faith in Europe proper when new missions were sent to the Near East to proselytize and seek new converts (Masters 2001, 70; see also Salibi [1988] 2003, 72; Degeorge 2004, 159–60). For a wider anthropological engagement with Greek Catholicism, see Mahieu and Naumescu (2008).

5. Bartlett (2013, 65ff.).

6. Orsi (2005, 184ff.).

7. Weber ([1905] 2001); Schmitt ([1923] 1996).

8. Bialecki (2008, 2014); Haynes (2012); and more generally Peebles (2012).

9. For a wider discussion of Christian perceptions of urban space and coexistence, see Bandak (2014) and also Mayeur-Jaouen (2012).

10. In particular the Christian quarters of the Old City of Damascus saw an enormous influx of money for the building of restaurants and boutique hotels in the 1990s and 2000s (Salamandra 2004).

11. See also Keane (2007, 270–84).

12. Riegelhaupt (1984) and Badone (1990).

13. Bandak and Boylston (2014).

14. Hermkens, Jansen, and Notermans (2009).

15. See van Dam (1996) and Perthes ([1995] 1997).

16. Lesch (2005).

17. Chalcraft (2009).

18. See also Wedeen (2013).

19. Matt. 19:21–24.

20. I concentrate here on the sermons delivered on November 7 and December 24, but see also his publications (e.g., Zahlawi [2009]; Bandak [2015]).

21. Luke 16:19–31.

22. See Bandak (2013).

23. Eade and Sallnow (1991).

24. See Cannell (2006).

25. See Brown (1981) and Geary (1990, 1994).

26. Mauss ([1954] 1990).

27. Morgan (2012a, 25).

28. See Orsi (1985, 1996, 2005).

29. Jean-Luc Marion (2008, see also 2002).

30. William A. Christian ([1972] 1989, 168).

31. Schmitt ([1923] 1996).

13

The Paradox of Charismatic Catholicism

Rupture and Continuity in a Q'eqchi'-Maya Parish

Eric Hoenes del Pinal

The title of this essay plays on the titles of a couple of influential articles written by Joel Robbins in which he critiques the tendency of anthropologists studying Christianity to highlight continuities between pre- and postmissionized cultures.[1] Robbins's argument stems from his work with Pentecostals in Papua New Guinea,[2] and he suggests that part of the reason that anthropologists have failed to recognize Christianity's role in processes of change has to do with the way that Pentecostal and charismatic forms of Christianity articulate with non-Christian cultures. Global Pentecostalism, he proposes, presents a sort of paradox in that it is a "religion that localizes easily yet claims to brook no compromise with traditional life and that at the same time seems to have at its heart a set of globalized practices that often look very local in their makeup."[3] The way that Pentecostalism paradoxically mixes the local and the global, the past and the present, has led anthropologists, who already have a "bias towards continuity thinking," to minimize instances of real change, and hence to undertheorize the extent to which Christianity can have transformative effects on traditional societies and cultures.[4] Moreover, these characterizations fly in the face of ethnographic consultants' claims about their conversion to Christianity. Instead, Robbins argues, scholars need to take seriously people's claims that conversion entails significant personal transformations and to acknowledge that Christianity has the power to be disruptive, not because it as an imposition from the outside, but precisely because people take it up in service of their own projects. Part of our task, then, is to understand how local actors frame Christianity in terms of marking their present lives as distinct from their former ones—or, to put it another way, to understand how continuity and rupture organize their stances toward what it means to be a Christian.

I want to follow this point about continuity and rupture here, but in taking Charismatic Catholicism as my object of study I find the need to amend some of what Robbins has said. Given that it has had a longer term of engagement with local cultures than the forms of Pentecostalism Robbins is primarily interested in, might we, in fact, find a different set of problems or paradoxes when we look at "global Catholicism"? Could we say, given its record in Latin America, that Catholicism is a religion that is in fact quite open to compromises with local cultures— what Catholic theologians sometimes talk about as the "inculturation" of the faith[5]—despite its claims to universality? Or that perhaps its claims to universality enable it as a global institution to accommodate competing and potentially diametrically opposed sets of ideas and practices in what Carl Schmitt (1996, 7) has characterized as a "*complexio oppositorum*"?[6]

Though I cannot offer final answers these questions here, I believe that Charismatic Catholicism might be especially worth thinking about as we approach the question of how to formulate an anthropology of Catholicism because of the way it sits uneasily between normative characterizations of both Catholicism and Pentecostal/charismatic Christianity more generally.[7] As some of my consultants in the Guatemalan parish I call San Felipe liked to point out, some of the practices of Charismatic Catholics are strikingly similar to those of Pentecostals;[8] and yet, rather than converting to these other "sects," Charismatics insist on retaining ties with the Catholic Church's established institutional bodies, even though in many villages and hamlets the Catholic lay leadership is overtly hostile to (and at the very least vocally critical of) the Charismatics and their claims to institutional belonging. If, as Robbins has suggested, a key concern in the anthropology of Christianity has been to correct our tendency to see continuities despite our informants' claims of rupture, the question that arises from this case is, How do we interpret our ethnographic subjects' claims of continuity when these appear to be contradicted by quite evident signs of disjuncture? To put it more concretely, how do we make sense of Catholic Charismatics' claims that they are Catholics—and the most devout ones at that—when their ritual practices would seem to place them firmly in the camp of Pentecostals?

In the next section I trace out some of the consequences of this paradox before offering some insight into how it is partially resolved in the discursive strategies that San Felipe's Catholic Charismatics employ to mediate between continuity and rupture as part of their project to renew Catholicism.

THE CATHOLIC CHARISMATIC RENEWAL MOVEMENT

Charismatic Catholicism's origins can be traced to a series of prayer meetings held by a group of Catholic faculty members and students in 1967 at Duquesne University in Pittsburgh, Pennsylvania. As the story goes, the group had been reading about and had become interested in ecstatic religious experience—in particular the doctrine of the gifts of the spirit ("charisms")—so in the spirit of ecumenism they invited a group of local Pentecostals to join them for a weekend retreat. At this retreat, several Catholic participants had experiences that they interpreted as being "baptized in the Spirit," which included manifesting glossolalia or "speaking in tongues."[9] Convinced that they had been touched directly by the Holy Spirit, they began to invite other Catholics to join them in sharing this experience of spiritual renewal. Many of those visitors did, and went on to establish new groups throughout the northeastern and midwestern United States. Though these groups tended to be independent lay-led groups, some of them received the explicit support of parish priests, and a number of clergy also became involved in the nascent movement. By 1970 the Catholic Charismatic Renewal Movement (CCRM), as it had come to be known, established a National Service Committee to coordinate the various prayer groups' activities and advocate for formal institutional recognition of its activities in the United States. Five years later a similar organization—the International Communications Office—began to do so on a global scale.

Although strong ecumenism was a characteristic of the movement's beginnings, as it grew members of the CCRM increasingly came to identify themselves first and foremost with the Catholic Church, and the movement distanced itself from other forms of Pentecostal/charismatic Christianity. Though members of the earliest groups often referred to themselves as "Catholic Pentecostals" or "Pentecostal Catholics," the "Pentecostal" label gradually gave way to "Charismatic" as a way for members to differentiate themselves from other Pentecostals.[10] Movement leaders became very concerned with maintaining an affiliation with the institutional Catholic Church and began lobbying the Vatican for formal recognition, which was eventually granted to them by Pope Paul VI in 1975.[11] Papal recognition, however, came with the condition that CCRM groups would remain under strict sacerdotal supervision wherever they convened in the hopes that this would ensure that the CCRM would not stray too far from Catholic orthodoxy.[12]

The CCRM grew rapidly over the next three decades, and by 2005 (roughly the ethnographic present for this essay's case study) the Vatican estimated that approximately 120 million people—or a little more than 11 percent of all Catholics worldwide—belonged to the movement.[13] Latin America in particular became a growth area for the CCRM, with somewhere upwards of 73 million or 60 percent of Charismatic Catholics living in the region.[14]

Charismatic Catholicism's origins and rapid growth came during a period of major reform within the Catholic Church. It is well known that the Second Vatican Council (which met between 1962 and 1965), ushered in significant reforms to Catholic practice that sought to establish and cultivate new forms of lay participation,[15] and despite the CCRM's claims to divine inspiration it is important to historicize its emergence in this context. Arguably, the CCRM was able to gain a foothold within the larger global institution of the Catholic Church in part because its organizational structure of lay-led prayer meetings dovetailed with those of other initiatives such as Catholic Action and to a lesser extent the Cursillo movement.[16] Moreover, the CCRM's relatively more conservative politics meant that Popes John Paul II and Benedictine XVI among others saw it as a positive counterbalance to more socially progressive movements that were trying to gain a foothold in the Latin American Church at the time.[17]

Nonetheless, because of its ecumenical origins and because the practices of its members were heterodox, it was not a given that the Vatican would accept the CCRM. Rather, it is important to recognize the extent to which the latter's integration into the Catholic Church (and the fact that it did not splinter off to join other forms of Pentecostal/charismatic Christianity) was facilitated by the advocacy of several highly regarded theologians. The Belgian bishop Cardinal Leo Jozef Suenens (1904–96), who was a leading voice at Vatican II, came to be a particularly strong advocate of the CCRM within the Catholic episcopacy. Suenens interpreted the CCRM's desire for spiritual renewal as working in tandem with the church's larger project for *aggiornamento*, and he authored several theological works to align the movement's lay-centered practices with the Vatican's vision of Catholicism's future. Suenens argued that the CCRM played an important role within Catholicism in that it fulfilled Vatican II's calls for holiness and mission.[18] Specifically, he argued that the charisms that members of the CCRM experienced were authentic signs of divine grace and constituted a new Pentecost for the church,[19] and that as such they should be understood as a spirit-filled part of the general institutional renewal that the church sought through its recommitment to lay participation.[20] Near the end of his life, Suenens stated, "To interpret the [Catholic Charismatic] Renewal as a 'movement' among other movements is to misunderstand its nature; it is a movement of the Spirit offered to the entire Church and destined to rejuvenate every part of the Church's life."[21] Thus, whatever may be said about the historical circumstances surrounding the CCRM's emergence and acceptance, and the extent to which acceptance of the CCRM was a strategic move to retain numbers in places where Pentecostalism was growing or counteract other movements within Catholicism, we must also recognize that within the church there was a strong effort to justify it on theological grounds.[22]

The institutional history of the CCRM can thus be read as one in which questions of rupture and continuity have been at the forefront from the beginning. The movement's divinely inspired foundation during the Duquesne retreat, if this is read as a singular rupturing event, might well have led to schismatic separation from the Catholic Church. Yet following that event, aligning the two became a guiding concern for the larger institutional organs of the church, as well as for individual Charismatic Catholic communities as they came under the umbrella of national and international organizational committees.

This alignment has continued to be a major cause for concern because, despite Charismatics' insistence on their self-identification as Catholics, their critics can readily point to apparent discontinuities between local normative assumptions about how Catholics should act and what Charismatics do (or are imagined to do) when they gather among themselves. When these criticisms specifically point to the observable praxiological and theological continuities between the CCRM and non-Catholic forms of Pentecostal/charismatic Christianity, it is not difficult for outsiders to claim that there is very little that is Catholic about Catholic Charismatics. The next section examines some of the ways that San Felipe's Catholic Charismatics negotiate this tension.

SAN FELIPE

In San Felipe questions of continuity and rupture are central to the way that members of Catholic Charismatic and Mainstream Catholic congregations relate to each other.[23] Though the CCRM was introduced to Guatemala in 1973, and at the time of my fieldwork (2004–6) Charismatic Catholicism accounted for perhaps 60 percent of the country's Catholics, it had been a presence in San Felipe only for about eight years and was undoubtedly a minority religious position within the parish.[24] There were only four active groups in the parish (compared to 122 Mainstream ecclesial base communities [CEBs]), the largest of which, in a village I call Sa'xreb'e, drew between sixty and ninety congregants to its semiweekly services. By comparison, there were four Mainstream CEBs in the same village, each of which had congregations that were at least twice as large as the sole Charismatic one. Nonetheless, Sa'xreb'e's congregation had been quite successful, growing from a handful of members who had first come into contact with the CCRM in a neighboring village to becoming the largest Charismatic congregation in the parish.

Sa'xreb'e's success was due in part to the fact that its home base was in a large village close to a major highway and so could draw from a sizable population to begin with, and in part to its two leaders' effectiveness in "animating" their twice-weekly meetings. Hermano Guillermo, who was older of the two, had joined the CCRM first,[25] and though he was less comfortable speaking Spanish than Q'eqchi' he often took the lead in preaching, as he had a facility for putting together relatively lengthy but interesting sermons. Hermano Rigo, the younger of the two, was fully bilingual in Spanish and Q'eqchi', and likewise an accomplished speaker, but he preached less because he was also the leader and keyboard player in the choir band that provided the musical accompaniment to their meetings. Additionally they counted on the support of a core group of about fifteen others who played in the choir band, led prayers, and performed other tasks to keep the congregation active. Before converting to the CCRM, both Guillermo and Rigo had been well-regarded Mainstream catechists. Hermano Rigo, in particular, was considered a sort of rising star by the parish leadership, and his former fellow catechists took his conversion as an especially worrisome instance of Charismatic Catholicism's ability to siphon off members from their own CEBs.

In addition to the worry that Charismatics would cease attending CEB meetings, Mainstream Catholics cited a number of other reasons for disliking Charismatic Catholicism, including that the latter's members abstained from participating in traditional rituals and that they had set up a parallel structure of lay authority that challenged their own. However, in interviews and conversation the most common reasons given involved Charismatics' newly adopted modalities of communicative and expressive behavior in ritual settings.[26] As one senior Mainstream catechist—Qawa Emanuel—put it while explaining why he objected to letting the Charismatics use the village chapel as Father Augustine said they could, "Parecen puros protestantes" (They seem just like Protestants). They seemed just like Protestants because they were always "yelling in Spanish," which, he complained, kept him up at night. Qawa Emanuel was far from alone in characterizing Charismatics in this way, and as CCRM groups had spread through the parish significant social conflicts had arisen between Mainstream and Charismatic Catholics. The crux of the problem, of course, wasn't just that Charismatics sounded like Protestants but that they did so while also demanding and (what was worse) receiving access to the Catholic Church's material resources—namely village chapels and the expensive electricity they used to power their sound system. *Evangélicos*—a broad category that encompasses all non-Catholic Christians but especially indexes Pentecostals in Guatemala—were a religious other and not particularly well liked, but, Qawa Emanuel reasoned, at least they'd been clear in their intentions to separate themselves from the church completely.[27] These Charismatic interlopers, on the other hand, wanted to have their proverbial cake and eat it, too, even though they looked and sounded like Pentecostals.

San Felipe's Catholic Charismatics, for their part, denied that they were Pentecostals and instead emphatically declared themselves not just to be Catholics but to be Catholics involved in an especially important project of spiritual renewal. Congregants were to various extents aware of the institutional history of the CCRM I outlined above and had incorporated key parts of it in their narratives about who they were and why their practices differed from those of Mainstream Catholics. One congregant, for example, explained that Mainstream Catholics had misinterpreted the story of the Duquesne retreat and that this was why they criticized Charismatics for being *evangélicos*.[28] Rigo and Guillermo knew about Cardinal Suenens and his defense of the movement from reading some of the CCRM's Spanish-language publications. For all Charismatics, too, the idea that they were part of a genuine renewal of Catholicism was central to their self-identity *qua* Catholics; and in fact they preferred to identify their organization simply as "la Renovación" (the renewal) to emphasize this.

However, adopting membership in la Renovación as a badge of identity, successfully claiming that affiliation in the face of a hostile majority that sees you as
outsiders, and articulating exactly what it means to be renewing Catholicism are
not necessarily the same things. Instead, we might understand these as discrete
parts of a complex narrative project with significant social stakes. Because Charismatics' identity is subject to monitoring from both within and outside the group's
boundaries, the group's leadership faces the daunting task of finding a way of figuring themselves and their congregations so that they can successfully claim a
place within the institutional bodies of the Catholic Church, while simultaneously
ensuring that their congregants recognize that their form of religiosity is distinct
from the majority's Mainstream Catholicism as well as that of *evangélicos*. How,
then, do San Felipe's Charismatics accomplish this? And how can we better understand this process? One way is to examine how group leaders mobilize linguistic
and discursive resources to enact their particular kind of religiosity.

Elsewhere I have examined the communicative practices of Mainstream and
Charismatic Q'eqchi'-Maya Catholics using the framework of language ideology to
argue that the congregations' differing communicative styles are metadiscursively
regimented by their particular theological commitments.[29] Here I take a slightly
different tack by focusing on exactly how Catholic Charismatics marshal specific
linguistic and discursive resources to constitute themselves as a discrete religious
community.

Linguistic anthropologists interested in examining how social actors dialogically
and intersubjectively take up positions with respect to the form and/or content of
their utterances have become increasingly interested in theorizing stance and stance
taking.[30] Stance is in some respects a slippery theoretical construct that has slightly
different meanings for anthropologists, linguists, and sociolinguists, but generally
the term is invoked to talk about how speaking subjects strategically manipulate
discourse to variously position themselves in relation to the other subjects, objects,
and systems of meaning implicated by their utterances.[31] A speaker's stance might be
a commentary on the sort of social voice(s) that she imagines her utterance connotes, on the social system in which the utterance is embedded, on the epistemic
quality of the utterance, or on present or imagined interlocutors. I find the concept
useful here because it provides us a way of analyzing the interactive mobilization of
discourse in identity formation,[32] so it offers a key for understanding how preachers
and prayer leaders articulate and put into circulation certain models of moral personhood (i.e., a vision for what it means to be a member of the CCRM) through talk.
By attending to how various subject positions are invoked in talk, we can examine
how Charismatics present, justify, or typify the social meanings and values that they
view as central to their religious identity. Specifically, we can see how they create a
discrete religious identity by variously aligning themselves and their congregants (a)
as members of a cohesive religious community, (b) as participants in a larger institu-

tional project (the CCRM), and (c) as authentic Christians, while (d) also distancing themselves from nonpresent religious others, including both Mainstream Catholics and *evangélicos*. We can thus get a clearer picture of how Catholic Charismatics mediate continuities and ruptures in their religious identity, though juggling these vectors of identification can be difficult even for experienced preachers. The following examples illustrate the first part of this process.

Example 1

At a Charismatic meeting a prayer leader asks the congregation to pray with him over a preacher (Hermano Guillermo) who is about to deliver the sermon. Underlined text denotes Q'eqchi', italicized text denotes Spanish, bold text denotes words that are bivalent in the two languages, and the author's comments are in plain text.

1. Junelik chi xyaal sa' komonil xeek'aakilal xwankilal li Santil Musiqe.
2. *Entonces* taakanab' li qu sa' xb'een li *hermano*
3. ut naaqaye chi re li **Dios** chi joka'in
4. *Padre bendito*
5. *En esta noche, Señor*
6. *Nos encontramos*
7. *De nuevo, Padre, en este lugar (.)*
8. *Una vez mas Señor Jesús::*
9. *Este varón se inclina (.) delante de ti (.)*
10. *Porque es un (.) un hijo tuyo*
11. *Que los has escogido Señor (.)*
12. *Y lo has elegido para predicar tu palabra*
13. *Pon lo, Señor, tu Palabra (.) en la boca de este hombre*
14. *Como le hiciste a Elías, Señor::*
15. *Como le hiciste a* [unintelligible], *Padre*
16. *Pon tu mano divina sobre este hombre, Señor Jesús*
17. *Dale palabras para predicar, Señor*

1. It is always true that among us [in a group] we feel the power of the Holy Spirit.
2. *Then* we will place our hands over the *brother*
3. and [we] say to **God** like this
4. *Blessed Father*
5. *On this night, Lord*
6. *We find ourselves*
7. *Once again, Father, in this place (.)*
8. *Once again, Lord Jesus::*
9. *This man kneels (.) in front of you (.)*
10. *Because he is a (.) a son of yours*
11. *That you have chosen, Lord (.)*
12. *And you have chosen him to preach your Word*
13. *Put it, Lord, your Word (.) in the mouth of this man*

14. *As you did to Elijah, Lord::*
15. *As you did to* [unintelligible], *Father*
16. *Put your divine hand over this man, Lord Jesus*
17. *Give him words to preach, Lord*

This excerpt can roughly be divided into two parts: (1) a brief introduction to the ritual addressed to the congregation (lines 1–3); and (2) the prayer proper (lines 4–17). The prayer can itself be broken down into three subsections that topicalize distinct aspects of what is to be accomplished: (a) the setting (lines 6–8); (b) the prayer's intended subject, namely the preacher (lines 9–12); and (c) the objective of the prayer (lines 13–18).

The prayer leader's introductory statements are notably marked off from the prayer proper by the code-switch he effects from Q'eqchi' in lines 1 through 3 to Spanish from line 4 onward.[33] The code-switch also marks changes in the intended audience as well as the speech genre being performed—from organizational talk addressed to his co-congregants to prayer addressed to God. This is to say that the speaker's shifts in footing and genre are reinforced by a change in the linguistic code he uses.[34] Moreover, the code-switch serves to align the actions of congregants by making certain patterns of linguistic use (e.g., the use of Spanish) a crucial part of their co-participation in the ritual and thus highlighting this linguistic choice as a salient feature of their religious identity. As I've noted above, much of the criticism that Charismatics endure from their neighbors is based precisely on their marked use of Spanish, and although Mainstream Catholics tend to hyperbolize the extent to which Charismatics speak Spanish, the use of Spanish, as this excerpt makes clear, is ritually meaningful in CCRM meetings.

A further alignment takes place at a grammatical level. The prayer leader begins using an indefinite third-person construction (line 1), but by line 2 he commits the congregation to take a particular course of action by using a first-person plural future tense construction ("We will lay our hands"). In line 3 he shifts to the present tense while retaining the first-person plural in the present ("We say . . . like this"). At one level this series of shifts is quite mundane, and speakers in a variety of contexts regularly perform similar moves, but in this context by following this order the prayer leader effectively aligns the congregation's course of action with his own words. When he moves to the prayer itself, the preacher takes up the first-person plural voice to address God and in doing so effectively speaks for the congregation as a collective (even though each of them is ideally offering his or her own individualized version of the prayer as well). This alignment of many people's actions with the words of a single speaker makes the congregational life of the group manifest. This is reinforced by the content of line 6, in which the speaker specifically expresses a sense of being together ("We find ourselves") and a little later, in lines not transcribed here, by a declaration of mutual intentionality ("We want to hear your word, / We want to hear your voice, Lord").

Equally important to the creation of a unified congregation (which is set off against Mainstream Catholics by code choice) is the establishment of several key doctrinal points that are put into the mouths and minds of the congregants through this shared prayer. Most obviously, the prayer invokes God's direct and immediate intervention into the ritual by asking God to touch the preacher (line 16) and put his words in the preacher's mouth (i.e., give him the skill to preach; lines 13, 17). Moreover, several lines later (not transcribed here) the prayer leader asks God to give the congregation the capacity to hear and fully understand the sermon. A corollary to this idea is present in lines 11 through 12, when the prayer leader states that this preacher has been chosen directly by God. This is important because CCRM preachers are self-selected, whereas the clergy select Mainstream Catholic lay leaders (catechists), who are thus more closely aligned with the institutional hierarchy of the church.[35] This kind of immediate intervention is not a feature of Mainstream Catholic prayer, and is part of the way in which the distinction is created between the groups.

Lines 14 through 15 establish the historical precedent for the subject of the prayer (i.e., giving the preacher the ability to preach clearly) and implicitly equate Hermano Guillermo with biblical prophets—a telling allusion because it provides an epistemic basis for the claim that this Charismatic congregation in the Guatemalan highlands is a legitimate descendant of a biblical lineage. Statements such as this one evince the idea that Charismatic Catholicism is a renewal movement that seeks to revive an earlier, more authentic version of Christianity. It also points to one of the more Catholic aspects of Charismatic Catholicism insofar as it draws a direct lineage from the biblical past to the present as a means of establishing that this as the one true universal church.

Example 2

Having been prayed over by the congregation, Hermano Guillermo begins to deliver his sermon and in the course of doing so comes to a point at which he wants to frame the work of the CCRM as an ethical project that congregants have to take up both for personal moral cultivation and for the cause of revitalizing Catholicism as a whole. As he is developing this idea, Guillermo begins to offer specific ways congregants may do this, eventually coming to a discussion of using mass media sources to further their religious development.[36] As we see below, in doing so he encounters a problem that must be resolved.

1. Wan *emisora, hermanos,* wan kaqreru wan::
2. *Radio Estrella,* aran taawab'i li *mejor predicación.*
3. Wi ink'a naroq sa' laa *radio* taaloq laa *casete* re *predicación*
4. re:: *osea* re *católica.*
5. Malaj re li *Renovación carismática católica* junajaj.
6. *pero* wan a'an naxnaw *casete* aj re:: ajwi chi *evangélica* naxloq a'an wi loq chi rab'inkil (.)

   7. Ink'a, mejor ma sach *hermanos*
   8. nab'al anwan yoo xq'eb'al *confiar* sa' li emisora a'an
   9. Ink'a *hermanos* taake taawix loq'al li Qawa **Dios** b'ar wan.
  10. Wan sa' li *Renovación carismática católica. Amén?*

   1. There is *[a] radio station, brothers,* there are some, there is::
   2. *Radio Estrella,* there you will hear *the best preaching*
   3. If it doesn't come in on your *radio,* go buy your *cassette* of *preaching*
   4. of:: *that is* of *Catholic [preaching].*
   5. Or of the *Charismatic Catholic Renewal* only.
   6. *But* there are, one knows, *cassettes* of:: also of *Evangelical [preaching],* buy that,
      if you buy that to listen to (.)
   7. No, *better* to forget *[it], brothers*
   8. Many now are giving their *trust* to those *stations*
   9. No, *brothers,* you will give your faith/respect to the Lord **God** where *[he]* is.
  10. He is in/with the *Catholic Charismatic Renewal. Amen?*

In proposing that congregants might make use of radio broadcasts and cassette tape sermons—the two most accessible and popular forms of media in San Felipe— Hermano Guillermo comes to the realization that there is a danger that those who take up such a project of self-study might carry it out incorrectly. His specific worry is one that echoes that of the CCRM's critics—namely that Catholics might mistakenly adopt *evangélico* products and practices as their own. To this end Hermano Guillermo offers a warning and clarification about which media congregants should use, but in doing so his message becomes a bit muddied. He begins by naming a specific radio station that carries the right sort of programming (Radio Estrella). He follows this up by suggesting that if congregants can't tune in to this radio station (a real possibility given the hilly topography of Sax'reb'e) they can buy cassettes of preaching instead (line 3). However, perhaps realizing that the majority of religious cassettes that circulate in the marketplace are produced by *evangélicos,* he repairs his statement by specifying that these should be Catholic tapes (line 4), but then qualifies this statement further by saying they should buy Charismatic Catholic tapes "only" (line 5). However, though he sets out that qualification, he then backtracks to discuss Protestant tapes again, making overt the implicit understanding that this other category of media exists. More troublingly, he seems to suggest that they should listen to *evangélico* cassettes. It is in fact not uncommon for Charismatics to consume *evangélico*-produced media, and Charismatic preachers even use such media to help prepare their sermons.[37] However, in this context the suggestion is dissonant with his larger point,[38] and he finds he must repair the statement. He does so in lines 7 and 8 by warning that though many others now trust and listen to Protestant radio and tapes, his interlocutors should not. Instead, they should praise God where he really is—with the Charismatic Catholic Renewal. He closes with an "Amen" in a rising intonation, thus formulating it as a question that looks to the congregation for confirmation that they have understood and are in agreement. The congregation's responding "Amen" closes this segment.

If the first example showed how a prayer leader sought to align congregants' actions to produce a sense of group cohesion, this second example helps illustrate the tenuous balancing act that is involved in doing being a Charismatic Catholic in San Felipe.[39] Coherently articulating the importance of moral self-formation, institutional allegiances, and the pressures of ecumenicalism can be problematic for the very people charged with leading the congregation. The formal similarities of Pentecostalism and Charismatic Catholicism mean that there is always a very real possibility that congregants may misrecognize *evangélico* media as their own precisely when the distinction between the two needs to be clearest. By overtly referencing religious media, Guillermo inadvertently indexes the reality of a larger religious marketplace in which parishioners as a matter of course don't always leave boundaries between categories uncrossed.[40] By trying to align congregants' future actions with the specific moral project of the CCRM, Guillermo thus inadvertently opens up the possibility that they might stray from normative expectations of how they are to accomplish this project and might instead fulfill their critics' condemnation of them as crypto-*evangélicos*. It is no surprise, then, that despite what appear to be the clear intentions of his sermon he has difficulty in putting it all together and finds he has to repair his speech several times to align disparate ideas.

By examining these examples and emphasizing the discursive moves that the group's leader must make to enact a vision of what it means to be a Catholic Charismatic in San Felipe, I hope to have problematized the question of how people come to see themselves as participating in Catholicism more broadly.

As I've shown here, the problem of just how Charismatic Catholicism interfaces with the larger body of the Catholic Church recurs at a number of levels—evincing a number of different formulations of continuity and rupture between the two. Justifying the movement's position within the larger church can remain problematic even for highly committed members like Hermano Guillermo; and despite the work that Cardinal Suenens did to legitimize the movement within the Vatican, in San Felipe its place was not yet guaranteed in the mid-2000s.[41]

The case of San Felipe's Catholic Charismatics points us to a number of potentially interesting issues for the anthropology of Catholicism. First, it serves as a reminder that we ought to be cognizant of the multiple ways in which Catholicism is enacted at a local level. Specifically, it alerts us to the need to examine when and how groups of Catholics make differences between themselves and others salient and to investigate the stakes of these claims to difference. As Edward Cleary has noted, "There is no 'pure' Catholic Charismatic model,"[42] and even within Latin America there are significant differences in the social and cultural dynamics of this one movement within the church. In fact, it was clear in Alta Verapaz that the tensions that troubled San Felipe's Catholics were absent in neighboring parishes, where Charismatics not only coexisted peacefully with other Catholic groups but also frequently overlapped in their memberships.

Second, the case suggests that we can productively expand on the first point by attending to how particular communities articulate their membership in the larger transnational body of Catholicism. Interrogating the social and moral projects that are implied by these articulations and analyzing the resources, discursive and otherwise, that are mobilized in their pursuit allow us to examine local instantiations of macro-level issues central to Catholicism. In what ways might appealing either to long-standing local affiliations, as Mainstream Catholics do in San Felipe, or to broader cosmopolitan imaginings of the Catholic Church, as Charismatics do, shape the ways that they enact Catholicism? Here we might also problematize the extent to which the practices of local communities of Catholics mediate understandings of Catholicism as at once universal and locally grounded and point to how we might think about the paradox of global Catholicism. Does the fact that, despite the Catholic Church's robust global institutions, its membership's practices evince overt differences even within a single ethnically homogeneous parish present a second paradox that we need to consider as we try to account for Catholicism's appeal around the world?

NOTES

1. Robbins (2003a, 2007).
2. Robbins (2004a).
3. Robbins (2003a, 224).
4. Robbins (2007, 10).
5. See, e.g., Irarrázaval (2000).
6. Schmitt ([1923] 1996, 4).
7. I think that this is true both for practicing Catholics themselves and for scholars who study them.
8. The parish name and all personal names are pseudonyms. See below for more details on the parish, as well as Hoenes de Pinal (2009, 2011). This work was initially funded by the Wenner-Gren Foundation and involved approximately twenty months of participant observation research with parishioners and clergy in Cobán, Guatemala. During this period I observed and recorded church services weekly, participated with lay leaders and clergy in nonritual parish activities, and conducted both formal and informal interviews with parishioners and clergy.
9. McGuire (1982); Csordas (1997).
10. McGuire (1982, 4).
11. The International Charismatic Catholic Renewal Services (ICCRS, formerly the International Communications Office) received an official charter from Pope John Paul II in 1993 recognizing it as the central organizing and coordinating institution of the CCRM within the Vatican.
12. Chesnut (2003).
13. International Catholic Charismatic Renewal Services, "About ICCRS," n.d., accessed June 27, 2016, www.iccrs.org/en/about-iccrs/.

14. International Catholic Charismatic Renewal Services, "The CCR," n.d., accessed June 27, 2016, www.iccrs.org/en/the-ccr/; Cleary (2011).

15. See, e.g., Wilde (2007); O'Malley (2008).

16. Nabhan-Warren (2013).

17. Chesnut (2003); Csordas (2007).

18. Cordes (1997).

19. The original Pentecost is described in Acts 2 as the events that occurred at a feast fifty days after the resurrection of Jesus, at which the Holy Spirit was supposed to have descended on the faithful. The sign of this was glossolalia (Acts 2:4).

20. Suenens ([1974] 1975).

21. Quoted in Whitehead (2006, 18).

22. On the Church's acceptance of the CCRM as a strategic move, see, e.g., Chesnut (2003).

23. I use the term *Mainstream Catholic* to refer to the majority, unmarked category of Catholics in the parish. Although the term is not used locally (the opposition is usually formulated in terms of Charismatics and Catechists there), I use it here because it foregrounds the way in which Charismatics are a locally understood as a new and divergent religious identification. It is worth noting, too, that Mainstream Catholicism in San Felipe actually encompasses a range of religious positions, including relatively more orthodox and relatively more syncretic beliefs and practices.

24. Cleary (2011, 242, 243).

25. *Hermano* and *Hermana* are Spanish for "brother" and "sister" and were customarily used by Charismatics as pronouns to address each other. I have retained their use here because this was on way that Charismatics distinguished themselves from Mainstream Catholics, who used Q'eqch'i terms.

26. Hoenes de Pinal (2011).

27. When talking about *evangélicos* San Felipe's Catholics tended to use the term *los hermanos separados* or "the separated brothers."

28. As far as I was able to determine, Mainstream Catholic leaders did not know the Duquesne story, nor did it factor into their dislike of Charismatics.

29. Hoenes de Pinal (2011).

30. Jaffe (2009).

31. Dubois (2007).

32. Bucholtz and Hall (2005).

33. There is also a distinct stylistic shift here, as the text-metricality of the two sections is quite distinct. Note, for example, the parallelism present in lines 7–8, 12–13, and 14–15.

34. On "footing," see Goffman (1981).

35. Hoenes de Pinal (2009).

36. Cf. Hirschkind (2006).

37. Hoenes de Pinal (2009).

38. It is possible that my presence factored into his need to amend his initial statements, since this was one of the first Charismatic meetings that I recorded in Sa'xreb'e. Though I had tried to explain to the groups who I was and what I was doing, the fact that I had spent nearly a year working closely with the clergy and Mainstream Catholics before working with the Charismatics meant that for a while many of them presumed I sympathized with their critics.

39. On "doing being," see Sacks (1984).

40. On the religious marketplace, see Chesnut (2003).

41. Though I have not returned to do formal research in nearly a decade, I had the opportunity to briefly visit the parish in 2013. A number of things had changed, not the least of which was that the parish now offered weekly mass in Spanish at Sax'reb'e's for the benefit of Charismatics in the area, whereas previously all masses had been in Q'eqchi' only.

42. Cleary (2011, 19).

14

The Virgin of Guadalupe and Spectacles of Catholic Evangelism in Mexico

Kristin Norget

The essence of the Baroque entails neither falling into nor emerging from illusion but rather realizing *something in illusion itself, or of tying it to a spiritual* presence *that endows its spaces and fragments with a collective unity.*

—GILLES DELEUZE, *THE FOLD: LIEBNITZ AND THE BAROQUE* (EMPHASIS IN ORIGINAL)

I make my way among the other pilgrims with my friend Margarita slowly up the Calzada de Guadalupe, the wide avenue leading to the Basilica of the Virgin of Guadalupe in Mexico City.[1] Most of us are in small groups, though I see single pilgrims, some barefoot, carrying large framed images of the Virgin on their backs. The closer we get to the Basilica, the thicker the river of pilgrims, the more excited the crowd. We pass clusters of trucks adorned with plastic flowers, images of the Virgin, and colorfully painted banners that identify them (Twenty-First Bicycle Pilgrimage to the Basilica of Our Lady of Guadalupe; Fourteenth Pilgrimage on Foot to Our Lady of Guadalupe; San Felipe Teotlaltzingo de Puebla; Barrio de Papantla Españita, Tlaxcala; San Alfonso Aquixtla, Puebla; Bomintzha, Hidalgo, and so on). People wave at a huge screen that has been erected where the Calzada intersects with Talismán Avenue: "*Look, look, there we are!*" I hear some pilgrims yell; like many others in the crowd, they take photos of themselves with their cell phones as they see their faces appear on the screen.

A couple of hours later, as we approach the very end of the Calzada, a huge speaker system at the basilica entrance emits an animating message to all pilgrims. Reaching the basilica's massive Plaza Mariana, we behold another large screen that has been set up to project the "Mass of the Roses" (*Misa de las Rosas*) that begins at midnight. The plaza is full to the brim, and there are street vendors and phalanxes of police and security agents and young Red Cross volunteers, sifting

FIGURE 14.1. Souvenir photo stall, Cerro de Tepeyac, Mexico City, December 11.

FIGURE 14.2. Pilgrims on Calzada de Guadalupe, Mexico City, 2012.

everywhere through the crowds. In the area close to the entrance to the huge 1970s basilica, metal barriers have been set up in a haphazard pattern to control movement. I scan the plaza, a sea of tents, cardboard sheets, colorful plastic tarps, blankets, and sleeping bags. Many groups wear the same-colored T-shirts—a few others, "pre-Hispanic" or other indigenous clothing. Some pilgrims are perilously close to our feet, huddled up, sound asleep. Most of those who, like us, are on their feet, are pressing toward the basilica itself. At the entrance it is stifling; we are squeezed right together. Finally we reach the security rope; thanks to the press passes Margarita secured earlier in the day, we pass under it and make our way into the cavernous basilica and upstairs, where elite groups are comfortably seated and the media camps—TVAzteca, Televisa, RadioMaría, ESNE (El Sembrador Nueva Evangelización) and so on—have set themselves up.[2] Television cameras are stationed in the balcony overlooking the main stage before the Virgin's image; others are clustered on a smaller outside balcony, taking shots of the river of pilgrims who are in the main plaza below. The scene is bordered along one side by the Old Basilica and other centuries-old buildings that stand in stark contrast to the modern basilica structure.[3] Every place is packed with people, and even up on the balcony it is hard to move.

To one side of the stage, a young seminarian enthusiastically invites various groups of pilgrims to come and offer "serenades" ("Migrants' Serenades," "Workers' Serenades," and so on), others to offer a cheer to the Virgin as if at a sporting event ("*A la Bio, a la Bao, a La Bim Bom Ba, la Virgen, la Virgen!*"). As the boys' choir assembles on the main stage, the huge lights behind the stage turn green, then purple above the massive pipes of the modern organ. The entire scenario is a state of continuous movement, noise, and alternating washes of colored light.

The mass begins with Norberto Rivera, cardinal and primate archbishop of Mexico and archbishop of Mexico City, speaking about the marvel of the Virgin's appearance almost five hundred years before, and the wonder of Pope Francis, selected as "the new missionary of God" some eight months earlier. He greets the pilgrims and the prelates—the bishop of Munich, others from Poland—who have been specially invited. Within the various liturgies themselves are sermons, messages, songs, in many languages, indigenous and European—Mazatec, Latin, Portuguese, French, Italian, Náhuatl, in addition to Spanish. We hear fireworks from outside exploding periodically throughout the ceremony, breaking the aura of solemnity inside the basilica. In his mass homily, Archbishop (and Basilica Rector) Enrique Glennie makes continuous reference to the Virgin's mythic role as transcendent, maternal, and redemptive arbiter-healer:

> Our Mexico is hurt. She suffers for the blood of so many of our Mexican brothers spilled by other brothers driven by the greed, hatred, evil interests, corruption and vices which have immersed our homeland [*patria*] in violence, insecurity and terror. . . . Only the Virgin of Guadalupe can resolve so many seemingly irreconcilable

aspects of our society to build a new culture of peace, respect for life, trust, and mutual aid. In the name of the Holy María de Guadalupe let us proclaim: Enough! [¡*Ya basta!*] Enough of arming ourselves to fight against one another! Enough of the spilling of the blood of innocents! Enough of poisoning our children and youth with drugs! Enough of living spreading corruption and injustice! Enough of murdering so many thousands of innocent babies in the wombs of their mothers!

Glennie's passionate, overtly politico-theological jeremiad, gesturing toward Mexico's narco-violence, the drug addiction of youth, and the "problem" of abortion, is followed by the abrupt entrance of a group of dancers dressed in brilliantly colored tunics and plumed headdresses. The crowd is silent as they advance along the central path in the nave, singing and dancing to the rhythm of shell rattles (*sonajas*) and string instruments, waving incense burners. They pause, spinning and leaping for a few minutes amid the clouds of smoke from incense burners, and then leave. The Mass continues. . . .

. . .

The above description is a compilation of notes from fieldwork conducted in 2013 at the annual celebration of the Virgin of Guadalupe, centered on December 12, in Mexico City.[4] The brown-skinned Virgin of Guadalupe is one of the densest—and dearest—symbols of Mexican nationhood. Commonly regarded as a syncretic fusion of the pre-Hispanic Aztec goddess Tonantzin and the Virgin Mary, she is said to have appeared first to the indigenous peasant (and now saint) Juan Diego in 1521, speaking Náhuatl, at the hill of Tepeyac, where the modern Basilica dedicated to her now sits in the north of Mexico City.[5] Her apparition myth is at the heart of nationalist narratives of *mestizaje* and has been dissected by several historians.[6] December 12, her annual feast day, marks one of the largest Catholic pilgrimages in the world. The event reflects both this historical depth and the Virgin's immense popularity: over the week around December 10 to December 14, the usual trickle of visitors to the Virgin's altar swells to a human deluge as millions from all over the country and beyond flock to the basilica—by bus, motorcycle, car, subway, bicycle, or truck convoy, on foot or on their knees—for an hour, for an afternoon, or sometimes for up to a few days, camping out on the historic plaza or in nearby streets. While there, they may take part in many of the masses that take place all day long, or may merely enter the basilica to visit the Virgin, or may not even take one step inside the church before returning home. The Virgin's feast day then encompasses a wide array of popular practices and actions that follow their own logic of piety, many of them centered in or oriented around local or domestic settings.[7] But the celebration of *La Guadalupana*[8] in Mexico City, still at the legendary site of Tepeyac, is much more than a popular devotional outpouring focused on a famous saint: it is also a richly layered example of the Roman Catholic Church's evangelical forms and of the political theological power of "special effects" in an increasingly mediatized, globalized world. For the main audience of the Virgin's celebration is not only the congregation in the basilica but also television audiences, including the Mexican diaspora, or other Latin Americans living at home or abroad.

The notion of "special effects" is here drawn from De Vries,[9] who underlines both the historical dependence of conceptions of the political domain on the religious and the inherent "natural," ontological relationship between religion and new technological media. While other forms of Christianity clearly also rely heavily on such special effects, I am interested here to explore what may be shaping Catholicism's particular mode of engagement with new media. I thus address in this essay the content of the current mass, multimediated celebration of the Virgin of Guadalupe in Mexico—its *spectacular* forms of representation, its spectrum of prominent indigenous and other culturally plural referents, and so on—as a window onto salient features of Catholic evangelism. For it is not only certain Protestant Christian religions that are busily persuading and stirring potential and already "captured" subjects. In the context of a reactionary response to Vatican II, since the pontificate of John Paul II, the Catholic Church has manifested a renewed missionary-evangelical zeal in efforts to maintain and grow Catholicism in a world where most Catholics now live outside of western Europe, the Church's symbolic heart.

For example, saints like the Virgin of Guadalupe, potent icons of local and national histories and material objects of passionate, sensory devotion, serve to galvanize and *emplace* popular faith in an international and transnational landscape. Prominent saint-focused celebrations, especially at national shrines like that of *La Guadalupana*, also display tendencies within religious forms to engage, seize, and cultivate subjects through and *in* now more expansive modes of experience and dimensions.[10] This is enabled by new media technologies, which also allow Catholicism to move into new corners of everyday life and to reconfigure both the social and the political roles of the institutional church. These modes are thus also *generative,* a salient form of the church's self-reproduction.

How can we theorize the complexity of contemporary public Catholic manifestations like the Virgin's Mexico City celebration—their apparent polycentric and multiperspectival nature, their seeming universal/local, modern/nonmodern contradictions, their pluri-cultural, hypermediated "color" and texture, and thus the sheer *excesses* of signification they set in motion, and in registers now multiplied? With his now classic concept of Catholicism as a "complex of opposites" (*complexio oppositorum*), Carl Schmitt attempted to illuminate precisely such complexity. Schmitt emphasized Catholicism's "elastic form" that can successfully accommodate no end of antitheses, be these concrete or abstract, matter or spirit, *praxis* or *doxa,* without any need for resolution or synthesis.[11] Yet especially as an aesthetic, communicative form, contemporary Catholicism is also unavoidably embedded in flows of information and images outside the conventionally imagined domains of the "religious." Like other global religious forms, Catholicism might therefore be seen as an ever-adapting complex political-theological system; yet there is something singular about the way that this system's ontology and architecture are manifested.

In this discussion I use the frame of the *neobaroque* as a way of productively illuminating dimensions of this unique complexity in a way that Schmitt's model does not. One might say that baroque Catholicism is the par excellence aesthetic form of the *complexio,* "encompassing incommensurables while keeping them in productive tension."[12] Recent scholarship has developed the idea of the baroque not just as a period of creativity and cultural synthesis in seventeenth-century Europe but also as a transhistoric mobile aesthetic form shaped by spectacularity and particular political and economic conditions of transition and "crisis."[13] A cultural system with the formal characteristics of grandeur, excess, complexity, chaos, contradiction, hyperbole, and sensationalism, the (neo)baroque is concerned to evoke "states of transcendence that amplify the viewer's experience of the illusion."[14] The neobaroque is thus *mediative* in a scalar and almost fractal fashion, absorbing contrasting elements and opposed forces while masking them, altering awareness and sensations, and hence having compelling material effects on those who engage with it.

MEDIATING CATHOLICISMS

Mediation is intrinsic to Catholicism's very nature: through an array of liturgies, theologies, substances, objects, and persons, Catholicism bridges earth and "the divinity of the stars," living and dead, devotees and Christ, person and collectivity.[15] On a more earthly plane, for the church, Catholic evangelism as a mediating design must deal with the irreconcilable tension between universalism and localism. This tension—appearing at the level of the church elite but not in terms of the myriad ways that Catholicism is lived—is given by the church's imperative of maintaining the authority of Catholic doctrine versus the missionary imperative of making the faith meaningful and rooting it in diverse local settings. Managing this, however, is no easy matter: in contrast with Protestantism's emphasis on inward belief (faith) and lay interpretations of the Bible—allowing the world to apparently be made over anew—the Catholic Church has always been concerned to tightly control reproduction of the Word, investing equal authority in the biblical message and in external channels of grace like the sacraments. In the "modern" era of the twentieth century, the church's wariness toward freedom of expression slowed its embracing of mass communications media (e.g., newspapers, radio, and television) as tools of evangelization. In fact, until the 1950s, the Vatican's official policies concerning such media remained cautious, defensive, and fairly limited in scope.[16] But from that point onward, this cautious stance evolved incrementally into a more eager embracing of mass media technology in spreading the Catholic word—and image(s).

During Vatican II, through the 1963 "Decree on the Means of Social Communication" (*Inter Mirifica*), the church addressed the use by Catholics of "social media" (at the time, radio, television, film, and printed mass media) to augment the apostolic ministry of the church. From the start of his pontificate, John Paul II (1978–2005) built on this opening. In the mid-1980s, for example, the pope actively pushed for a new globalization strategy for the Vatican's channels of communication, a push that harmonized with theological-pastoral ideologies that he had promoted since the beginning of his papacy. This impetus was part of efforts to restore the authority and moral doctrines of the pre–Vatican II era, marking a change in the institutional church's global discourse for reinvigorating Catholics' faith called the New Evangelization—"a call to conversion" to all Catholics.[17] The New Evangelization urged Catholics to a serious reengagement with Catholic scripture and doctrine that would emphasize unity, solidarity, and homogeneity and—in the interests of authority and universality—the active re-missionization of the faith by clergy and lay Catholics.

Thus the New Evangelization's appeal for an intensification of the rate and expansion of "centrifugal" flows of Catholic images and words globally was coupled with a "centripetal" reining in of Catholic doctrine. It is worth noting that the pope's efforts in this regard responded to the post–Vatican II trend toward so-called "vernacular" interpretations of Catholic identity and doctrine such as liberation theology and indigenous theology, which troubled John Paul's urgent exhortation for Catholics to return to the core of their faith.[18] In his millennial apostolic letter *Novo Millennio Ineunte* (2000), for example, the pope stressed what he proclaimed as the Universal Call to Holiness. In this plea, the image of the "Pilgrim Church" was key to launching a new evangelizing mission that urged each Catholic to live out his or her spirituality in close imitation of Christ (*imitatio Cristi*). The inward piety and a personal relationship with God stressed in this mission contrasted starkly with the social (and politically transformative) emphasis of Vatican II and its hallmark concept of the "People's Church."

This new style of post–Vatican II evangelism was aimed particularly at those countries in the Catholic "religious regime" where John Paul II saw that a new missionization was urgently needed—especially in the Americas, where the vast majority of Catholics now reside.[19] Thus, embodying such missionary zeal, the "Traveling Pope" (*el Papa Viajero*), as he came to be known, undertook more pastoral trips than all former popes combined, to a total of 129 countries (he visited Mexico five times).[20] He also beatified 1,340 people and canonized 483, more than all the popes together over the previous five centuries. The aesthetics of this campaign are important; they emerge from the church's embracing of media as part of the New Evangelization's mission of a reborn, all-loving, resolutely modern, global church.

The concern for the church's integration of media into evangelization only grew under Joseph Ratzinger, first as John Paul II's prefect of the Congregation for Doctrine and Faith, then under his tenure as Pope Benedict XVI, which began in 2005. As pope, Benedict gave the "means of mass communication" a key role in charitable activity (the new emphasis in the Call for Holiness) in three encyclicals, *Deus Caritas Est* (2005), *Spe Salvi* (2007), and, in particular, in his "signature" and final letter, *Caritas in Veritate* (2009).[21] In these and other writings and public addresses, Benedict continued his stress on an ethics of charity (*caritas,* "love") to "authentic" integral human and social development. This interpretation thus sustained the shift in emphasis begun by John Paul II, from the post–Conciliar Church in the World to a more spiritualized, emotional, and ethics-driven Catholic faith centered on the theology of the Holy Spirit and the image of a universalist Catholic *Humanitas* or "unity in diversity."[22]

More importantly, this established the conditions for the emergence of a different phenomenology of the faith—a new way of *feeling* and *being* Catholic—and for the church to influence more overtly secular spaces of society. This shift in sensibility diverges from the image of the church as an institution wielding its power with dogmatism, threat, and force—in the Americas, an image lingering since the Conquest. Instead, emerging at the current historical conjuncture is the church of baroque spectacle, a highly mediated political-theological form preoccupied with sentimental illusion, cultural pluralism, and reconfiguration of Catholics' way of apprehending their faith, as a technology of subtle yet forceful persuasion. Thus, whereas the spirit of opening and relativism characterizing post–Vatican II theology was a response to the view of the church's need to resituate itself in the modern age, neobaroque Catholic evangelism is a reflection of a centralizing, revisionist backlash to such views. Neobaroque evangelism is evident worldwide and can be seen as a form that is responsive to what has been called a general "southern shift" in Christianity.[23]

Media technologies and techno-aesthetics are eminently popular and "democratized" in terms of both people's ready access to media and their capacity to produce independently such mediatic forms (e.g., via Twitter, YouTube, etc.).[24] At the same time, certain techniques of presentation, televisual and digital technologies, and media of global communications are also critical constituents of neobaroque evangelical praxis. The Vatican and the national ecclesiastic hierarchy (the Mexican Bishops' Council or CEM—Concilio Episcopal Mexicano) direct the liturgical content of large hypermediated ceremonies like that of the Virgin of Guadalupe in Mexico City. Early celebrations over much of the colonial period saw pilgrims visiting the Villa de Guadalupe and the old basilica that housed the Virgin's image (completed in 1706), where they made votive offerings to the Virgin of poetry, music, song, and flowers, both inside and outside the basilica.[25]

The gradual involvement of media in the celebrations since early in the twentieth century can be seen to have influenced significantly their development and the gradual emergence of their "spectacular" dimensions. While radio channels have been trans-mitting programs related to the Virgin's celebration in Mexico since the 1930s, the arrival of television in the 1950s allowed one national television channel (XEW-TV) to begin to transmit coverage of the celebrations from the basilica site—though not within the building. This soon included well-known stars of the channel singing to the Virgin as a means of promoting themselves. At this time artists of radio and television took part in the short urban pilgrimage (that I did in 2013) and in a program called "Morning Songs [*Mañanitas*] to the Virgin of Guadalupe"; this early program saw such stars singing to the Virgin just outside the (old) basilica atrium. Sometime in the early 1960s Abbott M. Guillermo Schulenberg formally permitted the artists to enter the basilica to sing directly to the Virgin's image. Yet this still did not include the transmis-sion of Masses or any other liturgical component.[26]

The penetration of televised media into the celebration intensified with the onset of Mexico's so-called "neoliberal" era at the end of the 1980s. Constitutional reforms passed in 1992 altered the relations between church and state, unleashing a new circulation of Catholic symbols between "secular" and "religious" spaces previously held apart, at least formally, within the public sphere.[27] This flow was also enabled by the electronic mass media. For example, under the new laws, which allowed for a greater public and media visibility to all (registered) religions, Catholic masses in Mexico, such as the Virgin's basilica mass on the night of December 11, could now be televised (either live or prerecorded). The reforms allowed a more concentrated media coverage of Vatican-sponsored events in Mex-ico such as papal visits, beatifications, and canonizations.

As this mediatization dovetailed with new church policies, including the rees-tablishment of a nominal alliance between the government and the Holy See, it changed the tenor of Catholic evangelization in Mexico more generally, bringing it into harmony with changes in the church's global campaign. In 2000, Mexico elected an openly devout Catholic president, Vicente Fox, eroding further the stark perceptual divide in postrevolutionary Mexico between church and state.[28] Thus, while the neobaroque aesthetics of contemporary Catholic evangelism is aimed at inducing in practitioners certain experiences of faith, this aesthetic in Mexico has also been enabled by a new media ecology produced by recent changes in political and legal policy. I suggest this allows us a new way of considering how the religious ("magical"), the technological, and the political, in De Vries's words, "come to occupy the same space, obey the same regime and the same logic."[29]

BAROQUE CATHOLICISMS

The lens of the baroque allows us to see Catholicism's endurance as an aesthetic form in a *longue durée* framework. As marked by the Council of Trent (1545–63) and the Spanish Inquisition, the baroque era in Europe coincided with the Counter-Reformation and the appearance of a zealous, authoritarian church obsessed with control and a rationalization of the faith. The baroque, for example, was the era of the strengthening of the authority of bishops and the intensification of religious instruction.[30] This evangelistic fervor spread throughout the Catholic regime, including in New Spain. Following a new "pedagogy of the sacred" emerging in the wake of Council of Trent reforms, clergy in the New World began to vigorously promote saint cults, colorful images, extravagant and lush demonstrations of wealth and beauty in churches, and feast day celebrations.[31] These were part of the crystallization of a distinctly *baroque* Catholicism that underlined the externals of faith, "the pathos rather than the ethos of religion."[32]

Thus baroque Catholicism in the New World relied on aesthetic splendor, the monumentality of great cathedrals built with facades of intricate detail, and the overwhelming effect of flamboyant, emotionally evocative performances in especially saint and other feast day celebrations to proclaim and underline its transcendent, universal empire and to encourage particular ways of "being Catholic." At the same time, the church-driven baroque sensibility became fused with indigenous senses of the sacred in ways that shaped the very course of syncretism. Indeed, Indians (*indios,* the colonial term) in the New World "made Baroque art their own in inventive ways." Thus the "Baroque was a style without strict rules, a style of excess, of lavish decoration and dramatic light and shadow that attempted to create an experience of the sacred, not merely to symbolize it."[33]

Napolitano emphasizes that the "transformative use" of the Virgin of Guadalupe as an ambivalent "contested sign" stretches back to the beginning of her cult in the mid-1500s, claimed as she was through the centuries by Catholic theologians, nationalists, and popular and indigenous populations.[34] Yet the Virgin's capacity to "hold" and condense racial and other tensions circulating through the transitional, diverse, and fluctuating colonial society of the 1700s also made her a catalyst in the emergence of baroque sensibility in the Mexican archbishopric. Historian Serge Gruzinski, for example, explains that the spreading of the Virgin's cult imprinted a firmer identification in Indian minds of the Virgin Mary of Tepeyac with the goddess Tonantzin.[35] The resulting hybrid Guadalupe, who quickly inspired heightened devotion, was a powerful unifier for a new "creole" society, creating a national consciousness in which the Catholic Church had a central role. The church can therefore be seen to have attempted, by means of *La Morenita* (the Little Brown One), a concerted, deliberate "indianization" of the Christian supernatural, planting the seeds for the eventual emergence of a decisively Catholic nation.

In a way that recalls historical baroque Catholic forms, the neobaroque spectacularity of today's evangelism has centered on church-produced saint celebrations as key arenas of the mediation of institutional church power and presence— its affective governmentality, in Napolitano's coinage, in the global context.[36] Indeed, it might be argued that Guadalupe provides a particular opportunity for expressing the neobaroque. She has been a darling of the modern, mediatic church since its beginnings. Pius XII, in a radio message on October 12, 1945, called her "Empress of the Americas." In 1960, right before Vatican II, John XXIII called her the "celestial missionary of the New World" and "Mother of the Americas." Pope Paul VI honored the Virgin in a televised message to the faithful gathered in the Basilica of Guadalupe on October 12, 1970. On his first visit to Mexico, in 1979, Pope John Paul II declared her "Mother of the Church in Latin America" but also the "Star of Evangelization" for the whole subcontinent.

True to this role, the Virgin's celebration manifests the *complexio oppositorum* in operation, enfolding within itself an endless series of tensions and oppositions: universal and local, "knowledge" and faith, center and periphery, external and internal, eternal and immediate, miraculous and mundane, "modernity" and "tradition," revelation and occlusion, into a single form. Musical styles (classical, popular, Latin American, and European) and languages (Mazatec, Náhuatl, Latin, Spanish, French, Italian) are multiple; temporalities (pre-Hispanic, modern) are mixed; different ethnicities (including, in Mexico and elsewhere, indigeneity) are enclosed, gestured to, and underlined in a cosmopolitan collage; open, transparent "rational" secular discourse referring to specifics of the here and now of the "real" world is collated with "timeless," transcendent religious rhetoric. And above it all, the patriarchal European-centered institutional church extols a brown-skinned mother.

Thus, at the Guadalupe basilica site, television cameras are located among the masses of pilgrims both inside the basilica and outside, covering all corners of the plaza, even swinging wildly over the sleeping tents and bodies huddled in blankets and sleeping bags. Pilgrims observe themselves on screens throughout the plaza and, as described earlier, en route to it. The spectacularity of the event is felt everywhere in the excitement that envelops the crowd, the periodic cheering, heightened emotion and noise, the omnipresence of television cameras, and the technical effects of bright lights and amplified sound (music, church discourses). The interior of the basilica is projected on a screen in the plaza outside, in the same way that such screens form a regular part of other huge secular events in Mexico City—concerts, political addresses—defying any impression of exclusivity. The neobaroque aesthetics of the event thus situate the pilgrim-participant closer to or even inside the "action," and yet outside and more distant from it at the same time. A moment in 2012, for example, serves to exemplify this point: We stood beside pilgrims in front of an enormous screen that that year had been erected at TVAzteca's base at the rear of the plaza. The pilgrims might have seen themselves and other visitors appearing intermittently on the screen, or observed the televised mass that was going on inside the basilica. Indeed, many followed the projected liturgy of the mass as if they were inside the church. Others recorded bits of the mass on their cell phones. The space of institutional Catholicism effectively had been extended out onto the "popular," mass space of the plaza, enclosing it into a space directed by its own logic—while the reverse would not have been possible. The illusion presented was that of people's direct involvement in and even creation of the event, though within preestablished limits.

BAROQUE INCULTURATIONS

Recently diverse scholars have discussed the (neo)baroque as an *architecture of perception,* one that engages audience members not just as passive viewers but as central, active interpretants of chaos-into-order. Drawing on Deleuze's reading of the baroque (through the thought of baroque philosopher Liebniz), Ndalianis explains that the lens of the neobaroque in particular "offers an architecture of vision that situates the viewer in a spatial relationship to the representation. Rather than providing a statically ordered perspectival arrangement, the 'center' continually shifts, the result being the articulation of complex spatial conditions."[37] This orientation toward a multiplicity of spaces and focuses of signification, toward unstable centers, toward constant movement and transformation, but especially toward a new focusing on viewers/participants, evokes the experience of the Virgin of Guadalupe celebration and suggests a new way of approaching such events. The "harmony of illusions" intrinsic to baroque aesthetics is built on a predilection for effusive emotionalism, extravagance, embellishment, and excess, but also the projection of power, detail, and hierarchy.

Indigeneity—the "pure" index of cultural relativism and locality—is a vital aspect of the new global baroque Catholicism and its particular display of complexity (here, cultural pluralism) and order. A desire to stem the tide of converts to Protestant faiths may explain some of the concern to appeal to indigenous communities through direct efforts at eliciting senses of identification. But such efforts are also symptomatic of church anxieties regarding the current demographic shift of Catholic devotees away from Europe and over to the "global South," especially Africa and Latin America,[38] or even reconversion among what Napolitano has called the "Atlantic Return"—the millions of Latin Americans now residing in western Europe, the "heart" of the church.[39] Thus these rites are part of a repertoire of church practices and discourses that explicitly acknowledge and gesture toward the non-European, "peripheral," local cultural communities far from Rome, while signifying these as authentically *Catholic.*[40]

The content of the events of neobaroque Catholicism is knit together by a renewed church universalism, a focus on a unifying, truly catholic *humanitas* in which difference as Otherness is acknowledged and subsumed within an apparent liberal cosmopolitanism.[41] Pope Benedict XVI's 2009 reflection on the church's "mission of truth," in his final papal encyclical *Caritas en Veritate,* is revealing in this regard: "The Mission of Truth is something that the Church can never renounce. Her social doctrine is a particular dimension of this proclamation: it is a service to the truth that sets us free. Open to the truth, from whichever branch of knowledge it comes, the Church's social doctrine receives it, assembles into a unity the fragments in which it is often found, and mediates it within the constantly changing life-patterns of the society of peoples and nations."[42]

If, to echo the epigraph by Deleuze at the beginning of this chapter, the Mission of Truth enunciates a *unity* of fragments, saints—affectively charged symbols of local identities and historicities—are metonymical signs of such fragments. Saint celebrations, critical nexuses of the universal church and local "life patterns," are therefore important sites for the work of neobaroque evangelism. Mexico's celebration of the Virgin of Guadalupe is a perfect space of mediation, reconfiguring differences of time, space and, through the principle of inculturation, local, cultural-ethnic differences, at least as these are ideally constructed by the church. While the Vatican II concept of inculturation—an adaptation of church teachings to the cosmovisions and understandings of Others, especially indigenous cultures—was the basis of progressive and radical Catholic movements, here we have a very different interpretation of the church's encounter with the periphery. It is one in which a benevolent and inclusive church is seen to be nourished by the authentic faith of local, autochthonous peoples as these are enfolded into the church's unifying, paternalistic embrace. In the words of Archbishop Glennie, from a Mass of the Roses homily in 2011: "Inculturation is the incarnation of the Gospel in autochthonous cultures and at the same time the introduction of those cultures into the life of the church, so the apparitions of the Virgin of Guadalupe in 1531 are not only a hopeful view [*mirada esperanzadora*] to the past of our Christian faith awaked at Tepeyac, but also a view towards the challenges of the present in the creation of a future consolidated under the guidance of the Holy Spirit."

Stripped of its Vatican II resonances of the "reciprocal" recognition of the Other within evangelism, inculturation in this neobaroque context—embodied by the brown-skinned Virgin of Guadalupe—becomes the consummate mediating principle, the nurturing, loving, forgiving, and redeeming bridge between past and present and between distinct "peoples." Glennie's homily points clearly to the Virgin's timeless, maternal, unifying role:

> *I am the Mother of Love; come to me, all those who love me.* We have all responded to this invitation of Saint Maria of Guadalupe: those of us fortunate enough to be here in this sacred enclosure and those who—especially through television—also present themselves before our beloved *Morenita;* those who today come to praise her, and those who for the last 480 years have recognized and venerated her continuously as the true Mother of God for whom we live and as our devout Mother; those from different races and cultures—just as it was with the Spanish and the indigenous peoples [*los naturales*] of Mexico.

The enframings of Marianism by the contemporary church, as echoed in Glennie's homily, point to the family as the emblem of *humanitas*, explaining the centrality of the Virgin of Guadalupe within certain strongly gendered discourses of the New Evangelization and today's evangelism more broadly.[43] Because of the ambiguity and excess of the Virgin of Guadalupe's signifying breadth, in Mexico her image is also mobilized by the church to marry secular and religious spheres to articulate a unity of the (Catholic) family and nation.

Guadalupe's status as the brown Virgin, however, expands still further her signifying power. Church-authored gestures toward indigeneity, like the mimicking of evangelical Christian "embodied" forms of devotion in a movement promoted strongly by the Mexican church hierarchy since the mid-1990s, the Charismatic Catholic Renewal, as revealed in the emphasis on dance, singing, and direct interaction with the Holy Spirit, might be seen as aimed at thwarting the appeal of such churches to potential converts and at producing a sensational, affective "binding" to Catholicism.[44] As noted above, the baroque church of New Spain attempted to control Indians' sacred imaginaries by similar efforts at mimesis or a reconfiguration of the meaning of certain syncretic representations, as exemplified by its discourse surrounding the seventeenth-century image of the Virgin of Guadalupe. In contrast, neobaroque evangelism "captures" particular signs and elements of indigenous cultures and represents them as being specifically and "purely" indigenous in the sense of folkloric rather than supernatural. As I have discussed elsewhere, here the church's practice parallels that of the Mexican state, which has customarily relied on "fixed" ideas of indigenous status through markers of skin color, place of residence, and other cultural indices and practices (e.g., language, dress, diet, ritual celebrations), ignoring the way that indigenous identity in practice is actually multiple, fluid, and contextually shaped.[45]

As Napolitano rightly points out, the theological concept of *humanitas* is an "apparently inclusive, but actually exclusive, attribute of sameness."[46] So, as with the "problem" of women, differences that disturb the stability of the center are signified, displayed, and performed in ways that attempt to occlude or neutralize their threatening force by collecting fragments of Otherness and projecting them within a facade of homogenizing unity. Masked are the complex, heterogeneous colonial and postcolonial histories and religiosities of these "marginal" Catholics, which still trouble the bodies of both church and nation.

I hope to have shown the limitations of interpreting Catholic public religious performances such as that dedicated to the Virgin of Guadalupe as "completed" syncretic rites whose significance stems largely from the local cultural setting in which they appear. My discussion has suggested that instead they need to be problematized along expanded dimensions: orchestrated partly from the institutional heart of the church (the Vatican in Rome), they take up media technologies and market forces and move along new conduits, creating new religious subjectivities, imaginaries, communities, and "publics."[47] Their performance thus takes on more dimension, "intertextuality," and cultural complexity than can be grasped within a single frame, or can be grasped if we assume one ritual version to be more "authentic" than another. With a church-focused perspective, we can see that the commemoration of the Virgin of Guadalupe in Mexico City, for example, resonates with her celebration in, say, Oaxaca (a southern Mexican region with a high indigenous population), and these to the Masses and other events devoted to Guadalupe in St. Peter's Basilica in Rome, where there is an altar dedicated specifically to her. These events refer to each other, and to others; they are part of the same assemblage of politico-theological policies, images, new media platforms and technologies (including sound, light, and digital media), ethical orientations, and heightened affect that are not just "representations" but interactive, constitutive aspects of the Catholic perceptual regime and political (including the national) imaginary.

A pronounced spectacularization of church events is visible even beyond aspects of saint celebrations like that of the Virgin of Guadalupe: from the pope's international tours and canonizations, to Catholic World Youth Days, to transnational lay movements like the Charismatic Catholic Revival, Opus Dei, or the Legionaries of Christ, we can see an intensification of kinds of aesthetic and cultural complexity, affective tone, and a preoccupation with mediatization. A focus on the homology of aesthetic forms of Catholic evangelism thus allows us to read the content of Catholic institutional discourses, policies, public performances, liturgical programs, and lay Catholic movements and events as material forms "in concert," yet always exceeding interpretation within a single frame. They cohere by virtue of dominant church theological orientations that are not static but continuously evolving. Yet I believe such a focus also helps us appreciate the materiality of the "unity of opposites" itself, the "pulsion" of Catholicism as a living, adaptive form, and the ongoing constitution of the body of the Roman Catholic *Mater Ecclesia* and her *imperium*.[48]

NOTES

This essay is based on research funded by the Social Sciences and Humanities Research Council of Canada. I am also grateful to the SSHRC Research Team, "The Hispanic Baroque: Complexity in the First Atlantic Culture," especially Jesús Pérez-Magallon, for stimulating my research in unexpected directions at an auspicious moment in time. Simon Coleman, David Lehmann, Jeremy Stolow, Katherine Lemons, Setrag Manoukian, Jonathan Sterne, Kelly McKinney, Bruce Mellett, and my coeditors of this volume helped me in thinking about the intersection of the baroque, materiality, media, and Catholicism.

1. In this research I am deeply indebted to Dr. Margarita Zires, my collaborator in a research project on mediatization and the Catholic Church in Mexico and Peru. This essay, however, is entirely my own.

2. Multimedia channels such as MonteMaría Television, Galavisión, and EWTN-Televisión Católica, all with offices in Mexico City, transmit coverage of such ceremonies and other Catholic pro-

THE VIRGIN OF GUADALUPE AND EVANGELISM   199

grams throughout Mexico, Latin America, and internationally. The most important players in the mediatization of the celebration are Televisa and TVAzteca, powerful multimedia conglomerates based in Mexico City. Each year they compete for broadcasting privileges of the festivities and collate transmission of liturgical aspects (for example, the midnight "Mass of the Roses," on December 11) with the channels' own programming (such as *Las Mañanitas,* in which entertainment stars serenade the Virgin with well-known romantic and folkloric ballads). The construction of the new basilica (which opened in 1976) was partly financed by Emilio Azcárraga Milmo, president of Televisa (Zires 2014).

3. The Convento de las Capuchinas, the Old Basílica, and the Capilla de Indias.

4. Fieldwork research for this essay was conducted in Mexico City in 2011, 2012, and 2013.

5. Juan Diego was canonized in 2002, on John Paul's final visit to Mexico.

6. See, for example, Brading (2003); Lafaye (1976); Poole (1995); W. Taylor (1987). Nonhistorical works include Wolf (1958); Napolitano (2009), and Zires (1994).

7. Zires (2014). For more on the texture of popular Catholicism in a broader ethnographic context, see Norget (2006).

8. *La Guadalupana* is a nickname for the image and the name of a famous popular song devoted to the Virgin.

9. DeVries (2001).

10. See, for example, Meyer (2009).

11. Marder (2008, 33).

12. Muehlebach (2009, 499).

13. See, for example, Zamora and Kaup (2010); Ndalianis (2004); Calabrese (1992); Deleuze (1993). See also Norget (2014).

14. Ndalianis (2004, 28).

15. The expression is borrowed from Peter Brown's classic book (1981) on the cult of the saints in late medieval antiquity.

16. Reyna Ruiz (2012); Mújica (2008). Catholic radio began in 1931, but it was not until 1948 that Pope Pius XII founded the Pontifical Commission for Social Communications, charged with using media communications (primarily radio and television) in spreading the Gospel (see De Vaujany [2006, 361–62]).

17. The first reference to the "New Evangelization" concept was heard in March of 1983 in Haiti when in a message to Latin American bishops he called for "a new evangelization: new in its ardour, its methods, and expressions" (quoted in Peterson and Vásquez 1998, 316).

18. In his first visit to Mexico as pope in 1979, for example, John Paul II openly denounced liberation theology, an opinion he reiterated during subsequent visits.

19. On Catholicism as a "religious regime," see Casanova (1997). Latin America contains 40 percent of the world's estimated 1.2 billion Catholics, far more than the percentage of Catholics in Europe. The numbers of Catholic adherents in Africa and Asia are also steadily growing. See "The Geography of the Catholic Church," *Washington Post,* March 13, 2013, www.washingtonpost.com/wp-srv/special/world/catholics-around-the-world/.

20. "Los viajes de Juan Pablo II a México," *Noticieros Televisa,* April 29, 2011, http://noticierostelevisa.esmas.com/especiales/283376/los-viajes-juan-pablo-ii-mexico.

21. In *Caritas,* for example, Pope John Paul II declared that the media should "put themselves at the service of the truth, of goodness and natural and supernatural fraternity." Popes have also announced their views on the media through the church's annual World Communications Days, which began in 1967.

22. Napolitano (2016, 44). See Napolitano (2016) for a fascinating and comprehensive explanation of the "culture of life" in the theology of the New Evangelization.

23. For example, Laing (2006). For more consideration of church-indigenous religious dialogue in the Baroque period in Oaxaca, Mexico, see Norget (2008).

24. The idea of "techno-aesthetics," emphasizing the pleasure and sensation of technologies, is from Simondon (2012).

25. Zires (2014).

26. Zires (2014).

27. In 1992, President Carlos Salinas pushed constitutional changes, granting the Catholic Church more public freedom, including amendments to Articles 3, 5, 24, 27, and 130. In 1993, a new Law of Religious Associations and Public Worship gave legal recognition to all Christian churches. The government also formally renewed its diplomatic relations with the Holy See (nonexistent since the nineteenth century), named a personal representative to the pope, and affirmed the papal *nuncio* as the president's representative of the Vatican in Mexico, thereby giving him diplomatic status.

28. All presidents since Fox, namely Felipe Calderón and Enrique Peña Nieto, have also been avowed Catholics.

29. De Vries (2001, 52).

30. Kamen (2014, 102).

31. Gruzinski (2001); W. Taylor (1996, 48–49).

32. W. Taylor (1996, 48).

33. W. Taylor (1996, 61).

34. Napolitano (2009, 98).

35. Gruzinski (2001).

36. Napolitano (2016).

37. Ndalianis (2004, 152).

38. See, for example, Jenkins (2007).

39. Napolitano (2016). For more on the "economy of sanctity" within post-Vatican II Catholicism, see Napolitano and Norget ([2009] 2011).

40. Norget (2014, 276).

41. D. Lehmann (1999).

42. Benedict XVI (2009).

43. See Napolitano (2009).

44. The idea of "binding" is from Meyer (2009).

45. See Norget (2010).

46. Napolitano (2016, 8).

47. Martín-Barbero (1995); Cody (2011).

48. Marder (2008).

15

The Rosary as a Meditation on Death at a Marian Apparition Shrine

Ellen Badone

From the inception of the anthropology of religion, death has assumed a critical role in the discipline. We owe the classic formulation to Bronislaw Malinowski: "Of all sources of religion, the supreme and final crisis of life—death—is of the greatest importance. . . . Death and its denial—Immortality—have always formed, as they form today, the most poignant theme of man's forebodings."[1] More recently, anthropology has avoided universalizing statements about "religion." However, Malinowski's claim is arguably relevant in the context of Christianity, and more particularly for Roman Catholicism. In this chapter, I offer some reflexive suggestions about the significance of death for the anthropology of Catholicism, based on the ritual performance of the Rosary at a Marian apparition site, Kerizinen, in northwestern Brittany, France.

Kerizinen was home to Jeanne-Louise Ramonet, a peasant woman born in 1910, who claimed to experience over seventy apparitions of the Virgin Mary, sometimes accompanied by Christ, between 1938 and 1965. Pilgrimage to Kerizinen started in the late 1940s, as neighboring villagers came on foot to say the Rosary with Jeanne-Louise in the evening, after finishing their daily farmwork. Interdictions placed on the shrine by diocesan bishops in 1956, 1961, 1973, and 1975 curtailed the enthusiasm of local people for Kerizinen, but numbers of pilgrims to the site increased through the 1960s and 1970s as the shrine drew on an increasingly broad national and international pilgrimage field. By the early 1970s, several single women and one married couple had moved to Kerizinen as volunteers to assist Jeanne-Louise in maintaining the shrine and dealing with the crowds of visitors that sometimes numbered into the thousands. An association, Les Amis de Kerizinen, was formed in 1972 to manage the financial and material infrastructure of the shrine. The early spontaneous *communitas* of the site gave way to routinization as first a small chapel was constructed, later an impressive oratory with seating for over one thousand, and finally a pilgrims' welcome center with a lunchroom, an audiovisual presentation about the shrine, and a small shop. Attached to the welcome center is a residence for the four women who constitute the unofficial religious order based at Kerizinen. Jeanne-Louise herself died in 1995, leaving behind a group of supporters who seek to fulfill her mission of achieving recognition by the Roman Catholic Church for the authenticity of her visions and their associated messages. Her followers hope that someday Mlle Ramonet will be canonized as Saint Jeanne-Louise and that they will be permitted to celebrate Mass in the oratory.[2]

In the meantime, since the shrine is not officially recognized by the church, and since under the terms of the interdictions priests and members of religious orders are specifically forbidden to visit Kerizinen, the only devotions that can be performed at the shrine are prayers, such as the Rosary and the Stations of the Cross. Every afternoon at 3:00 p.m. the women living at the site lead visitors in the repetition of the Rosary, as Jeanne-Louise did daily during her lifetime. On liturgical festivals such as Assumption (August 15), busloads of pilgrims travel to the shrine, and three hundred or more people participate in the Rosary. On other weekdays, especially during the winter, however, there may be a dozen or fewer visitors present for the Rosary. These occasions are intimate, as the handful of pilgrims clusters together in the small oratory, the original small chapel built on the site that is now encompassed within the walls of the newer large oratory. The small oratory is located at the front of the larger building, and it houses statues of the Virgin, Christ, and St. Joseph, surrounded by potted plants and fresh-cut flower arrangements. The walls of the small oratory are covered with marble votive plaques, giving thanks to the Virgin for cures, both spiritual and physical, and other graces received. Canes, leg braces, and pairs of discarded crutches are also suspended from the walls. On winter afternoons, wind and rain buffet the high sloping roof of the large oratory; the lofty rafters creak in the cold, for the building is unheated, and sometimes the words of the Rosary are almost drowned out by the hammering of hail on the rooftop slates.

Those, like myself, who have not been raised in the Roman Catholic Church, are probably unaware that the Rosary consists of a sequence of 150 Avé Marias (Hail Marys) interspersed with the Gloria and Lord's Prayer, which are repeated in honor of the Virgin and to request her intercession.[3] The 150 Avés are organized into three groups of fifty, the chaplets, which are further subdivided into five groups of ten, or decades. Each chaplet is dedicated to a series of "mysteries" or events in the interlaced narratives of the lives of Christ and the Virgin. The first chaplet draws attention to the Joyful Mysteries, and its five decades call upon the faithful to meditate in succession on the Annunciation; the Visitation of Mary to Elizabeth, mother of

John the Baptist; the Nativity; the Presentation; and the Finding of Jesus in the Temple. The second chaplet focuses on the Sorrowful Mysteries: the Agony in the Garden; the Scourging at the Pillar; the Crowning with Thorns; the Carrying of the Cross; and the Crucifixion. The final chaplet is dedicated to the Glorious Mysteries, which include the Resurrection, the Ascension, the Descent of the Holy Spirit, the Assumption of the Virgin, and the Coronation of Mary in Heaven. For each Avé, the person leading the prayer recites the formula "Hail Mary, full of grace, the Lord is with thee; blessed art thou among women, and blessed is the fruit of thy womb, Jesus." The congregation responds, "Holy Mary, Mother of God, pray for us sinners, now and at the hour of our death." To complete a decade, this pattern is repeated ten times. When praying the Rosary, many Catholics use rosary beads to count off the Avés, decades, and chaplets, thus keeping track of their place in the sequence of prayers.

Clearly, the process of reciting the entire Rosary is a demanding exercise, both physically and mentally. The repetition of the Avé Marias can appear mechanical: indeed, one visitor to Kerizinen recounts with humor that she once overheard a child at the shrine asking, "But is it a robot [i.e., saying the prayers]?" It is difficult to maintain one's concentration, although ideally the believer should meditate on the mystery of the faith that corresponds to each decade. Although no one with whom I spoke at Kerizinen phrased it in such terms, it is possible to suggest that the act of coming to Kerizinen to say the entire Rosary could be conceived of as a form of self-mortification or sacrifice offered to the Virgin in return for her grace. Some pilgrims stand or kneel for lengthy sections of the Rosary, such as the entire second chaplet dedicated to the Sorrowful Mysteries, which increases the physical strain involved in the prayer.

The idea of death is implicit in the concept of self-mortification, as the etymology of the word, deriving from the French *mort*, death, indicates. A religious act of self-mortification, such as making a pilgrimage to Kerizinen to participate in the Rosary, thus involves for the pilgrim something like a foretaste of death. The pilgrim deliberately places his or her body in a state of relative discomfort for a period of time, denying gratification of its needs. The mental effort of repeating the prayers and concentrating on their meaning constitutes a parallel trial, which is linked kinesthetically to the participant's physical condition in the overall, embodied experience of reciting the Rosary. From the perspective of the believer, the denial of the body, the foretaste of physical death that is experienced in pilgrimage practices such as reciting the Rosary at Kerizinen (or, in more extreme examples, coming to a shrine barefoot or on one's knees) privileges the life of the spirit.[4] Moreover, such sacrifice, such temporary and partial killing of the self, can, paradoxically, lead to an enhancement of physical life, one's own or that of others, if the supernatural persona toward whom the prestation is directed responds by interceding to provide a cure for physical distress.

Throughout the Rosary at Kerizinen, the thoughts of the participants are repeatedly directed toward death. This emphasis on death is particularly prominent in the last line of the Avé, repeated by the entire congregation: "Holy Mary, Mother of God, pray for us sinners, now and at the hour of our death." At Kerizinen, the third chaplet is always concluded with the prayer requested by the Blessed Virgin at Fatima, which underscores themes of death and the possibility of physical suffering in the afterlife: "O my Jesus, forgive us our sins, save us from the fires of hell, lead all souls to heaven, especially those who have most need of your mercy." Moreover, the traditional Roman Catholic prayer for the dead, the De Profundis, is frequently recited, either in French or in Latin, at the end of the third chaplet. Finally, the imagery of the Sorrowful Mysteries, which deal with the torture and crucifixion of Christ, calls to mind the vulnerability of the human body and its fragility in the face of pain. The decade focusing on the Scourging is introduced by the following phrases at Kerizinen:

> The Holy Victim sheds his blood. His sublime love for us is poured out.
>   Let us request mortification and forgiveness for our sensuality.

Likewise, the decade focusing on the Crowning with Thorns is preceded by the phrases:

> Cruel tiara, you bruise his brow. Jesus who loves us accepts the insult.
>   Let us ask for forgiveness for our vanity and our sinful desires.

These sections of the Rosary convey the message that physical gratification and sensual pleasures are ephemeral and must be renounced.

The transient nature of the physical body and the material world is contrasted with the immortality and timelessness of God, represented in the repetition of the Gloria at four points during the Rosary: "Glory be to the Father, and to the Son and to the Holy Spirit, As it was at the beginning, is now and ever shall be, World without end. Amen."

The interlinked physical and mental processes involved in participating in the Rosary at Kerizinen have the effect of foregrounding for pilgrims themes of self-abnegation, death, the ephemerality of the material world, and the necessity of separating the self from that world, which is defined as sinful. At the same time, the Rosary directs the thoughts of participants toward the afterlife. Indeed, the focal point of the Gospel narrative summarized in the Mysteries of the Rosary is Christ's triumph over death and consequent promise of eternal life for believers. The obverse, damnation for unbelievers, consists of the physical agony associated with the process of dying prolonged for eternity, as indicated in the reference to the "fires of hell" in the Fatima prayer. The introductory formulas for the Glorious Mysteries of the Ascension, Assumption, and the Coronation of the Virgin provide a portrait of heaven and outline the virtues that help to prepare the pilgrim for the afterlife: detachment from the world, desire for heaven, perseverance, and "*une sainte mort*," a holy death.[5]

The denial of death's finality constitutes the central message of the Glorious Mysteries. A Lévi-Straussian might well see in the Rosary narrative a prime example of an insoluble contradiction—Life: Death —giving rise to a mediating third term—Afterlife. Other theorists, like sociologists Zygmunt Bauman and Clive Seale, suggest that all social life is predicated on the psychological effort to deny the reality of death, simply because the routine business of quotidian living would become paralyzed were we continually to confront the prospect of life's termination.[6] In a theoretical tradition extending from Sigmund Freud, Ernst Becker, and Robert Jay Lifton and Eric Olson through Maurice Bloch and Jonathan Parry and others, Seale argues that religion constitutes a defense against the fear and uncertainty provoked by death and therefore that ritual seeks to "transform mortality into fertility and renewal."[7]

Likewise, I suggest that religious practices such as the Rosary, especially when performed in the liminal context of pilgrimage shrines like Kerizinen, provide an institutionalized setting in which participants can contemplate death and meditate on life's fragility. In this way, such practices—at least for some pilgrims—may "tame" or "domesticate" death anxiety, keeping it at bay by providing a forum where death may be symbolically confronted, and symbolically overcome.[8] Perhaps meditating on death while repeating the Rosary renders the end of existence as we know it less terrifying, more approachable, and more possible to encompass conceptually than it would be in the absence of religious ritual. Or perhaps it is simply that—much in the same way as the anxiety-driven repetitive rituals of the obsessive-compulsive—religious rituals involving repetition like the Rosary do not really confront fear of death but rather protectively displace it from center stage of the participants' preoccupations.[9]

Certainly, many visitors are attracted to Kerizinen precisely because they are encountering death: either the death of the self or that of significant others. Witness Mme Le Roux, a middle-aged woman from a nearby town, who describes herself as "*une sauvage*" alienated from the official church, who started attending the Rosary at Kerizinen every week during her mother's six-month struggle with cancer. At Kerizinen, Mme Le Roux recalls she prayed for her mother and felt that, in losing her mother, she could identify with the sorrow of the Virgin who lost her Son. After her mother's death, Mme Le Roux's experience at Kerizinen healed her grief by giving her the certainty that her mother had found heaven. Now, after being diagnosed with cancer herself and undergoing surgery, Mme Le Roux continues to find a sense of peace in the face of her own uncertain future through participation in the Rosary at Kerizinen.

Similarly, Bernadette, an older woman originally from Marseille who attends the Rosary almost daily, told me the story of her family's afflictions and explained how she had been drawn to Kerizinen. Her son-in-law, in his late thirties, suffers from a kidney disease. A kidney transplant gave him hope of recovery, but the disease has recurred in the donated organ, and he is undergoing dialysis treatment. Adding to the family's distress, Bernadette's young grandson has been diagnosed with the same kidney condition that afflicts his father. To pursue medical treatment, Bernadette moved with her daughter's family from Marseille to a coastal Breton town near Kerizinen, where a highly regarded clinic specializes in treating renal disorders. Bernadette recounted that she had initially found it difficult to adapt to living in a new part of France and that she had been extremely depressed by the dismal prognoses for her son-in-law and grandson. Now, however, as she told me, she has "found her rhythm," attending Mass each morning in the town where she lives and driving to Kerizinen for the Rosary in the afternoon. Faced with the threat of death that looms over both her son-in-law and grandson, Bernadette explained that the only thing she can do is to pray. Through prayer and the support of the women at Kerizinen, Bernadette feels strengthened: she has overcome her depression and is able to cope.

It is not only women who seek help in confronting death at Kerizinen. Yves Madec, a tall, powerful man in his early sixties who runs a modern and highly successful vegetable production enterprise in the Kerizinen area, is a member of the board of directors of Les Amis de Kerizinen and one of the shrine's most active promoters. Yves first thought seriously about Kerizinen in the mid-1980s, when his nine-year-old daughter Michelle contracted cancer. For six months, Michelle underwent debilitating treatments in hospitals in both Paris and Brittany. Toward the end of this difficult period, Yves approached Jeanne-Louise at Kerizinen and asked for her help in praying for his daughter's recovery. Michelle was taken on pilgrimage to Kerizinen from the hospital, wearing her nightgown and hooked up to her intravenous medications, and she was warmly greeted by Jeanne-Louise. Yves looks back to the final two weeks of Michelle's life as a kind of epiphany. He was with her constantly in hospital, and it was a period of strong emotions and great joy for him. Yves feels that together he and Michelle were able to live her death in peace and serenity, and he believes that this gift was a blessing obtained through the prayers offered at Kerizinen. Yves explains that when he was young he enjoyed running in races, and it was always a great moment of fulfillment to finish in the lead. For Yves, Michelle's death felt like winning a race, only the emotions were much stronger and the sense of victory more powerful. Yves's account of his daughter's passing echoes the prayer in the third chaplet of the Rosary, repeated so often at Kerizinen, which asks the Virgin for the blessing of a holy death.

So prayer at Kerizinen is empowering, at least in the narratives summarized here. For Mme Le Roux, Bernadette, and Yves Madec, as for many people whom I encountered at Kerizinen, pilgrimage to the shrine has enabled acceptance of death, that of the Self and that of the Other. As Rosaldo points out, however, the impact of any given ritual will not be uniform for all participants, owing to their differences as positioned subjects.[10] Significantly, Hélène Madec, Yves's wife and mother of Michelle, did not experience the sense of serene joy and fulfillment that her husband recalls in connection with the death of their daughter. When I translated this paper for Hélène, she explained that her own memories of Michelle's death were colored by the stress and fatigue of spending months at Michelle's side in hospital. Even so, Hélène told me that she recalled feeling that Michelle's death was "almost a liberation, as though I had returned [to God] the child I had received, with the strong faith that I would find her again later [i.e., in the afterlife]."

Earlier I speculated that praying the Rosary at Kerizinen—and by extension in other Catholic contexts—familiarizes the faithful with the prospect of death and thus renders the inevitable end of existence less terrifying. In contrast, Hélène's reference to reunion with lost loved ones and with God after death evokes more positive—and more theologically orthodox—aspects of the Rosary and broader Catholic teachings on death. Commenting on this paper, Hélène and another woman who is deeply committed to Kerizinen emphasized that in their view the Rosary promotes meditation not only on death but also on life in its most complete spiritual sense. For the believer, the ritual of saying the Rosary provides an avenue for contact with living spiritual beings, Christ and the Virgin. As Hélène and her companion explained, "Christ asks us to die to ourselves, to renounce all that is not God, in order to live more fully." They also pointed out that the Joyful Mysteries of the Rosary that deal with Christ's resurrection and Catholicism's promise of eternal life are as important as those Mysteries that focus more explicitly on themes of death and mortality.

Significantly, Hélène's perspective on death corresponds closely to the teachings in the *Catechism of the Catholic Church*:

THE MEANING OF CHRISTIAN DEATH

1010 Because of Christ, Christian death has a positive meaning: "For to me to live is Christ, and to die is gain." "The saying is sure: if we have died with him, we will also live with him." What is essentially new about Christian death is this: through Baptism, the Christian has already "died with Christ" sacramentally, in order to live a new life: and if we die in Christ's grace, physical death completes this "dying with Christ" and so completes our incorporation into him in his redeeming act. . . .

1012 The Christian vision of death receives privileged expression in the liturgy of the Church

Lord, for your faithful people life is changed, not ended.
When the body of our earthly dwelling lies in death
We gain an everlasting dwelling place in heaven.[11]

For myself, as an ethnographer, reading the *Catechism* and listening to believers like Hélène reinforce my sense of being both insider and outsider. On the one hand, when I was a devout Anglican in my teens, I shared the "Christian vision of death" outlined above. On the other hand, as an agnostic anthropologist approaching my sixties, I feel alienated from the church's promise of immortality. Moreover, I cannot ignore the fact that many of those who pray the Rosary at Kerizinen seek miracles of bodily healing—for themselves or others—and thus strive to prolong life rather than to embrace death. Yves Madec, Mme Le Roux, and Bernadette prayed initially for curing of the body, rather than for healing of the soul. Through the lens of faith, however, the absence of a physical cure is represented in their accounts, not as evidence of divine failure, but as a subtler, more complex and bittersweet kind of miracle: the redemption of the spirit through acceptance of God's will. Yet, the skeptic might ask, is it not a form of self-deception to convince oneself that a miracle has actually happened precisely because another, asked-for miracle did *not* take place?

My initial fieldwork in Brittany, which focused on ideas about death and the afterlife, took place when I was in my midtwenties.[12] Death looks different as one gets older. The immediacy of the concept increases, and it no longer appears like a vague prospect on a far horizon. For the most part, however, I have found that it is possible to maintain the fiction that one is securely insulated from death by the ubiquity of biomedical interventions "at home." Elsewhere, in places where life is shorter and more precarious, death must always seem more imminent. How then, do people continue to live? Lifton and Olson argue that "it is possible to think of human life at every moment as moving between two poles: imagery of total severance (death imagery) and imagery of continuity (symbolic immortality). Both are present in a kind of balance: neither is able totally to abolish the other."[13] I suggest that the enduring appeal of the Rosary for pilgrims to Kerizinen, and for Catholics around the world, resides precisely in its ability to maintain this kind of balance between imagery of death and visions of immortality.

During my fieldwork, I frequently asked myself whether Kerizinen ultimately helps the people who go there or simply provides them with a community in which their problems are reinforced. In this connection, I am reminded of my close friend Jeannette, who used to spend Sunday afternoons at Kerizinen during a painful period of depression after her son decided to emigrate to the United States instead of taking over the family farm. Jeannette recalls that she would go to Kerizinen and cry throughout the Rosary, aware that all around her other women were also shedding tears, each preoccupied with her own particular problems. After some months, acting on the advice of her family doctor who told her she needed to expand her social horizons, Jeannette joined a domino club for senior citizens. She now spends Sunday afternoons at domino tournaments, and her depression has lifted.

There are others at Kerizinen who appear even more deeply troubled than Jeannette, Bernadette, or Yves Madec: the young man who comes to the shrine for relief from the voices inside his mind that urge him to inflict harm on the people around him; the musician in his forties smelling strongly of alcohol who recounts his battles with Satan; and the young couple struggling with unemployment and alienation from the local social milieu because the husband is a former street person. From one vantage point, I ask myself, are these people and others like them comfortable at Kerizinen simply because they have no place else to go—because they are socially marginalized and struggling with mental illness? Do the themes of death and the devaluation of temporal pleasure that characterize the religious experience at Kerizinen reinforce the morbid preoccupations, anxiety, and depressive tendencies of such pilgrims, especially if we assume that all anxieties are ultimately rooted in the fear of death? As Seale suggests, "If we were to be constantly preoccupied with thoughts of our own death, participation in society and culture would lose all meaning, as indeed it does for some people who by virtue of psychological illness are flooded by existential anxieties, which too often . . . lead to actions of self-destruction."[14]

In my conversation with Hélène and her companion at Kerizinen, we discussed the difficulty of distinguishing between healthy religion and what they termed "religion as a symptom" of psychological illness. I am inclined to conclude that there is no difference between these categories, that religion is always a symptom. Yet as Seale and others point out, religious affiliation can provide a "symbolic route to immortality."[15] Rather than promoting a pathological perspective, at least for some pilgrims, rituals like the Rosary at Kerizinen may, through a judicious blending of denial of death and confrontation with it, afford hope and transcendence of paralyzing terror when they are faced with the transient nature of embodied existence. Performing the Rosary and similar rituals would thus generate serenity, confidence, and mental well-being for believers. Indeed, some evidence from the social sciences suggests that people with religious faith have less depression, stress, and anxiety than their nonreligious counterparts.[16]

As with the anthropology of religion, death and its transcendence have been crucial components of Roman Catholic doctrine from its beginnings. The *Catechism* teaches that "death entered the world on account of man's sin" and also states: "We firmly believe . . . that, just as Christ is truly risen from the dead and lives for ever, so after death the righteous will live for ever with the risen Christ."[17] The death and resurrection of Christ are the key elements in the Catholic narrative. This narrative is recounted through the performance of the Rosary and also is celebrated through the Eucharist, which constitutes the fundamental focus of the Catholic Mass everywhere that it is performed throughout the world. In receiving the bread and wine of the Eucharist, the faithful partake of the body and blood of Christ, thereby gaining the promise of eternal life.[18] As anthropologists studying Catholicism and Catholics, we do not want to recreate the naive functionalism of Malinowski. Yet we cannot ignore the profound and profoundly moving centrality of death—and life—at the heart of the religious system we study.

NOTES

Research for this paper was funded by a grant from the Social Sciences and Humanities Research Council of Canada.

1. Malinowski ([1925] 2004, 19).

2. Badone (2007).

3. "The Holy Rosary," www.theholyrosary.org, n.d., accessed January 26, 2015.

4. For examples of these practices, see, among others, Dubisch (1995) and Gemzöe (2009).

5. As with the Joyful Mysteries and the Sorrowful Mysteries, the verbal imagery of the Glorious Mysteries is given tangible form through the medium of the stained-glass windows around the walls of the large oratory.

6. Bauman (1992); Seale (1998, 3, 70).

7. Freud ([1915] 1957, [1930] 1961); Becker (1973); Lifton and Olson ([1974] 2004); Bloch and Parry (1982); Seale (1998, 66).

8. Aries (1982).

9. See Rapoport (1989, 263–64). The existence of a parallel between religious rituals and those of the obsessive-compulsive was first hypothesized by Sigmund Freud ([1907] 1959, [1927] 1961). For a recent discussion of obsessive-compulsive disorder based on clinical experience that alludes to the differences between religious rituals and obsessive-compulsive ones, see Aboujaoude (2008, 34). Note that as of the publication, in May 2013, of the latest version of the American Psychiatric Association's *Diagnostic and Statistical Manual of Mental Disorders* (*DSM-5*), obsessive-compulsive disorder is no longer classified as an anxiety disorder but now appears in a new category of "Obsessive Compulsive and Related Disorders." American Psychiatric Association (2013). Michael Carroll (1989) provides a psychoanalytic reading of popular Catholic rituals, including the Rosary, that differs from my own perspective.

10. Rosaldo (1989).

11. Holy See (1995, 285–86).

12. Badone (1989).

13. Lifton and Olson (2004, 38).

14. Seale (1998, 70).

15. Seale (1998, 70). See also Lifton and Olson (2004).

16. Significantly, Luhrmann (2012, 289–92) cites research indicating that when God is perceived as "close and intimate" prayer is associated with positive mental health benefits but that if God is perceived to be "remote or not loving" there is "a direct relationship between prayer and psychopathology." More generally, Luhrmann explores the relationships between mental illness and spirituality (227–66).

17. Holy See (1995, 280, 284).

18. Holy See (1995, 368–96).

16

A Catholic Body?

Miracles, Secularity, and the Porous Self in Malta

Jon P. Mitchell

In the burgeoning anthropology of Christianity, the most written-about branch of Christianity is Pentecostalism.[1] Pentecostalism is widely cited as the fastest-growing religious movement in the world and alongside forms of reformist Islam is often seen as evidence of, or indeed responsible for, a substantive re-enchantment or desecularization of the world.[2] A number of scholars have pointed toward the modernity of Pentecostalism—the extent to which its teachings harmonize with the social and economic transformations brought about through modernization—individualization, capitalist accumulation, and so on.[3] Josh Brahinsky has argued that we might see the Pentecostal emphasis on the experiential as part of this modernism. He suggests that we might analyze Pentecostal forms of experience to uncover a "Pentecostal sensorium," informed by particular understandings of the body and of the relationships between experience, evidence, and discernment.[4]

This chapter asks whether we might accomplish a similar sensorial understanding of Catholicism, focusing on the body logics underpinning Catholic understandings of the world, which, although appearing nonmodern or countermodern, might nevertheless be reconciled with our understandings of modernity. My conclusion is that in certain circumstances this might be possible but that the kinds of contexts in which this reconciliation is possible depend on social and historical, rather than ontological, considerations. Where substantive expert testimony confirms the modernity of the Catholic sensorium, its logic appears as harmonious with current social understandings of modernity. Where on the other hand this expert testimony is absent, or contested, its logic appears at odds with modernity.

My ethnographic location is Malta, and my focus the relationships of Maltese Catholics to saints and miraculous phenomena. I explore these relationships in two contexts. The first is that of medicine, and particularly people's understanding of the role of saints in interceding with regard to surgical procedure. Here the chapter uses Sultana's ethnography of Maltese amputees but also Baldacchino's exploration of the canonization of Gorg Preca, Malta's only saint, whose intervention in eye surgery formed part of the justification for his sanctity.[5] Preca's canonization was largely uncontroversial in Malta; the position of saints within medical contexts is treated as axiomatic. The second context is that of a contemporary Maltese visionary, Angelik Caruana, who since 2006 has owned a statue of Our Lady— the Virgin Mary—that appears to be crying blood. He has been seeing visions and receiving messages from Our Lady, as well as experiencing spiritual attacks from demons and the devil, and the pain of the Passion of Christ. His case became controversial when public debate revealed disagreement between experts over the etiology of the apparently miraculous phenomena he was experiencing. Religious assessment of miracles depends on the corroboration of secular experts, who confirm that the phenomena under scrutiny can have only supernatural origin. Where evaluation is equivocal, credibility is undermined, and—at least in Malta— recourse is made to the authority of established elites, both religious and secular.

A CATHOLIC SENSORIUM?

In his historical treatment of Pentecostal body logics, Brahinsky argues for a distinct Pentecostal sensorium, which figures the body at the center of Pentecostal struggles to realize—or rather, cultivate—the presence of the Holy Spirit. In his account, this involves creating the appropriate gestural and experiential repertoire to generate senses of presence, and moving toward spontaneous experience through bodily self-cultivation. He follows the Assembly of God, a US-based Pentecostal movement that originated in the Midwest, moving to California in the early 1900s. The group's early meetings involved concentrated efforts to bring about glossolalia, as an intervention of the Holy Spirit, through lengthy prayer and singing sessions lasting for weeks of all-day, and sometimes all-night, worship.[6] The arrival of tongues was a physical, experiential manifestation of God: "physicality reveals spirit."[7] This logic was carried forward as the central principle behind Assembly of God practice. By the early twenty-first century, the movement was working with small-scale meetings at its own Bible school and large-scale mass meetings in hired football stadia. In both contexts, participants held on to the experiential as evidence of the presence of the Holy Spirit. When asked what gave them confidence that God was real, the overwhelming response lay with "empirical sensory experiences that might be described as supernatural yet embodied."[8] These ranged from feelings of tingling, warmth, or heat to a more inchoate sense of the "presence" of the spirit.[9]

Charles Taylor, in *A Secular Age*, argues that we might usefully distinguish three levels of the secular in contemporary society: first, a withdrawal of religion from public social life; second, a decline of religious beliefs and practices; and third, a reconfiguration of contemporary understandings and experiences of selfhood. The self of the secular age, he argues, is "buffered" from the kinds of bodily incursion at the center of the Pentecostal sensorium. Rather, experiencing the Holy Spirit figures a "porous" self that is "open and porous and vulnerable to a world of spirits and powers."[10] The distinction of "buffered" and "porous," for Taylor, frames not merely a distinction between secular and religious concepts of self, but at a larger level frames the distinction between modern and nonmodern, or premodern, subjectivity.

In a secular age, Pentecostalism, like romanticism, appears countermodern—significant in the endurance of its appeal to the body as against the mind-centered logics of the modern "buffered" self.[11] For Brahinsky, though, the Pentecostal logic seeks an accommodation with modernity, borrowing both the language and principles of scientific materialism—and particularly a concern with experiential evidence. The body logics of the sensorium, he argues, offered "authoritative language for a society energized by scientific materialism—early Pentecostals even borrowed scientific lingo, calling tongues the 'initial evidence' of the spirit."[12]

My question here is whether we might also construct a vision of a Catholic sensorium, and if so, what might it look like. The Pentecostal sensorium clearly depends on a particular vision of porousness. While the Pentecostal self is porous to the effects and influences of the Holy Spirit—which arrives unmediated at times of ritual crescendo—it is buffered (at least in Brahinsky's treatment) in relation to the effects and influences of the material world itself. Materialities are not in themselves also porous, and so are not the media through which the porousness of the body is accomplished.

In Catholicism, the body can also be entered by the forces of good or evil, but this porousness extends beyond the straightforward vulnerability of the body to spiritual incursion. The body's boundary can also be transgressed sensorially, which is to say that the ordinary senses can be used to perceive extraordinary presence that inheres in the material environment. Vision, hearing, smell, and touch can pick up the presence of the Holy, as distributed in the environment. Statues, images, relics, rosaries—the material culture of Catholicism—are transmitters, conduits, or "media of presence,"[13] themselves porous and vulnerable to spirits and powers. To this extent, the Catholic sensorium is not limited to the body but is "distributed" beyond the body,[14] and spiritual powers are—at least potentially—immanent in all things. David Howes argues that we should see religion as a sensorial process, but not one that involves a straightforward or simple process of perception or conception—sensing. Taking a lead from theories of "distributed cognition" and "extended mind," he argues that sensing is not confined to the brain but rather consists of a "looping" process between mind, body, and environment, in which sensory cognition occurs in the relationship of brain and body to the world around. In examining religion, he argues, "we need to focus on the 'loops'—that is, on the mediation of experience by specific cultural practices . . . [and artifacts] . . . for the senses have a vital role to play in framing—or *mediating*—the relationship between mind and environment, self and society, idea and object.[15] Understanding this "extended sensorium" as a particular mode of porousness is essential to understanding the Catholic body, the Catholic self. As the Italian philosopher Mario Perniola has argued, Catholics live in an "enchanted world," in which the presence of God and the saints is constantly making itself known.[16] For Catholics, he argues, the power of God "lurks" in the material world, in such a way that "the experience of the world is an essential aspect of Catholicism."[17]

As Brahinsky argues in relation to the Pentecostal sensorium, the Catholic vision also makes accommodation with modernity, through the empiricist materialism of the social and, particularly, the medical sciences. The former have been put to use, in Malta at least, in discerning the enduring presence of the word of God. Established in the early 1990s, the church-affiliated Institute for Research into the Signs of the Times—DISCERN—is a sociology-based research and policy unity dedicated to tracing the role of faith in contemporary Maltese society. The latter, meanwhile, are central to the Vatican's procedures for establishing the authenticity of miracles. In both cases, deductive reasoning, materialist laws of cause and effect, and procedures of scientific falsification are rigorously applied, in interrogation of the "lurking God" and the porous self.

Located at the geographical center of the Mediterranean, Malta offers a unique—perhaps privileged—perspective from which to explore these issues. Through history, this position has placed it on the borderlands between Christian Europe and Islamic North Africa. Despite worshipping a God they call *Alla,* Maltese allegiance has been resolutely Christian—though not straightforwardly European. Through a history of de facto colonization by the pan-European Knights of Saint John (1530–1798), actual colonization by Britain (1800–1964), and accession to the European Union (2004), Malta has maintained an ambivalent attitude toward Europe[18]—particularly inasmuch as Europe has come to be associated with secular modernity. In terms of Taylor's three levels of secularism, Malta looks decidedly unsecular. The church has not substantially withdrawn from public social life, and Catholicism is constitutionally protected as the national religion.[19] As DISCERN surveys have attested, although some religious practices have declined, belief has remained high and commitment to the main sacraments—christening, first Holy Communion, confirmation, marriage—keeps 98 percent of Maltese in the church.[20] Add to this a porous self, and Malta appears a nonsecular, nonmodern society. However, despite perhaps placing Malta outside the secularist narrative of Europe, Malta's Catholicism has been used historically to place it *within* Europe[21]—Catholicism is, after all, a European religion, the more so when one lives at its southern extreme. Reconciling its Catholicism with European modernity, Maltese sociologist and sometime DISCERN researcher Anthony Abela has suggested that rather than "traditional" or "modern," Malta should be considered "neo-traditional"—sufficiently modern to be considered European but sufficiently traditional to be European in a particular way.[22] At the very edge of a secular space, then, the Maltese case can help us to understand the position of Catholicism within the contemporary secular age.

BODIES, MEDICINE, AND MIRACLES

If Brahinsky historicizes the Pentecostal sensorium, the closest thing we have to an historicized Maltese Catholic sensorium is Per Binde's work on southern Italian Catholic understandings of body and vitality.[23] He focuses on what he calls "traditional" southern Italy—encompassing the regions south from Abruzzo and including Sicily, from the unification of Italy in 1861 until the Second World War. Although there are significant historical particularities to Malta that make it distinct within the southern Italian context, there are nevertheless important linkages in terms of practices, orientations, and ideas. Malta was part of the Diocese of Sicily until the early nineteenth century, and many of its churches and chapels are dedicated to popular southern Italian saints: Saint Lucy, Saint Rita, Saint Agatha. Like Italy, Malta developed a strong tradition of lay confraternities that operated as trade guilds and organized saints' feasts—*festi*. Indeed, both the practices of *festa* and the strong, deep devotion shown by persons toward saints are shared across Malta and southern Italy, to the extent that we might argue that they share historical underpinnings. Moreover, as with Brahinsky's Pentecostals, the historical antecedents of the contemporary sensorium endure into the present.

In the southern Italy described by Binde, the body was conceived as a conduit and carrier of vitality—or life force—that must be carefully managed to ensure an appropriate balance. Linked in his analysis to the classical medicine of humors, bodily vitality was associated with humidity and was figured as a limited good, of which humans were born with a finite quantity.[24] Humidity decreased as time went by, so that aging was conceived as a process of drying. Death—and the dead—were associated with complete dryness.[25]

Although the body and its vitality were considered ideally as a system of equilibrium, it was not a closed system. Rather, the body was porous. Its vitality—its humidity/moisture—could be threatened from outside, particularly by supernatural agents, such as witches and demons, who were considered inherently dry and inherently thirsty: desperate to steal or suck up the vitality of the healthy living person.[26] Similarly, vitality could be boosted through the ingestion of vitality-giving foods; through proximate contact with animals or animal parts; through washing or bathing in natural moisture—dew, lakes, rivers, or the sea; or through engagement with saints.[27]

Saints are carriers of grace—*grazia*—which is a form of spiritual vitality that both complements and in certain contexts replaces bodily vitality. Indeed, at the end of life, when the moist bodily vitality is spent, one ideally takes on a full state of grace in the afterlife. This replacement can also take place in the here and now. Where bodily vitality is reduced, *grazia* can enter the body to "fill the gap" left by bodily vitality. This is the logic behind Catholic ascetic practices, where people deliberately sap their bodily vitality to bring about an inflow of *grazia.* It also demonstrates the essential virtue of bodily suffering, which offers up the space to receive *grazia* and is often at the center of saints' possession of *grazia.*[28] Saints, who were once themselves living, either were piously self-deprecating, were victims of bodily suffering, or were martyred, guaranteeing them eternal *grazia.* Unlike bodily vitality, spiritual vitality is an unlimited good. Saints possess it in infinite supply and so can deliver it back—so to speak—from the heavenly realm into the earthly, in the form of intercession as return for prayer, devotion, or votive offerings.

This enduring presence of saints is central to the extended Catholic sensorium. Since antiquity, Catholicism has been preoccupied with the issue of presence—the presence of the sacred or holy in the here-and-now.[29] From the third and fourth centuries of the Common Era, pilgrimage centers developed around living saints, often hermit "holy men," and at the sites of the tombs of Christian martyrs.[30] Such sites were places where the religious could experience the power and *grazia* of the saints through a spiritual engagement with their presence–or *praesentia.*[31] *Praesentia,* however, was not limited to the pilgrimage site. Saints could also be present in the smallest relic of their lives,[32] or in their images and statues. The precise nature of the *praesentia* inherent in depictions of the saints has been a matter of considerable theological debate, though through repeated movements and councils of reform, and even into the latest liberal teachings of the Second Vatican Council, it is confirmed that there is a direct link between the image of a holy person and that person him- or herself in heaven: "The honor rendered to an image passes to its prototype and whoever venerates an image venerates the person portrayed in it";[33] vice versa, the *grazia* emanating from the prototype passes through the image to the person who honors it.

This attachment to a porous body and porous images of saints can appear jarring in contemporary Malta. Jean-Paul Baldacchino, a Maltese anthropologist of Malta, describes a visit in 2009 to the country's newly built general hospital. He was called away from fieldwork—researching the local devotion to Saint Gorg Preca, Malta's only saint, who had been canonized in 2007—to visit a family member who was an in-patient. This was his first visit to the facility, and he was impressed by its state-of-the-art medical modernity. However, while he sat in his relative's ward, his sense of admiration at the surroundings was punctuated by what he describes as the "irruption of the sacred."[34] A bell rang, and a woman in medical white coat entered, accompanied by a hospital orderly, but holding a chalice and Eucharist. They were here to administer Communion—spiritual aid, rather than medical. Initially taken aback, on reflection Baldacchino realized that he should not have been surprised. The hospital was named, and dedicated to, *Mater Dei*—Mother of God—and like almost all Maltese public (and private) spaces was replete with the paraphernalia of Catholicism: crucifixes, statues, wall shrines, and so on.

Victoria Sultana also emphasizes the centrality of these Catholic understandings of body, spirit and saint in the Maltese medical process. In her research on Maltese amputees, she describes how in the newly built hospital rumors had initially circulated that the sterile and utilitarian building would not be filled with saints, but in time the corridors and wards became populated with the indices of the sacred.[35] Four months after its opening, the large antique crucifix that was thought to have occupied Malta's main hospitals since the seventeenth century was moved to Mater Dei, uniting mother and son, to considerable relief in the hospital.

The amputees Sultana describes think through their bodily loss in relation to concepts of vitality, grace, death, and resurrection. On the one hand, amputation involves bodily loss and suffering. On the other hand, this suffering is virtuous and can "draw in" grace. Sultana's informants refer to the necessity of suffering for redemption:

> I'm certain that without suffering we cannot go to heaven. Therefore, I accept the problem with joy. I join my personal suffering with the passion and death of Christ so that I will reap greater merits in heaven.[36]

> Louisa, a bilateral amputee who lost her limbs due to meningitis, recounted a visit to her ward from the Archbishop of Malta. He came to her bedside with the hospital chaplain, as she recovered from her surgery. She had, she said, resigned herself fairly quickly to her limb loss, and felt an inner peace and acceptance of her situation. The Archbishop, she said, did not offer her prayers, but rather asked her to pray for him, effectively acknowledging the extraordinary state of grace that her suffering and loss—her loss of bodily vitality—had brought her into.[37]

The experience of illness and amputation can be "sacramental," Sultana argues, as it frequently brings an amputee closer to God. Moreover, the bodiliness of amputation makes it particularly salient both because the sacraments, as physical manifestations of *grazia*, are premised on bodily presence and imparted through physical objects and actions and because the canonical images of Catholicism— the statues and paintings of saints—are deeply corporeal. They represent, or indeed embody, bodies of perfection but also the body in pain, mutilation, and sometimes also amputation. For amputees their surgery usually provokes a deep reflection on their relationship with not only their own bodies but also those of the saints and leads to amputees "gaining strength in their belief in God, inner courage and a new 'state of grace.'"[38]

Part of this reflection involves what Sultana describes as a "negotiation" between saints and persons.[39] Individual saints "specialize" in particular pathologies or afflictions—often related to their worldly profession, their suffering or martyrdom.

For example, Saint Agatha, whose breasts were removed during torture, is powerful against afflictions of the breast; Saint Blaise, a physician-turned-bishop, helps with laryngeal ailments; Saint Lucy helps with the eyes. Individual persons have their favorite saints—chosen either by association with their local parish or church or because of their reliability in giving *grazia*. Negotiation involves transaction and reciprocity. The afflicted make promises—of money, devotion, or penance (*weghda* in Maltese)—in return for intercession and grace. For example, one of Sultana's informants paid €100 to Saint Anthony, who is known to be helpful in finding lost things, after he answered a prayer that his cardiologist would find him well enough not to require surgery.[40] Others offer the *weghda* of walking barefoot in pilgrimage during the annual procession of Our Lady of Sorrows (*Id-Duluri*). *Id-Duluri* is a particularly important devotion, as she commemorates Our Lady's sorrow and suffering at Christ's passion—the very origin of saintly *grazia*. Others still make votive offerings—gifts of paintings, jewelry, clothing, or crafted silver depictions of an afflicted body part (leg, chest, eye, heart). More recently, these "ex-voto" gifts have taken the form of biomedical objects—orthopedic casts, crutches, splints, together with photographs of and letters from the afflicted, giving thanks to the interceding saint.[41]

The small intercessionary miracles that these votive offerings mark are testimony to the free flow of power and grace between persons and saints, bodies and things. As Baldacchino puts it: "In the hospital waiting room, the body did not figure as a closed objectified reality. On the contrary, through the aegis of prayers and miracles, the body was intimately connected to 'forces' outside itself."[42]

Miracles, as well as confirming the sanctity and *grazia* of the saints, are central to the process of conferring sanctity. For Saint Gorg Preca (1880–1962), Malta's saint, the first of two qualifying miracles involved the inexplicable reattachment of a detached retina in 1964.[43] Charles Zammit Endrich was myopic and prone to retinal detachment. Initially operated on by Dr. Censu Tabone—ophthalmic surgeon and future president of Malta—his retina soon detached again, and a second operation was planned. Before the surgery, Endrich received a visit from a friend, who was a member of the MUSEUM—a Maltese lay organization dedicated to teaching catechism and preparing children for Holy Communion and confirmation. MUSEUM was established by Dun Gorg Preca—not yet a saint, merely Dun, a priest—and Endrich's friend brought with him a shoelace that had been worn by the late Dun Gorg. Placing it under his pillow (or on his cheek according to some accounts), Endrich's friend prayed for intercession from Preca, and when Tabone examined his patient he found him to be fully cured. In his testimony, cited by Baldacchino, Tabone appears to confirm the miracle:

> Mr Zammit Endrich and his wife looked at each other and simultaneously, in a peculiar tone, repeatedly asked me if I was sure . . . [of the cure] . . . because this had to be a miracle due to their prayers. I don't remember who they said they prayed to for

intercession but I definitely remember that they attributed the recovery to a grace or a miracle. This remained an implicit understanding between us for the rest of Mr Zammit Endrich's life. . . . I could also add that the reputation of sanctity of the servant of God Fr George Preca is known by everybody in Malta. I in all my long years of experience could confirm that I have never come across a case of spontaneous recovery under similar conditions in the professional literature.[44]

Baldacchino describes in some detail the scrutiny to which this and the other evidence of Dun Gorg's sanctity were put by the Consulta Medica—the council of physicians established by the Vatican to examine the medical evidence in respect of miracles.[45] He contrasts this meticulous empiricism and scientistic rationalism to the apparent irrationalism of the Catholic porous self, concluding that, rather than being opposed to science—as modern and premodern, or rational and irrational—contemporary Catholicism might be characterized by an oscillation between forms of scientific rationalism on the one hand and mysticism on the other.[46] From this he identifies within Malta a distinctively Catholic modernity, which in some senses reconciles the modernity of scientific rationalism and the apparent premodernity of bodily porousness.

Moreover, he identifies Saint Preca as a fundamentally modern saint, not only because he was canonized under the post–Vatican II procedures of empirical scrutiny, but also because of his role in the development of Maltese society. Prior to the process of canonization, Preca had been heralded as a pioneer of language education, and education in general, introducing free Maltese-language catechism lessons to the poorest and least educated of Maltese children—this at a time when language and education were contentious political issues between the local elites and the British colonial authorities.[47] On both sides of the highly polarized Maltese political scene, Preca was heralded as a "man of the people" and an "apostle of the workers."[48] His canonization united the Maltese: "When the Maltese got to proclaim 'St George of Malta' as the first Maltese saint, there could be no doubt that nation and religion were seen to be in perfect harmony."[49]

The populism of Saint Gorg matches the populism of sainthood more generally. As Kenneth Woodward argues, all saints must originate among "the people."[50] Although they may finish with adjudication and proclamation from the Vatican, they begin in much more everyday contexts. Revelation begins in the mundane: the transcendent is rooted in the immanent. Such is the nature of the Catholic sensorium.

STATUES, VISIONS, AND LOCUTIONS

Angelik Caruana comes from the same southern Maltese dock-working region that Saint Gorg Preca's educational ministry was intended to benefit. As a young man he joined Preca's MUSEUM movement but subsequently left to marry his wife, Catherine, with whom he set up a home in the coastal town of Birzebuggia and began a family.

In January 2006, Catherine bought a statue of Our Lady of the Immaculate Conception. She had gone to the local store to buy paint for the redecoration of the family kitchen when the statue caught her eye. Although she could ill afford the €89 price tag, there was something about the statue that drew her toward it. She arranged with the shopkeeper to pay in installments and took the statue home with her. Within days, the statue—which was unremarkable in every other respect—appeared to cry tears of blood. Catherine and Angelik contacted the local church authorities, who took the statue to the Curia for testing. They confirmed that the tears were blood, but because the crying stopped when the statue was in their custody they concluded that there was no evidence that its origin was supernatural. The crying resumed when the statue was returned to the Caruanas. They were advised by the Curia to place the statue in a glass box to prevent human interference. The crying continued. A few months later, the glass box burst outwards, with oil and salt collecting at its base and oozing outwards.

Statues in the Catholic world have long been more than mere representations of holy personages. As Robert Orsi argues, they are "media of presence,"[51] carrying the presence and the *grazia* of the saint him- or herself. This flows out from the statue spiritually, but also materially. Binde describes such phenomena as a consequence of the excess *grazia* derived from the saint and embodied in the statue. Unable to contain the excess, statues emit "bodily fluids that heal and reinvigorate human beings."[52]

In April 2006, Angelik Caruana began to have visions of Our Lady. While showing visitors a photograph of the statue, he fell to the ground and lost consciousness of his surroundings. A bright light appeared, in the middle of which was a woman, who pleaded with him to encourage conversion through praying the Rosary. Initially in the family home, the visions also began occurring at meetings of the prayer group Mir[53]—which had been set up following a 2005 pilgrimage to Medjugorje. Like Our Lady's messages to Angelik, the focus of the Mir meetings is conversion, but a particular conception of conversion derived from the Catholic Charismatic Renewal, which emphasizes a process of continuous conversion and consistent commitment to behaviors and sentiments in pursuit of the love of God. Angelik's visions of and messages from Our Lady continued regularly at the Mir meetings and elsewhere. In December 2006, Our Lady asked Angelik to establish a shrine on the nearby prehistoric hill-temple of Borg-in-Nadur, outside Birzebuggia. Here the visions became more routinized. Six couples from the Mir group, including Catherine and Angelik, established themselves as a cenacle called Theotokos[54]—the Greek name for Our Lady, "bearer of God." They erected a large crucifix at the top of the hill, with a small altar below, which would serve as a focus for Angelik's visions of what now became Our Lady of Borg-in-Nadur, and drew crowds of up to a thousand people to witness his ecstatic episodes. Looking up to the sky, or up to the crucifix, he often takes on the bodily postures of the crucified Christ or Our Lady herself. He sometimes appears to interact with another person, most recently (December 2014) cradling an infant Christ in his arms. On occasion, he falls to the ground in apparent agony, describing later how demons or the devil attacked and jostled him.

The visions are preceded by intense heat, bright light, and a distinctive but sweet and pleasant odor, which are described both by Angelik and by other attendees. In the "extended" Catholic sensorium, *praesentia* and *grazia* are sensorially signaled. The body picks up the markers of presence as they breach into this world from the next. This is not so much the "sixth sense" of picking up supernatural or spiritual presence as the utilization of established senses to pick up presence through its indexical markers.[55] Powers of evil also leave markers—in visions, coldness, and foul smells. Angelik describes the smell of demons as similar to that of burning tires. This shifts, however, as he is drawn into the apparition proper. His apparent mimicry—or perhaps better, mimesis—of the classical depictions of the Holy persons signals an embodied acknowledgment of visceral *praesentia,* as the body is taken over by the *grazia* of Our Lady or of the Holy Spirit itself.[56] "Filled with the spirit"—in Maltese, *mimli bl'is-Spirtu*—he enters a momentarily altered state of consciousness, in which the normal senses are overridden. He feels no pain, for example, if he is poked or prodded. He then speaks the words of Our Lady before collapsing onto a chair, exhausted.

The Vatican established guidelines in 1978 for the evaluation of alleged apparitions such as those reported by Angelik.[57] These specify that the local church authority should make an initial evaluation based on the moral standing and mental health of the visionary, the theological accuracy of the revelations—messages must contain no doctrinal errors—and the strength of devotion that the apparitions generate. If satisfied, they will declare *pro nunc nihil obstare*—or "For now, nothing stands in the way" of practices associated with the alleged apparition, while the situation will continue to be monitored. After the initial Curia investigation, this monitoring was effectively devolved. Theotokos was led spiritually by a local Cappuchin monk—also the leader of Mir—who provided support and interpretation of Our Lady's messages, placing them in the context of church doctrine. He was later also joined by a Jesuit, who assisted in interpretation but also reported to the Curia. A local psychiatrist was appointed as scientific investigator. Trained in the United Kingdom, he was concerned with establishing a nonpsychiatric diagnosis for Angelik—ruling out forms of dissociative or delusional disorder, or schizophrenia—but also collecting testimony among attendees at Borg-in-Nadur of witness to potentially miraculous phenomena. Through these experts, Theotokos sought to establish and maintain the criteria for *pro nunc nihil obstare.* However, the rule of their expertise was soon to be challenged as the case was opened up to broader public debate. While few would criticize Angelik on the grounds of doctrinal error or strength of devotion—features of the 1978 guidelines that remained in the domain of religious expertise—questions were raised about the morality of his motivation and about his mental state. In each case, reference was made to secular experts, mobilized against Theotokos.

From an early stage, the visions, messages and manifestations at Borg-in-Nadur were broadcast via social media by Theotokos themselves, on a blog http://ladyborginnadur.blogspot.co.uk/ (no longer operational) and on YouTube. By mid-2007, they had attracted the attention of the Maltese media, particularly the popular weekly investigative news program *Xarabank*. In May 2007 they broadcast the first of three programs dedicated to the Angelik phenomenon. *Xarabank* is a lengthy discussion show that runs for over two prime-time hours on a Friday night. It combines investigative film segments with expert panel discussion, formal interviews, a question-and-answer period with a large studio audience, and often both telephone and social media participation and voting from the public at home. It replicates the particular dynamics of the Maltese public sphere as a whole, which connects mass media with face-to-face interaction to a greater extent than in most other places.[58] In this context, public celebrities are intimately known as neighbors or friends of friends.[59] There is a long tradition of letters to the editors of national newspapers, and the advent of online social media has even further blurred the boundaries between the personal and the public. In this context, very few Maltese do not have some connection with the participants at Borg-in-Nadur, either through Angelik and Theotokos or through those who regularly attend the weekly manifestations. Such programs are therefore woven into the fabric of broader public debate.

The first *Xarabank* program revolved around the statue and the opinion of a local forensic scientist, who was asked to comment on the pattern of blood on the statue's face and the broken glass box. He concluded that the evidence suggested that the blood—which turned out to resemble that of Angelik himself—appeared to have been dabbed onto the statue, rather than crying from inside it, and that the box, which had reportedly burst from inside, appeared to show signs of having been struck from the outside in several places. Against this scientific evidence was pitted the testimony of a prominent national journalist who had spent a lot of time with Angelik and was convinced of the authenticity of the phenomena at hand. Angelik himself declined to participate. The second program focused on evidence from Angelik's psychiatrist. He explained the tests that he had performed on Angelik while in a state of ecstasy and at other times, concluding that there was no evidence of fraud, deceit, or, significantly, mental illness. The program showed him pricking Angelik's eyes with a needle and shining lights into his eyes to demonstrate the suspension of normal sensory function. In his opinion, the only possible source of Angelik's experiences was divine.

Heated public debate ensued in the pages of Malta's newspapers, online and in print, and on the country's many current affairs–based blog sites, as well as in coffee shops, grocery stores, and village squares throughout the country. The *Xarabank* programs established the terms for this debate: on the one hand, a focus on the forensic evidence from material objects—the statue, the glass box—which may demonstrate evidence of porousness in having been affected by, or perhaps transmitting, supernatural agency, or alternatively evidence of having been tampered with; on the other hand, a focus on the medical evidence of Angelik's body itself, which might similarly demonstrate its porousness to supernatural powers, or alternatively symptoms of mental illness.

Questions were raised about Angelik's reputation. Rumors circulated that Angelik had previously been involved in criminal activity and had amassed problematic debts with dangerous people. Gaining popularity would both protect him from harm and enable him to raise funds to repay the debts. It is not uncommon for people regarded as "blessed" in their close relationship to the Holy Family to themselves be called upon to bless others and to receive donations in return, particularly when they can also circulate oil and salt that are blessed with *grazia*. Some were incredulous that Angelik really could be a conduit for Our Lady's messages. He appeared to be a relatively uneducated man, with a strong accent, and to come from the rural and less respectable villages of Malta's south—what some Maltese would call a "rough" person—*hamallu*. As one informant put it, "How can it be . . . he's such a graceless man [*ragel bla-grazju*]." Surely somebody in regular touch with Our Lady would demonstrate more obvious signs of *grazia*. A number of commentators also challenged the psychiatric evaluations presented by the Theotokos scientific investigator. He was publicly challenged in the second *Xarabank* program by a more senior Maltese medic, who had also been a prominent national politician. The manifest symptoms suggested a psychiatric diagnosis, he argued, and he issued a warning about the professional reputation of the psychiatrist.

The dominant critique, however, revolved around the implications of the Borg-in-Nadur movement for Malta's identity as a modern European nation and returns us to the issue of secular modernity. A number of commentators questioned whether phenomena such as this were really credible in the twenty-first century. One prominent journalist dismissed the "medieval hysteria" of Angelik and his followers, criticizing the backwardness and credulity of the Borg-in-Nadur movement.[60] Her line of attack was not so much the charlatanry or delusion as the ignorance it displayed—or more specifically, the way it painted Malta and the Maltese as ignorant.

THE POLITICS OF POROUSNESS

We therefore have two examples of porousness—everyday medical porousness sanctified in the figure of Saint Gorg Preca and the more extraordinary porousness of Angelik at Borg-in-Nadur. The first is broadly accepted as authentic; the second problematized, if not vilified, for its nonmodernity. That the same commentators are able to hold such conflicting opinions about phenomena that, by Taylor's reckoning, are equally premodern, because equally porous, suggests that the evaluation of these phenomena—the terms by which they are judged modern or not—are not so much ontological as sociological. In both cases, the fact—or potential fact—of porousness is fully accepted. Images, objects, statues, *are* open to the flow of *grazia* from the saints they depict, and bodies *are* open to the ensuing sensational forms. Such is the nature of the Catholic sensorium. But the modern Catholic sensorium requires corroboration from secular experts—the Consulta Medica or other medical experts and forensic scientists—to confirm the validity of particular examples of porousness.

If miracles and sainthood originate with "the people," they are legitimized by the authorities and elite experts. We must not underestimate the authority of the church and the status of expertise as rooted in social class. While Vatican commissions legitimized and confirmed the *grazia* of Saint Preca and confirmed the authenticity of his miracles, the church has kept Angelik and Borg-in-Nadur at arm's length. They have consistently professed skepticism, reserved judgment, and indeed curtailed Angelik's public activities. Theotokos cenacle meanwhile has attempted to put together its own dossiers of supporting evidence—its own legitimizing expertise—through its own psychiatrist, but also by inviting overseas experts, including Rene Laurentin, renowned French theologian and expert on Marian devotions. As Baldacchino argues, the oscillation between mysticism and rational empiricism at the heart of contemporary Catholicism is partly driven by class differentiation.[61] While mysticism is associated with a more "popular" or "populist" religiosity, the empiricism of the Vatican Consulta and others is driven by the educated elite. Where the two coincide—where, for example, one sees a mystical or miraculous phenomenon that is corroborated by the educated elite, authenticity is difficult to deny. This was precisely the case with Charles Zammit Endrich's miraculous retinal cure—which was confirmed by a prominent physician who was to become none other than the president of Malta—Professor Censu Tabone. Angelik's miracles had no such establishment support. Although the supporting psychiatrist was well known as a public figure, this was largely through populist TV shows and "self-help" newspaper columns; he lacked the gravitas of figures such as Tabone, or the senior medic-politician who criticized him on *Xarabank*.

As with the expert, so also with the visionary. In a sense the canonization of Saint Gorg Preca, and the confirmation of authenticity of his miraculous *grazia,* were overdetermined. He was a prominent national figure himself, a forward-thinking—even revolutionary—activist who was equally lauded across the political spectrum. His canonization was a logical—even inevitable—next step in the history of Malta; his genuine grace and miraculous capabilities were beyond question. Angelik, on the other hand, remains very much a figure of scrutiny, an anomaly. His social position, above all else, frames him as the victim—or at least on the wrong side of—a politics of evaluating different cases of porousness.

On the one hand, then, we have a porousness that is accepted as modern; on the other hand a porousness that is vilified as premodern, medieval hysteria. To read porousness as a diagnostic of nonmodernity in this context is perhaps missing the point—that as José Casanova suggests, modernity and secularity are narratives, but ones that in context people seek to reconcile with their own histories, their own trajectories, and their own understandings of not only the relationship between selfhood and sainthood but also the relationship between religious and secular experts and authorities.[62]

NOTES

I am grateful to the British Academy for funding the research upon which this chapter is based.

1. On the anthropology of Christianity, see Cannell (2006); Engelke and Tomlinson (2006).
2. Berger (1999); Hefner (2013); Robbins (2004b).
3. Robbins (2004b).
4. Brahinsky (2012).
5. Sultana (2011); Baldacchino (2011).
6. Brahinsky (2012, 220–21).
7. Brahinsky (2012, 221).
8. Brahinsky (2012, 222).
9. Brahinsky (2012, 227).
10. C. Taylor (2007, 27).
11. C. Taylor (2007, 766–67).
12. Brahinsky (2012, 229).
13. Orsi (2005, 49).
14. Howes (2015).
15. Howes (2015, 155).
16. Perniola (2003, 310).
17. Perniola (2003, 313, 311).
18. J. Mitchell (2002).
19. Government of Malta (1964).
20. DISCERN (2007, 6).
21. Casanova (2006a).
22. Abela (1991).
23. Binde (1999).
24. Binde (1999, 37).
25. Binde (1999, 39, 40).
26. Binde (1999, 95, 109).
27. Binde (1999, 50–53).
28. Binde (1999, 163).
29. Brown (1981); Kaufman (2005); Orsi (2005); Primiano (1999).
30. Brown (1981); Frank (2000).

31. Brown (1981, 88).
32. Geary (1986).
33. Catholic Church (1993, art. 2132).
34. Baldacchino (2011, 104).
35. Sultana (2011, 108–9).
36. Sultana (2011, 86).
37. Sultana (2011, 114).
38. Sultana (2011, 86).
39. Sultana (2011, 103).
40. Sultana (2011, 103).
41. Sultana (2011, 106).
42. Baldacchino (2011, 106).
43. Baldacchino (2011, 106).
44. Baldacchino (2011, 111–12).
45. See also Woodward (1990, 191–220).
46. Baldacchino (2011, 118); see also Unamuno (1921).
47. Baldacchino (2011, 107); Hull (1993).
48. Baldacchino (2011, 108).
49. Baldacchino (2011, 108).
50. Woodward (1990, 17).
51. Orsi (2005, 49).
52. Binde (1999, 129).
53. *Mir* is the Croatian word for "peace."
54. The cenacle is the upper room of a house in Jerusalem that is thought to have hosted the Last Supper. Naming themselves a cenacle, then, connotes a group of people preparing for the Passion.
55. On the "sixth sense," see Howes (2009). I use the Peircean term *index* here to signal a form of representation that is causally related to the thing it represents. As argued below, in Catholic understandings of representation the image is related to the prototype not only by resemblance. The image contains something of the power of the prototype and acts as a conduit, such that, for example, a statue of Our Lady of the Immaculate Conception can itself channel the power of Our Lady and feed back communication to her—requests for intercession, for example.
56. I prefer the term *mimesis* as it signals a generative process of "creating anew" and sidesteps the implications of trickery inherent in mimicry, or copying. See J. Mitchell (2015).
57. Sacred Congregation for the Doctrine of the Faith (1978).
58. See J. Mitchell (2002, 20–22).
59. Boissevain (1974).
60. Galizia (2009).
61. Baldacchino (2011, 115).
62. Casanova (2006b).

17

Experiments of Inculturation in a Catholic Charismatic Movement in Cameroon

Ludovic Lado

Following its spread in sub-Saharan Africa from the nineteenth century onwards, Christianity has gradually become an African religion, not only in the sense that all over the continent millions of Africans claim to be Christians, but also in the sense that it is being appropriated by Africans, many of whom are now founders of Christian churches, generally described in the literature as "African Independent Churches."[1] These churches have attracted the attention of a number of anthropologists and historians, underlining the many ways in which Africans are not just passive receivers but producers of local versions of Christianity, some of which have attempted to bridge the gap maintained by mission churches between Christianity and African "traditional" cultures and religions.[2] Comparatively, far less attention has been given by anthropologists to similar processes within mission churches, most probably "because the independent churches are seen as so much more *African*."[3]

The present contribution looks at a particular instance of the local production of Catholicism in Cameroon by focusing on the agency of a ritual specialist and promoter of inculturation, Father Hebga, a Jesuit Charismatic priest, who negotiates the related contradictions through ambiguous processes of hybridization similar to those described by David Mosse (in this volume) among the Tamil in the South of India. The leading pastoral concern at the heart of this praxis is the satisfaction of the needs of the faithful searching for healing in the framework of the Catholic Charismatic Renewal. The wider ideological framework is the discourse of inculturation that has dominated theological debates in Africa Catholicism since the 1970s and of which I attempt here an anthropological critique. Father Hebga as an ethnological object is portrayed as a cultural broker in the framework of postcolonial discourses attempting to restore the dignity of Africans violated by symbolic violence associated with slave trade, colonization, and missionary Christianity.

Protestant Christianity was established among the coastal people of southern Cameroon before the colonial period of Cameroon's history was launched by the Germans in 1884. Jamaican and British Baptist missionaries were the first to arrive in the region in 1841.[4] In their missionary policy, they strongly opposed the slave trade and built schools that became venues of evangelization and new channels of social emancipation, thereby upsetting existing social hierarchies and their means of reproduction. With the arrival of Germans in 1884, British missionaries progressively retreated and handed over their stations to Swiss and German missionaries of the Basler Mission in 1888. A few native pastors and elders were not happy with this new arrangement and refused to work under the Basler Mission. They parted ways with the Germans and went on to found their own Baptist churches and to conduct parallel missionary activities. One of the earliest ones was the Native Baptist Church, founded by one of the first indigenous Baptist pastors in the early 1890s. Many other native Protestant churches were to emerge alongside German, Swiss, American, and French missions. Progressively Protestantism spread from the coast to the interior of southern Cameroon.

The German Pallotines (Societas Apostolatus Catholici) were the first Catholic missionaries to arrive in Cameroon in 1890. The German colonial administration expected Christian missionaries to participate in their colonial project, since for them Christianization meant nothing else than civilization, the vulgarization of German culture.[5] The Pallotines settled in a village on the banks of the river Sanaga that they renamed Marienberg. From there, they evangelized other areas of Cameroon, including the neighboring village of Edéa, where a mission station was established as early as 1891, thirty-seven years before the birth of Father Hebga, the proponent of inculturation who is the focus in this chapter. The missionary policy of the Pallotines included the creation of schools, the formation of native catechists, and the translation of the Bible, catechisms, and prayer books from German into local languages. The Pallotines evangelized Cameroon until 1916, when they were forced to depart following the ousting of Germany from Cameroon by France and England after World War II. They were then replaced by English and French missionaries whose societies are still active in Cameroon today, with many of them now run by the local clergy. This sketch shows how European macropolitics conditioned missionary activity in Cameroon at the end of the nineteenth century and in the early twentieth century. The Catholic Church in Cameroon today has a membership of about four million people, roughly 25 percent of the total population. It is divided into twenty-five dioceses, which are now almost all headed by Cameroonian bishops, an indication of the predominance of the local clergy. Its demographic growth is steady, and it is now one of the main social actors in Cameroon, especially in the areas of education and health care.

Located in central Africa, Cameroon has a population (est. 2011) of approximately twenty-two million, of whom today about half claim Christian identity. Statistics on religious belonging in Africa, however, can be highly misleading, as they fail to capture the porosity of boundaries between religious groups, which in the Cameroonian context also include Muslims and followers of traditional religions. Indeed, religious belonging and practice in Cameroon are much more complex than apparently clear-cut statistics would indicate because of the reality of multiple loyalties. Cameroonian Christianity is today as plural as anywhere else in Africa. Although missionary churches, both Catholic and Protestant, are still dominant, they are now facing fierce competition from the recent wave of charismatic (or neo-Pentecostal) churches.

The empirical data used in this essay were collected during fieldwork undertaken in Cameroun from 2004 to 2005 in a Catholic Charismatic group named Ephphata,[6] which was founded in 1976 in Yaoundé, the capital city of Cameroon, by Meinrad Hebga, a Jesuit priest. The material was gathered mainly in Yaoundé (urban) and Mangèn (rural) because most the activities of the movement took place in these locations. Father Hebga lived in the area of Yaoundé, the capital city of Cameron, where most Ephphata prayer groups were concentrated, and he traveled twice a month to Mangèn (about fifty miles away from Yaoundé) for ritual practice in the spiritual "clinic" of the movement.

FATHER HEBGA AND EPHPHATA

Father Hebga's trajectory pictures him as a multifaceted personality produced by colonial, missionary, and postcolonial processes. He embodies the very hybridity and ambiguities manifest in his theory and praxis. He was born in Cameroon in 1928 and raised in a very practicing Catholic family, which after his primary studies sent him to the seminary to train for priesthood. His writings reflect his inner struggles with the asymmetrical relationships between white missionaries and local seminarians, sometimes marked by racism.[7] He was ordained as a diocesan priest but later decided to become a Jesuit and remained one until his death in 2008. Ideologically, he became a staunch proponent of African philosophy and African theology seen as the way out of Western intellectual domination. Among his many works, the most cited, because a virulent critique of missionary Christianity, is "Emancipation d'églises sous tutelle" (Emancipation of churches under tutelage), published in 1976. In those days, such a publication was a daring move. As a consequence of it, he lost his teaching position at the Pontifical Gregorian University in Rome, because Roman authorities felt that he had gone too far in his critique of the missionary establishment in Africa. He then returned to Cameroon and was hired to teach Western philosophy at the public university in Yaoundé.

Hegba first came into contact with Catholic Charismatics in the United States in 1972 at John Carroll University in Cleveland (Ohio), where he was a visiting lecturer. The Catholic Church was just beginning to make sense of Charismatic Renewal experiences, which were new and challenging for many church authorities. Father Hebga maintained interest in the emerging movement and finally was "baptized in the spirit" in a classical Pentecostal church, the Assemblies of God, in Abidjan (Ivory Coast) in 1976. This was another daring step, but this time in the ecumenical field. He then went on to found Ephphata in Cameroon in the same year. This was just the beginning of a long battle with church authorities to get the Charismatic Renewal movement accepted as an orthodox Catholic practice in Cameroon in particular and in the Catholic Church in Africa in general. As David Mosse rightly points out (this volume), local productions of Christianity often involve a struggle with hybridity and heterodoxy, a struggle with the guardians of orthodoxy.

With the founding of Ephphata, Hebga became the pioneer of Catholic Charismatic Renewal in Cameroon. But it was not until 1978 that the movement began to attract attention when the reputation of Father Hebga as an efficacious healer began to spread in Yaoundé and beyond. Membership quickly rose,[8] and Father Hebga felt the need to organize the movement by setting up formal structures to control the spread of Ephphata Charismatic groups in various dioceses where bishops were willing to make space for this novelty. His was a hierarchical structure, with Father Hebga himself as the founder and national chaplain, and below him lay people heading chapters and subchapters made of prayer groups in parishes. The running of Ephphata centered on Father Hebga, who had the last word on everything of importance to the movement. Infighting between lay collaborators to win his trust and some share of power and influence was commonplace. Ephphata quickly became a national movement with representations in many dioceses in Cameroon, and Father Hebga often traveled to visit them. To secure the legitimacy of Ephphata as a Catholic movement, he managed to obtain the ecclesiastical recognition of the movement by the bishop of his native region where he was to establish the headquarters of the movement, specifically in Mangèn, a rural area that became the main ritual center of the Ephphata. The bishop became the tutor of the movement, and Father Hebga could rely on him to shield it from the attacks of unsympathetic bishops.

The ritual life of Ephphata consisted mainly of weekly prayer meetings and fortnightly charismatic gatherings in Mangèn during which ritual healing was intensively practiced. Father Hebga was aided in this by a team of well-trained lay collaborators. Mangèn operated as a sort of spiritual clinic with a permanent staff paid by the movement to look after the center and the patients sent there for follow-up or intense therapy. The permanent staff of the center were also trained in ritual healing and guided the daily prayers for patients at the center. Obviously such a spiritual clinic was also a novelty, one that had both its sympathizers and

FIGURE 17.1. Father Hebga honored by UNESCO in Youndé for his intellectual contribution to humanities and culture.

detractors among the local church hierarchy. By the 1990s Father Hebga had established a nationwide reputation as a ritual healer in the Catholic Church in Cameroon, and by then a number of other Catholic Charismatic groups had sprung up alongside Ephphata. In 1993, Ephphata was established in Paris by Cameroonian migrants who had been members of the movement in Cameroon. This was followed by the emergence of other Ephphata prayer groups in London and the United States. Father Hebga paid yearly visits to these cells of the movements; these were always occasions of intense healing rituals for various sorts of ailments, especially those related to witchcraft. It is worth noticing that the trajectory of the movement is itself an embodiment of the transnational character both of Catholicism as global phenomenon and of Ephphata as a local production. From its American roots to Cameroon and back to the United States through Paris and London, the local product escapes its local trappings to reconnect with the global scene through migration.

THE HYBRIDITY OF RELIGIOUS EXPERIENCE

According to John Parratt, the sharp dichotomy maintained by early missionaries between Western missionary Christianity and "pagan" African culture accounts for the dilemma of many African Christians. Although they have embraced Christianity, they find it difficult to break completely with their religious and cultural traditions and end up holding on to both.[9] Because of the failure of mission churches to heed some of the existential anxieties of African converts, many have developed the ability to articulate multiple religious loyalties.[10] I also contend that this situation, described by Desmond Tutu as "religious schizophrenia," is a form of subversion,[11] a practical form of religious indocility within mission churches that contrasts with more radical forms of "subversive bricolages" that the African Independent Churches are usually seen to represent.[12] The discourse and praxis of inculturation of which Father Hebga was an advocate can be interpreted as an attempt from the Catholic elite to address this subversion.

For the sake of ethnographic illustration, I refer here to the work of René Bureau (among others) on the Sawa people of Cameroon, which addresses the clash of symbols and meanings between missionary Christianities and African cultures.[13] This echoes the pioneering work of Godfrey Lienhardt on the ambiguities of cultural translations at the heart of Catholic missionary enterprise among the Dinka of South Sudan.[14] The Sawa are a coastal Bantu people of Cameroon in central Africa. Bureau shows that conversion to Catholicism among the Sawa was not only progressive but also selective.[15] The first Christian missionaries to arrive in Cameroon were sent by the Baptist Missionary Society of London, and they settled on the Cameroonian coast among the Sawa people in January 1841. The Germans settled as a colonial power in 1884.[16] At the Conference of Berlin in 1885, Cameroon was formally placed under the protection of Germany.[17] Following this course of political events, the German Pallotine fathers arrived in Cameroon in 1889.

Evangelization meant for early missionaries a mere displacement of local religions, which had catered to the religious needs of the Sawa before the arrival of Christianity. According to Bureau, the precolonial Sawa believed that the universe included not only the earth and its inhabitants but also suprahuman entities who controlled life and power, those precious values that human beings long for.[18] Well-being and health, for the Sawa, were a function of the quality of their relationships with these suprahuman powers. In other words, before the arrival of Catholic missionaries, religion for the Sawa was the main means of preserving life and combating evil in all its forms, especially bewitchment and sickness. Such local beliefs and cults, however, met with radical opposition from Christian missionaries. Concerning healing in particular, missionaries in collaboration with colonial establishments sought to replace African traditional systems of healing with Western medicine in the lives of converts. But one of the main challenges for missionaries remained accounting satisfactorily for the effects traditionally attributed to witchcraft. Thus, after an initial rush for the new religion, the Sawa soon experienced not only a cultural void but also the inability of Christianity to fill it. Therefore, many of the new converts retained the possibility of resorting to their ancestral means of healing without necessarily rejecting Christianity and modern medicine. This selective and clandestine commerce with tradition is a form of subversion of official religion "from below" that has gradually forced the Catholic clergy to review its methods and to seek ways of initiating a dialogue between African traditions and Christian traditions. Hastings (1989) roughly distinguishes five major periods in the history of relationships between Western Christianity and African cultures. This applies to the Cameroonian context. The first period is that of the meeting of African culture and Christianity in a precolonial situation. The next is the colonial period, during which African cultures are still predominant but now are subjected to the violence of powerful colonial and missionary institutions. The third period, which covers roughly the first half of the twentieth century, corresponds to the heyday of colonial domination and to the flowering of Christian institutions in Africa. Then comes the fourth period, the turbulent years of decolonization, marked among other things by calls for African cultural renaissance, the years of the cultural movement of "Négritude."[19] Religion becomes also a prime arena for the implementation of a program of cultural authenticity. This period of resistance is characterized by a fierce critique of missionary Christianity, resulting in calls for the advent of an "authentic African Christianity." It is in this context that the discourse of inculturation came to dominate theological debates in Africa. Father Hebga took part in this debate as an acknowledged African theologian whose ideas are still inspiring younger generations of African theologians.

INCULTURATION AS A POSTCOLONIAL
DISCOURSE IN AFRICA

The concept of inculturation appeared in Catholic theological writings in the early 1960s and refers broadly to processes through which the Christian faith shapes and is shaped by a particular culture in a specific social context. The Belgian Jesuit Joseph Masson, former professor of theology at the Pontifical Gregorian University in Rome, was most probably the first to use the term *inculturer* in a theological sense in 1962. He argued in his 1962 article for the necessity to promote a "Catholicisme inculturée,"[20] especially in non-Western countries. At stake in the discourse of inculturation was the ability of Catholicism to come to terms with modern pluralism.[21] Although the Second Vatican Council took place from 1962 to 1965, the terminology of inculturation did not find its way into the official documents of the time, which instead used the term *adaptation*.[22] It was in the late 1970s that the word *inculturation* began to appear in papal documents.[23] It has come to be preferred over others such as *accommodation* and *adaptation*, which preceded it in expressing the need for a new "working accommodation" between Western Christianity and cultures, but within the confines of authorized doctrine.[24]

During their 1994 gathering in Rome, the Catholic bishops of Africa, following the lead of many theologians and together with Pope John Paul II, described inculturation as "an urgent priority in the life of the particular Churches, for a firm rooting of the Gospel in Africa" and as "one of the greatest challenges for the Church on the Continent on the eve of the Third Millennium."[25] I argue below that inculturation in Africa as a postcolonial, religious, and elitist identity discourse is rooted in essentialist assumptions and assimilationist approaches that tend to undermine the historicity of African Christianity in general and African Catholicism in particular.

Whether through slave trade, colonization, evangelization, or the postcolonial rhetoric of development, Western interventions in Africa were or are built on "the production and reproduction of particular images about 'Africa' and 'Africans,'"[26] most of which are derogatory. In the nineteenth century, Christianity reached black Africa as part of the Western campaign of "civilization" meant to "redeem" the "dark continent" from the claws of ignorance and devilish superstitions.[27] During the nineteenth century, the evolutionist reading of the history of humanity was also central to the nascent discipline of anthropology, which at the time needed the concept of "primitive society" for its own identity.[28] Concerning the anthropology of religion, Peter Van der Veer interestingly remarks that evolutionists, "despite their secular character, accepted that Christian monotheism was the apogee of religious evolution."[29] With regard to the geopolitics of missionary activities, "Missionary societies tended to work in areas where their home governments were directly involved,"[30] and some missionaries tended to act also as "cultural agents of their own nations."[31]

Postcoloniality in Africa is characterized not by homogeneity but by hybridity. Following Achille Mbembe, who underlines the ability of the "postcolonial 'subject'" to mobilize "not just a single 'identity,' but several fluid identities which, by their very nature must be constantly 'revised' in order to achieve maximum instrumentality and efficacy as and when required," Richard Werbner speaks of "multiple identities, plural arenas" in relation to postcolonial identities in Africa. African postcolonial societies are confronted today with a number of "dilemmas of identity."[32] One of these has to do with Christianity as a legacy of the colonial experience. The decolonization of Africa under the banner of nationalist movements from the end of the 1950s was often described in terms of the rejection of Western imperialism. Still, what Patrick Chabal named the "politics of the mirror" has survived in postcolonial Africa and is best exemplified by the rhetoric of development, which still seeks to fashion Africa in the image of the West.[33]

Valentine-Ives Mudimbe defines African postcoloniality in terms of *marginality*, which, according to him, designates the "intermediate space between the so-called African tradition and the projected modernity of colonialism."[34] Against the background of this postcolonial complexity, the appropriation of the religious discourse of inculturation in Africa has to be seen as part of the struggles of African Christians to come to terms with the ambiguities of their Western encounter. In other words, the question of "whether any African who is really Christian can possibly share in an African identity" is still haunting a number of African intellectuals.[35] Rejecting the colonial confusion of Christianization with Westernization, theologians of inculturation in Africa argue that it is time for Christianity in Africa to stop being Western and to become "really" African.[36] But this is more of an elitist concern, for at the grassroots level the local production of Christianity is a continuous phenomenon.

Furthermore, understandings of culture and religion inherent to definitions of inculturation in African Catholic theology are predominantly essentialist. For they seem to presuppose a transcultural "essence" of the Christian faith that can be transferred from Western cultures to African cultures in the process of acculturation.[37] In the last four decades, the theology of inculturation has been a dominant discourse in African Catholicism,[38] and recently the "official guardians of orthodoxy" in the Catholic Church have come to endorse its claims.[39]

Writing to the Catholic churches in Africa in 1995, Pope John Paul II remarks:

> By reason of its deep conviction that "*the synthesis between culture and faith is not only a demand of culture but also of faith*," because "a faith that does not become culture is not fully accepted, not entirely thought out, not faithfully lived," the special Assembly for Africa of the Synod of Bishops considered inculturation a priority and an urgent task in the life of Africa's particular Churches. Only in this way can the Gospel be firmly implanted in the Continent's Christian Communities. Following in the footsteps of the Second Vatican Council, the Synod Fathers interpreted inculturation as a process that includes the whole Christian existence—theology, liturgy, customs, structures—without of course compromising what is of divine right and the great discipline of the Church. . . . The Challenge of Inculturation in Africa consists in ensuring that the followers of Christ will ever more fully assimilate the *Gospel message*, while remaining faithful to all *authentic African values*.[40]

Such a definition raises some interesting questions. What does the term *authentic African values* refer to in a postcolonial Africa? This terminology betrays an essentialist perspective on culture or collective identity, a perspective that is common among a number of African theologians. For example, both Tharcisse Tchibangu and Vincent Mulago think that "Africanity" or "Africanness" can be roughly defined by the following elements: (a) cultic veneration of the ancestors; (b) belief in the existence and power of mystical forces that influence the lives of human beings; (c) a life-centered philosophy of life; and (d) a sense of solidarity that characterizes relationships with fellow human beings and the universe.[41] This brand of essentialism presupposes the cultural unity of Africa, a highly debatable assumption. We need to recall that religion is, to use an expression borrowed from Clifford Geertz, a "cultural system,"[42] an integral part of culture. Therefore, as theologian Aylward Shorter puts it, "The Christian Faith cannot exist except in a cultural form. *When we speak of Christian faith or Christian life, we are necessarily speaking of a cultural phenomenon.* It is a distinctive way of life that can only operate culturally."[43] The immediate implication of this intimate link between religion and culture is that evangelization necessarily involves the encounter and interaction between, on the one hand, the social and cultural world of the missionary and, on the other hand, the social and cultural world of the evangelized. The following example drawn from the ritual practice of Father Hebga is a good illustration of the ambiguities related to inculturation as a localizing process engineered from above.

AN INCULTURATED TYPOLOGY OF
SPIRIT POSSESSION

Regarding the inculturation of Christian healing in Africa, in 1991 Hebga published an article entitled "Healing in Africa."[44] Its outline is typical of most theological writings on inculturation in Africa. The first section, entitled "The Nature of Treatment in Africa," is introduced as follows: "To understand healing in Africa it is necessary to consider it in its own framework, in its socio-cultural context, and not through the distorting lenses of foreign anthropologies or cultures, set up as a universal norm of reference."[45] Again, the language of protest and resistance is manifest. In this first section, Hebga describes what he sees as the "African" conception of life, sickness, and healing. The text's second section, entitled "African Treatment and Christianity," seeks to "investigate the relevance of the Christianization of African therapeutic rites and the inculturation of the official rituals received from the Western churches."[46] Hebga goes on to suggest how a Basaa rite of purification (*likan li bihut*) from incest pollution could be Christianized.[47] In the Christianized version, traditional symbols and figures are replaced by Christian symbols. Animal sacrifice and other features such as the repetition of the incest act, the publicity of the rite, and so on are left out "for reasons of Christian morality."[48] This cautious selection points clearly to "authorizing processes" at work in the Catholic Church.

The theological discourse of inculturation has inspired new experiments in religious practice in contemporary African Catholicism. Father Hebga's healing practices are a case in point. From his healing ministry in Ephphata, especially the experiences of his patients, Father Hebga developed a localized typology of spirit possession integrating both Christians and local conceptions of possession. It is based on two main elements: on the one hand, idioms of possession current in the Catholic Church, especially a demonology characteristic of Charismatic Renewal as a working subculture within Catholicism, and, on the other hand, local understandings and experiences of possessions. Regarding the nature of the possessing

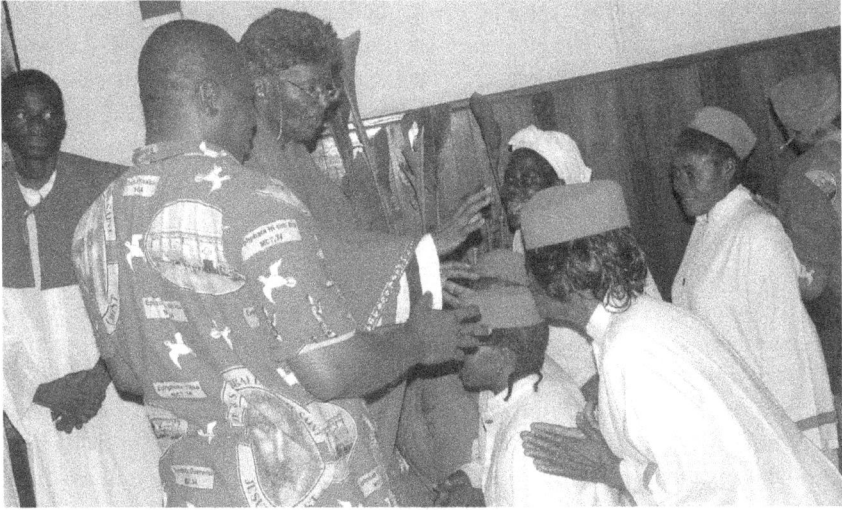

FIGURE 17.2. Father Hebga laying hands on choir members of Ephphata after a mass celebration at the headquarters of the movement in Mangèn.

entity, the terminology of the official doctrine of the Catholic Church has remained as close as possible to that of the Bible, which speaks of "Satan," "devil," "demon," "evil spirit," and "unclean spirit" without any further specifications. To refer to possessing evil spirits, the Catholic rite of exorcism uses additional categories such as "dragon," "roaring lion," "beast," "fallen and apostate tyrant," "enemy," "transgressor," and "seducer," among others. Moving beyond official idioms, Father Hebga goes on to distinguish four categories of possession in his native Cameroon, with the nature of the possessing entity functioning as the discriminating factor: spirits of the dead (*esprits des défunts*), genii (*génies*), living witches or sorcerers (*sorciers vivants*), and demons (*démons*).[49]

Indeed, in a number of cases of exorcism that I witnessed during Hebga's ministry of healing, the alleged possessors identified themselves as *mamiwata* (water spirits or ladies), falling under the second category. In one of the cases, they claimed to have been invited into the patient, a secondary school girl, by the "Queen of the Sea" for the purpose of endowing her with the gift of divination. These spirits wanted the girl to work for them, which implied for her giving up school and taking up practice as a diviner. It took several sessions to exorcise her. The belief in *mamiwata* is a widespread collective representation in the southern part of Cameroon, especially among the coastal Sawa people we referred to earlier.

Nevertheless, Father Hebga's demonology, which lumps together witches, sorcerers, spirits of the dead, and genii as evil entities, is not unproblematic, at least from the local perspective. Such an amalgamation undermines important distinctions inherent in local collective representations and constitutes a potential causal factor in the selective reception of normative religious discourse at the grassroots level. For example, among the Sawa of Cameroon the *miengu* (water spirits) that Hebga classifies as evil entities have very little to do with evil or witchcraft, at least according to local views. On the contrary, *miengu* are regarded by Sawa fishermen as benefactors of the community, as providers of fish for the well-being of human beings. By demonizing the spirits of the dead and some other spirits, Hebga seems to pursue willingly or unwillingly the early missionary policy of devaluating African traditional deities.[50] This demonization is rather paradoxical, coming as it does from such a staunch advocate of Africanization, who elsewhere harshly criticizes Western iconoclastic missionary policies in Africa.[51]

Such contradictions are not uncommon among African theologians struggling to reframe the Christian heritage through the lenses of African cultures. They are by no means specific to African Catholicism. Sharon Hutchinson describes similar processes in her study of the paradoxes of the encounter between Protestant Christianity and Nuer culture and religion, especially the impact of the prohibition of cattle sacrifices, by missionaries, on the religious conscience and behavior of Nuer converts to Christianity.[52]

Mission churches in Africa are faced with the clash between institutional orthodoxy and the heteropraxis of the masses. The institution can control the discourses it produces in the name of orthodoxy, but it has proven difficult to domesticate the praxis of the masses. Pierre Bourdieu has argued that practice is a matter not simply of obedience to rules but also of *habitus* (embodied and enduring social dispositions), of ad hoc solutions to problems, and of survival strategies dependent on the accommodating potential of the agency of individuals.[53] Between institutional discourse and actual practice, there is space for human agency. I am suggesting that the divided loyalty of Christian converts in Africa can also be explained in terms of the tension between structural constraints and the subversive potential of the agency of the masses.

INCULTURATION AND "AUTHORIZING PROCESSES"

The politics of the practice of inculturation are deeply entangled with the relationship between power and religious discourse.[54] According to Talal Asad, "The connection between religious theory and practice is fundamentally a matter of intervention—of constructing religion in the world (not in the mind) through definitional discourses, interpreting true meanings, excluding some utterances and practices, and including others. Hence my repeated question . . . How does power create religion?"[55]

Inculturation is a program of religious acculturation closely monitored by the leadership of the Catholic Church. It is one thing to affirm the necessity of a "synthesis" between the Christian message and African cultures but quite another to achieve it. What does a "synthesis" between Christianity and African cultures really mean? How are we to distinguish "acceptable" forms of religiosity from unacceptable ones? And who is in charge of the process? All of these questions pertain to power relationships constitutive of the concept of orthodoxy. They refer "to the authorizing process by which 'religion' is created," to the issue of how religious power creates religious truth.[56]

Pope John Paul II endorsed the discourse of inculturation, but did so with a strong caveat: "Considering the rapid changes in the cultural, social, economic and political domains, our *local* Churches must be involved in the process of inculturation in an ongoing manner, respecting the two following criteria: compatibility with the Christian message and communion with the *universal* Church. . . . In all cases, *care must be taken to avoid syncretism.*"[57] Thus the pope wanted "synthesis" but not syncretism—a concept often used pejoratively by church leaders to describe the Christianity of the African Independent Churches. But the difference between these two concepts is difficult to define. Aylward Shorter speaks of inculturation as a "phenomenon that transcends mere acculturation," but he fails to describe what this "transcendence" might consist of. For him acculturation (in his terms, the adaptation to or borrowing of traits from another culture) is only a step toward inculturation, for the former "may lead merely to a juxtaposition of unassimilated cultural expressions, coming from various directions or origins. This may lead, further on, to a form of syncretism, in which an illegitimate symbiosis occurs that is harmful to authentic Christian meaning."[58] Here Shorter identifies "syncretism" with "illegitimate symbiosis" incompatible with the supposedly "authentic" Christian message. The implication is that the aim of inculturation is to achieve a "legitimate" symbiosis—but the exact content of this symbiosis remains nebulous.

Indeed, anthropologists use the concept of syncretism most commonly to refer to "hybrid" religious systems, especially those consolidating "in response to the disruption of European colonialism."[59] So defined, the distinction between the "synthesis" or "symbiosis" advocated by the discourse of inculturation and "syncretism" is not easily identifiable. But for the Catholic Church, *syncretism* is a derogative term used to "condemn the adulteration of true Christian belief."[60] In the above statement by the pope, "compatibility with the Christian message" refers to orthodoxy of which the bishops and the Vatican officials are the guardians. So between the discourse of inculturation and its practice there are processes that involve power relationships. In the Catholic Church, there is a close connection between its understanding of "truth" and its hierarchical structure, between "truth" and the distribution of power. The ability to produce doctrinal "truth" depends on one's position in the hierarchy.

The discourse of inculturation has been very much a work of theologians and of the teaching office of the Catholic Church. In this sense, it is not a popular religious discourse in the sense of being truly "of the people." And only very few members of the laity in Africa would know what inculturation is all about. It has been elaborated for them but not with them or by them. Various experiments in inculturation have been carried out here and there in African Catholicism, but again, it has remained an elitist concern. In African Catholicism, lay people rarely study theology because until very recently it was taught only in seminaries to candidates for the priesthood. The result is that the clergy end up monopolizing the theological knowledge that is the key to doctrinal debates. This means in principle that the large majority of African Catholics cannot take part in the debates concerning their religious practice. Moreover, since priesthood is an option only for male Catholics, women are excluded from the production of theological knowledge.[61] In this sense, the discourse of inculturation is a masculine discourse in African Catholicism. Here, as it appears, one monopoly breeds another: priestly monopoly of what Max Weber called "religious intellectualism" implies the priestly monopoly of doctrinal interpretation, which presupposes the priestly monopoly of the exercise of authority.[62]

In this essay, for the sake of illustration, I have used Father Hebga's localizing experiments in a Catholic Charismatic movement in Cameroon to attempt an anthropological critique of the discourses and practices of inculturation in African Catholicism in general. I have discussed the religious discourse of inculturation in the light of anthropological conceptual tools such as religious hybridity, cultural translation, identity, and power relationships. I have attempted to do so in a way that better highlights the historicity of Catholicism in Africa—or how time, place, events, people, and power relationships in the continent have shaped or "created" religion.

Inculturation is a process of unilateral cultural translation for which the use of the word *dialogue* could be misleading, given the past and present contexts of asymmetric relationships between the West and the so-called Third World: Which dialogue, in whose language and between which partners? Furthermore, the ideology of inculturation approaches other religions and cultures as systems destined to achieve their fulfillment in Christianity, therefore privileging the assimilationist approach. The discourse of inculturation that has taken root in Africa is at its heart an attempt to "distinguish the message of Christianity from the cultural trappings of the West."[63] One of the reasons why church-authored Catholicism has come to embrace modern pluralism only reluctantly is the fear of religious "syncretism" and cultural "relativism." Inculturation is an attempt by the Catholic Church elite to control the process of acculturation generated by the Christian encounter in non-Western societies. This encounter has generated various forms of religious "bricolages" both within and outside mission churches. Questions remain as to how far these processes can be controlled from above and how subversive of "authorizing discourses" the religious agency of the masses can be.

It is worth recalling that the idea that religion can be differentiated from other spheres of life is a product of Western history, of the Western process of secularization. The discourse of inculturation is based on a theory of culture and religion strongly determined by the historical trajectory of Christianity within European culture, therefore of the idea of the "Gospel" as an independent element of culture able to move from one culture to another. Constitutive of the process of inculturation is an attempt by African Christians to come to terms with their own historicity. One of its goals is the healing of colonial memories of shattered identities so that African Christians can be reconciled with their own past and with themselves. In this sense, the process involves a certain amount of cultural retrieval. But it comes with the risk of handling African cultures as "museum pieces," or ahistorical realities.[64]

NOTES

1. They are usually the result of the initiative of a former member of a mission church. They are called "independent" to signify their autonomy with regard to missionary churches.

2. Sundkler (1948); Peel (1968); Comaroff (1985); Ranger (1986); Spear and Kimambo (1999); Magesa (1997).

3. Ranger (1987, 31).

4. Messina and van Slageren (2005, 27).

5. Messina and van Slageren (2005, 137–38); cf. also Ngongo (1982).

6. *Ephphata* is a biblical word meaning "open up" and is used by Jesus in the Gospel of Mark (7:34) to heal a dumb man.

7. Hebga (1976).

8. Reaching about five thousand in 2005.

9. Parratt ([1987] 1997, 4).

10. Comaroff (1985, 253).

11. Tutu ([1987] 1997).

12. Comaroff (1985).

13. Bureau (1962, 1996).

14. Lienhardt (1982).

15. Bureau (1962, 1996).

16. Fanso (1989, 81).

17. During this conference Western colonial powers formally partitioned and shared Africa among themselves.

18. Bureau (1996).

19. Movement of a renaissance of black culture and an affirmation of black identity that was started by black intellectuals in France.

20. Masson (1962); Shorter (1988, 10); Boka di Mpasi Londi (2000).

21. Tracy (1981, 1994); Shorter (1988, 18).

22. Standaert (1988).

23. Shorter (1988, 10).

24. Standaert (1988); James (1995, 9); James and Johnson (1988); Lienhardt (1982); Hastings (1989, 26).

25. John Paul II (1995, 59).

26. Sanders (2003, 53); Chabal (1996, 45).

27. Bediako (1992, 225ff.); Mudimbe (1988, 44ff.); Hastings (1967, 60).

28. Barnard (2000, 27ff.); Kuper (1988, 5); Asad (1974); S. Moore (1994, 8).

29. van der Veer (1996, 486).

30. Mugambi (1989, 14).

31. Beidelman (1982); Eboussi Boulaga (1981); Éla (1988).

32. Mbembe (1992, 5); Werbner (1996).

33. Chabal (1996, 45).

34. Mudimbe (1988, 5).

35. Ranger (1987, 29).

36. Jaouen (1995); Ntetem (1987); Nyamiti (1984); Orobator (2008).

37. Norget (2004) draws the same conclusion about experiments of inculturation in the Catholic Church in Oaxaca in southern Mexico.

38. Arrupe ([1978] 1981); Shorter (1988); Bibaki (1993); Bujo (1992); Hillman (1993); Owoahene-Acheampong (1988); Penoukou (1994); Pobee (1979); Ukpong (1994); Uzukwu (1994); Watio (1986).

39. Weber ([1922] 1963); International Theological Commission (1989).

40. John Paul II (1995, 78); my emphasis.

41. Tchibangu (1987, 33); Mulago (1965).

42. Geertz ([1973] 1993).

43. Shorter (1988, 12); my emphasis.

44. Hebga (1991).

45. Hebga (1991, 60).

46. Hebga (1991, 60).

47. The Basaa are a major ethnic group in Cameroon.

48. Hebga (1991, 66).

49. For a broader perspective on this issue, see Lado (2009).

50. Behrend and Luig (1999, xv).

51. Hebga (1976).

52. Hutchinson (1996).

53. Bourdieu ([1987] 1990, 10); C. Taylor (1999, 41).

54. Asad (1993, 33).

55. Asad (1993, 44).

56. Asad (1993, 37).

57. John Paul II (1995, 62); my emphasis.

58. Shorter (1988, 12).

59. Lindstrom (1996, 540).

60. Lindstrom (1996, 540).

61. Weber ([1922] 1963, 104).

62. Weber ([1922] 1963, 118).

63. Maddox (1999, 27).

64. Schreiter (1985, 29).

18

On a Political Economy of
Political Theology

El Señor de los Milagros

Valentina Napolitano

Candido and I are sitting in a small café. Close to Ponte Garibaldi there are many little places that cater to the waves of tourists who pass through Trastevere and the locals who live here or who come to work from the sprawling suburbs of Rome. Candido has been in Italy for over seventeen years; he orders a Campari, and I, a barley café—both so ordinary in Italian cafes but not so elsewhere—migration is experienced through changing tastes too.

He speaks Spanish rapidly, with an accent from northern Peru. His hands are strong, well kept—no tattoos on his arms that I can see. I quickly learn that he has worked for over ten years as a butler for a well-known noble family in Rome who, in his words, have treated him really well—so much so that he has been able to afford a mortgage and buy a small flat for his family in Rome, a purchase unusual among the large group of Latin Americans and Peruvians who attend the Latin American Catholic Mission, a few blocks away. He is "successful" in the eyes of his peers and the priests who have been running the mission and who attend to the spiritual care of the Brotherhood of the Señor de los Milagros. These are some of the reasons why the other members elected him two years earlier as the *mayordomo* of the Brotherhood of the Señor de los Milagros of Rome.

We trade stories about the Lord, the Catholic Church, and the difficulties and opportunities of living in Rome as a Latin American migrant. After I ask him how he sees the Brotherhood changing here in Rome, he launches into a short story about something that happened long before he became *mayordomo*, and that, he argues, could not happen today. A "troublesome" (*que tenía problemas*) fellow Peruvian was standing by at the annual procession, dressed casually. The man was asked on the spot by the *capataz* (the head of the procession) to join in carrying the Lord of the Miracles, since some of the carriers were struggling to carry the heavy sedan (*anda*) supporting the image. The man, who was not wearing the typical purple garment of the Brotherhood's members, was resistant to the proposition. Candido described him as afraid to carry the Lord because he felt *indigno* (unworthy). But again the *capataz* called him in and urged him to carry the sedan with the others, even though he wasn't wearing a proper vestment. Finally, the man joined in. As his body "gave in" to the Lord, his face changed and he wept throughout the whole procession. From then on, he became part of the Brotherhood—he left his "problems" and stealing habits behind. In Candido's words, the Lord "had changed" him, and he became *digno*—he could now hold down a job in Rome, to help his family back in Peru. He had become *digno* in multiple ways while rhythmically bearing an excruciating weight through a few streets of central Rome.

Like others active in the Latin American Catholic Mission, Candido is aware of the proliferation of civil Latin American migrant associations in Rome, but the Brotherhood of the Señor de Los Milagros is for him a different form of being altogether, *estar bien con uno mismo* (to be well with oneself). When you wear the garments, *el hábito,* and touch the Lord's vestments, and when you finally carry the crucifix, the Lord "helps you to see further" (*tener la mirada mas adelante*): you see that others have more problems than you have and that "we have all the right to be here."

I engage in this chapter with the Peruvian devotion of the Señor de Los Milagros (Lord of the Miracles) in Rome to explore the intersection between Catholicism, masculinity, and transnational labor. Through this I perform a multidisciplinary analysis of the articulation of political economies and political theologies. In this exploration, I am interested in studying the Brotherhood of the Lord of the Miracles in Rome not as a religious migrant movement (an example of one among many, a well-worn analytical frame in the sociology of religion) but as a movement of the religious *through* migrants, how gendered migrant bodies are invested with a *Catholic officium* (in the sense of being invested with an office related to a liturgy). I wish here to focus on the body in (religious) motion, to interrogate some of its orientations and plot its emergence out of local affective terrains and particular labor conditions (in this case the conditions of transnational labor). Devotional bodies are oriented toward and respond to contingent and historical worlds in such a way that they are themselves shaped, as Sarah Ahmed suggests, by dwelling in those worlds. Ahmed argues not only that we orient toward certain (devotional) objects (such as an icon) but that we orient our bodies around them, while we develop attachments of toward-ness or away-ness. These orientations help us understand the affective nature of attachments to these objects with, but also beyond, an exegetical understanding of the role of these same religious objects in ritual action.[1]

Caroline Walker Bynum, in an analysis of the material devotion of late Middle Ages, has suggested that we need to rethink religious icons (and relics) through an expanded framework that incorporates an ontological paradox: some Christian religious materialities are the "changing stuff of no-God and the locus of a God revealed"[2]—so much so that, I would argue, we need to analytically explore and follow the "left over," the traces of a Catholic *corpus*.[3] Part of a *longue durée* of Catholic histories, specific devotional objects may foreground, as they may also dwindle and background, this paradox in a present. This is particularly so in the manifestation of material expressions of devotion to Christ.[4]

If visionary religious culture has been central to aesthetic and anthropological readings of Christian religious modernity, so the materiality of tactility and the sensoriality of (divine) matter have been central to premodern forms (see Largier in this volume), as well as to healing and terrorizing powers.[5] Hence the anthropology of Catholicism, in particular, engages with an imbrication of past histories (their copresence and tactile sutures) in the present, the conundrum of incarnation (of the divine into the human in the figure of Jesus and as ritually reproduced by the ingestion of the Eucharist), and the economies that are at play through a liturgy of being invested with a sacred *officium*.

I have written elsewhere how the Catholic Church, animated by Latin American transnational migrants in Rome, fosters particular forms of governmentality as a "passionate machine"—a governmentality that goes beyond the regularizing rationality of some of its Foucauldian interpretations.[6] The governing apparatus of the church and its catechesis "operate by educating desires and configuring habits, aspirations and beliefs," with an orientation toward righteousness (Catholic) living and well-being.[7] Indeed, the Catholic Church at large has a long history of animating bodies, affect, souls, things, and landscapes around particular forms of evangelization and government—and with particular political agendas of inclusion and exclusion.[8] It is within this field of regimentation and inspiration that this Peruvian Brotherhood in Rome should be understood.

THE BROTHERHOOD IN ROME

The Señor de los Milagros is the focus of one of the fastest-growing Catholic devotional cults. He was painted in Peru around 1665, by African (Angolan) slaves working in the plantations in the Pachamilla Valley, close to Lima. The Cristo Morado, Señor de Pachamilla, Señor de las Meravillas, or Lord of the Miracles (other names for the Señor de Los Milagros) survived undamaged through both the 1665 and 1746 earthquakes in Lima and became a very popular focus of devotion among urban mestizos.[9]

In the late seventeenth century the painted image, which started to accrue a strong devotion in the Valley of Pachamilla, was entrusted to the care of the Sisters of Nazarenas. Their first convent was founded by the Guayaquil-born Sor Antonia Lucia del Espiritu Santo, but she did not actually live to see the completion of the work, nor did the main sponsor of the convent, the Basque Sebastiano de Antuñāno. As the popular devotion grew, in the late 1680s the image began to be taken out on processions in the streets around the convent in Lima. In 1715 the Lord of the Miracles was made the *patron jurado*, the patron saint of the city. Allegedly, in honor of Sor Antonia Lucia, in the late eighteenth century the image of the Virgen de la Nube (an Ecuadorian Virgin who had first appeared to Sancho de Andrade y Figueroa in 1695 in Quito) was placed on the other side of the image of the Christ in the annual procession. The Virgen de la Nube is represented standing on a half moon and holding a branch of olive tree, signaling a symbolic connection with the Holy Land. In Rome she is actually reread by a few members of the Señor de los Milagros Brotherhood in Rome as a symbol (together with the Lord of the Miracles) of the role that a Catholic faith coming from the Americas has in the re-evangelization of the Holy Land and the Middle East.

Transnational devotion to the Señor de los Milagros is intensifying in different parts of the world, from North America to Spain, Australia, and Japan, showing a productive articulation between the globalization of the devotion, the migrants' claim for visibility in public, urban spaces, and the achievement of a moral status in often unwelcoming hosting societies.[10] Representatives of the Ufficio delle Confraternite e delle Attivita' dei Laici (Office of Confraternities and the Activities of the Laity) of the Dioceses of Rome see this Brotherhood, which started to take form in Rome in the early 1990s, as one the most numerous and fast growing in the capital, and a process of its becoming an official *confraternita* of the dioceses is well under way. Its noticeable growth is seen by the Vicariate as a positive example of the New Evangelization. The New Evangelization is a post–Vatican II theological and catechistic movement, initiated by John Paul II, based on rethinking and reenacting the central role of Christ, especially in relation to Europe's need of "re-evangelization." Europe, from this perspective, is perceived as having become too "cold," too secular, and desperately in need of a renewed Catholic heart and blood (for this dynamic of the New Evangelization, see also Norget in this volume).

The pinnacle of the life of the Brotherhood is to take out the Lord of the Miracles in street processions. The Brotherhood of the Señor de las Milagros in Rome is composed of four groups called *quadrillas*—who take turns carrying the heavy sedan that the Christ rests on during processions—and a single group of women, who traditionally do not carry the image but hold incense and lead the singing of the litanies. The women carrying the incense are called *sahumadoras*, and the singing ones are the *cantoras*. The *cuadrillas* are lead by a *capataz*, and there is also a *capataz general* who leads all the *cuadrillas* when out in the procession. In Rome the head figure of the *mayordomo* is elected every two years.

More than three hundred families are now active in the Brotherhood of the Señor de los Milagros in Rome, and the organization attempts rather successfully to attend to the needs and the emergencies of fellow brother/sister (Peruvian) migrants. The Brotherhood has very strict rules: as in Lima (Peru), aspirants need to apply formally and are vetted in relation to their "family values"; they must maintain a strong Catholic discipline and put in frequent appearances at the Brotherhood for rehearsals. Men must train to carry the image of the Lord: impeccably dressed in a purple garment with a white cordon knotted around their waist once, they "take out El Señor" (*sacar al Señor*), thirty-two members at any given time carrying on their shoulders the image on the elaborately decorated *anda*, which weighs over two tons. The carriers are divided in four distinct groups according to their height, skills, and physical strength. The women wear a characteristic white embroidered shawl, and there are *sahumadoras* (incense holders) and *cantoras* (singers) ahead and behind the carried icon in the procession.[11] Many of the organizers think that that there is a crisis of the clergy in Rome, that there are not enough priests attending to even the most basic needs of people. So migrants who arrive here, Roberto explains in perfect Italian, experience a "spiritual shock," since the church does not give enough support: "It does not and cannot help."[12]

Like other Catholic religious devotions, the Brotherhood of the Señor de los Milagros has been studied as a form of popular devotion whose practices renew a faith handed down through generations and powerfully support and "unify" Peruvians in the *patria* and in the diaspora in times of economic and historical crisis.[13] Further, El Señor de los Milagros has been interpreted as a *vínculo* (strong link, connector) between the figure of Jesus and the devotees in the act of carrying: Jesus carrying "humanity" in his crucifixion and his devotees carrying him, reenacting the passion of Christ. However, I wish here to address this "bearing" of Christ as an exploration of a continuum between bodies, flesh, and (religious) objects, as part of a particular affective labor economy of shame, self-abandon, and redemption,[14] and hence as an ethnographic index of a political theology of investiture through histories of race, migration, and affects.

THE RELIGIOUS IN MOTION

It is the last Sunday of October 2012, in the early afternoon. We have been walking in the procession in windy and drizzling weather for over seven hours, in a loop from and back to the Church of Saint Giovanni dei Fiorentini on the one side of the River Tevere. We hold up our umbrellas while squeezing onto the pavement beside the row of men carrying the Christ. Bodies are touching, rubbing against each other, some really fatigued, moving slowly, but still desiring to be close the sedan.

We are chanting once again the Señor de los Milagros's hymn:

Señor de los Milagros, a ti venimos en procesión
tus fieles devotos a implorar tu bendición
con paso firme de buen cristiano hagamos grande nuestro Perú
unido todos con una fuerza te suplicamos no des tu honor.

[Lord of the Miracles, we come to you in procession
Your faithful devotees to implore for your blessing,
With a steady walk of a good Christian we are making stronger our Peru
Together we strongly beg you to give us your honor.]

Some fellow pilgrims do not share this national connection to Peru, being from other parts of the Americas, but they chant anyway. I know that the solidarity expressed by this communal chanting does not necessarily go very deep. Migrants do not always accept the pan–Latin Americanism championed by the priests who lead the Latin American Mission in Rome. Church pedagogies that aspire to cultivate pan-Latin Americanism among Latin American transnational migrants often cannot overcome existing national divisions (Napolitano 2016).

A few hours earlier we had left the section of Piazza Saint Peter that is in Vatican territory. The only ones who should carry Him (*El*) on that territory are the most distinguished members of the Brotherhood. During the procession *fiscales* (a sort of Brotherhood police force) can check on those members—dressed in their devotional violet tunics—who may go astray (usually moving too far from the procession, or engaging in unnecessary or disrespectful behavior) while waiting their turn to carry the Christ. If caught going astray, they may receive a fine, while the worst offense would bring an interdiction against carrying the Christ for a given period. This would be a deep source of shame.

The kind of shame here does not belong to the old debate on the nature of honor in Mediterranean. Jacqueline Rose reminds us that shame is a transitive and intransitive form of circulation and transmission of affect that is inflicted and can be self-inflicted (as in being ashamed). In Rose's words, "It shunts back and forth, crossing the boundaries between inner and outer."[15] This shame may have intersected with the history of the Angolan slaves who painted the Señor de los Milagros in Lima, and certainly it accompanies the gendered migrant itineraries of Peruvians now in Rome.

Latin American male migrants in Italy suffer a well-documented feminization of migrant labor.[16] Many find employment only in caring for elderly, often housebound people. Their strength lifts bodies in pain. They have to use cream on their hands to handle with care. Yet calloused hands are what migrants expected to show—once back in Peru—as a trace of hard labor in respected labor niches such as the construction industry. Hands that are too soft are a source of shame. Touching in the wrong way with these same hands is also the source of another shame. Let me explain.

FIGURE 18.1. Hands in procession.

In Roberto's words again:

> One of its [the Brotherhood's] aims is to transform from illegality to legality through the sacraments. One has to have proof of having received them, or to take them if one has not done so yet, so it is a form of evangelization or catechesis. It is a form of life. So it is not a legality of the state, there are people who belong to the Hermandad who are in prison, we know they have stolen because they needed to send money to Peru and they did not know how to do it otherwise, but we talk of the *legality of the soul*.[17]

Through caring for and carrying the Lord of the Miracles, both men and women "give of themselves" as true Catholics. They become the passionate engine of a renewed Catholic Church. Roberto again:

> If you really cannot do it anymore you ask for a change, but this is a shame [*verguenza*], the same as when you are not permitted to carry Him because of the discipline within the brotherhood. When you are carrying the Señor de los Milagros you are not thinking, this is just another thing. What we carry on our shoulders is not a symbol of the Señor de los Milagros, it *is* the Señor de los Milagros, so we cannot touch Him with our own hands, we just have to hold Him on our shoulders. Because the hands are dirty, and would you touch a *señor puro* with dirty hands?

So there are dirty hands, devotional hands, hands that are too clean, hands that want to carry, and hands that are ashamed to carry—all signaling different points on an affective continuum of the flesh.

On that windy afternoon, the carriers look increasingly fatigued. The faces of a few are twisted in grimaces of pain, while their steps shuffle together rhythmically. As a member puts it to me later, you have to abandon your body to Him. Then that self-abandon is carved on the flesh and the faces of the carriers. The fatigue is also breaking barriers. In the church's refectory, at the end of the pilgrimage, fatigued but happy men share a meal with their family and fellow brothers. There is laughter, pride, and joy to have carried Him. Fatigue and self-abandon also bring people closer and heal some of the wounds of shameful labor (recall the soft hands cared for with cream). Hence a part of this received Catholic *officium* is also a form of "heroic" carrying, a "masculine" capacity to bear a crushing weight, part of an ennobling that a man experiences by keeping or performing a promise to the Señor (*cumplir con El*).

Abandonment is a transitive action; you can abandon something or someone, but you can also abandon your self *to* something, in the sense of losing yourself in it or merging with it. It is an act of interrelatedness that inspires not only devotion but also the sociality that articulates the Brotherhood. The care of the Señor de los Milagros, of the body of Christ, is a form of interrelatedness that animates the affective space between things—not only Christ's icon but also worshippers' rosaries, scarves, mobile phones, and so on, that are entrusted to members of the Brotherhood, who wipe them around the Christ's foot stigmata at the climax of the celebration. This happens, for instance, at the end of October when the sedan is laid to rest a while in Saint Peter Square, at the midpoint of the main annual procession in Rome.

But the presence of the Señor de los Milagros in Rome signals a critical ambiguity. On the one hand, migrant men wish to be visible, to show that they can carry "Him," that they have "legality of the soul," and to be seen by the (pretty) women following the procession. At a time when transnational migrant labor from the global South in Italy is invisible in the sense of having few of the entitlements of citizenship, spiritual citizenship interjects another imaginary of power and potency into a (powerless) "secular" one. On the other hand, to care for the Señor de los Milagros is *entregarse a El* (to offer oneself to Him), to abandon oneself to Him, and to trust to Him what is especially precious—one's own children (the only ones who are lifted to touch Him when the sedan is laid to rest at the end of the procession). It is a self-abandon that gradually reveals itself in the faces and the increasingly shuffling steps of the exhausted migrants, under the drizzling rain. And within this ambiguity of migrants' visibility and invisibility in Italy the (migrant) body is invested with this Catholic office.[18] The weight of the Señor de los Milagros lifts the carriers to a lighter moral level, but it is also a constant reminder of the limitations (and excesses) of carnality. As a priest in Rome who follows these migrants put it: "Some of these men do not even know what to recite in the Mass. For them the Señor de los Milagros is something else, they do not need us [the priests]." Hence, as in other migrant devotional fields here, the Señor de los Milagros reinstates while also displacing the "centrality" of the Catholic Church in Rome.

By *centrality* I refer to the priestly role of mediation in the Catholic Church. Following that mandate, the Catholic Church has also stressed with the Second

Vatican Council the importance of the involvement of the laity in the processes of catechism and evangelization. That has opened new possibilities of engagement but also new problems around the role of lay leadership. Moreover, with its nearly military-like structure, the Brotherhood is ridden by its own tensions related to the politics of memory. Some of the members of the Brotherhood allege that other members are associated with the Shining Path movement, and still another is described as having being part of the secret police of a former president, Alberto Fujimori, who ran a very violent extermination campaign against Shining Path members during his mandate.[19] Here two opposite political stories present within the same transnational organization. Moreover, the Brotherhood contains another tension: between those who are more in tune with the social and festive mandate of the group and those who wish to cultivate more traditional religious aspirations (for instance, to uphold a stricter sacramental life).

Yet the Brotherhood seems to be thriving in this Italian Catholic landscape. Another female Peruvian devotee, part of the group of the *cantoras*, says, "There are tensions between the different national churches here in Rome, and there are few places to meet, but this is our struggle, also the struggle of Christ and the Señor de los Milagros. We are also the new blood of the Church here in Rome: we are the pulsating heart. Look at some churches here: no passions, no devotions—they would be dead spaces if it were not for us immigrants." The Señor Los Milagros blesses the city, and even if one does not have a legal residence permit one can become a *regolare dello spirito* (one regularized in the spirit). The power and presence of the Señor de los Milagros can grant a "legality of the soul" and "spiritual citizenship" to the urban (often undocumented) migrants who dwell in a contested and policed terrain at the interface of the Italian state and the Catholic Church. The donning of the Brother-hood's special garments realigns the boundaries of legality/illegality and indexes an ongoing slippage between Catholic political theology and Italian political economy. I address this in more detail in the remainder of this chapter.

THE LABOR OF THE RELIGIOUS

Candido, until 2014 the *mayordomo* of the Brotherhood in Rome, stresses that "we are not living under laws, but under grace, and grace has its beginning in love." Living under grace is not believed to make one immune from the troubles of life— indeed, recently the golden ornaments of the Señor were stolen from the church. Candido had to commission new ones, which now are kept in a safe and are added to the image only when it is taken in procession and not when it normally rests in one of the naves of the small church of Santa Maria della Luce in Trastevere—the headquarters of the Latin American Mission in Rome. Candido explains that in the last two years the Brotherhood has raised funds to refurbish part of the sedan, and they have just acquired a large beautifully embroidered *manta* (handmade blanket) directly from Peru. But not "living under the laws" implies another form of subjection.

The Lord should be *imponente* (imposing, bearing a majestic aspect); he has a weight on the carrying flesh: "The Lord is so pure and beautiful, and we want to make him more powerful [*poderoso*] and glorious [*glorioso*], so that everybody respects him, even the Roman traffic wardens and the police of the *questura* [who gives out permits to carry out the procession in the streets of Rome]."

The *presencia* (presence) of the Lord is important in such a way that it makes you feel, not so much "mas hombre" in carrying him, as more "minuscule and fragile." As a man, one has to make oneself "little" to be able to receive Him. Carrying produces a circulation of affects of shame and pride that bring up associations with servitude, magnitude, and glory.

The labor of religious care animates the flesh. The Latin American Mission in Rome and the Catholic Church at large aim to shape this transnational migrant labor as suffering and sacrificial, and ultimately as a productive labor force.[20] However, being chosen to care for and to carry the Señor de los Milagros shows that more tensions are at play. To be entrusted to or to be ashamed by "Him" opens up a terrain of masculinity where, at a specific sociopolitical conjuncture, *carrying* emerges as a form of self-abandon and shame (if you are picked up by a *fiscal*), or a release from it (you can live with your soft hands). So the growing visibility of religious "cultural expressions" such as El Cristo Morado (the Purple Christ, another name for the Señor de los Milagros) cannot be read only in the light of the dynamics of changes brought about by globalization;[21] they must also be read in the matter(ing) of histories and the orientation of bodies and the flesh.

To borrow Sara Ahmed's term, a touch (and at times the interdiction of touching) between the material image of the Lord and the bodies of the devotees is a "fleshy metonymy," a relation of closeness and proximity "between particular bodies and the 'body' of the social in that each comes into a precarious being only through being touched by the other."[22] This fleshy metonymy characterizes a Catholic sensorium. To study such a sensorium requires a focus on orientations of aesthetics and politics of touch (and contacts) that characterizes Catholicism in its multiple political, embodied, aesthetic, and economic registers. This tactile sensorium informs particularly Catholicism and its study of carnality as well as potential (and real) orientations of excesses of the flesh (part of a long history of erotic, mystical encounters, but of course also of the ambiguous "touching" of sexual abuse).

To conclude, I have focused here on how Catholic faith and practices produce orientations and attachments between bodies, flesh, and objects. To put it another way, I have explored an articulation between investment with a (liturgical) office and historical, affective regimes of (in this case migrant) labor. Such a focus also opens a perspective on the study of the animation of materiality in Catholicism along a continuum from a performance of liturgy to one of labor, a distribution of what Pitt Rivers (in this volume) would have called an economy of grace.

Eric Santner, following Ernst Kantorowicz, has cogently proposed that we need to explore not only how the mystic body of Christ has been transferred to a (mystical) body of a (premodern) kin, and distributed through his royal remains but also how the force of a *corpus mysticum* of Christ (as an immanent, yet spectral presence of transcendental value) can be studied through systems of circulation of the flesh and the excesses it produces.[23] Together with Giorgio Agamben they have both clearly shown that the economy and the management of a circulation of glory and splendor is not just a premodern (and royal) economic form—it informs present modes of living too.[24] Developing Foucault's argument on the shift from royal sovereignty to modern governmentality, Santner argues that this shift is not complete: there is always a residue of the mystical, royal body, a mystical and vital force of the flesh that we have to contend with in the present.

So by foregrounding an affective study of a migrant and liturgical praxis (being invested with the office to carry El Señor and keeping the promise to do so), I have explored here how this form of migrant Catholicism is in tension with affects of shame, self-abandon, orientations of touch (and the hands), and suffering. I argue that through a focus on the flesh, its orientation, its interdiction (where hands should not be placed), and the circulation of affect, devotion to the Lord of the Miracles in Rome liturgically invests the gendered bodies of migrant devotees. Affective tensions constitute a force field around devotional objects that orients subject(s) matter—those constitute an area of research where an anthropology of Catholicism can shed new light on the link between political theology and political economies.

If a gendered orientation of the migrant body and flesh is also an investiture of the body with the remains of the mystic Corpus of Christ (in this case through a Cristo Morado), the movement of the religious migrant highlights an economy of the flesh that rests between somatic experience (of the body) and normative experience (of state and cleric governmentalities). Migrants invested by a liturgical power of the office of the Brotherhood are also laboring bodies in economies of shame and perceived feminization (the carrying hands are shamefully soft). In the performative space of Roman streets, as in Saint Peter's square, the members of the Brotherhood are imbued with a glory of Christ, an authority to "govern" as people who have received a spiritual form of citizenship that is present regardless of their normative migration status (migrants can be documented or undocumented, yet they are *always* spiritual citizens).

So rather than examining El Señor de los Milagros in Rome as a religious migrants' movement, I have elected here to focus on migrants' investment by an office—the *sacrum officium* of a catholic brotherhood; this is a study of the religious in movement. By doing this I have foregrounded the orientation of migrant flesh and the gendered body within an economy of glory and royal remains (to use

Santner's words) that the presence of the Señor de los Milagros and the Peruvian *pátria* put in motion.

If, as Santner and Kantorowicz might argue, there is a residue here, an excess in the passage from an authority of the king to the authority of the political economy of the state (and its forms of management), I have delved into where this excess may be, and in which flesh. This residue is harnessed through the office that the migrants get invested and invited into by carrying the Señor de Los Milagros, which exceeds the normative authority of the present Italian nation-state. Parallel to an economy of productive immigrant labor stands an economy of migrant *spiritual citizenship* that articulates the intersection of the material and the spiritual, attempting to harbor a spectral dimension of a (Christic) flesh.[25] How successfully this competes with clerical liturgical attempts to secure a harbor in this same mystic and spectral power of the flesh of Christ is an open question.

NOTES

1. "Bodies may become oriented in this responsiveness to the world around them, given this capacity to be affected. In turn, given the history of such responses, which accumulate as impressions on the skin, bodies do not dwell in spaces that are exterior but rather are shaped by their dwellings and take shape by dwellings" (Ahmed 2006, 9).

2. Bynum (2011, 35).

3. See Napolitano (2015).

4. See Bynum (2011, 33): "The expression of and reaction to Christ's humanity, even his bodylines, were part of a larger religious discourse about the material itself and how it might manifest or embody God."

5. I refer here in turns to the work of Morgan (1998, 2005); see also Keane (1997, 2008), Matthew Engelke (2007), and Taussig (1992, 1997).

6. Napolitano (2015).

7. Napolitano (2016, 5). Consider the allegations that some of the leading figures of the IOR (Instituto per le Opere Religiose) are not so holy and have been corrupted by "careerism"—Tarciso Bertone, for example, secretary of state of the Holy See between June 2006 and August 2013, named by the press as one of the key cardinals in the Holy See who, willingly or unwillingly, pushed Benedict XVI to resign the papacy.

8. And it engenders ethical forms of interrelatedness that, more than ever, underpin neoliberal expressions of flexible (e.g., voluntary and charitable) work, as well as the founding values of the European Union (Muehlebach 2012; Holmes 2000).

9. Paerregaard (2008).

10. Paerregaard (2008, 2010).

11. Normally there is a clear gendered division of labor, but since Peruvian female migration has been prominent in Rome, women here do carry smaller icons, as was the case with the "enthroning" of Señor de La Justicia in the Church of Santa Maria della Luce in spring 2011. Enthroning a particular image means that from then on it is officially "seated": it belongs to that church and must be looked after by the lay and religious constituents of that parish.

12. Roberto is a very articulate, perfectly bilingual lawyer in his late twenties who grew up on the outskirts of Rome from the age of thirteen, in a family whose grandmother was totally devoted to El Señor de los Milagros.

13. See Molero and Oshier (2005); Paerregaard (2008, 2010).

14. For a further connection between bearing and suffering, see Mayblin (2010).

15. J. Rose (2003, 2).

16. According to available census data of 2013/2014, Latin American immigrants in Italy constituted 7.7 percent of the overall immigrant population in Italy. Peruvian immigrants numbered around ninety-nine thousand people clustered in and around major urban centers such as Genoa, Milan, and Rome. Peruvian immigration to Italy began in the early 1980s, and although it was initially overwhelmingly female, by 2014 the sex ratio was around 65 percent female and 35 percent male. Of this overall Peruvian immigrant population, 93 percent were employed in theservice sector and only 7 percent in industry and agriculture. Among the Peruvian population residing in Rome, the proportion of those employed in the service sector is even higher (see Dossier Statistico Immigrazione 2014).

17. For similar language and insights regarding the hidden theological core of the state, see Garces (2010).

18. For a discussion of the visibility/invisibility of migrants in Rome and the Catholic Church, see Napolitano (forthcoming).

19. Shining Path (Sendero Luminoso) was a Maoist liberation movement that supported the violent liberation of indigenous peoples and peasants in Andean Peru during the 1980s and early 1990s. It was supported by an urban intelligentsia but failed to canvass a response from, and actually clashed with, the indigenous population. Alberto Fujimori led a major repressive and military reaction to this movement during his presidency (1990–2000).

20. Napolitano (2016).

21. See Molero and Oshier (2005) for a case analyzing the devotion to the Señor de Qoyllur Rit'i in New York City.

22. Ahmed (2000, 49).

23. Santner (2011); Kantorowicz (1997).

24. Agamben (2001).

25. On the reading of Christ as the ultimate example of a becoming-flesh specter, see Derrida ([1993] 1994, 180): "If every specter, as we have amply seen, is distinguished from spirit by an incorporation, by the phenomenal form of quasi-incarnation, then Christ is the most spectral of specters."

19

Making a Home in an Unfortunate Place

Phenomenology and Religion

J. Michelle Molina

If to do philosophy is to discover the primary sense of being, then one does not philosophize in quitting the human situation; it is necessary rather to plunge into it.

—MAURICE MERLEAU-PONTY, "IN PRAISE OF PHILOSOPHY"

"I remained an unfortunate place to myself."[1] Augustine of Hippo lamented the scattered and distended nature of human subjectivity. Forever distracted, human existence entails being pulled in opposing directions by memories of the past and anticipations of a future. Further, we are never in accord with our physical selves: we grasp impossibly at past and future, while the body itself transforms and disintegrates in a here and now. Augustine's misfortune is that he cannot coincide with himself.[2] Unity with God is difficult when one is not a unified being. Unified being with God, according to Augustine, is an unattainable endeavor for mere humans, although the sainted body provides an exception to the rule of human depravity. At best, unity of mind/soul/body with God is to be deferred, arrived at only in heaven. Thus, after the Fall, anxiety, but also hope, structure Christian life, as one can lean toward the End Times that promise release from the bonds of nature.[3]

Here Augustine stands as a way-marker. The difficulty of "unity" that he points toward, however, does not belong only to Christian seekers. Approaches to the study of religious experience suffer from a "disunity" problem that stems from a legacy of mind-body dualism. Scholarship on religion could be characterized as distended, as scholars who seek to understand lived religion engage in an exhausting jog, as if between bases, now tagging "mind," then circling back to acknowledge "body," and, more recently, moving to incorporate "materiality" or "matter." While recent religious studies scholarship advocates the materialist turn as a solution to a mind-body dualism that is too "Protestant" in its expression (and thus for some, a means of recuperating Catholic devotional life), I suggest that, in a quest to better unify mind-body-matter in the study of lived human experience in the world, a critical anthropology of Catholicism could profitably incorporate phenomenology of embodiment as articulated by the mid-twentieth-century French philosopher Maurice Merleau-Ponty.[4] For Augustine, embodiment is a problem, a hindrance to the ultimate unity with God that has Augustine pointing toward the afterlife. Yet for Merleau-Ponty embodiment provides an avenue that emphasizes unity, but in an *enfleshed* world that is in many ways as mysterious as any afterlife Augustine could imagine. In what follows, I situate my thoughts about Merleau-Ponty within a discussion of how his phenomenology can connect two distinct conversations taking place in religious studies today, one about religious relationships and the other pertaining to material religions. I suggest that we utilize phenomenology as a descriptive method but also adopt it as a philosophic practice,[5] that is, an intellectual stance. Doing so, I contend, poses a specific challenge to scholars to loosen their hold upon the category of "religion" and rather, as intrepid trail followers, to use phenomenological methods to take note of the variety of concepts and objects, selves and others that emerge from embodied experience.

PROBLEMS: BODY, MIND, MATTER, MEANING

In a rigorous and insightful "state-of-the-field" evaluation, Constance Furey offers an overview of how the most prevalent questions in the last two decades of religious studies scholarship have revolved around the vexed position of "the body," as the locus of meaning, the vector of practice, the object of representation, or the subject of ritual action.[6] She echoes Robert Orsi's lament that the lived body appears too often as the socialized body, the disciplined body.[7] For Furey and Orsi praxis has trumped subjectivity. Meaning is out, practice is in, inner experience is passé and too Protestant a notion, the socialized body is the only aspect of lived religiosity for which scholars can—responsibly? safely?—account. Even recent interventions on the topic of "ethical self-formation" are still too hesitant when it comes to imputing religious meaning, but unnecessarily so, Furey contends, circling this scholarship back upon itself with the sage observation that, ultimately, "what is at stake in these studies of *praxis* is ... the question of *meaning.*"[8] Both Orsi and Furey offer a way out of this either-or conundrum, arguing that a rich and nuanced account of religiosity can be found by privileging relationships, a suggestion taken up by Brenna Moore, whose recent essay on friendship demonstrates how religiosity can be understood through "the personal domain of mutual bonds."[9] This mode of analysis and description puts the living human at the center of a complex web of practices and representations, felt experience, and desire, as well as contingent social forces, in sum, capturing *meaning* and *materiality* within religious experience.

I want to pause over this word *materiality*. Scholars across the humanities, including religious studies, have been taking a new look at material culture, asking us to consider not what a thing *is* but rather what it *does*.[10] Notions of vibrant materiality draw our attention to assemblages of actors—human and material—but without positing a subject-object dichotomy. As Jane Bennett states the aims of this approach, "There was never a time when human agency was anything other than an interfolding network of humanity and nonhumanity; today this mingling has become harder to ignore."[11] In her efforts to highlight this part-whole relationship, Bennett brackets the human, seeking a horizontal, nonhierarchical, and less human-centered notion of agentive activity.[12] Attuned to a more distributive notion of agency, she asks scholars to begin to see the capacious and entangled nature of a materiality in which human subjectivity is subsumed as just one more vital element within assemblages of agentive things. In sum, "vital materiality" is the name of a fast-moving theoretical highway that leads toward understanding the "life of things."

Some scholars of religion are quite optimistic that analytic approaches to "thing-power" could have the capacity to open up new horizons in religious studies scholarship.[13] Notably, there are some especially high hopes for how the study of Catholicism might fare within this new analytical frame. As Jennifer Hughes wrote recently, "The Protestant-normative, Reformationist, Western, and utterly 'American' ethos of religious studies, with the invisible *mysterium* over the material *tremendum,* its reverence for the interior and disdain for the exterior—these have hindered the development of a theoretical apparatus capable of approximating and interpreting the complex role of living matter in diverse religious practices."[14] In sum, Hughes sees embracing the materialist turn as a refusal to impose European (colonial) terms: "Rather than systematically imposing Western ontological categories on religious and cultural phenomena that can hardly be encompassed adequately within these parameters, scholars might manifest an openness or willingness to revise or suspend these ontological understandings when confronting cultural systems that contrast starkly with Western philosophical norms."[15]

Clearly, the high-speed thought surrounding new materialism is a bit thrilling, and I am similarly intrigued by the new materialist turn, yet I am apprehensive about this brand of enthusiasm. A simple worry is that religionists will be diverted from the relational dimensions of religiosity outlined by Furey and Orsi. Is the body of lived religion to remain forever disciplined because scholarly attention has shifted to "the life of things"? Bennett's call to "bracket the human" can be most problematic for scholars of religion in that one might simply invert the vexed categories of inner/outer and mind/matter, with "outer" and "matter" now more worthy of study than "inner" and "mind."

Yet more disquieting is the valorization of the mystery of vital matter, the *mysterium materiae,* as Hughes puts it, that sets up the vitality of the material world within a just-so story in which Catholic materiality triumphantly resists the West-ern colonial legacy while simultaneously dethroning Protestant theology's domin-ion over religious studies terms and concepts—all in one fell swoop. The desire for an authentic mode of being that has evaded a colonial history or a Protestant-hued modernity is a strong fantasy indeed, but one that often results in intrepid aca-demic *writing* more than any kind of liberation from the entangled webs of history. Of greatest concern is that this view mistakenly positions not only Catholicism but also Latin America as having evaded the domain of Western philosophy instead of having been part of its foundation. Hughes is herself inspired by Bennett, whose attention to materiality draws upon philosophers ranging from Lucretius to Spinoza to Latour to understand Latin American Catholic devotional life, and I see no problem with this. Put more simply, the range of Western philosophic thought and practice is quite broad and does not speak in a single voice.

Better in my view to ask, what philosophic connections has Catholicism's glo-bal history made possible? How and when have philosophic ideas percolated into everyday Catholic practice? Here I am taking a page from David Scott's work on colonial governmentality. At the turn of our new century, Scott insisted that the critical questions about our global present could no longer be framed as decidedly anticolonial scholarly projects. He argued not so much for rejecting Europe and its centrality as for configuring it differently—much as Dipesh Chakrabarty spoke of "provincializing" it—and for doing scholarship that would attend to the many ways in which European modes of self-governance became integral aspects of colonial lives.[16] His work informs my own intellectual commitment to understand Europe and Latin America as vitally connected: to tap into the life-worlds of Latin Americans past and present, we must take into account not only a coercive and at times brutal Catholic colonialism but also the introduction of forms of philo-sophic practice embedded in what has been called the "care of souls" tradition. This genealogy includes ancient philosophers like Cicero but also church fathers like Cassian and Gregory the Great, as well as modern modes of philosophic thought from Descartes to Heidegger.[17] Accordingly, my own scholarship has attempted to historicize the ways in which the circulation of Catholic devotional practices globalized the philosophical imperatives to know and care for, indeed, to *discover* a self. In writing about Jesuit ethical formation, I found the phenomenol-ogy of embodiment a particularly apt mode of analysis for writing an *embodied* history of how colonial subjects began to experience themselves as split between mind and body.[18]

My aim in this essay is to draw attention to the Western philosophy of phenom-enology because it *has* questioned the radical distinction between subject and object and, in sum, has grappled with the problem of body/mind/matter but, sig-nificantly, without choosing sides, so to speak. Rather, phenomenology provides tools to think about the materiality of both human and nonhuman subjects, offering an approach that is inclusive of the *intersubjective relations* that Furey has insisted are critical to understanding human religiosity, but notably, phenomenology views human/nonhuman relationality *as itself intersubjective* because embodied action is how bodies/space/matter come into being. If religious studies is moving from an emphasis on the human experiential dimension of "lived religion" to explore the "vital materiality" of the world of things, then the phenomenological approach to embodiment can provide a means to interrogate the "divide" between the two while also forging something of a bridge to span the chasm that divides these disparate literatures. In particular, the phenomenology of embodiment closes down the distance between humans and matter, enabling an interrogation of human being as deeply rooted, in fact, *as* a form of material life. As we will see shortly, Merleau-Ponty's notion of "flesh" provides an orientation toward understanding human being-in-the world as a vital materiality. To this end, new scholarship on materiality is very suggestive and yet potentially problematic for the scholar of religion, for the category "religion" emerges from the primordial foundation of being and knowing, that is, from *human* embodied perception that is impossible to bracket when one is attempting to understand what materializes as *religious* about an experience.

Merleau-Ponty's philosophy, with embodiment as its central problematic, provides an avenue to carefully examine this conundrum. Merleau-Ponty described the lived world as a *knot of relations*. His human-centered philosophy of being-in-the world attends to the materiality of being and opens a way to think about human and nonhuman situated within a single frame. Following Husserl, Merleau-Ponty works with a revised notion of "intentionality" that does not reside in conscious awareness. Rather, Merleau-Ponty locates intentionality as the attitude and orientation of body geared into world. His notion of being or being-in-the-world posits the phenomenal body as a starting point and argues that to perceive is to bring objects and concepts into shape as they are grasped. *Body* is anchored in the world, *consciousness* trails in its wake, never truly experiencing that moment of embodied fusion, rarely conscious of itself as geared or anchored. Selves and objects emerge from the movement of a body geared into world by motility (*motricité*), that is, the mobile body is itself the perceiving subject. Unity, the primordial experience of the lived body, remains elusive, impossible to consciously inhabit.

Embodied action is always intertwined within the matrices of time (habit-body) and space (body-of-this-moment). Thus the emergence of *meaning* emphasizes both sedimentary layers of history and culture (insights that predated and influenced Pierre Bourdieu's emphasis on *habitus* as spontaneous iteration of a sedimented embodied history), but meaning is grasped in a momentary coherence in which ground and figure shape one another in a "now." In other words, there is a certain experiential thickness that does not belong solely to either "individual," "community," or "thing." History is folded into motility, not as a "datum," but rather as a tension. In fact, Merleau-Ponty's notion of a momentary coherence (outlined so beautifully in his essay on Cézanne's style of painting) captures the sense of the historian's catchword—*contingency*—a word whose meaning is best encapsulated in Paul Valéry's quip that history is the science of that which never happens twice. And yet we attempt to herd those unique unrepeatable moments into patterns of meaning.

> Seeing, speaking, even thinking (with certain reservations, for as soon as we distinguish thought from speaking absolutely we are already in the order of reflection), are experiences of this kind, both irrecusable and enigmatic. They have a name in all languages, but a name which in all of them also conveys significations in tufts, thickets of proper meanings and figurative meanings, so that, unlike those of science, not one of these names clarifies by attributing to what is named a circumscribed signification. Rather, they are the repeated index, the insistent reminder of a mystery as familiar as it is unexplained, of a light which, illuminating the rest, remains at its source in obscurity.[19]

Accordingly, "concepts" are always reductive because embodied experience overflows conceptual frameworks, or, as he says above, "Not one of these names clarifies by attributing to what is named a circumscribed signification." Further, Merleau-Ponty's "body-of-this-moment" emphasizes an openness and possibility that we forfeit when we insist upon starting as "subjects" taking up our "objects" of study. *Thought* cannot contain the richness — nor the evasive mystery, in Merleau-Ponty's terms—of embodied experience. In the next section, I suggest that the anthropology of Catholicism pay close attention to his insistence that body/mind/matter absolutely *cannot* be taken up separately because they are fused, of one and the same thing, a unity.

FLESH

Where are we to put the limit between the body and the world, since the world is flesh?

—MAURICE MERLEAU-PONTY, "THE INTERTWINING—THE CHIASM."

Let us circle back, momentarily, to the problematic of embodied existence that so vexed Augustine. If worldly existence was potential distraction, fascination with nature was all the more so. Nature, while evidence of God's omnipotence and thus justifiably an object of reverent awe, ought not to become an object of curiosity. "What excuse can I make for myself when often, as I sit at home, I cannot turn my eyes from the sight of a lizard catching flies or a spider entangling them as they fly into her web?. . . My life is full of such faults and my only hope is in your boundless mercy. For when our hearts become repositories piled high with such worthless stock as this, it is the cause of interruption and distraction from our prayers."[20] Curiosity enacts yet another form of distraction for the already distended and scattered human. Augustine deemed curiosity about nature a potentially "ungodly" situation in which "the mind has fallen in love with bodies outside itself through the senses of the flesh and has become involved with them through a long familiarity."[21] Yet what Augustine deemed "ungodly" caught the imagination of Merleau-Ponty, that is to say, the senses of the flesh, body's "long familiarity" with the world; this idolatrous situation provided the terms through which Merleau-Ponty theorized a form of embodied *unity*. Where Augustine had implored, "Do not wish to go out; go back into yourself. Truth dwells in the inner man," Merleau-Ponty summarily rejected the notion of "inner" experience and "outer" material world, instead observing that there is no inner man. "Man is in the world" and this human does not *search* for meaning, he is *condemned* to it.[22]

To reiterate, Merleau-Ponty's phenomenology utilizes a notion of a lived world that accounts for humans and objects simultaneously as a "knot of relations."[23] In his late writing, he began to develop an ontology of "flesh" as an element or substrate from which "subjects" and "objects" emerge,[24] a body of work that was sketched out but remained unfinished at the time of his death in 1961. Yet even his early writings on Cézanne's painting (1945) gave his readers a sense of the intertwining of matter and man. About Cézanne, he wrote: "But he himself was never at the center of himself. . . . It was in the world that he had to realize his freedom, with colors upon a canvas."[25] His *Phenomenology of Perception* describes the body as anchored or geared into the world in such a way that being-in-the-world limits consciousness's ability to determine itself. "Consciousness must be brought face to face with its unreflective life in things and must awaken to its own, forgotten, history—that is the true role of philosophical reflection and this is how a true theory of attention is established."[26]

Over the course of his life, Merleau-Ponty dug deeper into nature and began to posit an ontology in which "subject" and "object" emerge as differentiations within fleshly unity.[27] Flesh is unitary being: intentionality is itself derived from this unity, and what he called *écart* (fold, break, or rupture in the unity) is what is experienced as "subject" and "object." This is not a divide but a folding over. As theologian Andreas Nordlander explains, subject/object differentiations of flesh are "a play of difference within unity."[28] Nordlander goes on to summarize what is at stake in this formulation: "It is therefore not a question of showing how two (consciousness and nature) united into one (the body) but of how one (being) separates into two (perceiver and perceived)."[29] This leads us to see that humans are, themselves, abundant objects and the reason why the turn toward materiality must simultaneously account for human being. "If to do philosophy is to discover the primary sense of being, then one does not philosophize in quitting the human situation; it is necessary rather to plunge into it."[30] Instead of splitting or bracketing the human, Merleau-Ponty's notion of flesh provides an orientation toward understanding human experience as a manifestation of uniquely vital matter.

CAVEAT: NOT "PHENOMENOLOGY OF RELIGION"

What I am advocating here is distinct from recent efforts to recuperate "the phenomenology of religion" of the early twentieth century. In a recent edition of the *Journal of the American Academy of Religion,* Jason Blum made a case for recovering the phenomenology of religion for the field of religious studies. The problem child in the phenomenology of religion is Mircea Eliade (1907–86). As Blum states succinctly, Eliade "suggests that there is something to religion that stands apart from its historical manifestations and which cannot be reduced to context, and it is that essence of religion with which the phenomenologist is primarily concerned."[31] Husserl's methodology of *epoché* was intended to prevent positing an object as natural. Yet Eliade utilized Husserl's *epoché* to distill the "essence" of religion and thus hold it apart from other forms of experience, a move that has been termed a "protectionist strategy to guard religion from social science."[32]

Blum wishes to move away from this kind of essentialism, but in my view he does not venture far enough. He contends that phenomenological description is a form of interpretation that can capture "the meaning of religion from the perspective of religious experience and consciousness."[33] "Conceptualized in this fashion, the meaning that phenomenology of religion seeks to disclose is not transcendent; it is the meaning encapsulated and expressed in the *religious discourse, text, or experience under analysis.*"[34] The terms *consciousness* and *experience of the religious subject* run throughout Blum's essay as if interchangeable, signaling the kind of *conscious* focus, attention, and/or intentionality of actors who are *aware* of their experiences as "religious." This is not objectionable, but neither is it phenomenology proper. Despite his stated intention, "religious experience" continues to sound like a defensive strategy—here the *epoché* functions once again as a hands-off maneuver, protecting the essential elements of religious life from critical analysis by naming in advance what the phenomenological method will produce.[35] Yes, "religion" is a concept that prompts those who study it to reach for certain sets of texts, institutions, practices, and objects that we understand in advance to be "religious." Yet naming "religion" as the hoped-for object in fact diminishes the methodological power of the *epoché,* as *religion itself* is the naturalized object that requires bracketing.

Phenomenology could be more appropriate to the issues that animate religious studies today—the tangled weave of body, mind, matter—if we retrieved phenomenology via Merleau-Ponty, who has largely been ignored in religious studies.[36] This strikes me as a real loss for scholars of religion, as Merleau-Ponty makes clear that phenomenological description is aimed at capturing *momentary coherences* and thus allowing scholars of religion to tackle the problem of essentialism head on. A close reading of his work would have us ask our questions differently. How does the concept "religion" emerge from an embodied experience that overflows that limited category? If we are condemned to meaning, as Merleau-Ponty contends, then all meaning making, all *thought*, is reductive, in that it "reduces" an unbounded phenomenal field to the more limited terrain of representation. Perhaps not remarkably, he once described perceiving as an act of faith.

> Faith—in the sense of an unreserved commitment which is never completely justified—enters the picture as soon as we leave the realm of pure geometrical ideas and have to deal with the existing world. *Each of our perceptions is an act of faith in that it affirms more than we strictly know, since objects are inexhaustible and our information limited.* Descartes even said that believing two and two makes four demands an act of will. How can the Catholic be blamed for living equivocally if everybody dwells in the same state and if bad faith is the very essence of consciousness?[37]

Instead of engaging in the vexed hand-wringing about "reductionism," Merleau-Ponty helps us see that the human condition is embodied orientation toward meaning making. There is no escaping reductionism.

PHENOMENOLOGY AS SPIRITUAL EXERCISE

Embodied experience: the source of possibility for Merleau-Ponty, the source of much vexation for Augustine. Yet the question—What is it to be a human anchored in the world?—serves as a reminder of what the ethnography and history of Catholicism can illuminate. We are, however, left with the question: What kind of anthropology is this? Michael Jackson has for some years worked to inject philosophy into anthropology. Specifically, he has drawn upon phenomenological description to better approximate human experience in his ethnographic writing. Jackson evokes Husserl's *epoché* or bracketing as vital to ethnographic method. "The phenomenological method involves 'placing in brackets' or 'setting aside' questions concerning the rational, ontological, or objective status of ideas and beliefs in order to fully describe and do justice to the ways in which people actually live, experience, and use them—the ways in which they appear to consciousness."[38]

But we must remember that phenomenology does not just provide a method of description. It is itself a philosophical *stance,* that is, a willed orientation and an exercise in honing and refining our tools of analysis: "If we could rediscover within the exercise of seeing and speaking some of the living references that assign them such a destiny in a language, *perhaps they would teach us how to form our new instruments, and first of all to understand our research, our interrogation, themselves.*"[39]

While attention to embodied practice can itself be analyzed in phenomenological terms (e.g., description of the scholar's embodied experiences in time), what we have, in fact, is a call to vigilance, to a scholarly radical reflexivity, a paying attention to attention in order to approximate in description a primordial lived intertwining of people and objects. While Augustine aimed toward momentary glimmers of unity with God through a program of spiritual exercises that included reading and writing, Merleau-Ponty's writings about the communion of body and world can similarly be understood as a kind of philosophic exercise—what Pierre Hadot referred to as *prosoche,* the Stoic word indicating attention to attention. Merleau-Ponty's philosophical exercise aims to see through the dark glass of human consciousness to catch a primordial unity unawares. Phenomenological method entails an orientation, an aim, and the ensuing description foregrounds itself as reiterative practice aimed at capturing a moment in formation. "If it is true that as soon as philosophy declares itself to be reflection or coincidence it prejudges what it will find, then once again it must recommence everything, reject the instruments reflection and intuition had provided themselves, and install itself in a locus where they have not yet been distinguished, in experiences that have not yet been 'worked over,' that offer us all at once, pell-mell, both 'subject' and 'object,' both existence and essence, and hence give philosophy resources to redefine them."[40] Concepts are shaped to a purpose—indeed this is true for scholars of religion as well as religious subjects—for whom the *ease* of reiterability is almost always at stake: scholars and practitioners both, in their own ways, attempt to capture and name patterns of experience as "religious" representations, "religious" texts, "religious" objects, et cetera, so as to enable others to latch on to them. Yet try as they might to hold them in place, these efforts do not change the fact that, from the phenomenological point of view, those concepts and objects are simply folded again into other momentary coherences that are themselves open and unlimited and have the *potential* to become . . . perhaps "religion," or perhaps the potential to be grasped within a new assemblage, a different momentary coherence.

Religion (as study or practice) is reiterative, which is the key to establishing predictable patterns. But phenomenology is a philosophy that requires scholars to become at home with a pattern of unpredictability. What, then, would it mean to let go of "religion" and "specialness" as conceptual starting points? "Special things" is Ann Taves's approach to steering clear of essentialism in religious studies. She breaks down concepts into smaller pieces in order to better contextualize them, yet she is still dealing in the realm of categories, of ideas and things singularized and set apart.[41] I am suggesting we ask instead (or in addition), "How do the ideas and things come into being?" Moreover, could we set aside worries about losing control over the object that defines the field of religious studies? Unique among human operations is the orientation of humans toward meaning that is arrived at through embodied mobility in the world. This is the mode to which all humans are condemned—*no matter what.*

Merleau-Ponty's phenomenology of embodiment calls for a meditative practice, if you will to take up objects and practices that are sometimes but not always "religious." This inherent ambiguity is what compels scholars to ask again and again—"What is happening here?"—and to seek new orientations from which to approach possible answers. Accordingly, as Tim Ingold suggests, scholars engage in "trail-following" rather than classification.[42] On the move, the scholar forges what William Connolly calls "imperfect stabilizations."[43] We trail after that intrepid trailblazer—in an embodied momentum toward meaning—and take note of the objects and subjects, mundane and sublime, that it leaves in its wake. The philosopher's task, in Merleau-Ponty's words, is to act as witness: "The philosopher pays attention to the serious man—of action, of religion, or of passion—perhaps more acutely than anyone. But precisely in doing this, one feels that he is different. His own actions are acts of witness."[44]

In the study of representations and concepts, we begin at the end, that is, with subjects already split from objects. Yet if we take Merleau-Ponty's phenomenological writing, as I think we should, in the spirit of philosophical *exercise,* we see that just as much as Augustine strove to transcend the embodied plight to inhabit those glimmers of God's presence, Merleau-Ponty endeavored to catch being-in-the-world, an equally elusive unity, by submerging himself more fully in embodiment. Both thinkers were concerned to understand the nature of human experience, and *both* continue to provide important keys for grappling with Catholic being-in-the-world. If Merleau-Ponty insists that humans are best understood as condemned to finding meaning through lived mobility in the world, then Augustine draws our attention to the ways in which memory, hope, and despair drive human desire to *transcend* embodied being. In other words, we need to take heed of Augustine's concerns because they enable us to conduct a phenomenological anthropology of the emergence of *the desire* to be outside of time and body. In other words, a phenomenology of embodied humans geared into a world must find a way to deal with the embodied experience of the hope to transcend it.

How do ideas and things come into being? If our explanatory categories do not sufficiently *explain* how we *sense* the world on a daily basis, then how do we make sense of the sense we make? When is the prickling of skin a "religious" experience versus a "chilling" thought versus a close brush with an air-conditioning unit? Mundane experience is itself mysterious, and this experiential richness is never fully captured by the concepts that emerge from grasping attempts. How can we use Merleau-Ponty's phenomenology to write about an experience that *becomes* religious? Attention to assemblages usefully prompts us to be even more vigilant about how the absolutely mundane figures into experience. We walk into a church and take note not only of the wooden pews that support the bodies at prayer but also of the wriggling child bumping into the folded metal chairs in the corner that in turn darken a portion of the textured peeling wall upon which hangs the dimly lit venerated crucifix. But note that the new materiality's vibrant assemblages are neutralizing as well: the wooden crucifix, crucially, is no more vibrant an entity than the wooden pews or the curved vitality of the folded chair. Rather, its meaning is emergent, knotted into embodied relations. This is not an extractive process in which we point to preselected "religious" objects; rather, oblique orientations are required, a squinting of the eyes to bring other figures into view—in fact, a flattening of "religion" for a fuller view of how mobile bodies are oriented in such a way that what emerges is sometimes "politics" or "shopping" or "boredom" and sometimes "God," "miracle," or "conversion."

I put these thoughts to use as I work through an eighteenth-century conversion narrative. In this account, a Swedish Lutheran merchant named Lorenzo Thjülen took an opportunity to leave for Portugal and Spain because, inspired by Enlightenment philosophy and French literature, he wished to know the world and to arrive at the truth about religion based upon reasoned disputation. The opportunity for discussion about religion presented itself when he traveled from Cádiz to Corsica in a caravel with 1,200 Jesuits recently expelled from the Americas. On his ship he counted approximately two hundred, all of whom were from the viceroyalty of New Spain (Mexico). The ensuing conversations with the Jesuits on the topic of "the true faith" culminated in his desire to convert to Catholicism and, later, his decision to take vows as a Jesuit. Crucially, a shipboard intimacy developed between Thjülen and Manuel Iturriaga, a Mexican Jesuit theologian. At the end of the five-week journey, Thjülen could not imagine departing from this man he called "the father of my soul."[45]

The story of this convert to Catholicism arrives in my hands, to use Merleau-Ponty's words, "already in the order of reflection." That is, Thjülen wrote the account approximately a year and a half later. In it he returns to the events that led to his conversion to Catholicism and decision to become a Jesuit. So how can my historical-ethnographic writing use his account to bring that fleshly "knot of relations" into view? Trail-following in the phenomenological mode asks the scholar to attend to embodied intentionality as knotted into the many moods of water and wood, to imagine men geared into salt and stench, to recognize embodied being folded into a world that was unstable not only because of the elements but also because human conviviality shifted from the warmth of shared Mexican chocolate during afternoon breaks to the heated tension that flushed cheeks and raised voices when conversations about doctrine took unexpected turns. We pay attention to the press of the rosary that discomfited the Lutheran merchant, the material aggravation of the beads: Why *did* he put them on, wear them under his shirt, why does he stand on deck, gathered into utterances that repel him? A surprise to himself that he found himself anchored in the density of Mexican-accented voices when, daily, the men clambered up on deck to recite the Rosary, the black robes themselves becoming sonorous when no longer the distinctive clothing of two hundred individual bodies but, momentarily, a fusion of cloth, voices, weight, wind—each day different—yet each day breaking apart once again, when the prayers were finished, splitting off into smaller entities, hands pushing beads back into pockets, while Thjülen's disavowal pressed into his chest, the irritation itself the pivot that propelled him to seek solace in another conversation with Father Iturriaga.

The attempt here, in brief, has been to bring all the pieces together: matter, mind, body, and the relationships between bodies human and nonhuman. As per Merleau-Ponty's discussion of Cézanne's style of painting, to perceive is to see all at once, to flatten and make full in a single move, to pay attention to how ground and figure form one another. Phenomenology can be utilized as a great leveler: it does not, in advance, look to single out "special things" but rather asks how and when certain objects, like the rosary, at once repulsive and attractive, emerge as "religious." Accordingly, with phenomenology we can aim to capture both the concreteness and the density of Thjülen's shipboard experience as it took shape against an enfleshed seascape, a move that has great possibility for understanding the "special things" that some people deem religious but that also lends a vitality or specialness to all materiality.

Humans are fecund and abundant "objects" in a phenomenal world. Hence the folly of bracketing "the human" to access "the material," since both are constituted by "a whole series of layers of wild being."[46] Ultimately, the quest to pay attention to the emergence of "religious" things or "Catholic" things is disorienting because it is a study of a here and now (or as a historian, a there and then). Attention to location, space, time, as I point out here, *must* include the absolutely mundane and seemingly unimportant. But at the same time one must also take note of the human inhabitants of that location/space/time who point to an elsewhere, another time, or even the end of time. In working in the mode of a trail-follower, we keep tabs on them, on materiality, on ourselves, and as we do so, Augustine's problem becomes ours: we are not at home with ourselves, but we can become at home in *not being at home.*

NOTES

I am very grateful to the colleagues whose thoughtful readings of this essay were crucial to developing this thought-piece. Thank you Mira Balberg, Jennifer Callaghan, Ryan Dohoney, Constance Furey, Andrew Jankowski, and Mary Weismantel.

1. Augustine (1961, bk. 4).

2. Andrea Nightingale (2011) beautifully captures this understudied aspect of Augustine's work in her recent book *Once Out of Nature.*

3. Notably, in Eden there was no need for hope, yet crucially, hope provides the proper orientation of human desire, a most necessary postlapsarian form of anticipation of a transcendent unity once one has escaped time and stilled the body in the hereafter.

4. This is, in fact, a "return" appropriate to anthropology, whose structuralist and subsequent cultural turns are indebted to Merleau-Ponty's lectures in the 1960s at the Collège de France. See Gutting (2001).

5. Here I am drawing upon Pierre Hadot's (1995) work on ancient philosophy as a means of striving toward the unattainable, that is, wisdom.

6. Furey (2012, 7–33).

7. Orsi (2014, 7–11).

8. Furey (2012); my italics.

9. B. Moore (2015).

10. Bynum (2011); Bennett (2010); Ritchey (2014); Vásquez (2010).

11. Bennett (2010, 31).

12. Bennett (2010, 23–24).

13. Sally Promey (2014) leads the way in the study of sensory material culture in religious studies in an impressive collection of essays titled *Sensational Religion*.

14. Hughes (2012, 16).

15. Hughes (2012, 19).

16. Scott (1999, 26); Chakrabarty ([2000] 2008).

17. Reich (1995).

18. Molina (2013).

19. Merleau-Ponty ([1964] 1969a, 130).

20. Augustine (1961, 243–44).

21. Augustine (2002), quoted in Nightingale (2011, 112).

22. For discussion of how Merleau-Ponty's project is shaped by Christian poetics, see Rivera (2015).

23. Merleau-Ponty ([1945] 2013, lxxxv).

24. Merleau-Ponty ([1964] 1969b).

25. Merleau-Ponty ([1948] 1992a, 25).

26. Merleau-Ponty ([1945] 2013, 34).

27. Merleau-Ponty ([1968] 2003).

28. Nordlander (2011, 167). See also Nordlander (2013).

29. Nordlander (2011, 164).

30. Merleau-Ponty ([1953] 1988, 15–16).

31. Blum (2012, 1028).

32. Hollywood (2004, 518).

33. Blum (2012, 1026).

34. Blum (2012, 1030); my emphasis.

35. As others have pointed out, the deployment of the category "experience" is not adequately interrogated. See Desjarlais (1996) and Sharf (1998).

36. A major exception is Csordas (2002). Csordas (1990) is an important essay where a call for attention to embodiment pairs Pierre Bourdieu's body disciplined by habitus with Merleau-Ponty's body of the moment.

37. Merleau-Ponty ([1948] 1992b, 179); my emphasis.

38. Jackson (1996, 10).

39. Merleau-Ponty ([1964] 1969a, 130).

40. Merleau-Ponty ([1964] 1969a, 130).

41. Taves (2012, 58–83).

42. Ingold (2013, 743).

43. Connolly (2011, 46).

44. Merleau-Ponty ([1953] 1988, 59). "The limping of philosophy is its virtue. True irony is not an alibi; it is a task; and the very detachment of the philosopher assigns to him a certain kind of action among men. Because we live in one of those situations that Hegel called diplomatic, in which every initiative risks being changed in meaning, we sometimes believe that we are serving the cause of philosophy by isolating it from the problems of the day" (61).

45. I have published preliminary findings on Thjülen's conversion. Molina (2015, 641–58). The bonds of their religious friendship are the subject of my initial analysis of the conversion narrative. Thjülen lived out the remainder of his life, as did the majority of the Mexican Jesuits, as an exile in Bologna.

46. Merleau-Ponty ([1964] 1969b, 177–78).

PART THREE

Interventions in the Anthropology of Catholicism

20

"We're All Catholics Now"

Simon Coleman

It is a brave act for the editors of this volume to try to map out, to designate, to *christen*, a new subfield of "the anthropology of Catholicism": brave not least because of our self-deconstructive tendencies, our chronic disciplinary disposition to anatomize concepts to death while disdaining those foolhardy enough to deploy them more positively; and yet also necessary because, like it or not, a conversation dedicated to the study of Catholicism is emerging in conferences, classrooms, and texts. If Protestantism emerged historically out of opposition to the Catholic domination of Europe, contemporary study of Catholicism is responding to the increasing intellectual dominion of an "anthropology of Christianity" that has, for the most part, meant the study of Pentecostalism and evangelical Protestantism.[1] As an ironic consequence of such developments, a focus on Catholicism per se raises the possibility of opening up rather than narrowing fields of inquiry.[2] But it also faces a challenge, because one of the great successes of the recent study of Protestantism *qua* Christianity has been its ability to speak to the discipline as a whole: inquiries into rupture, ritual, materiality, modernity, globalization, and personhood have challenged the limiting intellectual frame of religion itself, even as they have helped anthropologists to probe some of the repressed intellectual and cultural genealogies of their own past.[3]

In the following I hope to contribute in a small way to the opening out of an anthropology of Catholicism. I do not pretend to characterize Catholicism as a whole, since the anthropological study of any subject does not constitute the subject itself. My strategy invokes the semiotics of anthropological theorizing and provides suggestions for possible distinctions between the subfields (or subsubfields) of the study of Protestantism and of Catholicism. I lay out three areas where I think difference might fruitfully be established, however provisionally: "ritual practice," "global diffusion," and "temporal experience." These themes take us into larger analytical realms of religious authority, religio-political economy, and perception of history. In addition, and in line with the overall aims of this volume, I think they take us respectively into three phases of the anthropological study of Catholicism: past debates that still have considerable salience; current developments; and potential investigation for the future into a topic that would reward further attention.

The title of my piece was originally intended to be a variation on the theme of a phrase—"We are *all* Protestants now"—uttered to the anthropologist Webb Keane by a Greek Orthodox friend.[4] In the speech event Keane describes, this statement refers to "a world-historical configuration" that far exceeds its particular doctrinal affiliations.[5] The speaker is not a Protestant in terms of formal membership, but his words indicate the power of a self-designation that is also a form of recognition: as moderns we are *always already* Protestant, so the phrase has the potential to move in locutionary terms between description, assertion, and possibly even resignation. In reflecting on these words as I considered this chapter, I first wondered whether Catholicism might also be said to have surpassed its conventional doctrinal frameworks in particular ways. Then I encountered a piece by Omri Elisha, intriguingly titled "All Catholics Now? Spectres of Catholicism in Evangelical Social Engagement," which took me in a slightly different direction.[6] Clearly I was not the only person interested in exploring the possibility that Catholicism might somehow be living up to the universal meaning of its name, though I was surprised by my partner in speculation: it turned out to be American evangelical politician Mike Huckabee, talking to a group of conservative lobbyists in 2012, and himself echoing the words of a Southern Baptist pastor. Huckabee and the pastor were not suddenly claiming a worldwide shift in religious affiliation but were expressing solidarity with Catholic bishops in their opposition to President Obama's proposals to require private employers to provide insurance coverage for contraception.

We see what might be at stake in examples of categorizing self and others in contexts of religious, political, and intellectual ambiguity. Part of Elisha's point, I think, concerns the *situational* character of religious identification. He shows how even within the cauldron of American public religious discourse evangelicals and Roman Catholics have been able to forge meaningful partnerships when necessary, so that at times a repugnant "you" can become a temporarily unified "we": a postmodern form of segmentary opposition, perhaps. But Elisha goes further. He reveals the subtle resonances and affinities between certain contemporary evangelical sentiments and Catholic sensibilities in the United States over issues of social welfare and justice, suffering, and even "the sacramentalist undercurrents in the ministries of socially engaged evangelicals, especially regarding benevolence and charitable giving."[7] One moral that we can take from Elisha's piece, then, is that in thinking of such entities as Catholicism and Protestantism we must consider the particular modality of religious/and or social action that is being invoked at any given point. I draw another lesson by comparing his piece with a paper by Chris Hann,[8] which argues against the idea that there are deep ontological barriers within Christianity: rather, in Hann's terms, we should be developing a comparative framework that allows us to see cases as distinctive crystallizations of a broader Christian "civilization," identified through examining a wider temporal and spatial canvas than is our ethnographic wont.

I worry a little over what Hann means by "civilization," but I side with him and Elisha in seeing many of our (and often our informants') categorizations and designations as matters of scale and social/ethnographic frame, as foci of both solidarity and shifts in emphasis. Both of these scholars may also share some common ground with Webb Keane's interlocutor in their recognition of the complex interleaving of multiple Christian identities, which may at other times and through other analytical frames seem incommensurate. If a fundamental paradox on which much of Christianity appears to be constructed is the presence, in a single person, of both the divine and the human, under the right circumstances a basic ethnographic paradox might be the coexistence of apparently contradictory identities within the same informant: *both* Greek Orthodox *and*—somehow—"Protestant."

I am not suggesting here that an anthropology of Catholicism per se is hopelessly compromised and thus doomed before it starts. Rather, I am exploring how naming and designating involve choices, with their inherent politics, particularistic framing, and limited temporality. Given that a key aspect of producing such an academic designation at the present time is the context of the current burgeoning anthropology of Protestant groups around the world, a valid approach might be to produce studies of Catholicism that choose themes *not* yet explored in great detail by the latter—gender being just one rather notable example.[9] Such an approach would still be influenced by prevailing studies of the Protestant through its self-conscious absencing of the latter, of course. At the same time, I am not convinced by the kind of argument that says, for instance, "Catholicism is focused on the body in a way that Protestantism is not." There is clearly *something* to this statement. But I think it confuses theological discourse with anthropological analysis. From an ethnographic perspective Protestantism is precisely as much about the body as Catholicism, even if at times its theologies might downplay discussion of embodiment: when an evangelical pastor puts on a dark suit and resembles nothing so much as a business executive, when my Pentecostal informants gaze proudly at the sea of people crowding into an otherwise largely empty church hall, when I listen to an Anglican priest in England and recognize the characteristic timbre of voice he or she adopts in addressing a congregation, all of these point to the deep salience of the body, even as they suggest significant though permeable distinctions from other forms of Christianity.

So my approach here is not to self-consciously ignore the anthropology of Prot-estantism but to ask how an anthropology of Catholicism might articulate with the latter, not only in search of common ground but also in a quest for fruitful distinc-tions. I am not denying the significance of still other forms of Christianity such as Orthodoxy,[10] but for current purposes I am focusing on a particular set of com-parisons and contrasts. Let me therefore go back to the three areas I mentioned above: ritual practice, global diffusion, and temporal experience.

RITUAL PRACTICE

Well before the emergence of the current anthropology of Christianity, a signifi-cant juxtaposition of views on the character of Christian ritual occurred within the discipline. The perspectives came from two scholars who had much in common: both were British (though they would move in the second part of their careers from the United Kingdom to the United States); both were committed Catholics as well as anthropologists, and developed theoretical perspectives where personal and intellectual convictions intertwined; both occasionally saw themselves as peripheral to mainstream secular academic discourse and yet became hugely influential; both deployed their analysis not only to draw attention to the study of Christianity but also to highlight and relativize rituals "at home" as they moved their ethnographic gaze from Africa to Euro-America; and both drew on long-standing anthropological perspectives that highlighted the power of ritual to cre-ate communities and boundaries, order and disorder. I refer, of course, to Mary Douglas and to Victor Turner.

Douglas and Turner wrote in the context not only of the current anthropologi-cal debates of their time—worries over functionalism, explorations of structural-ism and semiotics, debates over meaning and symbol—but also of much wider public discussions regarding the distinctive yet changing role of ritual in the Cath-olic Church. In doing so, both oriented their work at least in part toward that problematic I mentioned above, though arguably they turned it into a question more than an assertion: "*Are* we all Protestants now?" Talking late in her life to the Canadian journalist Eleanor Wachtel about such books as *Natural Symbols*, Doug-las notes: "Well, it was the 1960s, wasn't it? There was a big anti-ritual move on—rituals were thought to be meaningless. It's really a non-conformist Protestant idea against any established church; it's a position of revolt. Established churches have rituals; if we want to get more directly to God by ourselves, we don't need rituals."[11]

For Douglas, this was not just a question of dispassionate analysis: Richard Far-don notes that *Natural Symbols* was written in part as an annoyed response to the reforms of the Second Vatican Council, and indeed an early article laying out her argument appeared in *New Blackfriars* under the no-nonsense title "The Con-tempt of Ritual."[12] Douglas's exploration of the culture of the group she names the

Bog Irish argues for the importance of ritual observances whose significance goes beyond the rationality and "unwitting" Protestantism of reforming clerics.[13] Her message is that we do *not* all have to be Protestants now, even in the West, and that anthropology is well equipped to reveal how the planned dissolution of "the strong boundary walls which once defended the fortress model of the Church" risks sacrificing distinctiveness for a kind of identity-dissolving democracy.[14]

What, then, of Victor Turner? His and Edith Turner's analysis of Catholic pilgrimage and the notion of *communitas* emerged a little later, in the late 1970s, though they were also clearly writing in the shadow of Vatican II.[15] For them, the shade cast by the reforms was much more benign. Pilgrimage revealed a possibility of freedom of expression within religion that also had counterparts in apparently secular countermovements of the time. In its religious form, *communitas* expressed a form of popular charisma in opposition to the bureaucracy of the church[16]—and of course the 1970s were also the decade of the emergence of Charismatic Catholicism in North America and then far beyond.

I have juxtaposed these two figures not only because they illustrate an anthropology of Catholicism before the name was invented but also because I think that Douglas and Turner echo and invert each other in intriguing and still salient ways as they wrestle with Catholicism, ritual, and the apparent Protestantization of their faith. Douglas focuses on a much more domestic form of Catholicism, rooted in ethnicity and community but also in religious authority as a necessary and ordering principle.[17] Protestant-style reformation of ritual is dangerous not only because it comes from the very center of the church but also because it uses its *own* authority to undermine the very liturgical bases on which it depends, attacking principles of differentiation and hierarchy in space, time, and ritual practice. The Turnerian analysis of major pilgrimage sites looks not to the "ordinary" but to the already differentiated, set-apart space and time of the sacred shrine, which forms an alternative "center out there."[18] *Communitas* thus forms its own complex riff on Protestant themes of boundary dissolution: it is confined within a liminoid boundary, but within the safety of that frame it can break down boundaries not only between persons and God but also between person and person. Mediation is challenged and a kind of Catholic sincerity created,[19] but one hedged about by particular forms of material culture and ritual, and dwelling not only on interior experience (tapping directly *into* divine inspiration) but also on external relations (establishing authentic relations *across* human realms).

We see here two scholars wrestling not only with relations between Protestantism and Catholicism but also with the protoanthropologies of these religious forms. Though adopting different political standpoints in relation to questions of authority, both invoke an underlying grammar of established center versus popular periphery, of significant differentiations of the sacred in time and space, of conflicts and yet ineluctable relationships between clergy and laypeople. This is a grammar that moves in and out of close articulation with seemingly more Protestant themes of sincerity and mistrust of mediation. And it is precisely out of these ambiguities of conjunction and disjunction, meaningful to informants as well as to analysts, that we learn to recognize some of the significant ways in which an anthropology of Catholicism, not merely per se but also in relation to how other ways of being religious, might be developed, at least in Western, supposedly secularizing contexts.

Moving forward to the present, Douglas's Bog Irish have become even less distinctive almost five decades after she analyzed their ritual lives, though to some degree they have been replaced by other Catholic migrants to the United Kingdom from Asia and West Africa. Furthermore, it is ever harder to maintain the semblance of *communitas* by building authoritative ritual borders around the liminoid tourist, heritage, and religious centers that make up many contemporary pilgrimage sites, such as the site of Walsingham in eastern England that I have been studying since the 1990s, which contains both a High Anglican and a Catholic shrine.[20] And yet I think that my contemporary observations of Catholic pilgrims at Walsingham show variations on a grammar that again plays on the complex relationships between authorized ritual center and unauthorized if creative peripheries. At Walsingham, ritual is not usually treated with outright contempt by visitors to either shrine, even by those who are largely ignorant of the religion into which they have nominally been born. Rather, it is approached with a manifold variety of stances, ranging from relatively unreflective "Bog Irishism" to irony to a kind of ambiguous respect combined with mistrust.[21] Elsewhere, I have described more extensively what I see as a "lateral" (as opposed to liminal or liminoid) approach to pilgrimage ritual that is adopted by many,[22] but my point here is that such visitors depend precisely on being aware, however dimly, of the existence of an authorized set of ritual forms in relation to which to define the self as an often distanced, or vicariously involved, or indeed slightly mystified "participant." The sense of participation here is very different from the ideal of devoted and sincere engagement of, say, evangelicals and Pentecostals. That is not to dismiss it as trivial or nonmodern, however, and while it represents an area of ritual sensibility that is much less spectacular than that of, say, Pentecostal ecstasy, it nonetheless embodies a very widespread if underanalyzed form of religious engagement. Indeed, it may represent one way in which even the relatively religious uncommitted are "more" Catholic than Protestant.

GLOBAL DIFFUSION

In discussing the context of the "We are *all* Protestants now" remark, Webb Keane notes that the democratic diffusion of Protestant notions of inwardness and an associated concern to "distinguish subject from object" may be connected in part with "the pressures of the contemporaneous globalizations of Protestantism."[23] I would add that, if the anthropology of Christianity has been associated closely with evangelicalism and Pentecostalism, its connections with these proselytizing religious forms have also tended to link it with images of dynamic cultural mobility and social change.[24] Many anthropologists may still feel decidedly ambivalent in the face of evangelical mission,[25] but they no longer ignore it.[26] Indeed, a focus on such believers has become—in these more self-reflexive times—a means to discuss questions of rupture and continuity not only in the culture of informants but also within the styles of thinking of anthropologists themselves.[27]

Given the direction of such debates, Catholicism—the religion most obviously of an age of previous colonialization and subsequent assimilation with local religious practices—has been in danger of being associated not only with the culturally moribund but also with the theoretically stagnant. Of course, there has also been some kickback against such a caricatured view. Jennifer Scheper Hughes's recent discussion of novelty within Mexican Catholicism argues that such religion is in fact in the midst of a striking period of both experimentation and expansion, and one that contradicts assumptions that the diffusion of Protestantism throughout Latin America has provided the only significant form of new religious imagining.[28] Also with a focus on Mexico, Toomas Gross traces the social costs of conversion to Protestantism in Zapotec communities in Oaxaca, indicating the active cultural work that may go into *not* choosing to convert: apparent cultural and religion stagnation may conceal complex and nuanced responses to change, just as apparent rupture may not in fact be irreversible.[29]

I add that it may also be a mistake to cede so much cultural and analytical territory (and trajectory) of globalization to analyses of contemporary Protestant proselytization. A key research question may be whether and how a Catholic-inspired landscape of global movement compares, interacts, interleaves, and indeed contrasts with Pentecostal and evangelical patterns. Thus, in his examination of the "geography of the Spirit" contained within Catholic Charismatic communities, Thomas Csordas explores the interaction between Pentecostal forms of diffusion and the specifically communitarian dimension of Catholic Charismatics.[30] There may even be distant links here with Douglas's and Turner's grammar of Catholic practice in which boundaries of community and ritual retain their salience. I think also of Valentina Napolitano's analysis of Mexican transnational migration to Italy, which draws on the image and icon of the Virgin of Guadalupe as a "nexus of affect."[31] But I also go back to the landscape of sacred shrines more generally, and the striking links between the new political economy of transnational migration and the historically deeply rooted, yet currently dynamic patterns of pilgrimage in the Catholic world. The differentiated landscape of sacred places, old and new, across Europe, the Americas, and other parts of the world provides fascinating arenas for the reception and negotiation of diasporic Catholic identities in such older shrines as Walsingham and Lourdes but also in fresher contexts of, say, Nuestra Señora de la Caridad in Miami.[32] The scope here is for the examination of globalizing networks of migrants and communitarian groups, moving across authorized and unauthorized shrines, mapping in complex ways onto a worldwide ecclesiastical cartography coordinated through Rome while also intersecting with non-Catholic forms of transnational religious and economic networks.

TEMPORAL EXPERIENCE

I have given myself virtually no space to mention my final analytical realm, but such brevity may be appropriate, since I simply wish to point to what I see as a relative gap in the current literature on Catholicism. Again, my strategy is one of juxtaposition and strategic distinction. The notion of rupture that has catalyzed so much research into Pentecostalism, evangelicalism, and their relationships to both modernity and change is in part a trope of temporality. Jon Bialecki, Naomi Haynes, and Joel Robbins wonder, indeed, whether "Christianity in many of its forms is a religion centered on sharp discontinuities—incarnation, conversion, apocalypse,"[33] and this view may have some validity. However, it also raises the question of how an analysis of Catholicism can explore questions of change and transformation in ways that expand and nuance our understandings of ritual experiences of time but also wider historical shifts—perhaps sometimes blunting the sharpness of apparent discontinuities without rendering them any less analytically significant.

Of course, much of what I have been describing so far has been implicitly or explicitly about time as well as space and community: Douglas and the Turners responding to Vatican II, Scheper Hughes and Gross complicating the link between Catholicism and stagnation in Mexico, and so on. A current research project I am engaged in may shed some light on this issue, as I and others examine the past and present role of Anglican and Roman Catholic cathedrals in the United Kingdom: such spaces are surely, among other things, remarkable machines for the production of different models of religious time, yet they are remarkably understudied by social scientists.[34] I conclude, however, with a further juxtaposition, which refers both to temporality and to the wider anthropology of Christianity. For one might argue that the anthropological discourse of Pentecostal and evangelical expansion itself echoes the triumphalist narratives of many such informants, whose identity is precisely bound up with taking "territories" for Christ and hastening the End of Time. It is notable, then, that a number of commentators remark on the wide prevalence of a (Western?) Catholic "decline and fall" narrative that takes its flavor both from a post-Reformation and from a much more recent post–Vatican II sensibility.[35] Our role as anthropologists must be to note but also to resist the temptations of adopting jagged narrative juxtapositions between triumph and decline. We need to call into being, to name, an anthropology of Catholicism that recognizes the power but also the politics of classifying any "new" field of study and that respectfully acknowledges but is not overtaken by the discourse of our informants.

NOTES

1. Bialecki, Haynes, and Robbins (2008). It is worth bearing in mind that the English term *Roman Catholic* is relatively modern in origin, emerging most strongly from the nineteenth century, and that it is often used by outsiders to the church such as Anglicans. In my own work at Walsingham, I work on at least two types of Catholic: so-called Anglo-Catholics and Roman Catholics.

2. Compare Hann (2007).

3. See, e.g., Cannell (2006); Robbins (2007).

4. Keane (2007, 201).

5. Keane (2007, 201).

6. Elisha (2013).

7. Elisha (2013, 74).

8. Hann (2014).

9. Though see, e.g., A. Stewart (2012).

10. On Orthodoxy, see Bandak and Boylston (2014).

11. Douglas (1970); Douglas and Wachtel (2013, 287).

12. Fardon (2013, 5); Douglas (1968).

13. Douglas (1968, 6).

14. Hornsby-Smith (1999, 294); compare Flanagan (1991); Gilley (1999).

15. Turner and Turner (1978).

16. See also Turner and Turner (1978, 32); Coleman (2014).

17. In turn, her use of Bernstein's (e.g., 1971) restricted and elaborated codes seems to refer to two aspects of her persona: an academic disposition for complex explanation and a religious desire for firm delineations of conduct and identity.

18. Turner (1973).

19. Though we should also bear in mind that the Turners borrow the imagery of "I-Thou" relations from a Jewish philosopher: Martin Buber.

20. See, e.g., Coleman (2009, 2014).

21. Coleman (2009).

22. Coleman (2013).

23. Keane (2007, 201).

24. Coleman (2014).

25. Harding (1991).

26. Coleman and Hackett (2015).

27. Robbins (2007).

28. Scheper Hughes (2012, 7).

29. Gross (2012, 357).

30. Csordas (2015).

31. Napolitano (2009).

32. Tweed (1997); see also Vásquez (2008).

33. Bialecki, Haynes, and Robbins (2008, 1144).

34. See the website "Pilgrimage and England's Cathedrals: Past and Present," www.pilgrimageand cathedrals.ac.uk/.

35. See, e.g., Gilley (1999); Janet (2001).

21

What Is Catholic about the Clergy Sex Abuse Crisis?

Robert A. Orsi

From the moment when stories of the abuse of children and adolescents by Catholic clergy and its cover-up by church officials and ordinary Catholic parishioners first began appearing in the media, American bishops and Catholic media pundits sought to sever any connection between Catholic history and culture and the abuse of youngsters by ordained men. This crisis was about the intrinsic evil of homosexuality, it was claimed, as if all gay men were prone to pedophilia and ephebophilia. Or the crisis was about psychopathology, about a sickness of the mind and body of the pedophile; or it was about the sexual licentiousness of the American 1970s. Vatican spokesmen complacently emphasized the *American* nature of the crisis, which in the Roman lexicon stood for "liberalism" and "modernity." In any case, the numbers of pedophile priests in the church were lower than in society at large, relative to their respective demographics; in this way, the hierarchy's bad faith was quantified. The closest any diagnosis came to Catholicism itself was the assertion that the crisis arose out of the more liberal ways of being Catholic that followed the Second Vatican Council.

So the brutalized bodies of children, to which American bishops had up to this point paid little attention, were deployed in the service of the agendas of the pontificates of John Paul II and Benedict XVI. By the logic of such arguments, the clergy sex abuse crisis is not a topic for historical or ethnographic inquiry into Catholicism. To claim otherwise, as I do, and as many survivors of clergy sex abuse do as well, is to open oneself to the charge of contributing to "the new anti-Catholicism," a phrase whose origins coincide with the breaking news of the abuse of children in the church.[1]

. . .

Many of the adult survivors of clerical sexual abuse I have gotten to know over the past several years scornfully refer to *healing* as the "h-word." They do not want to be asked by people who have not been sexually abused by priests if they have been healed, which sounds diagnostic; or told that they need to be healed, which is condescending; or to be assured that they will be healed, which has an ominous ring to it. "Don't tell me that I just need healing / Until you feel what I am feeling," Frank H., a Roman Catholic priest who was abused by priests first as a boy and again as a seminarian, warns in aphoristic verse. From the mouths of others, "healing" comes as an injunction to silence. It posits an end to their pain that survivors do not recognize from their lives. They do not deny that there is much to be healed, but "healing" is not a simple or innocent matter.[2]

Just how fraught "healing" is among survivors became excruciatingly clear to me one evening during a meeting of a group of Chicagoland survivors who have known each other since the early 1990s, when they helped found a now-disbanded national organization called the Linkup (for "Victims of Clerical Sexual Abuse Linkup"). The Linkup offered spiritual support and counseling to survivors and their families, as well as public occasions for survivors to tell their stories to each other and to the media. This group has been meeting on the third Monday of the month ever since. It was in each other's stories that they first recognized themselves as the victims of predator priests, and this created a deep and enduring bond among them. They believe they understand each other's lives in a way no one else does, not even family members. The group's informal leader and one of its most beloved members is a seventy-seven-year-old man I will call Pete S. It was Pete who proposed to the others that I be invited to attend the Monday meetings, and after discussion among themselves and with me they agreed. I went almost every month for about two years, and members of the group are among my closest conversation partners. On this particular evening there were two visitors, a man and woman who had been involved in the Linkup years ago but were now only in intermittent contact with the Chicago group. One of the topics of conversation this Monday was the Healing Garden that the Archdiocese of Chicago had just opened at the historic Holy Family Church on the city's near west side for survivors of all forms of sexual abuse.[3]

As it happened, I had been invited to attend the garden's opening, which coincided with the archdiocese's annual Mass of Atonement and Hope, by one of the moving forces behind the conceptualization and landscaping of the site, Kevin H. A Chicago priest, Father Robert E. Mayer, had sexually abused Kevin between the ages of twelve and sixteen. To avoid public scandal, and with no concern for children at risk, diocesan officials protectively moved Father Mayer from parish to parish across the greater Chicago area for years before and after he abused Kevin. Mayer was

FIGURE 21.1. Statue of the Holy Family, Healing Garden, Archdiocese of Chicago. Photo: Mark Black, Chicago Daily Herald.

caught and convicted in 1993. Kevin and I talked at length about his plans for the Healing Garden, every detail of which was profoundly important to him.[4]

At the garden's entry is a plaque with a message from Chicago's late Francis Cardinal George. The garden committee "didn't tell him what to write," Kevin says, which he believes gave special import to the cardinal's decision to inscribe on the plaque an apology "to those who have been sexually abused by priests or others in the Archdiocese of Chicago." Kevin was not uncritical of the cardinal. He objects, for example, to the prelate's solicitous attention to a priest imprisoned for sexual abuse, which Kevin sees as "supporting the abuser." But about the plaque Kevin says that the cardinal "spoke from the heart." A second plaque expresses the committee's vision for the garden. "The creation of this healing garden," the text reads in part, "is an attempt by us, clergy abuse survivors of the Archdiocese of Chicago, to heal, learn from and grow from the physical, mental, emotional and spiritual harm done to us." The most impressive feature of the garden is a metal statue of the Holy Family in modern dress, holding hands and dancing in a circle. The presence of this joyous group in the Garden, Kevin explained, expresses the confident hope that family bonds disrupted by sexual abuse will be healed one day.[5]

This is not how the Monday night group saw it. Jackie S., a woman whose judgment I respect, derided the statue as "Ring-around-the-Rosie." There was complaint that because the garden was for all survivors of sexual abuse it drew attention away from clerical sexual abuse in particular, the cardinal's apology notwithstanding. One of the visitors, a man whose rage erupted repeatedly that evening in graphic fantasies of violence against priests, mocked the location of the garden in "a parking lot," although Pete demurred, pointing out that the garden was close to the parish school and visible from the street. Ignoring this, Billy L., as I will call him, added that he wanted to be filmed desecrating the garden, which again made the regular members of the group visibly uncomfortable. The other visitor, Susan M., a volatile woman in her late sixties held in wary respect by the group because her life after the abuse was especially horrific, ridiculed the healing place as "an empty little garden outside the church in an inner-city Chicago neighborhood." Both visitors asserted that it was not possible any actual survivors were involved in the garden's making. When I said that I knew one of the people who planned the garden and that he was a survivor, Susan replied that the garden nevertheless failed to make clear "how widespread the abuse was," without which any apology was meaningless. Billy interjected that the archdiocese ought to tear down the stations of the cross at Holy Family Church and in their place erect a memorial to victims of clerical abuse. Jackie added that a more appropriate symbol for the garden would have been a millstone, an allusion to the fate Jesus warned awaited those who harmed children.[6]

The conversation circled the garden a while longer, with people proposing various alternatives to its design, until finally Billy suggested that the group go over later that night with a hacksaw and sever the hands of the members of the Holy Family from each other. He proposed to leave them dangling by threads of sharp metal, with their fingers just barely touching, which Billy said would truly represent what abuser priests did to their victims' families. Anxious that Billy was serious, one of the Monday night regulars gamely suggested that he consider photoshopping this image. Jackie said that the garden's caretakers ought to let the grounds become overrun with weeds. From memory she quoted the fourteenth-century churchwoman and reformer Saint Catherine of Siena, who told Pope Gregory XI during a time of protracted schism and corruption within the church to "uproot from the garden the stinking weeds full of impurity and avarice and bloated with pride." The stinking weeds, Jackie explained, referred to priests and bishops. The conversation ended with the somber conclusion that the Healing Garden was yet another way the church was attempting to silence victims of clerical sexual abuse by empty gestures of "healing."

· · ·

"There is no one" among the victims of clerical sexual abuse, a survivor named Monica told me, "who was not abused in a Catholic way." Monica, who is in her early fifties today, was sexually abused over a period of many years, starting when she was a little girl, by a ring of pedophile priests living together in the rectory of her home parish in northern New England. "In a Catholic way" means many things. It may refer, for example, to the abuse of children and adolescents in the particular spaces and times of Catholic worship. But specifically against those who deny this, "in a Catholic way" opens the abuse crisis to historical and ethnographic inquiry, precisely into what it reveals about Catholicism itself. The sexual violence of priests, the widespread collusion of bishops in it, the silence of so many lay Catholics, and especially the struggles of survivors over the years with the manifold consequences of what was done to them (and by extension to those around them) have torn away the tightly woven density of doctrine, metaphysics, sacrament, authority, obedience, inheritance, and devotion that all together in the ordinary course of things constitute Catholic bodies, relationships, memories, and imaginations. It has done so, moreover, more fully than any other catastrophe in modern history in which the church has been caught up—revolution and war, for instance—because the sex abuse crisis is situated exactly where the most intimate aspects of Catholic life meet the political and ecclesiastical realities of the church, the nexus of subjective/objective, internal/external, which is where "the Catholic tradition" lives.

This is not to say that the crisis simply gives up its revelations about Catholicism, as if suddenly everything that was once obscure and opaque has now been rendered utterly transparent. This requires searching. So against those defenders of a hypostasized "Catholic tradition" who deny that there is anything to learn about modern and contemporary Catholicism from the clergy sex abuse crisis, I maintain that there is everything to learn. This includes, among other things, how persons, when they are very young, are formed within the tradition; how this formation gets so deeply pressed into their bodies and imaginations that it becomes a subjectively internalized and experienced objectivity; and then how ordinary Catholics live with bodies, minds, and imaginations that, as a result of their formation, they often encounter, especially in times of rupture with the church, as separate and apart from themselves. Some clue to what the editors refer in the introduction to this volume as the mystery of Catholicism's endurance over time is to be found in this dimension of the crisis and in its wake.

· · ·

Kevin is impatient with survivors who are unable to find "what gets you past the anger." He acknowledges that when the revelations of abuse first surfaced in the 1980s "the path of anger" was necessary to compel the church to recognize the abuse and take steps to protect children in the future. But the situation is different today. The first priest he told about his abuse after deciding in July 2006 to come forward with his story wept with him; archdiocesan officials listened attentively and respectfully and never challenged his credibility; the cardinal made time to see him privately. "I am happy now to go to church," Kevin told me, "because I have experienced good church." The time for talk of weeds and hacksaws is past. "We're protecting children now." Today it is time for what Kevin calls "the path of reconciliation." His vision for the garden reflects his experience of the church as a place of healing.

But the Linkup group maintains that the Healing Garden trivializes survivors' experience ("Ring-around-the-Rosie"). The absorption of priests' victims into the general population of the sexually abused excuses the church from having to contend with the specifically Catholic nature of clerical sexual abuse. Billy's comment about the shoddy location of the garden articulates survivors' apprehension of being marginalized by the church and rendered irrelevant to its life. His idea that the stations of the cross ought to be pulled down and replaced with images of survivors establishes a powerful Christological analogy. To speak of "healing" the pain that shaped survivors' lives and continues to do is as absurd as it is to speak of "healing" the suffering of Christ's passion. The plan to brutalize the statue of the Holy Family brings the violence of sexual abuse into the center of the Garden. "How can there be healing," asks Frank H., who is a member of the old Linkup group although he lives too far away to make the Monday meetings, "if you don't know what the hurt is, what the damage is?" The church, Frank says, has "failed to acknowledge the severity of the trauma." The disfigured statues would have objectified this damage in a powerful way. Touching the jagged edges of the severed hands, if they chose to do so, visitors would feel in their own bodies something of the pain survivors suffered in theirs.

. . .

All the survivors I know continued going to Mass into adulthood, long past the time when it was within their power to choose otherwise. By their accounts they were good and faithful Catholics. But over time they began to feel disassociated from themselves, alien and out of place at the Eucharist and the sacraments and in their parishes. Survivors struggled to appear normal to the people around them, but they did not feel normal. "I didn't belong," Mary Rose, a Linkup survivor in her midseventies, described going to Mass as a young mother, "and people knew I didn't belong. It's like they knew but didn't know." Survivors were ashamed of the abuse. They felt responsible for it. They feared it was a sin to accuse a priest of such evil; no one would believe them in any case. Survivors lacked the language to comprehend or to describe what had happened to them. These were the long years of the "absence of words" when survivors were unable to speak about their abuse to anyone. In silence they contended with broken marriages, substance abuse, and psychological turmoil, confused and mystified by their lives.[7]

Church was not safe, moreover. Predator priests sexually abused their victims in sacred spaces, on the altar or close to it, sometimes during Mass, or in the sacristy adjoining the sanctuary, where the golden vessels of the Mass were stored and the priests' ceremonial robes hung; or in the confessional, where priests alone had the power to absolve sins; or in the rectory, where priests lived and ordinary parishioners seldom went. Some priests turned the abuse into a perverse act of devotion; others demanded their victims pray with them or for them. Even when abusers did not draw the connection to the Catholic devotional and sacramental imaginary so explicitly, to be abused by a priest, the *alter Christus* in Catholic theology, the other Christ, was to be abused at one remove from God. There was an ontological specificity to clerical sexual abuse, as Monica's comment about "a Catholic way" underscores.

So the stones of churches, the smells and colors of Catholic sacred interiors, carry memories of the abuse. In her early adulthood, Monica felt so raw and vulnerable in church, so utterly exposed—being sexually abused, Monica says, is "like having the skin ripped off your body"—that the only way she was able to continue going to Mass was by hiding behind the great pillars in the nave or sitting at the end of the long pews to be able to escape quickly if she needed to do so. "Everything about my life was how to find safety," Monica says of these years. Monica was afraid that the people around her could literally see into her, to see 'my sin,'" as she thought of the abuse at the time (she still does sometimes). She felt "at the mercy" of the people in the pews beside her. "If it was even possible to go to church," she went on, "it felt like the tips of [my] nerves were on fire." Sitting in the parking lots of churches, which was often as close as she was able to get to the sanctuary, Monica waited for the resonant ambient silence that signaled it was the time of the consecration of the Mass within, when, she says, the walls separating her from the altar faded away and "I would be close to God on the altar." She resented the Catholics coming and going with what seemed to her bored and blasé looks on their faces.

• • •

Being sexually abused by the *alter Christi* pulled victims deeply into the Catholic sacred world and at the same time distanced them from its ordinary everyday reality, which otherwise, like the Catholics Monica watched from her car, they might have taken for granted. This was especially so for members of the Linkup generation, formed in the full tradition before the Second Vatican Council, by vowed women religious whose sole occupation was children's religious instruction. This was not Kevin's Catholicism. He does not remember the Latin Mass or any of the popular devotions of the earlier era. But the older generation's experience of the ontological dissonance of the abuse was extreme. Bernard R., a retired engineer in his midsixties who as a boy was drawn into a sexually intense relationship by a priest, says of survivors, "We've been dealt another reality. We look at things differently. Our reality is a little different from other people's reality." "Other people" here means other Catholics. If not immediately, then certainly over time the sacral disconnect of the abuse made victims exiles within the church and unwelcome strangers to their fellow Catholics. When this experience of being simultaneously present and absent at Mass became too much to bear, they stayed away, for a while or forever.

By way of illustrating survivors' unique location in the contemporary church, Frank regularly references the scene in *The Wizard of Oz* in which Dorothy, dragged behind a curtain by Toto, her dog, discovers an ordinary, foolish little man manipulating the levers that produced the awesome spectacle of the great and powerful Oz's power. Survivors have also seen the machinery of false authority, the predators working the levers of the theology of the *alter Christus.* The "awesome . . . almost miraculous vocation of the priesthood," in the words of a popular pre-Conciliar devotional volume written for seminarians, makes priests ontologically different from and superior to all other creatures, including the angels. Written just when older survivors were starting parochial school, in 1950, *Dear Seminarian,* by the Baroness Catherine de Hueck, ends with a litany that reads in part, "A priest is a holy man because he walks before the Face of the Almighty. . . . The heart of a priest is a chalice of love. . . . The heart of a priest is the trysting place of human and divine love. . . . A priest is the reflection of God's love." Survivors know that such grandiloquence hides the ordinary and bad little men who abused them and the bishops who protected these men.[8]

Bernard's use of the passive voice—"We've been dealt another reality"—underscores the fact that survivors had no or little choice: to have seen behind the curtain was a sentence imposed on them when they were powerless to resist. Many of the survivors I know speak of seeing behind the veil in terms of deep sadness.

Rosemary, an old friend of Frank's, said that the church was a great comfort to her as a child until she was raped in high school by a priest who was a close friend of her parents. Since then, the comfort "isn't there anymore." This priest had converted her mother to Catholicism, and Rosemary was afraid that if her mother found out what he had done, she "would lose her faith . . . and really be damned to hell." So she kept the rape a secret for years. Today, Rosemary says, it is "painful and almost intolerable" to enter a Catholic church. "I just can't make myself believe in what I see as smoke and mirrors." There is no satisfaction in rejecting the church. "The effect of this loss," Rosemary says, "is like watching the Technicolor go out of something."

Rosemary's visual metaphor is another reference to *The Wizard of Oz.* The black-and-white of Dorothy's ordinary life in Kansas is transformed in the movie into glorious color when she arrives in Oz. The temporality of the transition is reversed in Rosemary's autobiography, however. She starts out in the sumptuous pre–Vatican II architectonics of the real presence;[9] then a priest rapes her, the color drains away, and she steps into a world that "is all gray." This is a "huge loss," Rosemary says, and an irrevocable one. She compares herself to Catholics who have not been abused by priests, who have not seen behind the curtain. They "fawn over priests whether they deserve it or not," she says, just "by the fact that they are priests." People in the pews "stick their heads in the sand." Survivors refer to Catholics who go in their faith as if they have not seen or heard what so many priests and bishops did to so many children—even though they have seen and heard—as "the sheeple of God."

·   ·   ·

Survivors do not speak with a single voice; they are forever revisiting and rethinking what they have learned about themselves, about the church, and about Catholicism as the circumstances of their lives change over time and in conversation with each other. To assemble what survivors have seen on the other side of the veil into an agenda for their personal growth or as a program for church reform obscures the complex and shifting dynamics of their voices. But what is the other reality Bernard, Frank, and the others claim to have been compelled to experience and to know?

As the comments above suggest, survivors are deeply troubled by Catholics who refuse to acknowledge the full reality of the tradition, its capacities for evil as well as for holiness, or to see how thoroughly evil gets entwined with sanctity in Catholicism. Bernard, Monica, and the others encountered this reality at one of its most intimate instantiations in the tradition, at the hands of men who alone had the authority to touch the body of God. They also know that the deceit has not only endured but deepened over time. "The problem with the priesthood today," Frank maintains, "is that it almost demands inauthenticity." The pivot of this deception is the matter of sexuality in the church. While it is well known that seminaries are sexually active places and many Catholics casually doubt that all or even most priests are faithfully celibate, the church maintains the pretense of clerical celibacy along with its regime of sexual prohibitions for the laity. As Monica once told me, her customary poise giving way to pure anger, the church told her it was a sin to live with her boyfriend while the priests who raped her continued in their ministry. "How can that church tell me not to sleep with this man, which is normal," she recalled asking herself, "when all those abnormal priests had already slept with me."[10]

"Nothing can be greater in this world of ours than a priest," De Hueck closes *Dear Seminarian.* "Nothing but God himself." As long as you are distracted by such deception, Frank says, as long as Catholics persist "in their blindly sentimental love affair with the illusion," then bishops, priests, and popes "can get away with anything." The only way to reform the church is to "break the illusion." "There's a lot of truth in the illusion. But the truth isn't gone" when things turn black-and-white again, Frank says. "The illusion is."

·   ·   ·

This is what many survivors take as their mission in the contemporary church, *precisely as men and women who were sexually abused as youngsters by priests.* "We are the people constantly picking at that curtain," Frank says about himself and other survivors. To have been abused and survived has given them a distinctive vocation among the people of God. The abuse ruptured their relationship with Catholic reality—not immediately, but inevitably—and since that time, standing in this broken place, they have seen themselves and the church in a new light. Jackie's speaking the words of Catherine of Siena from memory was an instance of the embodiment of this singular vocation and this particular location vis-à-vis the tradition. Likewise, Bernard says he "rails against" Catholics in love with the illusion, which he likens to "another medication, as in pills and booze." These Catholics are "hiding behind religion." Frank descries what he calls "Rush Limbaugh Catholics" who believe—Frank deepens his voice here to sound either like a prelate or the Wizard of Oz (Frank would say both)—"All you have to do is listen. You don't have to think. We've done all the thinking for you, because you don't know anything."

So powerful and insistent is the idea among survivors that what they have been violently compelled to see is necessary for the church that some of them are led to ask—*only in this context and only for this reason*—the unthinkable. Was being sexually abused by a priest "a curse or a gift"? These are Bernard's words. I think he would say that the answer to his question is that the abuse was both curse and gift. Survivors have been cursed with this gift. It was the alternative reality forced on them as children that they accepted as their vocation as adults.

· · ·

None of the survivors I know are hopeful that the Catholic doctrine of the priesthood and the practices of deference, acquiescence, and undeserved reverence that grew out of it will change soon. Even the ever-hopeful Monica believes that a generation of priests and prelates must die off before any real change happens. "There's so many people fighting the coming to life," Frank says about the contemporary church. "They love the illusion. When we try to bring the light of truth to the darkness that is the church, they prefer the darkness. Somehow the darkness is more beautiful than the truth." Survivors know they make other Catholics profoundly uneasy. Not long ago, members of a suburban Chicago sought to have two women who had prayed during Mass one Sunday for children abused by a priest there exorcised because they believed that the women's stance in opposition to the pastor, who wanted no mention of this at all, was a sign that they were possessed by evil. Frank told me that another survivor once confided in him that he felt like "a poison in the church." "Light is poison to darkness," Frank assured him.

Many survivors are convinced that priests and prelates today "just want [us] gone," a phrase I have heard from many survivors. This sentiment is especially strong in the Linkup group, which tends to be more suspicious of the church, but survivors whose relationship with Catholic tradition appears less troubled share it. They are afraid the hierarchy is biding its time until they pass away, time closes over this moment in Catholic history, and memory fades. This speaks to the limits of the tradition's "elasticity," the hard edge of resistance to challenges from within. But to be the poisonous light in the contemporary church is survivors' charism, to use a technical Catholic word for a special gift of the Holy Spirit. This is how they see it and this is why they resist the "h-word." They are the unhealed. In Monica's words, "The abyss is always there. . . . I choose between light and darkness on any one day." It is as the unhealed that they persist in their fierce, unforgiving, and open-eyed engagement with Catholicism.

NOTES

1. See, for example, Jenkins (2003) and Massa (2003).

2. All the conversations referenced in this work began in the summer of 2012 and are ongoing. I have used pseudonyms throughout. Conversations took place in a number of venues, around Chicago and elsewhere in the United States. Funding for this research was provided by the Social Science Research Council and Northwestern University. I dedicate "The Problem of Healing among Survivors of Clerical Sexual Abuse" to the memory of Rick Springer. For a trenchant and powerful critique of the cultural politics of healing, see Kleinman (2006, esp. 27–45).

3. On the history of Linkup, see Clites (2015).

4. The full title of the liturgical celebration at Holy Family Catholic Church on September 15, 2012, was "Mass of Atonement and Hope for the Ongoing Healing Required for Child and Youth Sexual Abuse Survivors, Their Families, the Church, Society, and for the Continued Vigilance toward the Protection of Children and Youth." There is ample online information about Rev. Robert E. Mayer; interested readers might start with BishopAccountability.org (2007).

5. For a discussion of the genesis of the Healing Garden by a member of the planning committee, see Hoffman (2013).

6. The scriptural reference is to Matthew 18:6.

7. The phrase "absence of words" is from Messler and Frawley (1994, 55). This section of the essay draws on chap. 7, "Events of Abundant Evil," in Orsi (2016, 215–48).

8. De Hueck (1950, 18, 86–87).

9. On "architectonics" I follow James W. Fernandez's (1982, 408) definition, writing of the Bwiti chapel, "Ritual activity warms the chapel up and makes it attractive to the ancestors. Description of the activity that takes place within architectural spaces enables us to understand the architectonic: the feelings and meanings of that a given space may evoke."

10. On the open secret of clerical sexuality, see the important book by Jordan (2000, especially 83–208). In a powerful and resonant phrase, Jordan refers to the modern Catholic Church as "the empire of secrets" (89). See also Jordan (2003).

22

Possession and Psychopathology, Faith and Reason

Thomas J. Csordas

Exorcists in the Roman Catholic Church explicitly trace their ministry back to biblical episodes in which Jesus casts out evil spirits, but exorcism has a complex history of development and periods in which it is more or less foregrounded in the life of the church. Demons were not officially defined by the church as spiritual entities until the Fourth Lateran Council in 1215 under Pope Innocent III. In the fifteenth century "exorcism manuals" became common and were extensively used in ritual healing prayer to cast out evil spirits. By the time the *Malleus Maleficarum* (The devil's hammer) was published, the concept of witchcraft was coming to prominence as an idiom of satanic activity among humans, though it never completely replaced the idea of demon possession.[1] A standardized rite of exorcism was officially promulgated in 1614, but the frequency and relevance of exorcism declined during the period from the Enlightenment through contemporary modernity.[2] In 1884 Pope Leo XIII had a vision of Satan after celebrating Mass and composed a special prayer to Saint Michael for defeat of the devil. He established it as a common conclusion to a Low Mass, but its use was discontinued by the Second Vatican Council in 1964. At that point formal exorcism was among the rituals identified for updating, but the revision process languished. In his 1972 *motu proprio* document entitled *Ministeria Quaedam* Pope Paul VI removed the title of exorcist as one of the standard "minor orders" with which all priests were endowed as a step toward ordination. Not only was this minor order devoid of practical significance, since exorcism already required a fully ordained priest with explicit authorization by a bishop, but in the United States in 1972 it was said that only one diocese had a priest formally appointed to the office of exorcist. In 1994 Pope John Paul II made mention of Leo's St. Michael prayer but made no move to reinstate it in the liturgy. It was not until 1999 that a revised rite of exorcism was promulgated, and recognition of its renewed relevance began to spread within the hierarchy.

The beginning of the twenty-first century witnessed a resurgence of interest in and practice of exorcism. In the wake of a satanism scare in Italy following a series of murders in 1998 and 2004 involving the heavy metal rock band Beasts of Satan, word spread that the Vatican wanted every diocese to appoint an exorcist, and a training course for exorcists launched at a pontifical university in Rome has been conducted annually since 2005. In 2010 the annual meeting of the Catholic bishops in the United States included a preconference explicitly addressed to the topic of exorcism and attracted sixty-six priests and fifty-six bishops. In 2011 a theology course on exorcism was taught in a US seminary for the first time since the Second Vatican Council fifty years earlier. In 2012 an Italian translation appeared of the work *Apparitionibus Daemonum*, originally published by Cardinal Federico Borromeo in 1624. In 2013 the eighth annual Course on Exorcism and Prayers of Liberation in Rome at the Atheneum Apostolurum, run by the religious order Legionaries of Christ and cosponsored by the Gruppo di Ricerca e Informazione Socio-religiosa (GRIS) headquartered in Bologna, attracted 163 participants from twenty-five countries. In June 2014 the International Association of Exorcists, founded in the 1990s, was granted official Vatican recognition by the Congregation for the Clergy.

The trajectory of this development, though for considerations of space I have presented it as a highly abbreviated sketch, suggests that exorcism be understood not only as a thriving form of religious practice but also as a dynamic social phenomenon. This observation demands explicit attention to the relation between the concrete experiences of social actors and the broader cultural processes and social forces in which they are embedded. Specifically, exorcism can be understood both experientially in terms of the therapeutic process put into play by the practice of ritual performance as an attempt to promote flourishing, and institutionally in terms of the conservative discourse of evil at large in the world that articulates a religio-political stance in the face of global cultural processes in social context. As the editors of this volume aptly comment in their introduction, the case of contemporary exorcism "reveals how the Catholic Church's discourse on evil works to mediate anxieties underlying broader social transformations, crises both within the church and in the world at large." I will briefly outline four domains in which the discourse of evil being mobilized by the church's expanding corps of exorcists highlights a particular tension, anxiety, or problematic, and then will elaborate in more detail on one of them.

I will adopt a Weberian idiom to assert that having control over, or at least practical and rhetorical command of, a powerful discourse of evil puts the corps of exorcists in a unique position in the Catholic world (1) vis-à-vis other interest groups, (2) in relation to morally charged categories, and (3) within discrete domains of action. First, the exorcist stands in stark contrast to the pedophile priest (technically the latter does not constitute an interest group but a social category) in relation to the moral category of patriarchy within the juridical domain. Whereas the abusive priest degrades the notion of spiritual father as protector, the exorcist engages in a strenuous cosmological struggle to protect and liberate the afflicted, sometimes at grave personal risk. The juridical domain in this sense pertains to the governance of exorcism by canon law and the violation of that law by abusive priests, while ironically both exorcists and abusive priests have run afoul of the secular legal apparatus. Second, exorcists establish a counterpoint to the global Catholic Charismatic Renewal movement in relation to the category of laity and its spiritual prerogatives within the pastoral domain. Since the movement's inception in 1967 its members have engaged in prayers for "deliverance" from evil spirits, while only priests under the authorization of a bishop can perform the solemn rite of exorcism. Tension over the boundaries between these practices and their pastoral supervision have waxed and waned, but it is noteworthy that few of the current cohort exorcists have themselves participated in the Renewal, while laypeople who assist them often have. Third, exorcism's discourse of evil defines a stance in relation to other religions and in relation to the possibility of religious diversity within the evangelical domain. Outside the other Abrahamic religions, any spirit or deity is by default subsumed under the category of the demonic, and any religious practice is subsumed under the category of the occult. Religious coexistence with Eastern, indigenous, and New Age religions is precluded in such a way that exorcism itself is in effect a form of evangelization and delegitimization of other religions. Finally, the practice of exorcism cultivates a distinctive mode of interaction with scientific medicine in relation to rationality in the therapeutic domain. Exorcists actively collaborate with psychiatrists and other mental health professionals who are themselves practicing Catholics. The goal is not only a differential diagnosis to determine whether a person in distress is mentally ill rather than demonically afflicted but also to determine how psychiatric disorder and demonic possession might interact when they are copresent.

In what follows I will address this latter aspect of contemporary exorcism practice, focusing on the relation between psychiatry and religion. Their intersection forms a critical conceptual boundary that appears to establish the epistemological limits of exorcism practice, and its consequences must therefore be explicated ethnographically. The boundary is somewhat ironically rendered virtually impenetrable precisely by the church's complete acceptance of psychiatry. Since in practice mental illness must be professionally ruled out or deemed to be copresent before a problem is recognized as due to demonic affliction, by definition the standard formulation of ethnopsychiatry that recognizes psychotherapy and religious healing as equivalent or alternative ways of addressing affliction cannot be applied within the logic of the system. In addressing the relation between suffering understood to be caused by a supernatural (or preternatural) agent and suffering caused by naturally occurring illness or psychopathology, exorcism raises not only the issue of how scientific medicine and ritual healing interact but also and especially for its practitioners an abiding concern with the relation between faith and reason.

THE PRACTICE OF EXORCISM

Catholic exorcists must be ordained priests, but some are diocesan priests and others are members of religious orders. Mental health professionals who advise on whether a person is afflicted by a psychiatric disorder rather than by an evil spirit, and who often assist in the prayer sessions, are typically practicing Catholics who accept the reality of demonic spirits. People determined to be under demonic influence also have specific characteristics with respect to their life history, spiritual background, and mental health status. Insofar as our current notion of human flourishing is traceable to the concept of *eudaimonia* as used by Aristotle and the Stoics, in the present context the relation between *daimon* and demon cannot go unremarked. Anthropology has a rich tradition of addressing similar concerns in the cross-cultural literature on ritual healing.[3] Catholic exorcism fits this category precisely, insofar as it is intended to have not only the negative function of removing the debilitating effect of evil, in the form of demonic affliction as an impediment to flourishing, but also the positive function of restoring a life of prayer and spirituality as the basis for flourishing. Critical to this undertaking is identifying variation in the cultural patterning of self and emotion in terms of which both affliction and flourishing can be recognized and defined.[4]

Catholic exorcism is a liturgical prayer in which the aim is relief from affliction due to possession by evil spirits, performed by a priest under explicit auspices from a bishop. It is critical to an ethnographic account that there are recognized degrees of demonic affliction within a distinction between ordinary and extraordinary action of the devil. The prime instance of ordinary action is temptation, while extraordinary action can take the form of manifestations that even one of the practicing exorcists said can be "Hollywoodesque." Violent aversion to the sacred, extrahuman strength, knowledge of the future or past, command of a language unfamiliar to the afflicted person, and alterations of vocal tone are among these. The exorcist focuses his attention on the phenomenological field of everyday life to determine how and whether the evil spirit has gained a purchase on the life of the afflicted. I paraphrase a priest from Italy with extensive experience as an exorcist who enumerated what must be attended to:

> Determine whether there are specific episodes in a person's life, including exposure to occult practices, whether voluntarily or involuntarily. Based on case studies we ascertained that ways that open the road for the devil are participating or being present at

séances, spending time with tarot, chiromancy, mediums, extrasensory perception; amulets if received from wizards consecrating them to spirits with specific rituals; objects bought as souvenirs of travel that are cursed; being present at ceremonies as a tourist; practices like transcendental meditation and Reiki; so-called magic communities; cult groups or associations practicing initiation to esoterism; listening to music with a message that invites to necrophilia, satanism, homicide, suicide, blood rites, Eucharistic thefts (which are in exponential increase), black masses and satanic rites with profaning of sacrament and sexual orgies, ritual homicide. But there are also other causes not connected to occult activity, like unconfessed grave sins or injustices, hate or rejecting forgiveness, disordered and perverse acts, especially attacking children or the Holy Spirit. Also, sexual violence, especially father on daughter or on children and adolescents. Not all the abused are subject to the extraordinary action of the devil, but many cases are associated with these moral wounds of sexual violence—we don't know the mechanism, but it allows extraordinary action. Fathers have beneficent effect of blessing greater than mothers, so fathers' abuse is more harmful, this is a hypothesis. Listen to the person and analyze their relation to God: do they pray, how often, how much, have they left something unsaid in confession like an abortion, do they attend sacraments and Mass, how their problems develop over time and what changed in behavior over time, whether the manifestation is continuous or discontinuous, appears and disappears suddenly, alternates randomly or appears always in same circumstances, related to places like in or out of home, church. If there is violence, in what situations is it manifested or accentuated? Did it begin after a particular event? If yes, they must describe the practices involved. What remedies have been used, such as doctor or psychiatrists, and do those specialists have causal explanations, have they gone from doctor to doctor and why, have they tried other healings like occult, alternative religious movements and oracles or teachings specifically applied to that person, were family members living or alive involved anyhow, have they manifest knowledge of unknown things or languages or knowledge of an event at distance or in future, forgotten manifestations or remembered only parts, exhibited strength beyond their age or gender, experienced reactions interior and exterior to sacred.

This searchlight scrutiny is described as discernment based on listening, but the sense in this priest's discourse of an urgency to leave no stone unturned suggests the necessity of interrogation across these categories that could reach an inquisitorial intensity. The dilemma faced by the exorcist is not whether the person is distressed and in need of help, which is invariably the case. The problem is that while it can be determined with some confidence that no extraordinary demonic activity or manifestation is present, it can also be the case that a demon is hiding, and the hidden demons are often the most powerful.

THREE RITUAL/CLINICAL VIGNETTES

The real distress experienced by those who seek the help of exorcists is assessed not only in terms of the presence or absence of demonic activity but also in terms of the presence or absence of mental illness. Psychiatrists and psychologists who are both practicing Catholics and convinced of the ontological reality of evil spirits consult and assist exorcists. The following three vignettes were offered by a Spanish psychiatrist I encountered at the Course on Exorcism and Prayers of Liberation in Rome. He was from a midsized city in Spain where the bishop had authorized him and two priests to lead an exorcism team in service to the diocese and had dispatched the three to attend the course in order to increase their knowledge in the area. He narrated the three vignettes in a conversation about how one can distinguish instances of mental illness from those of possession. The first is a case he ascribed to mental illness, the second to demonic possession, and the third at the time of his narration was still ambiguous and as yet to be determined.

Case 1

A thirty-six-year-old woman with Down syndrome went through fifty sessions of exorcism without result until the priest finally called his psychiatric consultant. He diagnosed paraphrenia with religious delusions, despite the presence of typical demonic manifestations including altered voice, agitated words in another language, inordinate strength, and a lot of religious content. The woman's father was dead, and her schoolteacher mother was very religious and along with a close friend was involved in a group focused on religious visions of the Virgin Mary. The mother, daughter, and friend lived together in a cramped two-room flat where the priest and psychiatrist visited to find every inch of the walls covered in religious images. The afflicted woman was wearing numerous religious medallions and a prayer around her neck, with a religious medal taped to her forehead, and her mother indicated that her demonic episodes always started at six in the evenings. When asked about her situation, the woman went wild, and in trying to pacify her the doctor observed her mouth was very dry and that in fact she was seriously dehydrated. She quickly drank two glasses of orange juice and ate some food, since she had also gone without eating for fifteen days. She soon became agitated again with a changed voice, but the doctor again pacified her. After four rounds of agitation-pacification the doctor realized he could start and stop the manifestations, the priest began to be skeptical, and the mother became annoyed. The doctor prescribed a one-week course of anxiolytic drugs and sleeping pills, instructed the mother and daughter to move out of the cramped flat, and said the daughter should wear only one religious medal. The mother obeyed but was unconvinced, for in fact she was a party to religious delusions, apparently aware that demons are said to attack those who are especially saintly, and wishing that her daughter would prove to be such a person. After a year of psychiatric management, the afflicted woman was back to being a "normal person with Down syndrome."

The report that the woman had undergone more than fifty exorcism sessions is not remarkable, in that exorcism is virtually never a one-time treatment, and indeed exorcists attest that a full liberation of a possessed person can take several years to achieve. Thus in itself this length of treatment does not rule out possession. Moreover, the standard manifestations mentioned are often quite clear-cut in cases of possession: violent strength beyond expectation given the person's age, physique, or gender; apparent knowledge of an exotic language or of facts the afflicted person would have no natural way of knowing; and aversion to anything sacred or inability to pray are among these. In some ways these overt and explicit manifestations make full-scale possession easier to "diagnose" than less severe forms of demonic affliction referred to as vexation or obsession. Critical in this instance is an evident hyper-religiosity, not only histrionic but linked with the idea that if one is demonically afflicted one may be especially holy and more likely to receive the attention not only of the ministering priest but of the merciful God who is the source of liberation. For the psychiatrist, evidence of this hyperreligiosity and clinical observation of the woman's apparent dehydration and the clockwork performative production of possession episodes ruled out veritable possession. Note that the determination was completely independent of the woman's diagnosis with Down syndrome, other than the implication that she might have been especially susceptible to manipulation and the further possible interpretation that her mother may have harbored a hope that the Down syndrome itself might have some demonic source that could be ameliorated by exorcism.

Case 2

A sixty-year-old woman understood as legitimately possessed exhibited eight to ten classic symptoms of possession: these included greater strength than her age or gender warranted, with four people needed to restrain her; changed voice and face; eyes rolled back and white; vomiting of a strange green liquid, speaking of an ancient language; and a strong negative reaction to holy water, the cross, and the priest's stole. Her first session lasted an hour and a half. Afterwards she remembered nothing and resumed a pleasant facial expression. She had attended Mass and taken communion before the exorcism session, which began after others had left the church. The devil then threw her to the floor, where protective cushions had already been placed. The doctor noted that she was normal both before and after the exorcism session. In this instance the afflicted person had come through the Charismatic Renewal looking for a priest to help her. She had a long history of experience with witchcraft or *brujería*—specifically in that when her mother was pregnant another woman did something to her—as well as with "voodoo." An electroencephalograph identified a small epileptic focus, which, however, was not active and was effectively controlled with anticonvulsant medication (a hand tremor disappeared with a low dose). The doctor noted that the occult exposure was all through her mother and not through her own activity, and later both within exorcism sessions and outside them she began to remember experiences she had

had as a little girl. In the previous three to four months she had continued prayers for deliverance with a priest but not formal exorcism.

The doctor's emphasis on the woman's dissociation and complete transformation during the exorcism rite framed by periods of normal comportment before and after indicates an impression that she had been inhabited by a preternatural entity. Indeed, it appears typical that demonic manifestations are most prominent during the rite when the demon is being confronted and provoked and finds it least easy to hide or remain inconspicuous—this is understood not as a feature of performativity but as characteristic of demonic behavior. That the woman had come to the rite through involvement in the Charismatic Renewal is significant, however, in that this Catholic Pentecostal movement explicitly relies on prayer for "deliverance" from evil spirits, understood as a practice that can be performed even by laypeople when demonic affliction is not so severe as to require the ministration of a priest authorized to perform an exorcism.[5] The psychiatrist distinguished all this as completely independent from the minor neurological condition that he understood as being well controlled by anticonvulsant medication. Far more important to him was the woman's exposure through her mother to occult activity in the form of magic, witchcraft, and "voodoo." In the logic of exorcism the occult is a very broad category ranging from fortune-telling with tarot cards to overt satanism, with ethnic and indigenous practices (e.g., paganism or animism) falling along a continuum invariably associated with demonic activity.

Case 3

An ongoing case of a twenty-six-year-old woman from Romania was creating some perplexity for the doctor and the two priests with whom he worked. Since age sixteen she had been diagnosed with schizophrenia, first in Romania, then in Spain. She was under treatment with neuroleptic drugs and spent Mondays through Fridays in a day hospital. Her parents were both pediatricians, and her father had died in a car accident. Her mother's grandmother had been involved in a form of traditional healing in Romania, and her mother was convinced she was possessed despite being a physician herself. Over the past several years the situation had improved, but then a dramatic change came about when the young woman began to experience episodes of intense pain in her hands and feet. Curiously, although she was rendered bedridden for three to four weeks, during this period her psychotic symptoms disappeared. Just a week before narrating this case the doctor went to her home because another such episode had occurred and she was bedridden with pain. Despite the fact that he had recently seen her with a "typical psychotic smile," on this occasion her face was normal except for the expression of physical pain, and she had no other apparent psychotic symptoms. He tested where the pain was by touching her hands and feet and determined that the greatest sensitivity was in the palms of her hands. In such a case he had to entertain the possibility that she was a stigmatic, that there could be a religious aspect, or that evil could be involved. One of the collaborating priests observed that the young woman had been involved in some unsuccessful love magic to attract boys and that her mother had at some point consulted a folk healer for diagnosis. What most perplexed the doctor was that true schizophrenia never remits, so that the episodes when pain replaced psychosis could indicate that schizophrenia was not the correct diagnosis. This possibility was reinforced by her mother's report that the young woman did not respond to her neuroleptic medication. If this was the case, however, it opened the possibility that the demonic symptoms were produced by demonic mimicry of psychopathology. Likewise, the pain episodes could be a product of hysteria, be caused by a demon, or be authentic divinely induced stigmata.

The complexity of this situation was palpable insofar as the boundaries between spiritual and psychiatric, divine and demonic, were at least for the moment inscrutably indeterminate to the psychiatrist and his priest colleagues. Multiple factors included exposure to immigrant healing techniques and involvement with love magic (both at best regarded as superstition and at worst as demonic practice), explicit diagnosis of schizophrenia, the complex effect of psychopharmaceutical agents, the fact of the woman's loss of her father in an automobile accident (which the psychiatrist appeared to see as more significant in this case than in the case of the woman with Down syndrome discussed above), and the fact that the mother was herself a physician presumed to have some degree of clinical judgment. Distinguishing among how symptoms of schizophrenia are understood to be expressed, how authentic stigmatic experience is manifested, and how demonic control is exerted is not simply a matter of separating three possible factors, for in the logic of exorcism an evil spirit is inherently deceptive and capable of mimicking symptoms of illness or holiness, as well as of masking its own presence.

FAITH AND REASONS

In what sense can a discussion such as this contribute to an anthropology of Catholicism? It depends on what you mean by the anthropology of Catholicism, because this phrase can be taken in at least three senses. First, it can be understood in the primary sense adopted in this volume, an ethnography of Catholicism per se as a religious, cultural, and institutional phenomenon. This is of considerable value except insofar as it becomes intellectually beholden to an "anthropology of Christianity" that is less a topic of investigation than a semiautonomous subfield within the anthropology of religion. Writers under this rubric constructively problematize the category of Christianity,[6] but the rhetorical/theoretical strategy they adopt in order to doing so is to downplay a substantial tradition of anthropological work on various forms of Christianity,[7] unduly claiming that Christianity has previously been neglected or even shunned by anthropology. A preoccupation with Protestantism led to the virtual exclusion until very recently of Catholic and Orthodox traditions, and aside from significant attention to the globally dynamic Pentecostal movement it still elides the broader importance of enthusiastic, apocalyptic, and millennial movements within Christianity. The main problem is that an anthropology of Catholicism framed in this way can easily be construed as a plea for inclusion in a sub-subdiscipline rather than a reminder of the scholarly richness in a broader anthropology of religion; a comparative study of Catholicism in its many variations can be just as productively arrived at through the field of religion and globalization, which spans anthropology and sociology.[8] Framing an anthropology of Christianity as a subdiscipline rather than as a topic is not only restrictive but potentially dangerous insofar as it has created a cohort of entering graduate students identifying themselves as anthropologists of Christianity rather than as anthropologists of religion interested in Christianity. In this respect an anthropology of Catholicism better serves the field by summoning the anthropology of Protestantism back into the larger fold of comparativist anthropology of religion rather than by becoming a sub-sub-subdiscipline within the anthropology of Christianity.

In a second sense of the term, an anthropology of Catholicism can be understood as a site where fundamental human or existential themes are elaborated in a culturally specific way. This is the approach I have adopted here in discussing the relation between religion and medicine in a form that it could take only in a specifically Catholic cultural context, while attempting to throw light on exorcism as a Catholic practice of ritual healing and a particular instance of the Catholic enactment of the dialectic of faith and reason. The problem of evil is another fundamental theme upon which particular light can be thrown by a consideration of Catholic exorcism. This is so in three respects, first among which is an understanding of evil as malevolent destructiveness, dramatized in the excruciating manifestations of possession among the afflicted and in the reputed ruining of lives by demonic influence, and reputedly perpetrated by humans in forms ranging from curses to satanic abuse and even murder. Second is the rendering of evil in the form of demons as highly "intelligent personal beings" who can establish relations of domination with humans but only with a degree of complicity, thus problematizing the relation between human evil and cosmological evil as well as the limits of free will when a person is possessed. Third is the constellation of evil, sin, and obedience insofar as it applies to both humans and demons, who are in actuality "fallen angels." The demons' fundamental and irredeemable sin was rejection of divine authority, though they can be compelled to obey by an omnipotent deity, and humans under divine authority are required to obey any divine command, no matter what it is. The biblical story of Abraham and Isaac shows God relenting in his demand for a father to kill his son (the expectation that the devil would go through with it is implicit in the notion of satanic ritual murder), but it indicates that God nevertheless reserves the right to make such a demand, which cannot be evil if it is God's will.

Third, the anthropology of Catholicism can be one of many interlocutors in a comparative/ethnological study that situates it among other religions as a form of both addressing and altering the human condition. Certainly a comparative study of evil across religions would be one place where the sketch I provided in the previous paragraph could enter a broader conversation bridging religious studies and philosophy. If demons and djinn hold parallel cosmological positions in Christianity and Islam, it would be important to examine the differing basis for the deep resentment each of them bears toward humans. For the Christian demons, this resentment can be traced to their recognition that although they were created far superior to humans, it is humans who are favored by God, whereas the djinn are said to resent humans because humans were created superior. Likewise, it is significant that demons are defined as unredeemable because of their irreversible rejection of God, whereas djinn can be saved and even helped by benevolent humans. Such analyses inevitably engage theology, but the comparative imperative makes it far easier to treat theology as a cultural system rather than as a parallel pursuit or cognate discipline, a temptation to which an insular anthropology of Christianity is all too susceptible. Finally, the significance of the contemporary resurgence of exorcism as a ritual practice in what is certainly one of the world's most intensely patriarchal institutions, where exorcists by definition are priests and hence male while a majority of the afflicted are female, can enter into a fruitful comparative critique of gender dynamics in religion.

Returning to the cases I have examined in this chapter, from a cultural, clinical, and pastoral standpoint far more could be said about how physicians and exorcists collaborate and how Catholic mental health professionals attempt to differentiate between natural illness and preternatural influence. In contemporary practice, not only do these individuals work across an empirical boundary, or perhaps threshold, between psychopathology and possession, but in synthesizing their own medical training and religious commitment they enact in actuality what theologians expound in principle as an intimate interaction between faith and reason. Thus their role in defining exorcism in the twenty-first century is perhaps just as important as the roles of the exorcist and the afflicted. From a moral, agentive, and existential standpoint, the discourse of evil opens a series of dichotomous relationships stemming from the basic opposition of faith and reason. Even if illness is not inherently evil, evil can cause illness. And if illness is evil, it is an impersonal natural evil, whereas demonic affliction is perpetrated by malevolent personal beings. Thus exorcism opens up for discussion the relations between personal and impersonal entities, endogenous and exogenous causes, natural and preternatural sources of affliction. Finally, from a comparative, ethnological, and interpretive standpoint, we anthropologists tend to be surprised when indigenous healers and patients tolerate what we see as contradiction and incommensurability. It appears exotic. Yet such a position is highly elaborated at the heart of civilization in the form of the dialogue between faith and reason, not only in theological discourse but also in the pragmatic domain of exorcism. Perhaps even more than in the typical ethnographic encounter with indigenous healers, it invites the question of under what circumstances a notion of "mystery" can be existentially viable, for that is how theology defines this relation between faith and reason. The problem is that for theology the mystery must be accepted as a matter of faith, whereas for anthropology a mystery is to be resolved through experience, thought, and the interpretation of data. This, however, is a problem beyond the scope of this chapter.

NOTES

Research for this work was supported by a grant from the Social Sciences Research Council's project on New Directions in the Study of Prayer.

1. Kramer and Sprenger ([1485] 1971); Caciola (2003).

2. Bax (1992); Sluhovsky (2007); Huxley ([1952] 1993); Certeau (2000); Cuneo (2001); Goodman (2005).

3. See Csordas and Lewton (1998) for a review.

4. Kitayama and Markus (1994); Csordas (1994).

5. Csordas (1997, 1994).

6. Robbins (2003b); Cannell (2006); Engelke and Tomlinson (2006).

7. See Hann (2014) for a summary of this literature and an accompanying critique.

8. Beyer (1994); Clarke (2006); Coleman and Collins (2004); Csordas (2009); Hefner (1998); Hopkins et al. (2001); Hüwelmeier and Krause (2009); Jenkins (2007); Juergensmeyer (2003); Poewe (1994); Robertson and Garrett (1991); van der Veer (1994); Vásquez and Marquardt (2003).

23

Catholicism and the Study of Religion

Birgit Meyer

In this essay I would like to reflect on the conceptual implications of the proposition of the editors to take (the study of) Catholicism more seriously. However, I would like to make clear from the outset that I do not follow their call to take part in inaugurating the anthropology of Catholicism. First, as a scholar whose work predominantly focuses on Protestant missions and Pentecostal movements in Africa, I would not be equipped to play a role in this regard. Second, I am suspicious of the trend to launch ever more "anthropologies" of specific phenomena (a criticism I also have with regard to the anthropology of Christianity). While I concede that this may be a useful strategic move to orchestrate joint attention to a particular phenomenon, there is a danger of getting stuck. On my part, I rather want to think about Catholicism in relation to debates in the broader, multidisciplinary field of the study of religion, where the current material and bodily turn seeks to offer new directions that move beyond the long-dominant mentalistic emphasis on belief, content, and meaning that has been identified as the proverbial "Protestant bias" of modern understandings of religion. What difference does a focus on Catholicism make for how we position the study of religion conceptually at a moment when its "Protestant" underpinnings are subject to fundamental critique?[1]

CATHOLICISM, PROTESTANTISM, AND THE MASTER NARRATIVE OF MODERNITY

Current commonsense discourses about religion—certainly in the Netherlands, Germany, and the United States—often mobilize stereotypical views of Catholic and Protestant religiosities that are grounded in long-standing tensions between these two strands of Christianity as they arose in the aftermath of the Reformation and the rise of a post-Enlightenment modern order. While Catholicism is usually associated with the worship of saints and relics, ritual and sacraments, and a corporeal religiosity, Protestantism—and especially Calvinism—is held to be centered on Bible reading and a search for abstract meaning, inducing a mentalistic religiosity. Depending on the attitude of the beholder, these contrasts may be valued positively or negatively. Their use is, of course, problematic because it maintains long-standing prejudices and promotes an essentializing dualism that ties each of these two Christian traditions to a distinct, hierarchized type of religiosity. While actual theological and other differences between Catholicism and Protestantism—each, in turn, standing for a highly diverse tradition—certainly should not be brushed over, it would be mistaken to view them through the lens of such decontextualized, crude oppositions as those mentioned above.

The reason why I invoke these clichés is that their use points to a fundamental underlying issue: the complex relation between mind and body, between the spiritual and the material, between thinking and sensing, and between cognition and carnality in post-Reformation Protestant and Catholic Christianity and modernity at large. The mobilization of these dualisms in talking about Protestants and Catholics reveals much about tensions in current understandings of and approaches to modern Christianity and religion in general. The neat, simple idea of the superiority of the left side of these dualisms over the right side cannot be maintained in the light of everyday religious practice. Rather, these dualisms could be seen as the poles of a continuum that includes Protestant *and* Catholic religiosities. In this context it is intriguing to note that *Protestant* and *Catholic* are often employed as adjectives—usually tongue-in-cheek—that are severed from the particular Christian tradition they evoke (see Coleman, this volume). While the former stands for a sober, inward-oriented religiosity of the mind, the latter refers to exuberant rituals, triggering the body and the senses, and a rich material culture—an outward-oriented religiosity of the body. Placed in a temporalizing framework that regards Protestantism as the vanguard of modernity, the qualification of certain aspects of Catholic religious practice as "Protestant" acknowledges that Catholics are, as it were, catching up (even though there may "still" be significant differences between the enlightened clergy that sought to modernize Catholicism after the Second Vatican Council and ordinary, conservative believers). Conversely, though more rarely, Protestants may be qualified as displaying "Catholic" features. I find the latter qualification more intriguing because it challenges the typically modernist temporal scheme according to which Protestantism is profiled as the modern religion par excellence that breaks with the Catholic past. This suggests cracks in the familiar image of Protestantism as instigating a religious subjectivity that privileges mind above body, duty above desire, *ratio* above passion—the model of modern personhood.

The scholarly version of this image was famously articulated by Max Weber in *The Protestant Ethic and the Spirit of Capitalism*. In his scenario of the rise of modern capitalism, the Reformation initiated a fundamental break between medieval Catholicism and modern Protestantism—epitomized by Calvinism and other Puritan movements, though to his dismay Lutheranism still was close to Catholicism—that eventually yielded a disenchanted society. For Weber, Catholic religiosity was characterized by the use of magical means—involving rituals, objects, body techniques, sacraments—in the pursuit of salvation that were authorized by the church and formed the basis of its power.[2] In his thinking, medieval Catholicism was based on superstition and thus stood in fundamental contrast to the rational outlook emerging in consequence of the Calvinist doctrine of predestination that robbed believers of the possibility to employ such means to influence God.[3] This introduced a new, rational relation between piety and worldly behavior (placement of one's conduct under the adage "Time is money," constant introspection, and methodological self-control) that eventually yielded the end of religion in a thoroughly rationalized society that became an iron cage.

From the outset, Weber's analysis, including his take on Catholicism, was contested. Apart from a number of remarks made in passing about Jesuits and Jansenists, Weber did not pay systematic attention to developments within post-Reformation Catholicism, such as the Council of Trent, the Counter-Reformation, and the baroque. By and large, he took Catholicism to be a less developed religion that had essentially not changed since the Middle Ages. Here it is not my intention to discuss how far his stance toward Catholicism was correct (in fact, he reproduced clichéd views as they were held in the German liberal Protestant milieu in the aftermath of the *Kulturkampf*) and how far his general thesis, which he refined and defended vigorously against a stream of criticisms until his death in 1920, can be maintained on empirical grounds.[4] The point is that Weber's thesis about the prominent role of Calvinist Protestantism as a harbinger of modern capitalism proved to be powerful in shaping social and cultural thought at large and the sociology of religion in particular. He articulated a dominant "master narrative" about modernity as rational, disenchanted, and ultimately secular,[5] and a view of Calvinist Protestantism as having transcended the importance attributed to practices, objects, the body, and sensations that had characterized medieval Catholicism. In short, the Calvinism of the "Protestant ethic" epitomized the rise of a dematerialized religiosity in an ever more materialistic world,[6] and modernity was profiled as a "secular form of Protestantism."[7] Catholicism, and all it was made to stand for, featured in this master narrative as Protestantism's Other and as a (to many, alas resilient and progress-impeding) matter of the past—a typical instance of what Johannes Fabian called "denial of co-evalness."[8]

As pointed out by the German cultural sociologist Andreas Reckwitz, in the aftermath of Weber (and other towering figures, including Durkheim, Parsons, and Habermas) mainstream social and cultural theory approached modern society as being disenchanted and rational, as if the initially Protestant spirit of capitalism had de facto unleashed a broader process of sobering up (in German *Ernüchterung*) that allowed scholars to neglect the body, emotions, space, and objects as relevant topics of social and cultural analysis.[9] Since the 1980s, this stance has been questioned ever more loudly and explicitly with the rise of postmodernism, which critiqued the claimed rationality and progressive orientation of the modernist project. This fueled the development of new epistemologies, theories, and concepts that move beyond the so far dominant approach to modern society in terms of abstract normative and symbolic orders. Various "turns" called attention to gender, the body and the senses, objects, space, emotions, and pictures, so as to affirm the importance of the material and concrete that had long and unduly been denied. Bruno Latour's statement "We have never been modern" aptly captured the growing realization of a cleavage between what modernity was presumed to be (as a project or master narrative) and what it actually came down to in everyday practice.[10] In this context, he identified the concept of the "fetish" as the prime symptom of a modern insistence on a clear dualism of persons and things that was ultimately impossible to be maintained in practice. Coining the notion of the "factish"—a mix of "fact" and "fetish"—and pointing out that "we help to fabricate the beings in which we believe," Latour went against the Protestant grain of modernity that was employed by Protestants to dismiss both Catholicism and non-Western religions as a superstitious worship of idols.[11]

Similarly, in their groundbreaking book *Re-forming the Body* the British sociologists Philip Mellor and Chris Shilling stress the ambivalent Janus-face of modernity, which, in their view, is characterized by a constant "resurgence of the flesh" that cannot be "easily contained within the cognitive orders of modernity."[12] Behind the official face that privileges the mind above the body and the passions, the other face (building upon Schopenhauer and Nietzsche) reasserts the importance of the body, passions, and the senses. If the former is grounded in the Protestant Reformation with its typical ascetic and mind-oriented subjectivity, the latter is grounded in the Catholic Counter-Reformation that unleashed the baroque with its "voluptuous corporeality" and "seduction of the senses."[13] They examine the differences and tensions between the re-formation of the body (understood as an actual, not merely metaphorical, corporeal process) and medieval Christianity, as well as between Protestantism *and* Catholicism in the modern period. Their admittedly schematic approach is lucid and provocative. While they accept the relevance of Weber's insights, they criticize sociology's exaggerated "focus on the legacy of Protestantism for the modern world" through which Catholicism is edited out of the master narrative of modernity.[14] Mellor and Shilling point out that "the Reformation's rejection of carnal knowing was inherently problematic: there was always the danger that touch, taste, smell, sight and hearing could lead to the acquisition of heretical knowledge. Similarly, modernity's promotion of cognitive apprehension cannot eliminate the passion and sensations of bodies, however much it has tried to manage or repress them."[15] They reject not only a reduction of modernity to a secular version of Protestantism but also a limited view of the latter in line with the ideal type (suggesting, in fact, that "Protestantism has never been Protestant"). Their analysis spotlights how bringing Catholicism— and thus the body, images, sensations, emotions, passions, and ritual practices— into the picture makes a crucial difference. Doing so derails familiar ways of narrating modernity that, as Mellor and Shilling point out, rely not only on an exaggerated Protestant bias but also on a biased Protestantism.

Above all, their work serves as a powerful reminder for scholars in the social and cultural sciences to take into account the importance of post-Reformation Catholicism and the baroque with its typical aesthetics of persuasion for contemporary modernity.[16] They spotlight the rise of a new expression of human corporality that "can be associated with the emergence of a 'baroque modern' form of embodiment: a form marked by a sensualisation of experience, partly analogous to that evident in the Counter-Reformation baroque cultures, which develops hand in hand with an extension of certain aspects of the Protestant modern body."[17] Indeed, the "lens of the baroque" is highly suitable for understanding the endurance of Catholicism as "a theological-political form" (as in the cult of the Virgin of Guadalupe; see Norget, this volume), and it throws into relief broader debates about the importance of the role of the senses, emotions, and experiences in binding people into current politico-aesthetic formations.[18]

A TURNING POINT: FROM CRITIQUING PROTESTANT BIAS TO APPRAISING CATHOLIC RELIGIOSITY

Of course, the overall critique deployed in mainstream social and cultural thought in analyzing modernity, as well as the various "turns" to the material and concrete, had parallels and repercussions in the study of religion. As Talal Asad argued powerfully, the modern study of religion is indebted to the legacy of post-Enlightenment Protestantism as framed within the master narrative of modernity.[19] This implied that scholarly concepts and approaches employed to analyze religious practices and ideas all over the world echoed Protestant suspicions with regard to Catholic religiosity, emphasizing instead a logocentric concern with the Word of God (through the Bible, preaching, reading, prayer) or gods. Synthesizing Protestant logocentrism with German idealism and phenomenological subjectivism gave rise to, as Manuel Vásquez puts it, "a somatophobic [and I would add: icono-, object- and practice-phobic] *Religionswissenschaft* whose seductive power still holds sway today."[20] Over the past twenty years, scholars have problematized the more or less unreflected projection onto other religions of arguably Protestant viewpoints that were mistaken for universal ones. The possibility of a universally applicable definition of religion was questioned, and a search for alternative approaches that take at face value the importance of the material and concrete is in full swing.

The critical concern to uncover the genealogy of the modern category of religion by pointing out its Protestant roots has great merits, but it also comes with its own intrinsic limitations. One problem I see is that the Protestant bias may easily be taken for real, rather than as an ideal type that reflects a particular theological and scholarly understanding. This yields a problematic affirmation of a caricature of Protestantism that is far removed from actual Protestant practice and lived religiosity. Indeed, "We should . . . be careful not to cast Protestantism as the villain in modern Christianity's denigration of the body and the external world."[21] Detailed ethnographic and historical works, partly conducted within the anthropology of Christianity, have uncovered aspects and dimensions of Protestant practice in Europe, America and the global South that do not conform to stereotypical views of this strand of Christianity as basically being centered on Bible reading and a search for abstract meaning, inducing a mentalistic religiosity.[22] This became even more obvious in the frontier zones of Western outreach where Protestant and Catholic missions confronted what they took as "heathendom" with their— significantly divergent—evangelizing projects.[23]

Second, the eagerness to spot and uncover a Protestant bias in the study of religion—over and over again—tends to sustain an appraisal of Protestantism as the cradle of modernity, at the very moment when critical scholarship unmasks and challenges this narrative, as pointed out above. The irony cannot be missed. If scholars in religious studies and the anthropology of religion have tended to mistakenly perceive concepts and assumptions as universal that were de facto rooted in a historically situated post-Enlightenment Protestant religiosity, scholars in the social and cultural sciences (whose main focus was the Western cultures and societies) have long tended to take more or less at face value the role of Calvinist Protestantism in the rise of modernity, understood in terms of rationalization and disenchantment. While uncovering the Protestant bias in the study of religion was a critical move that stated something hitherto ill-realized, the affirmation of the crucial role of Protestantism echoes a long-standing appraisal of the "Protestant Ethic" as the dominant scenario to account for the shape of modern society. In short, there is some degree of a mismatch between critical thought about the role of Protestantism in the study of religion, on the one hand, and in the social and cultural sciences, on the other. I think that it is time to move not only beyond critique of the "Protestant bias" but also beyond what is in my view its all too frequent invocation.[24]

So, if Protestantism cannot be reduced to how it was pictured in the Weberian scenario that shaped social and cultural theory, and if "we have never been modern" in a straightforward, progressive, rational sense, it is necessary for scholars to move further and open up the alternative archive of post-Reformation Catholicism. Of course, I do not propose to exchange the Protestant for a Catholic bias. The point is that the explicit role assigned to the body, the senses, objects, pictures, and rituals in the Catholic tradition can alert researchers to the broader relevance of materiality in religious practice at large and can prompt them to place Protestantism in a new light.[25] To flesh out a material take on religion and society, Catholic religiosity—in past and present—warrants a closer look. One of the laudable achievements of this volume is that it showcases a host of old and new materials to do so.

CATHOLIC MEDIATIONS—FRESH PERSPECTIVES

As noted above, I am not an expert in the study of Catholicism and have no intention to delve into a separate anthropology devoted to this particular strand of Christianity. But I think that deeper knowledge about Catholic religiosity—regarding theological ideas and rituals as well as everyday practice—is important to allow for a shift in perspective so as to bring into the picture aspects that remain blind spots as long as religion is explored through a mentalistic (Protestant) lens. The background of this interest is that in my work on Protestant missions and Pentecostal movements in Ghana I encountered many instances that challenged facile assumptions about the nature of Protestantism as well as the idea that Pentecostals are the ultimate (post) modern exponents of Protestantism. This pertains both to the striving for a modern, far from sober and ascetic lifestyle (already in the early days of evangelizing and even more with the rise of Pentecostalism since the 1990s) and to the strong role of bodily sensations, the performance of ritual, and the value attributed to certain power objects (the Bible, the membership book) in religious practice.[26] In short, I encountered the limits of what I took to be characteristic of Protestantism, and this prompted me to deploy an alternative, material approach that takes the body, sensations, objects, images, and rituals seriously as authorized harbingers that convey to believers a sense of divine presence, making God real.

Actually, my inclination to go for a material approach was grounded in a deep puzzlement about how to find a conceptual space to accommodate the explicit and deliberate human engagement in "doing" religion and effecting a genesis of divine presence that I encountered in my research among Protestants and Pentecostals. Gradually I realized that there was indeed a legacy of a Protestant-Calvinist inclination to privilege meaning, while making secondary the "outward" forms through which it was established and performed. From a Catholic perspective, the human ways of representing and approaching God would, of course, appear in another light. However, as far as I could see, there was no Catholic bias in place that could seriously compete with the Protestant one and that entailed alternative concepts and approaches in the study of religion that would suggest alternative takes on materiality and the human role in constructing religion.

The current conceptualization of religion as a practice of mediation and of multiple media (understood in a broad sense) as intrinsic to that practice and as employed for "materializing the sacred" arose in this void.[27] It is telling that Robert Orsi, as a scholar with long-standing expertise on Catholicism, played a lead role in this regard. Mediation, as is often remarked with a smile, is a "Catholic" thing. Indeed, Catholicism offers an explicit theology of mediation in which the body, objects, and practices are indispensable and are mobilized to bring about a sense of the "real presence of God,"[28] as highlighted in the doctrine of the transubstantiation of the host and wine into the body of Christ, the veneration of saints, the prominent role of images in devotional practice, and so on. But an approach to religion as mediation is even more revealing if mediation—and thus the human input into the "fabrication of the beings in which we believe"—is *not* acknowledged or emphasized on the *emic* level. This makes it possible to uncover the semiotic ideologies through which the actual use of media is deemphasized, in favor of generating a sense of immediacy, in Protestant religious practice.[29] As pointed out more extensively in other publications, I approach media that are authorized within specific religious traditions as "sensational forms" allowing believers to make the divine tangible in various shapes and to experience it as real.[30] In the study of religion the medium of the book has traditionally received a great deal of attention (without being necessarily appraised as a medium, certainly within a Calvinist theological framework that stresses immediacy) and has produced an impressive philological and hermeneutical expertise. By contrast, the study of other media—for instance, images—has long been marginalized and thus has generated much less analytical know-how. To further develop the study of religion as a phenomenon that involves multiple media, a focus on Catholic images and attitudes to art can serve as a highly illuminating example.

The Reformation entailed a more or less violent media shift, from the central role of relics and images in (everyday) Catholic religiosity to the Reformers' emphasis on the Bible. In turn, the Counter-Reformation launched the baroque as a powerful statement against the iconoclastic stance of Calvinism.[31] Communicating Catholic beliefs through the sensational display of art, the baroque style entailed a lavish aesthetics of persuasion that was spread across the world with, especially, Jesuit missions. This included the spread and reproduction of the most famous image of the Sacred Heart of Jesus painted by the Italian Pompeo Batoni (1760). Placed in an altar of the baroque Jesuit Church of Gesù in Rome, the image depicts the apparition of Jesus holding his bleeding heart to the French nun Margaret Mary Alacoque, who lived about one hundred years before the date of the painting.[32] The image became the endlessly reproduced icon of the Catholic devotion to the Sacred Heart of Jesus. It has remained popular among Catholics up to today, as I also found through my research in Ghana.[33]

A stronger contrast between baroque art (and this image in particular) and Calvinism's sober style is barely imaginable. Protestant Calvinism rejected the representation of divinity in any form and dismissed the devotional use of images.[34] This brought about the rise of a separate domain of art and aesthetics that was independent from the sphere of religion. As a consequence, art history and religious studies were worlds apart. With the rise of the pictorial or iconic turn in art history and visual studies, on the one hand, and an approach to images as religious media and an increased interest in the "icon" in the study of religion, on the other, new synergies have emerged since the 1990s between these so far disconnected fields.[35] For good reasons. Scholars in visual studies seek to come to grips with the apparent capacity of images to appear animated and enchanted and to think about how to account for their "power," life," or "agency."[36] There is a remarkable recycling and reproduction, via ever new media, of iconographic traditions and pictorial genres from the Catholic past.[37] And there is an apparent resilience and proliferation of visual regimes grounded in the Catholic baroque, at a time when northern Europe is caught up in a process of unchurching. Indeed, to invoke Mellor and Shilling once again, the "tension between cognition and carnality that shaped the post-Reformation era is at the heart of the advanced modern experience of the world: seductive images have returned in the modern information age, and it is even possible to talk of the emergence of a form of embodiment which is both 'baroque' and 'modern.'"[38] A deep understanding of these processes demands sustained collaboration between scholars in visual culture and religious studies, which in my view is beneficial to both sides. To gain such understanding, a focus on Catholic religiosity and its rich visual culture is an indispensable requirement.

Focusing on images as prominent religious media, I also want to make a more general point. As I pointed out, my motivation to look at Catholicism is not grounded in an interest in this brand of Christianity per se; rather, it stems from the idea that doing so offers a much-needed corrective. So, to take up the question posed in the beginning of this essay: What difference does a focus on Catholicism make for how we position the study of religion conceptually? Turning to Catholicism as an alternative archive allows for a critique of the Protestant legacy that shaped the master narrative of modernity as well as the study of religion across the world *and* offers fresh insights for conceptualizing and approaching religion from a material angle. Of course, I do not wish to affirm a stereotyped dualism that maps Protestantism and Catholicism on simple oppositions such as mentalistic and material. As I hope to have made clear, actual lived Protestant religiosity does not conform to such a view (and the same holds for Catholicism). The point is that paying attention to Catholic religiosity is helpful to further flesh out an approach to religion that acknowledges the role of the body, objects, and human practice in generating a sense of divine presence. This approach should ultimately transcend the mental-material distinction, as well as the spectrum of Christianity.

NOTES

I would like to thank the editors for inviting me to write this essay, and Jojada Verrips and Bruno Reinhardt for stimulating comments on an earlier version.

1. Asad (1993).

2. Weber ([1905] 2001, 61). See also Otto (2005, 236–37).

3. Weber ([1905] 2001, 71).

4. See H. Lehmann (2009, 107–15); Schluchter (2005, 68–72).

5. Van Rooden (1996, 203). See also Cox (2001).

6. Meyer (2010a, 743–50); Meyer and Houtman (2012, 9–13); see also Keane (2003, 411); Keane (2007).

7. As aptly put by Seidler, quoted in Mellor and Shilling (1997, 144).

8. Fabian (1983). The exclusivist mobilization of time remained central to modernist discourse up until today, as contemporary characterizations of Islam as "backward" show.

9. Reckwitz (2012). Their existence was, of course, not denied, but their analysis was regarded as relevant, not to sociology, but to fields other than sociology (e.g., emotions were relegated to psychology, understood as a science directed to the individual).

10. Latour (1993).

11. Latour (2010, 39).See also Keane (2007, 79–81); Meyer (2014).

12. Mellor and Shilling (1997, 156).

13. Mellor and Shilling (1997, 134–38).

14. Mellor and Shilling (1997, 8).

15. Mellor and Shilling (1997, 156).

16. See also Ndalianis (2004); van de Port (2013).

17. Mellor and Shilling (1997, 11).

18. Meyer (2009). See also Böhme (1995); Rancière (2006).

19. Asad (1993).

20. Vásquez (2011, 32).

21. Vásquez (2011, 32).

22. E.g., Klassen (2011); McDannell (1995); Verrips (2013).

23. E.g., Keane (2007); Meyer (1999).

24. This critique is also directed to myself; see Meyer (2014).

25. Engelke (2011, 221).

26. See Meyer (2014, 213–14); see also Meyer (1997, 311–37).

27. Orsi (2012, 147).

28. Butticci (2016). See also Butticci's fascinating website on Pentecostal aesthetics: www .pentecostalaesthetics.net.

29. Meyer (2011, 29).

30. Meyer (2006; 2011, 217–18). In this context I would like to note that Niklaus Largier's fascinating exposé of the bodily and sensorial practices of medieval mystics (this volume) and their deployment in romanticism strikes me as showing surprising similarities with contemporary Pentecostal religious practice and its specific sensational forms. This surprising recognition underlines the importance of spotting continuities, rather than mistaking the Reformation as a watershed that entailed a full break with medieval religiosity.

31. Belting (1990, 538–45); Schwebel (2002, 71–73).

32. Morgan (2012b, 90–111).

33. Napolitano (2007, 71–87). Cheap reproductions (made in China) are available throughout southern Ghana. Such posters are also popular among non-Catholics. While the image is employed as an icon that conveys to believers a sense of the presence of God and the power of Jesus, others reject it

as an illicit material form that operates as an "idol" or "fetish." The uses and debates about this image illustrate the extent to which long-standing tensions between Protestant and Catholic stances to images—as idols or icons—have spread on a global scale and inform current attitudes to (religious) visual culture. See Meyer (2010b, 100–130); Woets (2016).

34. It would be mistaken to characterize Protestantism as iconophobic. Images played a role in Protestant religious practice up to the present. The Protestant spectrum is differentiated, and especially in Lutheran churches pictures are displayed and parts of the pre-Reformation Catholic heritage are maintained. Generally shared among Protestants are illustrations in Bibles and pictures of biblical scenes and Jesus. The crucial point concerns the theological rejection of images as harbingers of divine presence. In everyday practice, as David Morgan (1998) showed, images of Jesus may be at the center of popular Protestant devotional piety.

35. On the interest in religious studies concerning images as religious media, see, e.g., Pentcheva (2006, 631–55); Lührmann (2010, 56–78). On new connections between this approach and the iconic turn in art history, see Meyer (2015, 6–14).

36. See, e.g., Freedberg (1989); Gell (1998); W. Mitchell (2004).

37. Weigel (2015).

38. Mellor and Shilling (1997, 157).

24

The Media of Sensation

Niklaus Largier

Approximately fifty years before Karl Rahner and Hans Urs von Balthasar redis-covered the significance of the patristic and medieval teachings about the "inner" or "spiritual senses" for twentieth-century Catholic theology, the French decadent writer Joris-Karl Huysmans revisited this poetics of sensation in his novel *À rebours* (Against nature).[1] While Rahner and Balthasar focus on the context of contemplation, spirituality, religious anthropology, and theological aesthetics, however, Huysmans used the medieval paradigms of sensual and affective stimula-tion as a model for the reinvention of sensation in a resolutely modernist attitude. In what we usually see as the "decadent" context and aspect of his work, some years before his explicit turn toward Catholicism in the later works, he thus already in *Against Nature* deployed a poetics of sensual intensities that, as I will show here, deeply resonates with medieval arts and notions of prayer. With its emphasis on the artificial stimulation of sensation and affect, the media that help to create it, and the new intensity that is being produced, Huysmans's position lies—speaking very schematically—somewhere between, on one side, the romantics' constructiv-ist desire to reinvent the nature of the senses, and, on the other, the modernist interest in a rediscovery of the phenomenology of sensation. The German roman-tic poet Novalis (1772–1801) might be seen as representing the former, and the Austrian novelist Robert Musil with his exploration of sensation and affect in the novel *The Man without Qualities* (1940), or Georges Bataille's collection of reflec-tions on experience under the title *Inner Experience* (1943), as representing the latter.

Thus we read in the reflections of the German romantic poet Novalis from 1798:

We have two sense systems which, however different they appear, are yet entwined extremely closely with one another. One system is called the body, one the soul. The former is dependent on external stimuli, whose essence we call nature or the external world. The latter originally is dependent on the essence of inner stimuli that we call spirit, or the world of spirits. Usually this last system stands in a nexus of association with the other system—and is affected by it. Nevertheless frequent traces of a converse relation are to be found, and one soon notices that both systems ought actually to stand in perfect reciprocal relation to one another, in which, while each of them is affected by its world, they should create harmony. . . . In short, both worlds, like both systems, are to create free harmony, not disharmony or monotony.[2]

In this programmatic statement it appears that Novalis describes body and soul, the senses, the emotions, and reason in a conversation with terms that are quite typical of romanticism and German idealism. In fact, however, Novalis draws here on a much older terminology and tradition as well. In particular, the specific concepts of "inner" and "outer" upon which his discussion of sensation depends, and which played a major role in medieval mysticism, were originally elaborated in the Middle Ages and early modernity. Novalis is in this regard exemplary of a particular engagement in romantic and postromantic thought on sensation with certain key conceptual moments, namely the distinction between internal and external stimuli, the idea of their "converse relation," and the desire for a new configuration of this relation in terms of a poetics of sensation ("free harmony"). What Novalis inherits from the tradition of the technologies of prayer that I will discuss below is the idea of an artificial, rhetorical stimulation and formation of the senses in and through specific practices. These have been developed in the context of prayer as well as in the very theory of "formation" (*Bildung*) that these practices entail and that Novalis knows mainly through pietist literature and education. It is, in other words, the very idea of a poetics of sensation and affect that Novalis develops in a conversation with the history and rhetoric of prayer.

As we read in many of the medieval treatises on prayer and contemplation, the goal of prayer does not lie in acts of praise, petition, or repentance. Instead, prayer and the media that are used—I am thinking of the liturgy, words, song, music, images, and gestures—enact the overcoming of the postlapsarian empirical and instrumental order of the world and the establishment of a pretaste (*praegustatio*) of the world to come. In other words, prayers are not just an address and a moment of dialogue: they produce qualities and intensities of sensual and affective experience that in their character anticipate moments of eschatological reconciliation— something that is to be compared to Novalis's notion of "free harmony." As David of Augsburg puts it in his treatise *The Seven Steps of Prayer*, prayer is the very "knocking" on heaven's door (quoting the "knocking at the door" from Matt. 7:7 and Luke 11:9): "When he tells us to pray, God does not mean that we should tell him with our words what we wish, since he anyway already knows what we need before we ask him for it. He rather means that we should *knock*. Through knocking we experience how sweet and good he is and thus we love him and join him in love and become one spirit with him."[3] This is David's explanation of the act of "rumination," the practice that not only remembers the scriptures but translates the act of remembering into an act of intense affective and sensual experience, or, in other words, the act that deploys the rhetorical effects of the words in order to make the scriptures alive in a new life of the soul—a new life that produces a convergence of inner and outer worlds. This happens in prayer in and through an art of figuration that draws on the scriptures and deploys its images and words in an exploration and reconfiguration of sensual possibilities. As Marshall McLuhan writes in a letter that comments on his own Catholicism in 1969, this very rhetoric of an affirmation of the sensual relies not on "concepts or ideas" but on an "analogical awareness that begins in the senses." Thus, he notes, "Your piece on me brings to mind that I am a Thomist for whom the sensory order resonates with the divine Logos. I don't think concepts have any relevance in religion. Analogy is not concept. It is community. It is resonance. It is inclusive. It is the cognitive process itself. That is the analogy of the divine Logos. I think of Jasper, Bergson, and Buber as very inferior conceptualist types, quite out of touch with the immediate analogical awareness that begins in the senses and is derailed by concepts or ideas."[4]

This "analogical awareness" is being produced—as it is in Novalis's vision of a reformation of the senses and the relation between "inner" and "outer"—through practices of prayer, contemplation, and a poetics of sensation, that is, through a use of media that transform the very realm of sensation and affect. Roughly one hundred years after Novalis, Huysmans's contemporary Maurice Barrès will write in *Un homme libre*, evoking the same thought and the practical aspects of this transformation: "If we knew how to produce the exact circumstances for the exercise of our faculties, we would be able to observe how our desires and our soul change and take shape. To create these circumstances, we don't have to use *reason* but a *mechanical method*. We have to surround ourselves with images—images that we put between ourselves and the superfluous world and that have a strong impact. As soon as we do this, we push our sensations and emotions from excess to excess."[5] It is this line of thought, a line that anticipates Georges Bataille's notion of inner experience as a place of transgressive experimentation and of an exploration of the limits of the possible, that I want to reconstruct here in my thoughts about prayer.

AGAINST NATURE

Before I return to the thought that in prayer we practice an art of analogical figuration in the service of a new world of sensation and affect, I want to stay with Huysmans for a moment. Published in 1884, Huysmans's novel portrays its decadent protagonist, Jean des Esseintes, as a figure who in his retreat from urban life imitates the monk who moves into a cell. Huysmans is well aware of the historical antecedents of this practice of sensation in medieval and early modern Catholic theological anthropology, characterizing his protagonist's "outbursts of feeling, impulses towards an ideal, towards an unknown universe, towards a far-off blessedness" in terms of something that is "as desirable as that which we are promised by the Holy Scripture."[6] His staging of a decadent culture of intense sensation and pleasure—in Nietzsche's words an "aesthetic justification" of existence—relies on practices that, as I will show below, have been elaborated in the context of an anthropology that is implied in medieval practices of reading, prayer, and contemplation. These practices entail essentially two movements: the segregation and abstraction from a given, seemingly "natural" and "literal" framework of sensation and affect, expressed in the figure of the retreat into the desert, the cell, or the solitude of contemplation; and the movement of production that relies on techniques of scriptural reading, the rumination of the text, and its deployment in a practice of animation that gives new shape to sensation and affect. In other words and using the simple example of reading: removing itself from the dryness of a literal reading of the scriptures, the soul rediscovers its life-giving force, not in the content that gives metaphysical meaning to its existence, but in a deployment of the spiritual sense of the text as the agent that gives new shape to the life of the soul in the world.

Huysmans compares the change in lifestyle, the highly self-conscious and stylized retreat of his protagonist from the boring dryness of the world, to that of the monk who takes refuge in his cell, removing himself from the world and allowing for nothing else than an artificial production of new states of mind, sensation, and intense experience. Jean des Esseintes does so, as does the monk or the nun, within a space that is clearly defined by architecture, texts, and specific artifacts. This does not mean, however, that the intensity of exposure to and the experience of the world would decrease in this context. The contrary proves to be true. With the assistance of contemplative techniques, simulacra, and the production of living images, the targeted evocations of taste, touch, and smell form a sphere of exploration and education of the senses and of the passions in an ever new way: a new way, that means, a way where sensation is understood, not in the everyday form as bound up with the naive empirical, utilitarian, and instrumental perception of things, but rather in forms that allow for ever new animations of sensation within specific frameworks of contemplative pleasure.

In Huysmans's text this takes shape in very concrete forms. Des Esseintes uses all kinds of tools to create his artificial world. To stage and evoke the experience of a cruise, he arranges aquariums with mechanical fish; images that evoke the bridge of a ship; sextants, compasses, chronographs; time tables and schedules of intercontinental shipping routes. Taken together, these things form an indexical, deictic space, allowing for an experience that removes itself from the experience of the world and that cultivates an entirely new world of experiential intensity by means that—as I will show more clearly below—can be compared to the monk's systematic and methodical use of images, texts, song, and scriptural quotes in the practice of prayer and contemplation. Huysmans writes:

> In this manner, without ever leaving his home, he was able to enjoy the rapidly suc-ceeding, indeed almost simultaneous, sensations of a long voyage; the pleasure of travel—existing as it largely does only in recollection and almost never in the present, at the actual moment when it is taking place—this pleasure he could savor fully, at his ease, without fatigue or worry, in this cabin whose contrived disorder, whose transient character and as it were temporary furnishings corresponded almost exactly with his brief sojourns in it, with the limited time spent on his meals, and which provided a complete contrast with his study, a permanent, orderly, well-estab-lished room, fitted out for the solid sustainment of a domestic existence.
>
> Besides, he considered travel to be pointless, believing that the imagination could easily compensate for the vulgar reality of actual experience. In his view, it was pos-sible to fulfill those desires reputed to be the most difficult to satisfy in normal life, by means of a trifling subterfuge, an approximate simulation of the object of those very desires.[7]

This applies not only to taking a virtual cruise but also to travels by train and in general to all forms of experience. This artificial world, or better, the experience produced by the use of artifacts, seems at first to be a world of radical modernity. It makes use of the most innovative applications of electricity, hydraulics, and pho-tographic reproduction, emphasizing the obsolete status of nature and, by way of this, of all kinds of naturalist machinations. Instead, Huysmans delves into a tex-ture of analogical figuration, images and words that refer to each other and that support and mediate a new intensity of sensation below the level of any herme-neutic engagement.

The modernity of this setup of media, however, is misleading. The media them-selves might be modern, but the technique has been developed much earlier. Drawing mainly on Ignatius of Loyola's model of scriptural meditation, Huysmans makes use of both key elements of the Jesuit's method: the *compositio loci*, the construction of a mental theater of imagination in order to stage and observe spe-cific scenes from the scriptures, and the *applicatio sensuum*, the investment in and arousal of the senses and affects in this practice of viewing and understanding.

Building on Ignatius, whose teachings form an important background also for Rahner's and Balthasar's notions of spiritual senses, Huysmans brings to our atten-tion two key aspects of this very specific understanding of sensation in Catholic anthropology, namely the movement against and beyond nature in its postlapsar-ian state and the very fact that all sensation and perception depends not only on what is naturally given but mainly on the means and media that are used to shape it. Meditation and contemplation are thus seen as deeply invested in media practices—practices that in a first step remove sensation and affect from their fallen natural order and in a second step give a new shape to sensation, anticipating the very taste and touch of an encounter with the divine in a redeemed world. Since this new shape is not a return to the natural world but its very perfection, it can—in the eyes of the theologian—only be a new world of grace, and since it is deeply informed by negative theology, acknowledging time and again the unknowability of the divine, it can emerge only in forms of *aisthesis,* a new form of perception beyond the categorical and conceptual order.

PRAYER

It is in the history of medieval thought about prayer that we encounter the most comprehensive explanation of this practice of shaping affect and sensation. A broad range of documents could be used here in order to illustrate this, and the texts that Huysmans and Bataille refer to explicitly—Ignatius, Angela of Foligno, Ruysbroec, and others—would be most certainly among them. To illustrate the mechanics of prayer I want to discuss just one of these texts, namely Hugh of Saint Victor's *Tractatus de virtute orandi* (On the power of prayer). As Hugh demonstrates in his treatise, the act of prayer is highly informed by rhetorical tradition and training, articulating the force of persuasion in terms of what we can call a self-formation as self-affection.

Prayer, meant to lead into a state of *excitatio* and *inflammatio*—ultimately of an overwhelming, intense, and absorbing love that is akin to the one medieval mystics like Mechthild of Magdeburg, Hadewijch of Antwerp, or Angela of Foligno are engaging with in their texts—is first and foremost an art of arousing affects and emotions: "Pure prayer is when from an abundance of devotion the mind is so enkindled that when it turns to ask something of God it forgets even its petition because of the greatness of His love; and while it vehemently desires to enjoy the love of Him whom it sees and wants to rest totally in Him now, it spontaneously sets aside its concern regarding that for which it came."[8] Pure prayer is prayer that forgets its own intention. It does so when it turns into a spiritual exercise that moves from reading to meditation, from the focus on meaning in forms of unexcited reading and understanding to affective and sensual moments of absorbing intensity in meditation. To produce this effect, to produce affective *excitatio,* Hugh writes, the reader of the scriptures and the person who prays has to engage in repeated mental re-evocation of the words he or she wants to concentrate on. That person does so by ruminating and masticating on these words in a way that brings forth the possibilities of their emotional and sensual impact.

At the very basis of this meditative exercise are rhetorical practices of figuration and amplification. At first the process simply consists in invention and enumeration, in the search for analogous figures, the construction of lists, the use of repetition and rhetorical questions, and the configuration of tropes drawn from the scriptures, from life experience, from lives of saints and martyrs, from memory, and from other available sources. The very construction of such lists presents the soul with a picture, with a series of figures that all have a specific effect on perception, affect, and sensation. These effects have to be further amplified through repetition, rhetorical questions, and elements of narration and narrative scripts that help to unfold the power of the figures. Thus, for example, drawing up a list of pains and enumerating all possible evils asks for an imaginative exercise in which such figures are produced on a stage that allows for the deployment of their affective force. This stage can be purely mental, but it can also include images and objects, music and liturgy, gestures and acts of bodily mortification. In all cases its construction implies a moment of exteriorization and spatialization, a space or a mental theater that is filled with media and that allows the effects of these media to unfold.

The more impressive and comprehensive the list, the more the soul will sigh, groan, and suffer in this act of animation that produces a space of affective intensity. Other lists and figural compositions—often in combination with narrative scripts, such as the Song of Songs, or the passion of Christ, or the story of Saint Anthony and his temptations—allow for the production of different affects: admiration and pleasure, humility and humiliation, terror and fear, devotion, dedication, hope, bitterness and sweetness.

In other words, the exercise of meditation presupposes complex practices of figuration and rhetorical amplification that in turn allow for the production of a broad range of affects and moments of sensation. These practices of figuration are based on archives including the scriptures, the lives of saints, and other material. In their deployment, however, they transcend the limiting scope of the archive and the meaning they have there. Consequently, Hugh emphasizes strategies that strip figures from the concrete literal meaning within the archive and from the intention-bound nature of prayer. Extracted from the archive, liberated from their immediate context and from intentions, the figures and tropes deployed serve nothing else than the production of an affective and sensual space that is open to divine love and that thus constitutes an affective texture of scriptural tropes, actual experience, and *praegustatio,* an eschatological foretaste of things to come—or, to evoke Novalis again, a "free harmony" in which the possibilities of sensation can be explored.

The process of the production of this sphere of religious and aesthetic experience must first be described in terms of externalization. As all the texts on prayer write—in accordance with traditions of negative theology—God and his realm are beyond language and concepts. To communicate with the divine abyss, affective and sensual forms of meditative prayer focus on tropes not only as images provided by the biblical text but as artifacts that can be used in specific ways, not to represent the divine, but to prepare and produce the absorption in the affect. Thus words and tropes drawn from the scriptures turn into sets of rhetorical stimuli that can be deployed in the form of material figures, words, images, and song.

This externalization also implies a nonhermeneutical approach to the tropes, an approach that in the very act of prayer strips the words of their representational and intentional nature and that liberates them in view of their affective and sensual effects. Thus they turn into staged external actors and help to produce a sphere of experience in between the "inner" and the "outer" where the soul transcends itself and its interiority in the act of being absorbed into the overwhelming love and pleasure that all the practices of figuration in prayer intend to produce. With the help of the externalized figures, the soul alienates itself from its earthly defined and "old" identity and interiority, choosing a state of exile that allows for the creation of a "new" state beyond the distinction of "inner" and "outer." It is this state that the rhetorical figures are ultimately meant to produce and explore.

As Hugh points out in his treatise on prayer, "The number of affects is infinite," and it is not possible to "list them all."[9] The same can be said about the experience of sensation in spiritual practice. Introduced in Origen's and Gregory of Nyssa's exegesis of the scriptures, the connection of contemplative reading and sensation has played a key role in the history of medieval spiritual practices.[10] It is in this context that we encounter the most elaborate thoughts about the "five inner senses." These "inner" senses, however, are not just opposed to the "outer" senses in a kind of spatial correlation. Instead, the distinction between "inner" and "outer" has to be understood in terms of a phenomenology of sensation. This phenomenology operates with the two terms to indicate, not two different realms of sensation, but two different ways of sensation. It focuses, not on the faculties of sensation, as does medieval faculty psychology, but on the very experiential fact of sensation as it presents itself when it happens. The "outer" way is seen as unfree and empirically determined inasmuch as it is caught up in the world of fallen nature and objects of desire. The "inner" way is seen as a path of liberation in view of a stimulation of sensation and affects that originates in the hidden meaning of the scriptures, that is enacted in the rhetoric of prayer, and that allows for an anticipation and the restitution of free sensation at the end of time. In the late Middle Ages, Peter of Ailly speaks of this as a way "to reach already in this life the pleasures of the eternal rewards in an experiential way, and to taste their sweetness with delight."[11] Rudolf of Biberach, in a treatise entitled *De septem itineribus aeternitatis* (The seven paths of eternity), emphasizes that "reaching the inner sense of taste, it opens it up toward the tasting of eternal sweetness."[12]

In other words, the "inner senses" are the senses insofar as they are receptive to a manipulation in the practices of reading and prayer. This manipulation liberates sensation from its empirical bounds, replaces the natural stimuli—the "old" world—through rhetorical ones, and leads to an absorption in divine taste and touch that is neither "inner" nor "outer."[13] As the affects can be aroused, shaped, and modified with the help of rhetorical stimuli and artifacts, so can sensation—touching, seeing, hearing, smelling, tasting—be aroused, shaped, and modified by rhetorical stimuli. Thus Origen's and Gregory of Nyssa's theories of the inner senses, developed in the context of questions of reading and hermeneutics, form the framework for a phenomenological understanding of sensation in the Middle Ages. This phenomenological understanding, however, focuses not on a primary level of experiential qualities and events but on the experiential qualities that are induced by the scriptures, scriptural tropes, and the liturgy. This is why I am speaking of a phenomenology of rhetorical effects. What Hugh's theory of prayer presents us with are ways scriptural tropes are being deployed in order to excite affects and sensation. They also present us with a phenomenological description of the ways the deployment of these tropes produce specific spheres and events of experience in an application of the senses. And they are open toward the experimental styles that we encounter in Mechthild of Magdeburg, Hadewijch of Antwerp, and others when they use rhetorical means to explore a wide range of experiential states.

PHENOMENOLOGY AND ANALOGICAL FIGURATION

Figuration and amplification are the fundamental aspects of the rhetorical practice that is at stake here. Figuration is, if we want, the very medium of prayer that deploys its effects in the "knocking" on heaven's door, which, as we know from Hugh of Saint Victor, is first and above all a "knocking" that unlocks the experiential possibilities of the soul to go beyond being caught up in everydayness. Inspired by romantic, decadent, and modernist adaptations of this model—above all Huysmans's "assimilation of the Jesuit influence"[14]—we can discuss this very practice as a set of media technologies or, maybe more consistently with medieval reflections on prayer, as media practices that rely on *artificia,* artificial means to support a self-transformation that necessarily also transforms the perception of the world. Prayer as the fundamental address to an unknown God in light of the revelation of the scriptures is thus not to be seen as a form of speech that represents the divine or the relation between the human and the divine. Instead, it is an art of unfolding the archive of the scriptures and of deploying it in figures that shape the life of the soul, its feelings, its sensuality, and cognition of the world itself and the divine. In this process, prayer relies on analogical figuration—a practice of forming textures of words, images, and sound—that does not have a primarily representational or hermeneutic function. Instead, the use of figures relies on their effects, namely the capacity to produce and explore the intensity of feeling and sensation: the sweetness and bitterness, the terror and the joy, in other words, heaven and hell. This takes place, however, only in a practice of transgression, excess, and excitation, a segregation that leaves behind the utilitarian and instrumental perception of the world and experiments with the possibilities to go beyond. The exploration of these possibilities is the task of the art of prayer when it unlocks the potentials of feeling and sensation not beyond but inside this world and its material form, producing a sphere of analogical figuration that constitutes the very space of resonance for the sensual experience of the divine in the world.

NOTES

1. McInroy (2012, 257–74).
2. Novalis ([1802] 1997, 61).
3. David of Augsburg (1933, 161).
4. MacLuhan (2010, 69).
5. Barrès ([1889] 1988, 105–6).
6. Huysmans (1998, 66).
7. Huysmans (1998, 18).
8. Hugh of Saint Victor (2014, 334); Latin text, Hugh of Saint Victor ([1997] 2014, 136).
9. Hugh of Saint Victor (2014, 341).
10. Largier (2003, 3–15); Largier (2008, 364–79).
11. Peter of Ailly (1634, 134).
12. Rudolf of Biberach ([1866] 1985, 467 [VI dist. V]).
13. Largier (2014, 58–71).
14. Huysmans (1998, 65).

Abdu, Samir. 2003. *Al-ṭawā'if al-masīḥiyya fī sūriyyā* [The Christian denominations in Syria]. Damascus: Dār ḥasan malaṣ lil-nushir.

Abela, Anthony M. 1991. *Transmitting Values in European Malta.* Malta: Jesuit Publications.

Aboujaoude, Elias. 2008. *Compulsive Acts: A Psychiatrist's Tales of Ritual and Obsession.* Berkeley: University of California Press.

Agamben, Giorgio. 1998. *Homo Sacer: Sovereign Power and Bare Life.* Translated by Daniel Heller-Roazen. Stanford, CA: Stanford University Press.

———. 2001. *The Kingdom and the Glory: For a Theological Genealogy of Economy and Government.* Stanford, CA: Stanford University Press.

———. 2013. *The Highest Poverty: Monastic Rules and Form-of-Life.* Translated by Adam Kotsko. Stanford, CA: Stanford University Press.

Ahmed, Sara. 2000. *Strange Encounters: Embodied Others in Post-coloniality.* London: Routledge.

———. 2006. *Queer Phenomenology.* Durham, NC: Duke University Press.

Albera, Dionigi, and John Eade. Forthcoming. "International Perspectives on Pilgrimage Research." In *International Perspectives on Pilgrimage Studies,* edited by Dionigi Albera and John Eade. London: Routledge.

Alberoni, Francesco. 1984. *Movement and Institution.* New York: Columbia University Press.

Al-Shahi, Ahmed. 1999. "Evans-Pritchard, Anthropology, and Catholicism at Oxford: Godfrey Lienhardt's View." *Journal of the Anthropological Society of Oxford* 30:67–72.

American Psychiatric Association. 2013. "Obsessive Compulsive and Related Disorders." www.dsm5.org/Documents/Obsessive%20Compulsive%20Disorders%20Fact%20Sheet.pdf.

Angrosino, Michael V. 1994. "The Culture Concept and the Mission of the Catholic Church." *American Anthropology* 96:824–32.

Apache-Ndé-Nneé Working Group. 2015. "Review of the Holy See: Shadow Report for the United Nations Convention on the Elimination of All Forms of Racial Discrimination." November. http://tbinternet.ohchr.org/Treaties/CERD/Shared%20Documents/VAT/INT_CERD_NGO_VAT_22151_E.pdf.

Appadurai, Arjun. 1988. "Introduction: Place and Voice in Anthropological Theory." *Cultural Anthropology* 3:16–20.

Ariès, Philippe. 1982. *The Hour of Our Death*. Translated by Helen Weaver. New York: Vintage.

Armstrong, Karen. 1997. *Through the Narrow Gate: A Memoir of Life in and out of the Convent*. New York: HarperCollins.

Arrupe, Pedro. [1978] 1981. "Letter on Inculturation to the Whole Society." In *Other Apostolates Today*, edited by Jerome Aixala. St. Louis, MO: Institute of Jesuit Sources.

Asad, Talal, ed. 1974. *Anthropology and the Colonial Encounter*. London: Ithaca.

———. 1993. *Genealogies of Religion: Discipline and Reasons of Power in Christianity and Islam*. Baltimore: John Hopkins University Press.

———. 2002. "The Construction of Religion as an Anthropological Category." In *A Reader in the Anthropology of Religion*, edited by Michael Lambek, 114–32. Oxford: Blackwell.

Augustine. 1961. *Confessions*. Translated by R. S. Pine-Coffin. New York: Penguin Classics.

———. 2002. *On the Trinity: Books 8–15*. Edited by Gareth B. Matthews. Cambridge: Cambridge University Press.

Bacchiddu, Giovanna. 2011. "Holding the Saint in One's Arms: Miracles and Exchange in Apiao, Southern Chile." In *Encounters of Body and Soul in Contemporary Religious Practices*, edited by Anna Fedele and Ruy Llera Blanes, 23–42. New York: Berghahn.

Badiou, Alain. 2003. *Saint Paul: The Foundations of Universalism*. Translated by Ray Brassier. Stanford, CA: Stanford University Press.

Badone, Ellen. 1989. *The Appointed Hour: Death, Worldview and Social Change in Brittany*. Berkeley: University of California Press.

———. 1990. *Religious Orthodoxy and Popular Faith in European Society*. Princeton, NJ: Princeton University Press.

———. 2007. "Echoes from Kerizinen: Pilgrimage, Narrative and the Construction of Sacred History at a Marian Shrine in Northwestern France." *Journal of the Royal Anthropological Institute* 13:453–70.

Baldacchino, Jean-Paul. 2011. "Miracles in the Waiting Room of Modernity: The Canonisation of Dun Gorg of Malta." *Australian Journal of Anthropology* 22:104–24.

Ballacchino, Katia. 2011. "Embodying Devotion, Embodying Passion: The Italian Tradition of the *Festa dei Gigli* in Nola." In *Encounters of Body and Soul in Contemporary Religious Practices*, edited by Anna Fedele and Ruy Llera Blanes, 43–67. New York: Berghahn.

Bandak, Andreas. 2013. "Our Lady of Soufanieh: On Knowledge, Ignorance and Indifference among Christians of Damascus." In *Politics of Worship in the Contemporary Middle East: Sainthood in Fragile States*, edited by Andreas Bandak and Mikkel Bille, 129–53. Leiden: Brill.

———. 2014. "Of Refrains and Rhythms in Contemporary Damascus: Urban Space and Christian-Muslim Coexistence." *Current Anthropology* 55 (S10): 248–61.

———. 2015. "Exemplary Series and Christian Typology: Modelling on Sainthood in Damascus." *Journal of the Royal Anthropological Institute* 21:S47–S63.

Bandak, Andreas, and Tom Boylston. 2014. "The 'Orthodoxy' of Orthodoxy: On Moral Imperfection, Correctness, and Deferral in Religious Worlds." *Religion and Society: Advances in Research* 5:25–46.

Barbeau, Marius. 1935. "Survival of French Canada." *Canadian Forum* 15 (176): 290, 313–14.

———. 1962. "Why I Publish Folk Songs." *Canadian Author and Bookman* 37 (4): 9.

Barker, John. 2014. "The One and the Many: Church-Centered Innovations in a Papua New Guinean Community." *Current Anthropology* 55 (S10): 172–81.

Barnard, Alan. 2000. *History and Theory in Anthropology.* Cambridge: Cambridge University Press.

Barrès, Maurice. [1889] 1988. *Un homme libre.* Edited by Ida-Marie Frandon. Paris: Imprimerie Nationale.

Barthes, Roland. 2012. *How to Live Together: Novelistic Simulations of Some Everyday Spaces.* New York: Columbia University Press.

Bartlett, Robert. 2013. *Why Can the Dead Do Such Great Things? Saints and Worshippers from the Martyrs to the Reformation.* Princeton, NJ: Princeton University Press.

Bauman, Zygmunt. 1992. *Mortality, Immortality and Other Life Strategies.* Cambridge: Polity Press.

Baumann, Gerd. 1997. "Dominant and Demotic Discourses of Culture: Their Relevance to Multi-ethnic Alliances." In *Debating Cultural Hybridity: Multi-cultural Identities and the Politics of Anti-racism,* edited by Pnina Werbner and Tariq Modood, 209–25. London: Zed Books.

Bax, Mart. 1992. "Female Suffering, Local Power Relations, and Religious Tourism: A Case Study from Yugoslavia." *Medical Anthropology Quarterly* 6 (2): 114–27.

Becker, Ernst. 1973. *The Denial of Death.* New York: Free Press.

Bediako, Kwame. 1992. *Theology and Identity: The Impact of Culture upon Christian Thought in the Second Century and Modern Africa.* Oxford: Regnum Books.

Behrend, Heike. 2011. *Resurrecting Cannibals: The Catholic Church, Witch-Hunts and the Production of Pagans in Western Uganda.* Woodbridge: James Curry.

Behrend, Heike, and Ute Luig. 1999. Introduction to *Spirit Possession: Modernity and Power in Africa,* edited by Heike Behrend and Ute Luig, xiii–xxii. Madison: University of Wisconsin Press.

Beidelman, Tom. 1982. *Colonial Evangelism.* Bloomington: Indiana University Press.

———. 1993. *Secrecy and Society: The Paradox of Knowing and the Knowing of Paradox.* Evanston, IL: Program of African Studies, Northwestern University.

Belting, Hans. 1990. *Bild und Kult: Eine Geschichte des Bildes vor dem Zeitalter der Kunst.* Munich: C. H. Beck.

Bender, Courtney, and Ann Taves, eds. 2012. *What Matters? Ethnographies of Value in a Not So Secular Age.* New York: Columbia University Press.

Benedict XVI. 2009. *Caritas in Veritate.* Encyclical letter, June 29. www.scborromeo.org /docs/caritas_in_veritate.pdf.

Bennett, Jane. 2010. *Vibrant Matter: A Political Ecology of Things.* Durham, NC: Duke University Press Books.

Berger, Peter, ed. 1999. *The Desecularization of the World: Resurgent Religion and World Politics.* Washington, DC: Ethics and Public Policy Center.

Bernstein, Basil. 1971. *Class, Codes and Control: Theoretical Studies towards a Sociology of Language*. London: Routledge and Kegan Paul.

Berryman, Phillip. 1987. *Liberation Theology: Essential Facts about the Revolutionary Movement in Latin America—and Beyond*. Philadelphia: Temple University Press.

Beyer, Peter. 1994. *Religion and Globalization*. London: Sage Publications.

Bialecki, Jon. 2008. "Between Stewardship and Sacrifice: Agency and Economy in a Southern California Charismatic Church." *Journal of the Royal Anthropological Institute* 14 (2): 372–90.

———. 2011. "No Caller ID for the Soul: Demonization, Charisms, and the Unstable Subject of Protestant Language Ideology." *Anthropological Quarterly* 84:679–703.

———. 2014. "After the Denominozoic: Evolution, Differentiation, Denominationalism." *Current Anthropology* 55:193–204.

Bialecki, Jon, Naomi Haynes, and Joel Robbins. 2008. "The Anthropology of Christianity." *Religion Compass* 2:1139–58.

Bibaki, Nzuzi. 1993. *Le Dieu-Mère: L'inculturation de la foi chez les Yombe*. Kinshasa: Éditions Loyola.

Bibby, Reginald W. 2008. "La religion à la carte au Québec: Un problème d'offre, de demande, ou des deux?" *Globe* 11:151–79.

Binde, Per. 1999. *Bodies of Vital Matter: Notions of Life Force and Transcendence in Traditional Southern Italy*. Gothenburg: University of Gothenburg.

BishopAccountability.org. 2007. "Accused Priests Who Worked in the Archdiocese of Chicago." www.bishop-accountability.org/il_chicago/.

Bloch, Maurice, and Jonathan Parry. 1982. *Death and the Regeneration of Life*. Cambridge: Cambridge University Press.

Blum, Jason. 2012. "Retrieving Phenomenology of Religion as a Method for the Study of Religion." *Journal of the American Academy of Religion* 80:1025–48.

Böhme, Gernot. 1995. *Atmosphäre: Essays zur Neuen Ästhetik*. Frankfurt: Suhrkamp.

Boissevain, Jeremy. 1974. *Friends of Friends: Networks, Manipulators and Coalitions*. New York: St. Martin's Press.

Boka di Mpasi Londi, Simon-Pierre. 2000. *Théologie Africaine: Inculturation de la théologie*. Abidjan: Inades.

Børresen, Kari Elisabeth. 1992. "The Ordination of Women: To Nurture Tradition by Continuing Inculturation." *Studia Theologica* 46:3–13.

Bourdieu, Pierre. [1987] 1990. *In Other Words: Essays towards a Reflexive Sociology*. Translated by M. Adamson. Cambridge: Polity Press.

Brading, David. 2003. *Mexican Phoenix: Our Lady of Guadalupe*. Cambridge: Cambridge University Press.

Brahinsky, Josh. 2012. "Pentecostal Body Logics: Cultivating a Modern Sensorium." *Cultural Anthropology* 27:215–38.

Brettell, Caroline. 1990. "The Priest and His People: The Contractual Basis for Religious Practice in Portugal." In *Religious Orthodoxy and Popular Faith in European Society*, edited by Ellen Badone, 55–75. Princeton, NJ: Princeton University Press.

Brosius, Christiane, and Karin Polit, eds. 2011. *Ritual, Heritage and Identity: The Politics of Culture and Performance in a Globalised World*. Delhi: Routledge.

Brown, Peter. 1981. *The Cult of Saints: Its Rise and Function in Latin Christianity.* Chicago: University of Chicago Press.

Brusco, Elizabeth. 2010. *Reformation of Machismo: Evangelical Conversion and Gender in Columbia.* Austin: University of Texas Press.

Bucholtz, Mary, and Kira Hall. 2005. "Identity and Interaction: A Sociocultural Linguistic Approach." *Discourse Studies* 7:585–614.

Bujo, Bénézet. 1992. *African Theology in Its Social Context.* Maryknoll, NY: Orbis Books.

Burdick, John. 1998. *Blessed Anastácia: Women, Race, and Popular Christianity in Brazil.* New York: Routledge.

Bureau, René. 1962. *Ethno-sociologie religieuse des Duala et apparentés.* Yaoundé: Institut de Recherches Scientifiques du Cameroun.

———. 1996. *Le peuple du fleuve: Sociologie de la conversion chez les Douala.* Paris: Karthala.

Butticci, Annalisa. 2016. *African Pentecostals in Catholic Europe: The Politics of Presence in the Twenty-First Century.* Cambridge, MA: Harvard University Press.

Bynum, Caroline Walker. 2011. *Christian Materiality: An Essay on Religion in Late Medieval Europe.* New York: Zone Books.

Caciola, Nancy. 2003. *Discerning Spirits: Divine and Demonic Possession in the Middle Ages.* Ithaca, NY: Cornell University Press.

Calabrese, Omar. 1992. *Neo-Baroque: A Sign of the Times.* Translated by Charles Lambert. Princeton, NJ: Princeton University Press.

Cannell, Fenella. 1999. *Power and Intimacy in the Christian Philippines.* Cambridge: University Cambridge Press.

———. 2006. "Introduction: The Anthropology of Christianity." In *The Anthropology of Christianity,* edited by Fenella Cannell, 1–50. Durham, NC: Duke University Press.

Caravelli, Anna. 1980. "Bridge between Worlds: The Greek Woman's Lament as Communicative Event." *Journal of American Folklore* 368 (93): 129–57.

Carpentier, Paul. 1981. *Les croix de chemin: Au-delà du signe.* Ottawa: National Museums of Canada.

Carroll, Michael. 1989. *Catholic Cults and Devotions: A Psychological Enquiry.* Montreal: McGill-Queen's University Press.

Casanova, José. 1997. "Globalizing Catholicism and the Return to a 'Universal' Church." In *Transnational Religion and Fading States,* edited by Suzanne Hoeber Rudolph and James Piscatori, 121–43. Boulder, CO: Westview Press.

———. 2006a. "Religion, European Secular Identities, and European Integration." In *Religion in an Expanding Europe,* edited by Timothy A. Byrnes and Peter J. Katzenstein, 65–92. Cambridge: Cambridge University Press.

———. 2006b. "Rethinking Secularization: A Global Comparative Perspective." *Hedgehog Review* 8 (Spring/Summer): 7–22.

Catholic Church. 1993. *Catechism of the Catholic Church.* Vatican City: Libreria Editrice Vaticana.

Certeau, Michel de. 1986. "The Politic of Silence: The Long March of the Indians." In *Heterologies: Discourses on the Other,* 225–36. Translated by Brain Massumi. Minneapolis: University of Minnesota Press.

———. 2000. *The Possession at Loudun.* Chicago: University of Chicago Press.

Chabal, Patrick. 1996. "The African Crisis: Context and Interpretation." In *Postcolonial Identities in Africa,* edited by Richard Werbner and Terence Ranger. London: Zed Books.

Chakrabarty, Dipesh. [2000] 2008. *Provincializing Europe: Postcolonial Thought and Historical Difference.* Princeton, NJ: Princeton University Press.

Chalcraft, John T. 2009. *The Invisible Cage: Syrian Migrant Workers in Lebanon.* Stanford, CA: Stanford University Press.

Chesnut, R. Andrew. 2003. *Competitive Spirits: Latin America's New Religious Economy.* Oxford: Oxford University Press.

Chidester, David. 2005. *Authentic Fakes: Religion and American Popular Culture.* Berkeley: University of California Press.

Christian, William A. [1972] 1989. *Person and God in a Spanish Valley.* Princeton, NJ: Princeton University Press.

———. 1981. *Local Religion in Sixteenth-Century Spain.* Princeton, NJ: Princeton University Press.

o———. 2012. *Divine Presence in Spain and Western Europe, 1500–1960: Visions, Religious Images and Photographs.* Budapest: CEU Press.

Chua, Liana. 2012. *The Christianity of Culture: Conversion, Ethnic Citizenship and the Matter of Religion in Malaysian Borneo.* Basingstoke: Palgrave Macmillan.

Clarke, Peter B. 2006. *New Religions in Global Perspective: A Study of Religious Change in the Modern World.* London: Routledge.

Cleary, Edward L. 2011. *The Rise of Charismatic Catholicism in Latin America.* Gainesville: University Press of Florida.

Clites, Brian J. 2015. "Breaking the Silence: The Catholic Sexual Abuse Survivor Movement in Chicago." PhD diss., Northwestern University.

Cody, Francis. 2011. "Publics and Politics." *Annual Review of Anthropology* 40:37–52.

Coleman, Simon. 2009. "On Mirrors, Masks and Traps: Ambiguity, Risk and Lateral Participation in Ritual." *Journal of Ritual Studies* 2:43–52.

———. 2013. "Ritual Remains: Studying Contemporary Pilgrimage." In *Companion to the Study of Religion,* edited by Janice Boddy and Michael Lambek, 294–308. Oxford: Wiley/Blackwell.

———. 2014. "Pilgrimage as Trope for an Anthropology of Christianity." *Current Anthropology* 55:281–91.

Coleman, Simon, and Peter Collins. 2004. *Religion, Identity and Change: Perspectives on Global Transformations.* Burlington, VT: Ashgate.

Coleman, Simon, and Rosalind Hackett, eds. 2015. *The Anthropology of Global Pentecostalism and Evangelicalism.* New York: New York University Press.

Comaroff, Jean. 1985. *Body of Power, Spirit of Resistance.* Chicago: University of Chicago Press.

Comaroff, John, and Jean Comaroff. 1991. *Christianity, Colonialism and Consciousness in South Africa.* Vol. 1 of *Of Revelation and Revolution.* Chicago: University of Chicago Press.

———. 1997. *Dialectics of Modernity on a South African Frontier.* Vol. 2 of *Of Revelation and Revolution.* Chicago: University of Chicago Press.

Congregation for the Doctrine of the Faith. 2007. General Decree Regarding the Delict of Attempted Sacred Ordination of a Woman. December 19. www.vatican.va/roman_curia

/congregations/cfaith/documents/rc_con_cfaith_doc_20071219_attentata-ord-donna_
en.html.

Connolly, William E. 2011. *A World of Becoming*. Durham, NC: Duke University Press.

Cordes, Paul Josef. 1997. *Call to Holiness: Reflections on the Charismatic Catholic Renewal.*
Collegeville, MN: Liturgical Press.

Corwin, Anna I. 2012. "Let Him Hold You: Spiritual and Social Support in a Catholic Convent Infirmary." *Anthropology of Aging Quarterly* 33 (4): 120–30.

Côté, Ralph. 2014. "125e de St-François-Xavier: L'historique des croix de chemin a suscité
l'intérêt de nombreux citoyens." *L'Étincelle*, February 3. www.letincelle.qc.ca/ actualites
/actualites/249807/125e-de-st-francois-xavier-lhistorique-des-croix-de-chemin-a-sus-
cite-linteret-de-nombreux-citoyens.

Courbage, Youssef, and Philippe Fargues. [1997] 1998. *Christians and Jews under Islam*. London: I. B. Tauris.

Cowan, Jane. 1990. *Dance and the Body Politic in Northern Greece*. Princeton, NJ: Princeton
University Press.

Cox, Jeffrey L. 2001. "Secularization and Other Master Narratives of Religion in Modern
Europe." *Kirchliche Zeitgeschichte* 14:24–35.

Csordas, Thomas. 1990. "Embodiment as a Paradigm for Anthropology." *Ethos* 18:5–47.

———. 1994. *The Sacred Self: A Cultural Phenomenology of Charismatic Healing*. Berkeley:
University of California Press.

———. 1997. *Language, Charisma, and Creativity: The Ritual Life of a Religious Movement*.
Berkeley: University of California Press.

———. 2002. *Body/Meaning/Healing*. New York: Palgrave Macmillan.

———. 2007. "Global Religion and the Re-enchantment of the World: The Case of the Catholic Charismatic Renewal." *Anthropological Theory* 7:295–314.

———. 2009. *Transnational Transcendence: Essays on Religion and Globalization*. Berkeley:
University of California Press.

———. 2015. "Mobility: A Global Geography of the Spirit among Catholic Charismatic
Communities." In *The Anthropology of Global Pentecostalism and Evangelicalism,* edited
by Simon Coleman and Rosalind Hackett, 129–45. New York: New York University
Press.

Csordas, Thomas, and Elizabeth Lewton. 1998. "Practice, Performance, and Experience in
Ritual Healing." *Transcultural Psychiatry* 35:435–512.

Cuneo, Michael W. 2001. *American Exorcism: Expelling Demons in the Land of Plenty*. New
York: Doubleday.

Curran, Charles. 2006. *Loyal Dissent: Memoirs of a Catholic Theologian*. Washington, DC:
Georgetown University Press.

Daniel, E. Valentine. 1984. *Fluid Signs: Being a Person the Tamil Way*. Berkeley: University
of California Press.

———. 2000. "The Arrogation of Being: Revisiting the Anthropology of Religion." *Macal-
ester International* 8:171–91.

David of Augsburg. 1933. "*Septem gradus orationis.*" In *Le "Septem gradus orationis" de David
d'Augsbourg,* edited by Jacques Heerinckx. *Revue d'ascétique et de mystique* 14:146–70.

Davidson, Donald. [1984] 2001. *Inquiries into Truth and Interpretation*. Oxford: Clarendon
Press.

Davie, Grace. 1994. *Religion in Britain since 1945: Believing without Belonging.* Oxford: Blackwell.

Day, Abigail. 2006. "Believing in Belonging in Contemporary Britain: A Case Study from Yorkshire." PhD diss., Lancaster University.

Degeorge, Gérard. 2004. *Damascus.* Paris: Flammarion, 2004.

De Hueck, Catherine. 1950. *Dear Seminarian.* Milwaukee: Bruce.

De la Torre, Renée. 2002. "The Catholic Diocese: A Transversal Institution." *Journal of Contemporary Religion* 17 (3): 203–316.

Deleuze, Gilles. 1993. *The Fold: Liebnitz and the Baroque.* Minneapolis: University of Minnesota Press.

De Martino, Ernesto. [1961] 2005. *The Land of Remorse: A Study of Southern Italian Tarantism.* Translated by Dorothea Louise Zinn. London: Free Association Books.

Dempsey, Corinne. 2001. *Kerala Christian Sainthood: Collisions of Culture and Worldview in South India.* Delhi: Oxford University Press.

Derrida, Jacques. [1993] 1994. *Specters of Marx: The State of the Debt, the Work of Mourning and the New International.* London: Routledge.

Desjarlais, Robert. 1996. "Struggling Along." In *Things as They Are: New Directions in Phenomenological Anthropology,* edited by Michael Jackson, 70–93. Bloomington: Indiana University Press.

De Vaujany, François-Xavier. 2006. "Between Eternity and Actualization: The Co-evolution of the Fields of Communication in the Vatican." *Communications of the Association for Information Systems* 18:355–91.

De Vries, Hent. 2001. "Of Miracles and Special Effects." *International Journal for the Philosophy of Religion* 50:41–56.

Díaz Balsera, Viviana. 2005. *The Pyramid under the Cross: Franciscan Discourses of Evangelization and the Nahua Christian Subject in Sixteenth-Century Mexico.* Tucson: University of Arizona Press.

DISCERN Institute for Research on the Signs of Times. 2007. *Word of God: A Research Survey for the Synod of Bishops 2008.* Malta: DISCERN.

Dominguez, Virginia R. 1986. "The Marketing of Heritage." *American Ethnologist* 13:546–55.

Dossier Statistico Immigrazione. 2014. "La collettivita' peruviana in Italia." www .dossierimmigrazione.it/docnews/file/2014_La%20collettivit%C3%A0%20peruviana_Scheda.pdf.

Douglas, Mary. 1968. "The Contempt of Ritual." *New Blackfriars* 49 (578): 528–35.

———. 1970. *Natural Symbols: Explorations in Cosmology.* London: Routledge.

———. 1986. *How Institutions Think.* Syracuse, NY: Syracuse University Press.

Douglas, Mary, and Eleanor Wachtel. 2013. "Original Minds: Mary Douglas in Conversation with Eleanor Wachtel." In *Mary Douglas: A Very Personal Method,* edited by Richard Fardon, 271–97. London: Sage Publications.

Doyle, Eric. 1983. "The Question of Women Priests and the Argument in Persona Christi." *Irish Theological Quarterly* 50:212–22.

Drogus, Carol Ann. 1997. *Women, Religion, and Social Change in Brazil's Popular Church.* Notre Dame, IN: University of Notre Dame Press.

Drouin, Martin, and Anne Richard-Bazire. 2011. *La selection patrimoniale.* Montreal: Multimondes.

Dubisch, Jill. 1995. *In A Different Place: Pilgrimage, Gender and Politics at a Greek Island. Shrine*. Princeton, NJ: Princeton University Press.

Dubois, John. 2007. "The Stance Triangle." In *Stancetaking in Discourse: Subjectivity, Evaluation, Interaction,* edited by Roberty Englebretson, 139–82. Amsterdam: John Benjamins.

Du Boulay, Juliet. 1974. *Portrait of Greek Mountain Village*. Oxford: Clarendon Press.

Dumont, Louis. [1966] 1980. *Homo Hierarchicus: The Caste System and Its Implications*. Translated by M. Sainsbury. Chicago: University of Chicago Press; London: Paladin.

Durão, Susana, and Daniel Seabra Lopes. 2011. "Introduction: Institutions Are Us?" *Social Anthropology* 19:363–77.

Eade, John, and Michael J. Sallnow, eds. 1991. *Contesting the Sacred: The Anthropology of Christian Pilgrimage*. London: Routledge.

Eboussi Boulaga, Fabien. 1981. *Christianisme sans fétiche: Révélation et domination*. Paris: Présence Africaine.

Egan, Keith. 2011. "I Want to Feel the Camino in My Legs: Trajectories of Walking on the Camino de Santiago." In *Encounters of Body and Soul in Contemporary Religious Practices,* edited by Anna Fedele and Ruy Llera Blanes, 3–22. New York: Berghahn.

Éla, Jean Marc. 1988. *My Faith as an African*. Maryknoll, NY: Orbis Books.

Elisha, Omri. 2013. "All Catholics Now? Spectres of Catholicism in Evangelical Social Engagement." In *The New Evangelical Social Engagement,* edited by Brian Steensland and Philip Goff, 73–93. Oxford: Oxford University Press.

Endres, Kirsten W. 2011. "From Wasteful Superstition to Beautiful Tradition: Changing Assessments of Popular Religion in Late Socialist Vietnam." In *Ritual, Heritage and Identity: The Politics of Culture and Performance in a Globalised World,* edited by Christiane Brosius and Karin Polit, 246–80. Delhi: Routledge.

Engelke, Matthew. 2004. "Discontinuity and the Discourse of Conversion." *Journal of Religion in Africa* 34 (1): 82–109.

———. 2007. *A Problem of Presence: Beyond Scriptures in African Church*. Berkeley: University of California Press.

———. 2011. "Material Religion." In *The Cambridge Companion to Religious Studies,* edited by Robert A. Orsi, 209–29. Cambridge: Cambridge University Press.oEngelke, Matthew, and Joel Robbins, eds. 2010. "Global Christianity, Global Critique." Special issue, *South Atlantic Quarterly* 109, (4):623–31.

Engelke, Matthew, and Matt Tomlinson, eds. 2006. *The Limits of Meaning: Case Studies in the Anthropology of Christianity*. Oxford: Berghahn Books.

Eriksen, Annelin. 2008. *Gender, Christianity and Change in Vanuatu: An Analysis of Social Movements in North Ambrym*. Farnham: Ashgate.

———. 2012. "The Pastor and the Prophetess: An Analysis of Gender and Christianity in Vanuatu." *Journal of the Royal Anthropological Institute* 18 (1): 103–22.

———. 2014. "Sarah's Sinfulness: Egalitarianism, Denied Difference, and Gender in Pentecostal Christianity." *Current Anthropology* 55 (10): 262–70.

Fabian, Johannes. 1983. *Time and the Other: How Anthropology Makes Its Object*. New York: Columbia University Press.

Fanso, Verkijika G. 1989. "Trade and Supremacy on the Cameroon Coast, 1879–1887." In *Introduction to the History of Cameroon: Nineteenth and Twentieth Centuries,* edited by Martin Njeuma, 63–87. London: Macmillan.

Fardon, Richard. 1999. *Mary Douglas: An Intellectual Biography*. Routledge: London.

———. 2013. "Introduction: Drawn from Life: Mary Douglas's Personal Method." In *Mary Douglas: A Very Personal Method*, edited by Richard Fardon, 1–12. London: Sage Publications.

Fedele, Anna, and Ruy Llera Blanes. 2011. Introduction to *Encounters of Body and Soul in Contemporary Religious Practices*, edited by Anna Fedele and Ruy Llera Blanes, x–xxvii. New York: Berghahn Books.

Fernandez, James W. 1982. *Bwiti: An Ethnography of the Religious Imagination in Africa*. Princeton, NJ: Princeton University Press.

Flanagan, Kieran. 1991. *Sociology and Liturgy: Representations of the Holy*. Basingstoke: Macmillan.

Fletcher-Marsh, Wendy. 1998. "Towards a Single Anthropology: Developments in Modern Protestantism." In *Equal at the Creation: Sexism, Society and Christian Thought*, edited by Joseph Martos and Pierre Hégy, 129–42. Toronto: University of Toronto Press.

Foucault, Michel. 1997. "The Birth of Biopolitics." In *Ethics: Subjectivity and Truth*, edited by Paul Rabinow, 73–79. New York: New Press.

Frank, Georgia. 2000. *The Memory of the Eyes: Pilgrims to Living Saints in Christian Late Antiquity*. Berkeley: University of California Press.

Freedberg, David. 1989. *The Power of Images: Studies in the History and Theory of Response*. Chicago: University of Chicago Press.

Freud, Sigmund. [1907] 1959. "Obsessive Actions and Religious Practices." In *The Standard Edition of the Complete Psychological Works of Sigmund Freud*, edited by James Strachey, 9:115–27. London: Hogarth Press.

———. [1915] 1957. "Thoughts for the Time on War and Death." In *The Standard Edition of the Complete Psychological Works of Sigmund Freud*, edited by James Strachey, 14:115–27. London: Hogarth Press.

———. [1927] 1961. "The Future of an Illusion." In *The Standard Edition of the Complete Psychological Works of Sigmund Freud*, edited by James Strachey, 21:5–56. London: Hogarth Press.

———. [1930] 1961. "Civilisation and Its Discontents." In *The Standard Edition of the Complete Psychological Works of Sigmund Freud*, edited by James Strachey, 21:64–145. London: Hogarth Press.

Furey, Constance M. 2012. "Body, Society, and Subjectivity in Religious Studies." *Journal of the American Academy of Religion* 80:7–33.

Gage, Matilda Joslyn. 1893. *Woman, Church and State: A Historical Account of the Status of Woman through the Christian Ages*. New York: Truth Seeker.

Galizia, Daphne Caruana. 2009. "Medieval Hysteria at Borg in-Nadur." *Running Commentary* (blog), April 7, 2009. http://daphnecaruanagalizia.com/2009/04/medieval-hysteria-at-borg-in-nadur/.

Garces, Chris. 2010. "The Cross Politics of the Ecuador's Penal State." *Cultural Anthropology* 25:459–96.

Gauvreau, Michael. 2013. "Without Making a Noise: The Dumont Commission and the Drama of Quebec's Dechristianization, 1968–1971." In *The Sixties and Beyond: Dechristianization in North America and Western Europe, 1945–2000*, edited by Michael Gauvreau and Nancy Christie, 186–216. Toronto: University of Toronto Press.

Geary, Patrick. 1986. "Sacred Commodities: The Circulation of Medieval Relics." In *The Social Life of Things: Commodities in Cultural Perspective,* edited by Arjun Appadurai, 169–91. Cambridge: Cambridge University Press.

———. 1990. *Furta Sacra: Theft of Relics in the Central Middle Ages.* Princeton, NJ: Princeton University Press.

———. 1994. *Living with the Dead in the Middle Ages.* Ithaca, NY: Cornell University Press.

Geaves, Ron. 2009. "Forget Transmitted Memory: The De-traditionalised 'Religion' of Prem Rawat." *Journal of Contemporary Religion* 24 (1): 19–33.

Geertz, Clifford. [1973] 1993. *The Interpretation of Cultures.* London: Fontana Press.

Gell, Alfred. 1998. *Art and Agency: An Anthropological Theory.* Oxford: Clarendon Press.

Gemzöe, Lena. 2009. "Caring for Others: Mary, Death and the Feminization of Religion in Portugal." In *Moved by Mary: The Power of Pilgrimage in the Modern World,* edited by Anna-Karina Hermkens, Willy Jansen, and Catrien Notermans, 149–63. Farnham: Ashgate20Gilley, Sheridan. 1999. "A Tradition and Culture Lost, to Be Regained?" In *Catholics in England, 1950–2000: Historical and Sociological Perspectives,* edited by Michael Hornsby-Smith, 29–45. London: Cassell.

Goffman, Erving. 1961. *Asylums: Essays on the Social Situation of Mental Patients and Other Inmates.* New York: Doubleday.

———. 1981. "Footing." In *Forms of Talk,* edited by Erving Goffman, 124–59. Philadelphia: University of Pennsylvania Press.

Goodman, Felicitas D. 2005. *The Exorcism of Anneliese Michel.* San Jose, CA: Resource Publications.

Government of Malta. 1964. Constitution of Malta.

Greeley, Andrew. 2001. *The Catholic Imagination.* Berkeley: University of California Press.

Gross, Toomas. 2012. "Changing Faith: The Social Costs of Protestant Conversion in Rural Oaxaca." *Ethnos: Journal of Anthropology* 77:344–71.

Groulx, Jocelyn. 2009. Preface to *Le patrimoine religieux du Québec,* edited by Solange Lefebvre, n.p. Quebec City: Presses de L'Université Laval.

Gruzinski, Serge. 2001. *Images at War.* Translated by Heather MacLean. Durham, NC: Duke University Press.

Gupta, Akhil, and James Ferguson. 1992. "Beyond Culture: Space, Identity, and the Politics of Difference." *Cultural Anthropology* 7 (1): 6–23.

Gutierrez, Gustavo. [1971] 1973. *A Theology of Liberation.* Maryknoll, NY: Orbis Books.

Gutting, Gary. 2001. *French Philosophy in the Twentieth Century.* Cambridge: Cambridge University Press.

Hadot, Pierre. 1995. *Philosophy as a Way of Life: Spiritual Exercises from Socrates to Foucault.* Edited by Arnold Davidson. Malden, MA: Wiley-Blackwell.

Halbwachs, Maurice. [1941] 1992. *On Collective Memory.* Translated by Lewis A. Coser. Chicago: University of Chicago Press.

Halemba, Agnieszka. 2015. *Negotiating Marian Apparitions: The Politics of Religion in Transcarpathian Ukraine.* New York: Central European University Press.

Hall, David D. 1997. *Lived Religion in America: Toward a History of Practice.* Princeton, NJ: Princeton University Press.

Handler, Richard. 2011. "The Ritualisation of Ritual in the Construction of Heritage." In *Ritual, Heritage and Identity: The Politics of Culture and Performance in a Globalised World,* edited by Christiane Brosius and Karin Polit, 39–54. Delhi: Routledge.

Hann, Chris. 2007. "The Anthropology of Christianity *Per Se.*" *European Journal of Sociology* 48:383–410.

———. 2012. "Personhood, Christianity, Modernity." *Anthropology of This Century,* no. 3. http://aotcpress.com/articles/personhood-christianity-modernity/.

———. 2014. "The Heart of the Matter: Christianity, Materiality, and Modernity." *Current Anthropology* 55 (10): 182–92.

Hann, Chris, and Hermann Goltz. 2010. "Introduction: The Other Christianity?" In *Eastern Christians in Anthropological Perspective,* edited by Chris Hann and Hermann Goltz. Berkeley: University of California Press.

Hansen, Thomas Blom, and Finn Stepputat. 2006. "Sovereignty Revisited." *Annual Review of Anthropology* 35:295–315.

Harding, Susan. 1991. "Representing Fundamentalism: The Problem of the Repugnant Cultural Other." Social Research 58:373–93.

Hart, Robert. 2008. "In Persona Christi." *The Continuum* (blog), November 4. http://anglicancontinuum.blogspot.com/2008/11/unless-someone-informs-me-of-their.html.

Hastings, Adrian. 1967. *The Church and Mission in Modern Africa.* London: Burns and Oates.

———. 1989. *African Catholicism: Essays in Discovery.* London: SCM Press; Philadelphia: Trinity Press International.

Haynes, Naomi. 2012. "Pentecostalism and the Morality of Money: Prosperity, Inequality, and Religious Sociality on the Zambian Copperbelt." *Journal of the Royal Anthropological Institute* 18:123–39.

Hebga, Meinrad. 1976. *Émancipation d'églises sous-tutelle: Essai sur l'ère post-missionaire.* Paris: Présence Africaine.

———. 1991. "Healing in Africa." *Concilium* 2:61–71.

Hefner, Robert. 1998. "Multiple Modernities: Christianity, Islam, and Hinduism in a Globalizing Age." *Annual Review of Anthropology* 27:83–104.

———, ed. 2013. *Global Pentecostalism in the 21st Century.* Bloomington: University of Indiana Press.

Henn, Alexander. 2014. *Hindu-Catholic Encounters in Goa: Religion, Colonialism, and Modernity.* Bloomington: Indiana University Press.

Hermkens, Anna-Karina, Willy Jansen, and Catrien Notermans, eds. 2009. *Moved by Mary: The Power of Pilgrimage in the Modern World.* Aldershot: Ashgate.

Hervieu-Léger, Danièle. 1996. "Productions religieuses de la modernité." In *Religion, sécularisation, modernité: Les expériences francophones en Amérique du Nord,* edited by Brigitte Caulier, 37–58. Quebec City: Presses de l'Université Laval.

———. 2000. *Religion as a Chain of Memory.* New Brunswick, NJ: Rutgers University Press.

———. 2008. "Religion as Memory: Reference to Tradition and the Constitution of a Heritage of Belief in Modern Societies." In *Religion: Beyond a Concept,* edited by Hent de Vries, 245–58. Bronx, NY: Fordham University Press.

Hillman, Eugene. 1993. *Towards an African Christianity: Inculturation Applied.* New York: Paulist Press.

Hoenes de Pinal, Eric. 2009. "How Q'eqchi'-Maya Catholics Become Legitimate Interpreters of the Bible: Two Models of Religious Authority in the Giving of Sermons." In *The Social Life of Scripture: Cross-cultural Perspectives on Biblicism*, edited by James Bielo, 80–99. New Brunswick, NJ: Rutgers University Press.

———. 2011. "Towards an Ideology of Gesture: Gestures, Body Movement and Language Ideology among Q'eqchi'-Maya Catholics." *Anthropological Quarterly* 84 (3): 595–630.

Hoffman, Michael D. 2013. *Acts of Recovery: The Story of One Man's Ongoing Healing from Sexual Abuse by a Priest*. Chicago: Acta Publications.

Hollywood, Amy. 2004. "Gender, Agency, and the Divine in Religious Historiography." *Journal of Religion* 84 (4): 514–28.

Holmes, Douglas R. 2000. *Integral Europe: Fast-Capitalism, Multiculturalism, Neofascism*. Princeton, NJ: Princeton University Press.

Holy See. 1995. *Catechism of the Catholic Church*. New York: Doubleday.

Hopkins, Dwight, Lois Ann Lorentzen, Eduardo Mendieta, and David Blatstone, eds. 2001. *Religions/Globalizations: Theories and Cases*. Durham, NC: Duke University Press.

Hornsby-Smith, Michael P. 1999. "English Catholics in the New Millennium." In *Catholics in England, 1950–2000: Historical and Sociological Perspectives*, edited by Michael Hornsby-Smith, 291–306. London: Cassell.

Howes, David, ed. 2009. *The Sixth Sense Reader*. London: Bloomsbury.

———. 2015. "Sensation and Transmission." In *Ritual, Performance and the Senses*, edited by Michael Bull and Jon P. Mitchell, 153–66. London: Bloomsbury.

Hubert, Henri, and Marcel Mauss. [1964] 1981. *Sacrifice: Its Nature and Functions*. Chicago: University of Chicago Press.

Hugh of Saint Victor. [1997] 2014. "*De virtute orandi*." In *L'oeuvre de Hugues de Saint-Victor*, vol. 1, edited by H. B. Feiss and P. Siccard, 126–71. Turnhout: Brepols.

———. 2014. "On the Power of Prayer." In *Writings on the Spiritual Life: A Selection of Works of Hugh, Adam, Achard, Richard, Walter, and Godfrey of St Victor*, edited by Christopher P. Evans, 331–47. Hyde Park, NY: New City Press.

Hughes, Jennifer. 2012. "Mysterium Materiae: Vital Matter and the Object as Evidence in the Study of Religion." *Bulletin for the Study of Religion* 41 (4): 16–24.

Hull, Geoffrey. 1993. *The Malta Language Question: A Case Study in Cultural Imperialism*. Malta: Said.

Hutchinson, Sharon. 1996. *Nuer Dilemmas: Coping with Money, War, and the State*. Berkeley: University of California Press.

Hüwelmeier, Gertrud, and Kristine Krause, eds. 2009. *Traveling Spirits: Migrants, Markets and Mobilities*. New York: Routledge.

Huxley, Aldous. [1952] 1993. *The Devils of Loudun*. New York: Penguin.

Huysmans, Joris-Karl. 1998. *Against Nature*. Translated by Margaret Mauldon. Oxford: Oxford University Press.

Ingold, Tim. 2013. "Dreaming of Dragons: On the Imagination of Real Life." *Journal of the Royal Anthropological Institute* 19:734–52.

International Theological Commission. 1989. "Faith and Inculturation." *Origins* 18:800–807.

Irarrázaval, Diego. 2000. *Inculturation: New Dawn of the Church in Latin America*. Translated by P. Berryman. Maryknoll, NY: Orbis Books.

Irvine, Richard. 2010. "The Mission and the Cloister: Identity, Tradition and Transformation in the English Benedictine Congregation." *Saeculum* 60 (2): 289–306.

Isnart, Cyril. 2009. "Recent Papers about Robert Hertz and St. Besse." *Etnográfica* 13 (1): 215–22.

Jackson, Michael. 1996. *Things as They Are: New Directions in Phenomenological Anthropology*. Edited by Michael Jackson. Bloomington: Indiana University Press.

Jaffe, Alexandra. 2009. "The Sociolinguistics of Stance." In *Stance: Sociolinguistic Perspectives*, edited by Alexandra Jaffe, 1–28. Oxford: Oxford University Press.

James, Wendy. 1995. "Introduction: Whatever Happened to the Enlightenment?" In *The Pursuit of Certainty: Religious and Cultural Formulations*, 1–14. London: Routledge.

James, Wendy, and Douglas Johnson, eds. 1988. *Vernacular Christianity*. New York: Lilian Barber Press.

Janet, Richard J. 2001. "'Cold, Bare Ruined Choirs'? Reflections on the Nature of Catholic History." In *Catholicism at the Millennium: The Church of Tradition in Transition,* edited by Gerald L. Miller and Wilburn T. Stancil, 3–18. Kansas City: Rockhurst University Press.

Jaouen, René. 1995. *L'Eucharistie du mil: Langages d'un people, expressions de la foi*. Paris: Karthala.

Jenkins, Philip. 2003. *The New Anti-Catholicism: The Last Acceptable Prejudice*. New York: Oxford University Press.

———. 2007. *The Next Christendom: The Coming of Global Christianity*. Rev. and exp. ed. New York: Oxford University Press.

Jesuit Madurai Province. 2002. *Golden Jubilee, 1952–2002 Souvenir*. Dindigul: Provincial Superior.

John Paul II. 1988. *Mulieris Dignitatem*. Papal encyclical, August 15. https://www.ewtn.com /library/PAPALDOC/JP2MULIE.HTM.

———. 1995. "Ecclesia in Africa: Post-synodal Apostolic Exhortation." www.sedosmission .org/web/en/mission-articles/doc_view/1299-ecclesia-in-africa-post-synodal-apos-tolic-exhortation-of-pope-john-paul-ii.

Johnson, Elizabeth A. 1996. "The Maleness of Christ." In *The Power of Naming*, edited by Elisabeth Schüssler Fiorenza, 307–15. Maryknoll, NY: Orbis Books.

Joly, Diane. 2008. "Des croix de chemin en quête de protecteurs." *Rabaska* 6:41–67.

Jordan, Mark D. 2000. *The Silence of Sodom: Homosexuality in Modern Catholicism*. Chicago: University of Chicago Press.

———. 2003. *Telling Truths in Church: Scandal, Flesh, and Christian Speech*. Boston: Beacon Press.

Juergensmeyer, Mark, ed. 2003. *Global Religions: An Introduction*. Oxford: Oxford University Press.

Kaell, Hillary. 2012. "Of Gifts and Grandchildren: American Holy Land Souvenirs." *Journal of Material Culture* 17 (2): 133–51.

Kamen, Henry. 2014. "Baroque Religion in Spain: Spanish or European?" In *The Transatlantic Hispanic Baroque,* edited by Harald E. Braun and Jesús Pérez-Magallon, 95–112. London: Ashgate.

Kantorowicz, Ernst Hartwig. 1997. *The King's Two Bodies: A study in Mediaeval Political Theology*. Princeton, NJ: Princeton University Press.

Kaufman, Suzanne K. 2005. *Consuming Visions: Mass Culture and the Lourdes Shrine.* Ithaca, NY: Cornell University Press.

Keane, Webb. 1997. "Religious Language." *Annual Review of Anthropology* 26:47–71.

———. 2003. "Semiotics and the Social Analysis of Material Things." *Language and Communication* 23:409–25.

———. 2007. *Christian Moderns: Freedom and Fetish in the Mission Encounter.* Berkeley: University of California Press.

———. 2008. "The Evidence of the Senses and the Materiality of Religion." *Journal of the Royal Anthropological Institute* 14:110–27.

———. 2010. "Minds, Surfaces, and Reasons in the Anthropology of Ethics." In *Ordinary Ethics: Anthropology, Language and Action,* edited by Michael Lambek, 64–83. Bronx, NY: Fordham University Press.

Kilde, Jeanne. 2013. "Approaching Religious Space: An Overview of Theories, Methods, and Challenges in Religious Studies." *Religion and Theology* 20:183–201.

Kitayama, Shinobu, and Hazel Markus, eds. 1994. *Emotion and Culture: Empirical Studies and Mutual Influences.* Washington, DC: American Psychological Association.

Klassen, Pamela E. 2011. *Spirits of Protestantism: Medicine, Healing, and Liberal Christianity.* Berkeley: University of California Press.

Kleinman, Arthur. 2006. *What Really Matters: Living a Moral Life amidst Uncertainty and Danger.* New York: Oxford University Press.

Knobauch, Hubert. 2001. Review of *Chain of Memory* by Danièle Hervieu-Léger. *Journal of Religion* 81 (3): 527–28.

Kohn, Eduardo. 2013. *How Forests Think: Toward an Anthropology beyond the Human.* Berkeley: University of California Press.

Kramer, Heinrich, and James Sprenger. [1485] 1971. *Malleus Maleficarum.* Translated by Montague Summers. New York: Dover.

Kritzman, Lawrence D. Foreword to *Realms of Memory: The Construction of the French Past,* vol. 1, *Conflicts and Divisions,* edited by Pierre Nora, translated by Arthur Goldhammer, ix–xiv. New York: Columbia University Press.

Kuper, Adam. 1988. *The Invention of Primitive Society: Transformations of an Illusion.* London: Routledge.

Lado, Ludovic. 2006. "The Roman Catholic Church and African Religions: A Problematic Encounter." *Way* 45 (3): 7–21.

———. 2009. *Catholic Pentecostalism and the Paradoxes of Africanization.* Leiden: Brill.

Lafaye, Jacques. 1976. *Quetzalcoatl and Guadalupe: The Formation of Mexican National Consciousness, 1531–1813.* Translated by Benjamin Keen. Chicago: Chicago University Press.

Laing, Mark. 2006. "The Changing Face of Mission: Implications for the Southern Shift in Christianity." *Missiology* 34 (2): 165–77.

Lancaster, Roger. 1988. *Thanks to God and the Revolution.* New York: Columbia University Press.

Largier, Niklaus. 2003. "Inner Senses—Outer Senses: The Practice of Emotions in Medieval Mysticism." In *Codierungen von Emotionen im Mittelalter / Emotions and Sensibilities in the Middle Ages,* edited by C. Stephen Jaeger and Ingrid Kasten, 3–15. Berlin: Walter de Gruyter.

———. 2008. "Medieval Mysticism." In *The Oxford Handbook of Religion and Emotion*, edited by John Corrigan, 364–79. New York: Oxford University Press.

———. 2014. "The Art of Prayer: Conversions of Interiority and Exteriority in Medieval Contemplative Practice." In *Rethinking Emotion: Interiority and Exteriority in Premodern, Modern, and Contemporary Thought*, edited by Rüdiger Campe and Julia Weber, 58–71. Berlin: Walter de Gruyter.

Larsen, Timothy. 2014. *The Slain God: Anthropologists and the Christian Faith*. Oxford: Oxford University Press.

Latour, Bruno. 1993. *We Have Never Been Modern*. Cambridge, MA: Harvard University Press.

———. 2010. *On the Modern Cult of the Factish Gods*. Durham, NC: Duke University Press.

Lehmann, David. 1999. "Fundamentalism and Globalism." *Third World Quarterly* 19:607–34.

———. 2013. "Religion as Heritage, Religion as Belief: Shifting Frontiers of Secularism in Europe, the USA and Brazil." *International Sociology* 28 (6): 645–62.

Lehmann, Harmut. 2009. *Die Entzauberung der Welt: Studien zu Themen von Max Weber*. Göttingen: Wallstein.

Lesch, David W. 2005. *The New Lion of Damascus: Bashar al-Asad and Modern Syria*. New Haven, CT: Yale University Press.

Lester, Rebecca. 2005. *Jesus in Our Wombs: Embodying Modernity in a Mexican Convent*. Berkeley: University of California Press.

Levine, Daniel H. 1992. *Popular Voices in Latin American Catholicism*. Princeton, NJ: Princeton University Press.

Lienhardt, Godfrey. 1982. "The Dinka and Catholicism." In *Religious Organization and Religious Experience*, edited by John Davis, 81–95. London: Academic Press.

Lifton, Robert Jay, and Eric Olson. [1974] 2004. "Symbolic Immortality." In *Death, Mourning and Burial: A Cross-cultural Reader, Living and Dying*, edited by Antonius C. G. M. Robben, 32–39. Oxford: Blackwell.

Lindsay, Michael, and George Gallup. 1999. *Surveying the Religious Landscape*. Harrisburg, PA: Morehouse.

Lindstrom, Lamont. 1996. "Syncretism." In *Encyclopedia of Social and Cultural Anthropology*, edited by Alan Barnard and Jonathan Spencer, 812–13. London: Routledge.

Loisy, Alfred. 1924. *My Duel with the Vatican: The Autobiography of a Catholic Modernist*. New York: E. P. Dutton.

Lührmann, Sonja. 2010. "A Dual Struggle of Images on Russia's Middle Volga: Icon Veneration in the Face of Protestant and Pagan Critique." In *Eastern Christians in Anthropological Perspective*, edited by Chris Hann and Hermann Goltz, 56–78. Berkeley: University of California Press.

Luhrmann, Tanya. 2012. *When God Talks Back: Understanding the American Evangelical Relationship with God*. New York: Knopf.

MacLuhan, Marshall. 2010. *The Medium and the Light: Reflections on Religion and Media*. Eugene, OR: Wipf and Stock.

Macy, Gary. 2008. *The Hidden History of Women's Ordination*. Oxford: Oxford University Press.

Maddox, Gregory H. 1999. "African Theology and the Search for the Universal." In *East African Expressions of Christianity*, edited by Thomas Spears and Isaria N. Kimambo, 25–36. Oxford: James Currey.

Mafra, Clara. 2011. "Saintliness and Sincerity in the Formation of the Christian Person." *Ethnos* 76 (4): 448–68.

Mager, Robert, and Serge Cantin, eds. 2010. *Modernité et religion au Québec: Où en sommes-nous?* Quebec City: Presses Université Laval, 2010.

Magesa, Laurenti. 1997. *African Religion: The Moral Traditions of Abundant Life.* New York: Orbis Books.

Mahieu, Stéphanie, and Vlad Naumescu. 2008. *Churches In-Between: Greek Catholic Churches in Postsocialist Europe.* Münster: LIT.

Mahmood, Saba. 2005. *Politics of Piety: The Islamic Revival and the Feminist Subject.* Princeton, NJ: Princeton University Press.

Malinowski, Bronislaw. [1925] 2004. "Magic, Science and Religion." In *Death, Mourning and Burial: A Cross-cultural Reader,* edited by Antonius C. G. M. Robben, 19–22. Oxford: Blackwell, 2004.

Marder, Michael. 2008. "Carl Schmitt's 'Cosmopolitan Restaurant': Culture, Multiculturalism, and *Complexio Oppositorum.*" *Telos* 142:29–47.

Marion, Jean-Luc. 2002. *Being Given: Toward a Phenomenology of Givenness.* Stanford, CA: Stanford University Press.

———. 2008. "Sketch of a Phenomenological Concept of the Gift." In *The Visible and the Revealed,* edited by J.-L. Marion, 80–100. New York: Fordham University Press.

Martin, Phyllis. 2009. *Catholic Women of Congo-Brazzaville: Mothers and Sisters in Troubled Times.* Bloomington: Indiana University Press.

Martín Barbero, Jesús. 1995. "Secularización, desencanto y reencantamiento mass-mediático." *Diálogos de la Comunicación* 41: n.p.

Massa, Mark S. 2003. *Anti-Catholicism in America: The Last Acceptable Prejudice.* New York: Crossroad.

Masson, Joseph. 1962. "L'Eglise ouverte sur le monde." *Nouvelle Revue Théologique* 84:1032–43.

Masters, Bruce A. 2001. *Christians and Jews in the Ottoman Arab World: The Roots of Sectarianism.* Cambridge: Cambridge University Press.

Mauss, Marcel. [1954] 1990. *The Gift: The Form and Reason for Exchange in Archaic Societies.* New York: Routledge.

Mayblin, Maya. 2010. *Gender, Catholicism, and Morality in Brazil: Virtuous Husbands, Powerful Wives.* London: Palgrave.

———. 2011. "Death by Marriage: Power, Pride and Morality in Northeast Brazil." *Journal of the Royal Anthropological Institute* 17:135–53.

———. 2014a. "People Like Us: Intimacy, Distance, and the Gender of Saints." *Current Anthropology* 55 (S10): 271–81.

———. 2014b. "The Untold Sacrifice: The Monotony and Incompleteness of Self-Sacrifice in Northeast Brazil." *Ethnos: Journal of Anthropology* 79:342–64.

Mayeur-Jaouen, Catherine. 2012. "What Do Egypt's Copts and Muslims Share? The Issue of Shrines." In *Sharing Sacred Spaces in the Mediterranean: Christians, Muslims, and Jews at Shrines and Sanctuaries,* edited by Dionigi Albera and Maria Couroucli, 148–73. Bloomington: Indiana University Press.

Mbembe, Achille. 1992. "Provisional Notes on the Postcolony." *Africa* 62 (1): 3–37.

McDannell, Colleen. 1995. *Material Christianity: Religion and Popular Culture in America.* New Haven, CT: Yale University Press.

McGuire, Meredith B. 1982. *Pentecostal Catholics: Power, Charisma, and Order in a Religious Movement.* Philadelphia: Temple University Press.

McInroy, Mark J. 2012. "Karl Rahner and Hans Urs von Balthasar." In *The Spiritual Senses: Perceiving God in Western Christianity,* edited by Paul L. Gavrilyuk and Sarah Coakley, 257–74. Cambridge: Cambridge University Press.

Méchoulan, Éric. 2008. *La culture de la mémoire, ou, Comment se débarrasser du passé?* Montreal: Presses de l'Université de Montreal.

Mellor, Philip A., and Chris Shilling. 1997. *Re-forming the Body: Religion, Community and Modernity.* London: Sage Publications.

Merleau-Ponty, Maurice. [1945] 2013. *Phenomenology of Perception.* Translated by Donald Landes. London: Routledge.

———. [1948] 1992a. "Cezanne's Doubt." In *Sense and Non-sense,* translated by Patricia A. Dreyfus and Hubert L. Dreyfus, 9–25. Evanston, IL: Northwestern University Press.

———. [1948] 1992b. "Faith and Good Faith." In *Sense and Non-sense,* translated by Patricia A. Dreyfus and Hubert L. Dreyfus, 172–81. Evanston, IL: Northwestern University Press.

———. [1953] 1988. "In Praise of Philosophy." In *In Praise of Philosophy and Other Essays,* translated by John Wild, James M. Edie, and John O'Neill, 3–70. Evanston, IL: Northwestern University Press.

———. [1964] 1969a. "The Intertwining—The Chiasm." In *The Visible and the Invisible,* translated by Alphonso Lingis, 130–55. Evanston, IL: Northwestern University Press.

———. [1964] 1969b. *The Visible and the Invisible.* Translated by Alphonso Lingis. Evanston, IL: Northwestern University Press.

———. [1968] 2003. *Nature: Course Notes from the Collège de France.* Translated by Robert Vallier. Evanston, IL: Northwestern University Press.

Messina, Jean-Paul, and Jaap van Slageren. 2005. *Histoire du Christianisme au Cameroon, des origins à nos jours: Approche oecuménique.* Paris: Karthala.

Messler Davis, Jody, and Mary Gail Frawley. 1994. *Treating the Adult Survivor of Childhood Sexual Abuse: A Psychoanalytic Perspective.* New York: Basic Books.

Meunier, Martin, Jean-François Laniel, and Jean-Christophe Demers. 2010. "Permanence et recomposition de la 'religion culturelle.'" In *Modernité et religion au Québec: Où en sommes-nous?,* edited by Robert Mager and Serge Cantin, 79–128. Quebec City: Presses Université Laval.

Meyer, Birgit. 1997. "Christian Mind and Worldly Matters: Religion and Materiality in Nineteenth-Century Gold Coast." *Journal of Material Culture* 2:311–37.

———. 1999. *Translating the Devil: Religion and Modernity among the Ewe in Ghana.* Edinburgh: Edinburgh University Press.

———. 2004. "Christianity in Africa: From African Independent to Pentecostal- Charismatic Churches." *Annual Review of Anthropology* 33:447–74.

———. 2006. "Religious Sensations: Why Media, Aesthetics and Power Matter in the Study of Contemporary Religion." Inaugural lecture presented at Vrije Universiteit, Amsterdam, October 6.

———. 2009. "From Imagined Communities to Aesthetic Formations: Religious Mediations, Sensational Forms, and Styles of Binding." In *Aesthetic Formations: Media, Religion and the Senses,* edited by Birgit Meyer, 1–28. Basingstoke: Palgrave Macmillan.

———. 2010a. "Aesthetics of Persuasion: Global Christianity and Pentecostalism's Sensational Forms." *South Atlantic Quarterly* 109:743–50.

———. 2010b. "'There Is a Spirit in That Image': Mass-Produced Jesus Pictures and Protestant-Pentecostal Animation in Ghana." *Comparative Studies in Society and History* 52:100–130.

———. 2010c. "Tradition and Colour at Its Best: 'Tradition' and 'Heritage' in Ghanaian Video-Movies." *Journal of African Cultural Studies* 22:7–23.

———. 2011. "Mediation and Immediacy: Sensational Forms, Semiotic Ideologies and the Question of the Medium." *Social Anthropology* 19 (1): 23–39.

———. 2014. "Mediation and the Genesis of Presence: Towards a Material Approach to Religion. With Comments by Hans Belting, Pamela Klassen, Monique Scheer, and Chris Pinney." *Religion and Society: Advances in Research* 5:205–54.

———. 2015. "Picturing the Invisible: Visual Culture and the Study of Religion." *Method and Theory in the Study of Religion* 27:6–14.

Meyer, Birgit, and Dick Houtman. 2012. "Material Religion—How Things Matter." In *Things: Religion and the Question of Materiality,* edited by Dick Houtman and Birgit Meyer, 9–13. New York: Fordham University Press.

Mignolo, Walter. 2002. "The Geopolitics of Knowledge and the Colonial Difference." *South Atlantic Quarterly* 101:56–96.

———. 2011. "Crossing Gazes and the Silence of the 'Indians': Theodor de Bry and Guamán Poma de Ayala." *Journal of Medieval and Early Modern Studies* 1 (41): 173–223.

Mines, Diane. 2005. *Fierce Gods: Inequality, Ritual, and the Politics of Dignity in a South Indian Village.* Bloomington: Indiana University Press.

Mitchell, Jon P. 2002. *Ambivalent Europeans: Ritual, Memory and the Public Sphere in Malta.* London: Routledge.

———. 2015. "Ontology, Mimesis and Divine Intervention: Understanding Catholic Visionaries." In *Ritual, Performance and the Senses,* edited by Michael Bull and Jon P. Mitchell, 11–30. London: Bloomsbury.

Mitchell, Timothy. 2002. *Rule of Experts: Egypt, Techno-Politics, Modernity.* Berkeley: University of California Press.

Mitchell, W. J. Thomas. 2004. *What Do Pictures Want? The Lives and Loves of Images.* Chicago: University of Chicago Press.

Molero, Javier Ávila, and Erica Oshier. 2005. "Worshipping the Señor de Qoyllur ritti in New York: A Transnational Andean Ethnography." *Latin American Perspectives* 32:174–92.

Molina, J. Michelle. 2013. *To Overcome Oneself: The Jesuit Ethic and Spirit of Global Expansion, 1520–1767.* Berkeley: University of California Press.

———. 2015. "Father of My Soul: Reason and Affect in a Shipboard Conversion Narrative." *Journal of Jesuit Studies* 2 (4): 641–58.

Moore, Brenna. 2015. "Friendship and the Cultivation of Religious Sensibilities." *Journal of American Academy of Religion* 83 (2): 437–63.

Moore, Sally Falk. 1994. *Anthropology and Africa: Changing Perspectives on a Changing Scene.* Charlottesville: University Press of Virginia.

Morgan, David. 1998. *Visual Piety: A History and Theory of Popular Religious Images.* Berkeley: University of California Press.

———. 2005. *The Sacred Gaze: Religious Visual Culture in Theory and Practice.* Berkeley: University of California Press.

———. 2009. "Aura and the Inversion of Marian Pilgrimage: Fatima and Her Statues." In *Moved by Mary: The Power of Pilgrimage in the Modern World,* edited by Anna-Karina Hermkens, Willy Jansen, and Catrien Notermans, 49–65. Aldershot: Ashgate.

———. 2010. "Materiality, Social Analysis and the Study of Religions." In *Religion and Material Culture: The Matter of Belief,* edited by David Morgan, 55–74. New York: Routledge.

———. 2012a. *The Embodied Eye: Religious Visual Culture and the Social Life of Feeling.* Berkeley: University of California Press.

———. 2012b. "Rhetoric of the Heart: Figuring the Body in Devotion to the Sacred Heart of Jesus." In *Things: Religion and the Question of Materiality,* edited by Dick Houtman and Birgit Meyer, 90–111. New York: Fordham University Press.

Mosse, David. 2006. "Possession and Confession: Affliction and Sacred Power in Colonial and Contemporary Catholic South India." In *The Anthropology of Christianity,* edited by Fenella Cannell, 99–133. Durham, NC: Duke University Press.

———. 2012. *The Saint in the Banyan Tree: Christianity and Caste Society in India.* Berkeley: University of California Press.

———. 2015. "Caste and the Conundrum of Religion and Development in India." In *The Routledge Handbook on Religions and Global Development,* edited by E. Tomalin, 200–214. London: Routledge.

Mudimbe, Valentine-Ives. 1988. *The Invention of Africa: Gnosis, Philosophy, and the Order of Knowledge.* Bloomington: Indiana University Press.

Muehlebach, Andrea. 2009. "Complexio Oppositorum: Notes on the Left in Neoliberal Italy." *Public Culture* 21:495–515.

———. 2012. *The Moral Neoliberal: Welfare and Citizenship in Italy.* Chicago: University of Chicago Press.

Mugambi, Jesse. 1989. *African Heritage and Contemporary Christianity.* Nairobi: Longman Kenya.

Mújica, Jorge. 2008. "Medios de comunicación e iglesia: Una relación con historia." http://es.catholic.net/op/articulos/41673/cat/878/medios-de-comunicacion-e-iglesia-una-relacion-con-historia.html.

Mulago, Vincent. 1965. *Un visage africain du Christianisme: L'union vitale Bantu face à l'unité vitale ecclésiale.* Paris: Présence Africaine.

Nabhan-Warren, Kristy. 2013. *The Cursillo Movement in America.* Chapel Hill: University of North Carolina Press.

Napolitano, Valentina. 2007. "Of Migrant Revelations and Anthropological Awakenings." *Social Anthropology* 15 (1): 71–87.

———. 2009. "The Virgin of Guadalupe: A Nexus of Affect." *Journal of the Royal Anthropological Institute* 15 (1): 92–118.

———. 2016. *Migrant Hearts and the Atlantic Return: Transnationalism and the Roman Catholic Church.* New York: Fordham University Press.

———. Forthcoming. "'The Globalization of Indifference': On Pope Francis, Migration and Global Acedia." In *Market and Morality,* edited by Filippo Osella and Daromir Rudnyckyj. Cambridge: Cambridge University Press.

Napolitano, Valentina, and Kristin Norget. [2009] 2011. "Introduction, Economies of Sanctity: The Translocal Roman Catholic Church in Latin America." *Postscripts* 5:251–64.

Ndalianis, Angela. 2004. *Neo-Baroque Aesthetics and Contemporary Entertainment.* Cambridge, MA: MIT Press.

Ngongo, Louis. 1982. *Histoire des forces religieuses au Cameroun: De la Première Guerre Mondiale à l'Indépendence (1916–1955).* Paris: Karthala.

Nightingale, Andrea. 2011. *Once Out of Nature: Augustine on Time and the Body.* Chicago: University of Chicago Press.

Noppen, Luc, and Lucie K. Morrisset. 2005. *Les églises du Québec, un patrimoine à. réinventer.* Quebec City: Presses de l'Université du Québec.

Nora, Pierre. 1996. "General Introduction: Between Memory and History." In *Realms of Memory: The Construction of the French Past*, vol. 1, *Conflicts and Divisions*, edited by Pierre Nora, translated by Arthur Goldhammer, 1–21. New York: Columbia University Press.

Nordlander, Andreas. 2011. "Figuring Flesh in Creation: Merleau-Ponty in Conversation with Philosophical Theology." PhD diss., Lund University.

———. 2013. "The Wonder of Immanence: Merleau-Ponty and the Problem of Creation." *Modern Theology* 29 (2): 104–23.

Norget, Kristin. 2004. "'Knowing Where We Enter': Indigenous Theology and the Catholic Church in Oaxaca, México." In *Resurgent Voices in Latin America: Indigenous Peoples, Political Mobilization, and Religious Change,* edited by Edward Cleary and Tim Steigenga, 154–86. New Brunswick, NJ: Rutgers University Press.

———. 2006. *Days of Death, Days of Life: Ritual in the Popular Culture of Oaxaca.* New York: Columbia University Press.

———. 2008. "Hard Habits to Baroque: Catholic Church and Popular-Indigenous Religious Dialogue in Oaxaca, Mexico." *Revista Canadiense de Estudios Hispánicos* 33:131–58.

———. 2009. "Popes, Saints, *Beato* Bones and Other Images at War: Religious Mediation and the Translocal Roman Catholic Church." *Postscripts* 5 (3): 337–64.

———. 2010. "A Cacophony of Autochthony: Representing Indigeneity in Oaxacan Popular Mobilization." *Journal of Latin American and Caribbean Anthropology* 15 (1): 115–43.

———. 2014. "Neo-Baroque Catholic Evangelism in Post-secular Mexico." In *The Transatlantic Hispanic Baroque: Complex Identities in the Atlantic World,* edited by Harald Braun and Jesús Perez-Magallon, 273–90. London: Ashgate.

Novalis. [1802] 1997. *Philosophical Writings.* Edited and translated by Margaret M. Stoljar. New York: State University of New York Press.

Ntetem, March. 1987. "Initiation, Traditional and Christian." In *A Reader in African Christian Theology,* edited by John Parratt, 103–9. London: Society for Promoting Christian Knowledge.

Nurse, Andrew. 1997. "Tradition and Modernity: The Cultural Work of Marius Barbeau." PhD diss., Queen's University.17Nyamiti, Charles. 1984. *Christ as Our Ancestor.* Zimbabwe: Mambo Press.

O'Malley, John W. 2008. *What Happened at Vatican II.* Cambridge, MA: Harvard University Press.

Orobator, Agbonkhianmeghe. 2008. *Theology Brewed in an African Pot.* Maryknoll, NY: Orbis Books.

Orsi, Robert. 1985. *The Madonna of 115th Street: Faith and Community in Italian Harlem, 1880–1950.* New Haven, CT: Yale University Press.

———. 1996. *Thank You, St. Jude: Women's Devotion to the Patron Saint of Hopeless Causes.* New Haven, CT: Yale University Press.

———. 2005. *Between Heaven and Earth: The Religious Worlds People Make and the Scholars Who Study Them.* Princeton, NJ: Princeton University Press.

———. 2012. "Material Children: Making God's Presence Real through Catholic Boys and Girls." In *Religion, Media and Culture: A Reader,* edited by Gordon Lynch, Jolyon P. Mitchell, and Anna Strhan, 147–58. London: Routledge.

———. 2014. "Speaking the Impossible 'No.'" *Bulletin for the Study of Religion* 43 (1): 7–11.

———. 2016. *History and Presence.* Cambridge, MA: Harvard University Press.

Orta, Andrew. 2004. *Catechizing Culture: Missionaries, Aymara and the "New Evangelization."* New York: Columbia University Press.

———. 2006. "Dusty Signs and Roots of Faith: The Limits of Christian Meaning in Highlands Bolivia." In *Christian Ritual and the Limits of Meaning,* edited by Matt Tomlinson and Mathew Engelke, 165–88. Lanham, MD: University Press of America.

Otto, Eckart. 2005. "Die hebräische Prophetie bei Weber, Troeltsch and Cohen." In *Asketischer Protestantismus und der "Geist" des modernen Kapitalismus,* edited by Wolfgang Schluchter and Friedrich Wilhelm Graf, 201–54. Tübingen: Mohr Siebeck.

Owoahene-Acheampong, Stephen. 1988. *Inculturation and Western Approaches to Medical Practice.* New York: Peter Lang.

Pacini, Andrea. 1998. *Christian Communities in the Arab Middle East: The Challenge of the Future.* Oxford: Clarendon Press.

Paerregaard, Karsten. 2008. "In the Footsteps of the Lord of Miracles: The Expatriation of Religious Icons in the Peruvian Diaspora." *Journal of Ethnic and Migration Studies* 34:1073–89.

———. 2010. "The Show Must Go On: The Role of Fiestas in Andean Transnational Migration." *Latin American Perspectives* 37:50–66.

Pandian, Anand. 2008. "Tradition in Fragments: Inherited Forms and Fractures in the Ethics of South India." *American Ethnologist* 35:466–80.

Parratt, John. [1987] 1997. Introduction to *A Reader in African Christian Theology,* edited by John Parratt, 1–8. London: Society for Promoting Christian Knowledge.

Paul VI. 1965. "Pastoral Constitution on the Church in the Modern World." December 7. www.vatican.va/archive/hist_councils/ii_vatican_council/documents/vat-ii_cons_19651207_gaudium-et-spes_en.html.

Peebles, Gustav. 2012. "Filth and Lucre: The Dirty Money Complex as a Taxation Regime." *Anthropological Quarterly* 85:1229–56.

Peel, John David. 1968. *Aladura: A Religious Movement among the Yoruba.* London: Oxford University Press for the International African Institute.

Peña, Elaine. 2011. *Performing Piety: Making Space Sacred with the Virgin of Guadalupe.* Berkeley: University of California Press.

Penoukou, Efoé Julien. 1994. *Églises d'Afrique: Propositions pour l'avenir.* Paris: Desclée.

Pentcheva, Bissera V. 2006. "The Performative Icon." *Art Bulletin* 88 (4): 631–55.

Perniola, Mario. 2003. "The Cultural Turn and Ritual Feeling in Catholicism." *Paragrana: Zeitschrift fur Historische Anthropologie* 12:309–25.

Perrault, Jean-Philippe. 2011. "De la *continuité tranquille?* Penser la jeunesse, le religieux et le catholicisme au Québec." *Recherches Sociographiques* 52:759–87.

Perthes, Volker. [1995] 1997. *The Political Economy of Syria under Asad.* London: I. B. Tauris.

Peter of Ailly. 1634. "Compendium contemplationis." In *Opuscula Spiritualia,* 67–139. Douai: Apud viduam Marci Wyon.

Peterson, Anna L., and Manuel A. Vásquez. 1998. "The New Evangelization in Latin American Perspective." *Cross Currents* 48:311–29.

Pew Research Center. 2015. "U.S. Catholics Open to Non-traditional Families." September 2. www.pewforum.org/2015/09/02/u-s-catholics-open-to-non-traditional-families/.

Pina-Cabral, Joao de. 1986. *Sons of Adam, Daughters of Eve: The Peasant Worldview of Alto Minho.* Gloucestershire: Clarendon Press.

Pitt-Rivers, Julian. [1992] 2011. "The Place of Grace in Anthropology." *HAU: Journal of Ethnographic Theory* 1 (1): 423–50.

Pobee, John. 1979. *Toward an African Theology.* Nashville, TN: Abingdon.

Poewe, Karla, ed. 1994. *Charismatic Christianity as a Global Culture.* Columbia: University of South Carolina Press.

Poole, Stafford. 1995. *Our Lady of Guadalupe: The Origins and Sources of a Mexican National Symbol, 1531–1797.* Tucson: University of Arizona Press.

Primiano, Leonard N. 1999. "Postmodern Sites of Catholic Sacred Materiality." In *Perspectives on American Religion and Culture,* edited by Peter W. Williams, 187–202. Oxford: Blackwell.

Promey, Sally. 2014. *Sensational Religion: Sensory Cultures in Material Practice.* New Haven, CT: Yale University Press.

Ram, Kalpana. 1991. *Mukkuvar Women: Gender, Hegemony and Capitalist Transformation in a South Indian Fishing Community.* Sydney: Allen and Irwin.

Raming, Ida. 1976. *The Exclusion of Women from the Priesthood: Divine Law or Sex Discrimination?* Metuchen, NJ: Scarecrow Press.

Rancière, Jacques. 2006. *The Politics of Aesthetics: The Distribution of the Sensible.* Translated by Gabriel Rockhill. London: Continuum.

Ranger, Terence O. 1986. "Religious Movements and Politics in Sub-Saharan Africa." *African Studies Review* 29 (2): 1–69.

———. 1987. "Religion, Development and African Christian Identity." In *Religion, Development and African Identity,* edited by Kirsten Petersen, 29–58. Uppsala: Scandinavian Institute of African Studies.

Rapley, Elizabeth. [2001] 2009. *A Social History of the Cloister: Daily Life in the Teaching Monasteries of the Old Regime.* Montreal: McGill Queen's University Press.

Rapoport, Judith L. 1989. *The Boy Who Couldn't Stop Washing: The Experience and Treatment of Obsessive-Compulsive Disorder.* New York: Penguin.

Ratzinger, Joseph. 2007. "Ecclesial Movements and Their Place in Theology." In *New Outpourings of the Spirit—Movements in the Church,* 17–61. San Francisco: Ignatius Press.

Reckwitz, Andreas. 2012. "Affective Spaces: A Praxeological Outlook." *Rethinking History* 16:241–46.

Redfield, Robert. 1956. *The Little Community and Peasant Society and Culture.* Chicago: University of Chicago Press.

Reich, Warren T. 1995. "History of the Notion of Care." In *Encyclopedia of Bioethics,* edited by Warren T. Reich, 319–31. New York: Macmillan.

Reyna Ruiz, Araceli Margarita. 2012. "Las frecuencias de Dios: Programas con contenido religioso en la radio en del Valle de México." PhD diss., Universidad Autonoma Metropolitana, Unidad Xochimilco, Mexico.

Riegelhaupt, Joyce. 1984. "Popular Anti-clericalism and Religiosity in Pre-1974 Portugal." In *Religion, Power, and Protest in Local Communities: The Northern Shore of the Mediterranean,* edited by Eric R. Wolf, 93–114. Berlin: Mouton.

Ritchey, Sara. 2014. *Holy Matter: Changing Perceptions of the Material World in Late Medieval Christianity.* Ithaca, NY: Cornell University Press.

Rivera, Mayra. 2015. *Poetics of the Flesh.* Durham, NC: Duke University Press.

Robbins, Joel. 2003a. "On the Paradoxes of Global Pentecostalism and the Perils of Continuity Thinking." *Religion* 33 (3): 221–31.

———. 2003b. "What Is a Christian? Notes toward an Anthropology of Christianity." *Religion* 33 (3): 191–99.

———. 2004a. *Becoming Sinners: Christianity and Moral Torment in a Papua New Guinea Society.* Berkeley: University of California Press.

———. 2004b. "The Globalization of Pentecostal and Charismatic Christianity." *Annual Review of Anthropology* 33:117–43.

———. 2007. "Continuity Thinking and the Problem of Christian Culture: Belief, Time, and the Anthropology of Christianity." *Current Anthropology* 48:5–38.

———. 2010. "Anthropology, Pentecostalism, and the New Paul: Conversion, Event, and Social Transformation." *South Atlantic Quarterly* 109 (4): 633–52.

———. 2014. "The Anthropology of Christianity: Unity, Diversity, New Directions: An Introduction to Supplement 10." *Current Anthropology* 55 (S10): 157–71.

Robertson, Roland, and William R. Garrett, eds. 1991. *Religion and Global Order.* New York: Paragon House.

Rocca, Francis X. 2013. "Why Not Women Priests? The Papal Theologian Explains." Catholic News Service, January 31. www.catholicnews.com/services/englishnews/2013/why-not-women-priests-the-papal-theologian-explains.cfm.

Rosaldo, Renato. 1989. "Introduction—Grief and a Headhunter's Rage." In *Culture and Truth: The Remaking of Social Analysis,* 1–21. Boston: Beacon Press.

Rose, Jacqueline. 1998. *States of Fantasy.* Oxford: Clarendon Press.

———. 2003. *On Not Being Able to Sleep: Psychoanalysis and the Modern World.* London: Chatto and Windus.

Rose, Nikolas. 1998. *Governing the Soul: The Shaping of the Private Self.* London: Routledge.

Routhier, Gilles. 2006a. "Les enjeux du débat actuel sur le patrimoine religieux." *Argument: Politique, Société et Histoire* 8 (2): n.p.

———. 2006b. "Governance of the Catholic Church in Quebec: An Expression of the Distinct Society?" In *The Churches and the Social Order in Nineteenth- and Twentieth-Century Canada,* edited by Michael Gauvreau and Ollivier Hubert, 292–314. Montreal: McGill-Queens University Press.

Rudolf of Biberach. [1866] 1985. *De septem itineribus aeternitatis.* Edited by Margot Schmidt. Stuttgart (Bad Cannstatt): Frommann-Holzboog.

Sacks, Harvey. 1984. "On Doing Being Ordinary." In *Structures of Social Action: Studies in Conversation Analysis,* edited by J. M. Atkinson and J. Heritage, 413–29. New York: Cambridge University Press.

Sacred Congregation for the Doctrine of the Faith. 1976. "Declaration *inter Insigniores* on the Question of Admission of Women to the Ministerial Priesthood." October 15. www .vatican.va/roman_curia/congregations/cfaith/documents/rc_con_cfaith_doc_19761015_ inter-insigniores_en.html.

———. 1978. "Norms Regarding the Manner of Proceeding in the Discernment of Presumed Apparitions or Revelations." February 25. www.vatican.va/roman_curia/congregations /cfaith/documents/rc_con_cfaith_doc_19780225_norme-apparizioni_en.html.

Sakaranaho, Tuula. 2011. "Religion and the Study of Social Memory." *Temenos* 47 (2): 135–58.

Salamandra, Christa. 2004. *A New Old Damascus: Authenticity and Distinction in Urban Syria.* Bloomington: Indiana University Press.

Salibi, Kamal. [1988] 2003. *A House of Many Mansions: The History of Lebanon Reconsidered.* London: I. B. Tauris.

Sanders, Todd. 2003. "Imagining the Dark Continent: The Met, the Media and the Thames Torso." *Cambridge Anthropology* 23 (3): 53–66.

Santner, Eric L. 2011. *The Royal Remains: The People's Two Bodies and the Endgames of Sovereignty.* Chicago: University of Chicago Press.

Scheper Hughes, Jennifer. 2012. "The Niño Jesús Doctor: Novelty and Innovation in Mexican Religion." *Nova Religio: The Journal of Alternative and Emergent Religions* 16: 4–28.

Schluchter, Wolfgang. 2005. "'Wie Ideen in der Geschichte wirken': Exemplarisches in der Studie über den asketischen Protestantismus." In *Asketischer Protestantismus,* edited by Wolfang Schluchter and Friedrich W. Graf, 49–73. Tübingen: Mohr Siebeck.

Schmitt, Carl. [1923] 1996. *Roman Catholicism and Political Form.* Translated by G. L. Ulmen. Westport, CT: Greenwood Press.

Schreiter, Robert. 1985. *Constructing Local Theologies.* Maryknoll, NY: Orbis Books.

Schwebel, Horst. 2002. *Die Kunst und das Christentum: Geschichte eines Konflikts.* Munich: C. H. Beck.

Scott, David. 1999. *Refashioning Futures.* Princeton, NJ: Princeton University Press.

Seale, Clive. 1998. *Constructing Death: The Sociology of Dying and Bereavement.* Cambridge: Cambridge University Press.

Seremetakis, Nadia C. 1991. *The Last Word: Women, Death, and Divination in Inner Mani.* Chicago: University of Chicago Press.

Sharf, Robert H. 1998. "Experience." In *Critical Terms for Religious Studies,* edited by Mark C. Taylor. 94–116. Chicago: University of Chicago Press.

Shaw, Rosalind, and Charles Stewart. 1994. "Introduction: Problematising Syncretism." In *Syncretism/Anti-syncretism: The Politics of Religious Synthesis,* edited by Charles Stewart and Rosalinda Shaw, 1–26. London: Routledge.

Shorter, Aylward. 1988. *Towards a Theology of Inculturation.* London: Geoffrey Chapman.

Simard, Jean. 1972. "Témoins d'un passé de foi." *Perspectives* 14:20–22.

———. 1979. *Un patrimoine méprisé: La religion populaire des Québécois*. LaSalle, Quebec: Éditions Hurtubise.

———. 1995. *L'art religieux des routes du Québec*. Quebec City: Gouvernement du Québec, Commission des Biens Culturels.

———. 1998. *Le patrimoine religieux au Québec*. Quebec City: Gouvernement du Québec, Commission des Biens Culturels.

Simondon, Gilbert. 2012. "On Techno-Aesthetics." Translated by Arne De Boever. *Parrhesia* 14:1–8.

Sluhovsky, Mose. 2007. *Believe Not Every Spirit: Possession, Mysticism, and Discernment in Early Modern Catholicism*. Chicago: University of Chicago Press.

Snyder, Patrick, and Martine Pelletier, eds. 2011. *Qu'est-ce que le religieux contemporain?* Montreal: Fides.

Spear, Thomas, and Isaria Kimambo, eds. 1999. *East African Expressions of Christianity*. Oxford: James Currey.

Standaert, Nicolas. 1988. "L'histoire d'un néologisme: Le terme 'inculturation' dans les documents Romains." *Nouvelle Revue Théologique* 110:555–70.

Stark, Werner. 1965. "The Routinization of Charisma: A Consideration of Catholicism." *Sociology of Religion* 26 (4): 203–11.

Stephens, Scott. 2011. "Catholic Sexual Abuse Study Greeted with Incurious Contempt." ABC Religion and Ethics, May 27. www.abc.net.au/religion/articles/2011/05/27/3229135.htm.

Stewart, Anna. 2012. "Gender, Faith and Storytelling: An Ethnography of the. Charismatic Internet." PhD diss., University of Sussex.

Stewart, Kathleen. 1992. "Nostalgia as Polemic." In *Rereading Cultural Anthropology*, edited by George E. Marcus, 252–66. Durham, NC: Duke University Press.

Stewart, Susan. [1984] 2001. *On Longing: Narratives of the Miniature, the Gigantic, the Souvenir, the Collection*. Durham, NC: Duke University Press,

Suenens, Leon Joseph. [1974] 1975. *A New Pentecost?* Translated by Francis Martin. New York: Seabury Press.

Sultana, Victoria. 2011. "Amputations and Invocations: A Study of Limb Amputation in Malta." PhD diss., University College London.

Sundkler, Bengt G. 1948. *Bantu Prophets in South Africa*. Oxford: Oxford University Press.

Taussig, Michael. 1992. *The Nervous System*. New York: Routledge.

———. 1997. *The Magic of the State*. New York: Routledge.

Taves, Ann. 2012. "Special Things as Building Blocks of Religions." In *The Cambridge Companion to Religious Studies*, edited by Robert A. Orsi, 58–83. Cambridge: Cambridge University Press.

Taylor, Charles. 1999. "To Follow a Rule . . ." In *Bourdieu: A Critical Reader*, edited by Richard Shusterman, 29–44. Oxford: Blackwell.

———. 2007. *A Secular Age*. Cambridge, MA: Harvard University Press.

Taylor, William B. 1987. "The Virgin of Guadalupe in New Spain: An Inquiry into the Social History of Marian Devotion." *American Ethnologist* 14 (1): 9–33.

———. 1996. *Magistrates of the Sacred: Priests and Parishioners in 18th Century Mexico*. Stanford, CA: Stanford University Press.

Tchibangu, Tharcisse. 1987. "The Task and Method of Theology in Africa." In *A Reader in African Christian Theology*, edited by John Parratt, 29–35. London: Society for Promoting Christian Knowledge.

Thorsen, Jacob Egeris. 2015. *Charismatic Practice and Catholic Parish Life: The Incipient Pentecostalization of the Church in Guatemala and Latin America*. Leiden: Brill.

Tomlinson, Matt, and Matthew Engelke. 2006. "Meaning, Anthropology, Christianity." In *The Limits of Meaning: Case Studies in the Anthropology of Christianity*, edited by Matthew Engelke and Matt Tomlinson, 1–37. Oxford: Berghahn Books.

Tonti-Fillipini, Nicholas. 2013. "The Catholic Church and Paedophilia: Learning from Failures." ABC Religion and Ethics, June 4. www.abc.net.au/religion/articles/2013/06/04/3774696.htm.www.abc.net.au/religion/articles/2013/06/04/3774696.htm.

Tracy, David. 1981. "The Analogical Imagination: Christian Theology and the Culture of Pluralism." *Religious Studies Review* 7:281–332.

———. 1994. *Plurality and Ambiguity: Hermeneutics, Religion, Hope*. Chicago: Chicago University Press.

Turner, Victor. 1973. "The Center Out There: Pilgrim's Goal." History of Religions 12 (3): 191–230.

Turner, Victor, and Edith Turner. 1978. *Image and Pilgrimage in Christian Culture*. New York: Columbia University Press.

Tutu, Desmond. [1987] 1997. "Black Theology and African Theology: Soulmates or Antagonists." In *A Reader in African Christian Theology*, edited by John Parratt, 36–44. London: Society for Promoting Christian Knowledge.

Tweed, Thomas. 1997. Our Lady of the Exile: Diasporic Religion at a Cuban Catholic Shrine in Miami. Oxford: Oxford University Press.

Ukpong, Justin. 1994. "Christology and Inculturation: A New Testament Perspective." In *Paths of African Theology*, edited by Rosino Gibellini, 40–61. Maryknoll, NY: Orbis Books.

Unamuno, Miguel. 1921. *Tragic Sense of Life*. New York: Dover.

Uzukwu, Elochukwu. 1994. "Inculturation and the Liturgy (Eucharist)." In *Paths of African Theology*, edited by Rosino Gibellini, 95–104. Maryknoll, NY: Orbis Books.

van Dam, Nikolaos. 1996. *The Struggle for Power in Syria: Politics and Society and the Ba'th Party*. London: I. B. Tauris.

van de Port, Mattijs. 2005. "Candomblé in Pink, Green and Black: Re-scripting the Afro-Brazilian Religious Heritage in the Public Sphere of Salvador, Bahia." *Social Anthropology* 13:1–24.

———. 2013. "The 'Natural' Is a Sham: The Baroque and Its Contemporary Avatars." *FORUM: University of Edinburgh Postgraduate Journal of Culture and the Arts* 16:1–10.

van der Veer, Peter, ed. 1994. *Conversion to Modernities: The Globalization of Christianity*. New York: Routledge.

———. 1996. "Religion." In *Encyclopedia of Social and Cultural Anthropology*, edited by Alan Barnard and Jonathan Spencer, 726–28. London: Routledge.

Van Rooden, Peter. 1996. *Religieuze regimes: Over godsdienst en maatschappij in Nederland, 1570–1990*. Amsterdam: Bert Bakker.

Vásquez, Manuel A. 2008. "Studying Religion in Motion: A Networks Approach." *Method and Theory in the Study of Religion* 20:151–84.

————. 2010. *A Materialist Theory of Religion.* Oxford: Oxford University Press.

————. 2011. *More Than Belief: A Materialist Theory of Religion.* Oxford: Oxford University Press.

Vásquez, Manuel, and Marie F. Marquardt. 2003. *Globalizing the Sacred: Religion across the Americas.* New Brunswick, NJ: Rutgers University Press.

Vatican Information Service. 2010. "Publication of CDF Norms on Most Serious Crimes." July 15. http://visnews-en.blogspot.com/2010/07/publication-of-cdf-norms-on-most .html.

Verrips, Jojada. 2013. "Speaking and Singing or How Ultra Orthodox Calvinists Tune Their Bodies." *Jaarboek Voor Liturgieonderzoek* 29:133–45.

Vincett, Giselle, and Linda Woodhead. 2009. "Spirituality." In *Religions in the Modern World: Traditions and Transformations,* edited by Linda Woodhead, Hiroko Kawanami, and Christopher Partridge, 319–38. London: Routledge.

Viswanath, Rupa. 2014. *The Pariah Problem: Caste, Religion, and the Social in Modern India.* New York: Columbia University Press.

von Vacano, Diego A. 2012. *The Color of Citizenship: Race, Modernity and Latin American / Hispanic Political Thought.* Oxford: Oxford University Press.

Watio, Dieudonné. 1986. "Le culte des ancêtres chez les Ngyemba (Ouest-Cameroun) et ses incidences pastorals." PhD diss., University of Paris Sorbonne (Paris-IV).

Weber, Max. [1905] 2001. *The Protestant Ethic and the Spirit of Capitalism.* Translated by Talcott Parsons. London: Routledge.

————. [1922] 1963. *The Sociology of Religion.* Boston: Beacon Press.

————. [1948] 1998. *From Max Weber: Essays in Sociology.* London: Routledge.

Wedeen, Lisa. 2013. "Ideology and Humor in Dark Times: Notes from Syria." *Critical Inquiry* 39:841–73.

Weigel, Sigrid. 2015. *Grammatologie der Bilder.* Berlin: Suhrkamp.

Werbner, Richard. 1996. "Introduction: Multiple Identities, Plural Arenas." In *Postcolonial Identities in Africa,* edited by Richard Werbner and Terence Ranger, 1–25. London: Zed Books.

Whitehead, Charles. 2006. "The Role of the Ecclesial Movements and New Communities in the Life of the Church." In *New Religious Movements in the Catholic Church,* edited by Michael A. Hayes, 15–29. London: Continuum Books.

Wilde, Melissa J. 2007. *Vatican II: A Sociological Analysis of Religious Change.* Princeton, NJ: Princeton University Press.

Wilson, Samuel, and Leighton Peters. 2002. "The Anthropology of Online Communities." *Annual Review of Anthropology* 31:449–67.

Woets, Rhoda. 2016. "The Moving Lives of Jesus Pictures in Ghana: Art, Authenticity and Animation." In *Creativity in Transition,* edited by Maruška Svašek and Birgit Meyer, n.p. New York: Berghahn Books.

Wolf, Eric. 1958. "The Virgin of Guadalupe: A Mexican National Symbol." *Journal of American Folklore* 71:34–39.

Woodward, Kenneth L. 1990. *Making Saints: How the Catholic Church Determines Who Becomes a Saint, Who Doesn't, and Why.* New York: Touchstone.

Zahlawi, Elias. 2009. *Ta☐mulāt* [Contemplations]. Damascus: Dār al-Majid lil-tabā'a wal-nushir wal-khadimāt al-tabā'aiyya Muhammad Insaf Tarabulsi.

Zamora, Lois P., and Monika Kaup, eds. 2010. *Baroque New Worlds: Representations, Transculturation, Counterconquest.* Durham, NC: Duke University Press.

Zires, Margarita. 1994. "Los mitos de la Vírgen de Guadalupe, su proceso de construcción y reinterpretación en el México pasado y contemporáneo." *Mexican Studies/ Estudios Mexicanos* 10 (2): 281–313.

———. 2014. "La mediatización televisiva de los rituales religiosos: Las mañanitas a la Vírgen de Guadalupe." *Revista Brasilera de História das Religiões* 7 (20): 5–34.

Zubrzycki, Geneviève. 2013. "Narrative Shock and (Re)Making Polish Memory in the Twenty-First Century." In *Memory and Postwar Memorials: Confronting the Violence of the Past,* edited by Florence Vatan and Marc Silberman, 95–115. New York: Palgrave.

Županov, Ines G. 1999. *Disputed Mission: Jesuit Experiments and Brahmanical Knowledge in Seventeenth-Century India.* New Delhi: Oxford University Press.

———. 2005. *Missionary Tropics: The Catholic Frontier in India (16th–17th Centuries).* Ann Arbor: University of Michigan Press.

CONTRIBUTORS

ELLEN BADONE is a Professor of Religious Studies at McMaster University. She works in the areas of pilgrimage, healing, and Catholic orthodoxy in France and Europe. She is a former President of the Society for the Anthropology of Religion.

ANDREAS BANDAK is an Assistant Professor in Cross Cultural and Regional Studies at the University of Copenhagen. He works on the politics of worship in the Middle East, with a particular focus on Syria.

STANLEY H. BRANDES is a Professor of Anthropology at the University of California, Berkeley. He has researched and published extensively on rituals, medicine, food, and the cultural anthropology of Mediterranean Europe and Latin America.

CAROLINE WALKER BYNUM is a University Professor Emerita at Columbia University and a Professor Emerita of Western Medieval History at the Institute for Advanced Study at Princeton. She is a leading scholar in the study of Christianity and gender.

WILLIAM A. CHRISTIAN is a renowned historian of religion and Christianity with a longtime interest in material religion and in vision and visionaries of the twentieth century in Spain and southern Europe.

SIMON COLEMAN is the Chancellor Jackman Professor in the Department of Religion at the University of Toronto. His work focuses on pilgrimage, material religion, words and worship, and anthropological theory.

THOMAS J. CSORDAS is a Professor in the Department of Anthropology at the University of California, San Diego. He specializes in medical and psychological anthropology, comparative religion, and anthropological theory, with a focus on Charismatics and Christianity.

ERNESTO DE MARTINO (1908–65) was an Italian anthropologist and an ethnologist of religion. A student of Benedetto Croce, he specialized in magic, healing, and rituals in southern Italy.

ROBERT HERTZ (1881–1915) was a French sociologist of religion and a student of Emile Durkheim and Marcel Mauss. He wrote *Death and the Right Hand,* a very influential text in twentieth-century anthropology.

ERIC HOENES DEL PINAL is a Lecturer in the Department of Religious Studies at the University of North Carolina, Charlottesville. He holds a PhD in anthropology from the University of California, San Diego, and specializes in politics, language, and the culture of Christianity in Mesoamerica.

HILLARY KAELL is an Assistant Professor of Religion at Concordia University in Montreal and holds a PhD in American studies from Harvard University. She specializes in the history and practice of North American Christianity.

LUDOVIC LADO is a Jesuit. He holds a doctorate in social anthropology from the University of Oxford (UK). He is currently head of the research office at the Center for Research and Action for Peace based in Abidjan in Côte d'Ivoire.

NIKLAUS LARGIER is the Sidney and Margaret Ancker Professor of German and Comparative Literature at the University of California at Berkeley. With a focus on medieval studies, he researches imagination, the history and formation of the senses, and the aesthetic experience of prayer from the Middle Ages to the Baroque era.

GODFREY LIENHARDT (1921–93) was a British social anthropologist who worked among the Dinka of Sudan. His classic work on African religion and rituals is *Divinity and Experience: The Religion of the Dinka* (1961).

MAYA MAYBLIN is a Lecturer in Anthropology at the University of Edinburgh. She specializes in politics, personhood, gender, morality, and anthropological theory, with a particular focus on Northeast Brazil.

BIRGIT MEYER is a German Professor of Religious Studies at Utrecht University. Her work focuses on global Pentecostalism, popular culture and heritage, religion, and media and the public sphere, as well as senses and aesthetics and anthropological theory.

JON P. MITCHELL is a Professor of Social Anthropology at the University of Sussex. His areas of expertise are ritual, the body and the senses, and the politics of the state and nationalism in Malta.

J. MICHELLE MOLINA is the John and Rosemary Croghan Chair Associate Professor in Catholic Studies in the Department of Religion at Northwestern University. Her research is on Jesuit spirituality and the early modern expansion of Jesuit order.

DAVID MOSSE is a Professor of Social Anthropology at the School of Oriental and African Studies, London. He has published extensively on the anthropology of religion, environment, and development and is a Fellow of the British Academy.

VALENTINA NAPOLITANO is an Associate Professor in the Department of Anthropology at the University of Toronto. Her areas of expertise are religion and diversity, urbanities in transformation, affects and migration, and the politics of traces.

KRISTIN NORGET is an Associate Professor in the Department of Anthropology at McGill University. Her research is on popular religious practice, the politics of indigeneity, and religion and media, focused on Mexico and more recently Peru.

ROBERT A. ORSI is Grace Craddock Nagle Chair in Catholic Studies in the Department of Religious Studies at Northwestern University. His work focuses on American Catholicism and on the theory and method of the study of religion. He is a former President of the American Academy of Religion.

JULIAN A. PITT-RIVERS (1919–2001) was a Professor of Anthropology at Oxford. His classic work on gender, honor, and kinship in rural Andalusia is *People of the Sierra*.

EDITH TURNER (1921–2016) was an English social anthropologist who worked at the University of Virginia and studied ritual, religion, healing, communitas, and humanistic anthropology.

VICTOR TURNER (1920–83) was a Scottish social anthropologist who shaped the anthropological study of symbolism, performance, and rituals. His ethnographically focused work was mainly on the Ndembu people of Zambia.

INDEX

Abela, Anthony, 215

Abraham, 165, 302

affects. *See* sensation and affect concept

Africa: Bwiti chapel, 292n9; Cameroonian Christianity, 228–29; and Christianity, 227; colonial, 7, 64; demographic shift, 195, 199n19; Ephphata group, 227; exorcism(s), 236–38; icons/images, 314n33; inculturation, 233–36; missionization of, 8, 64, 231–33, 305; nationalism in, 124; partition of, 241n17; Pentecostalism in, 24, 305; and politics of inculturation, 238–241; Protestantism in, 305; ritual activity in, 135; symbols in, 78; women priests in, 26n15

Against Nature (À rebours) (Huysmans), 316–19

Agamben, Giorgio, 13–14, 27n43, 253

Agatha, Saint, 215, 218

Ahmed, Sarah, 244, 252, 254n1

aithesis, 321

Alacoque, Marguerite-Marie, 312

Alberoni, Francesco, 15

Alpaïs of Cudot, 100

Ambedkar, B. R., 117

amplification, and prayer, 321–22, 324

analogical figuration, 318, 320, 324–25

Angela of Foligno, 98, 99, 321

Anglicans, 6, 117, 275, 278, 280, 281n1

Anna Vorchtin of Engethal, 98

Anthony of Egypt, Saint, 322

Anthony of Padua, Saint, 218

anthropology: criticisms of, 305; and Protestantism, 302

apparitions: and Eucharist, 22, 96, 99; Sacred Heart devotion, 82, 312. *See also* Marian apparitions

applicatio sensuum method, 320

architectonics, 289, 292n9

archival sources, use of, 33, 40, 311, 313, 322, 324

À rebours (Against nature) (Huysmans), 316, 318–321

Aristotle, 295

artifacts, 124, 214, 319–320, 322, 324

Asad, Talal, 14, 16, 238, 309

Assembly of God movement, 212

Augustine of Hippo, Saint, 54, 256–57, 261–62, 264, 266

Badone, Ellen, 24, 160

Baldacchino, Jean-Paul, 212, 216–19

Balthasar, Hans Urs von, 316, 320

Bandak, Andreas, 17, 19, 155

Barbeau, Marius, 126, 129, 137n34

Barker, John, 12

Baroque Catholicisms, 192–95

Barrès, Maurice, 317–18, 318

Barthes, Roland, 27n43

Bataille, Georges, 316, 318, 321

Bauman, Zygmunt, 205